A Century of Urban Life

The Norwegian-American Historical Association

Lawrence O. Hauge, PRESIDENT

BOARD OF PUBLICATIONS

A Century

# of Urban Life

The Norwegians in Chicago before 1930

by Odd S. Lovoll

PUBLISHED BY The Norwegian-American Historical Association   1988

DISTRIBUTED BY The University of Illinois Press

Photographs on pages iv and v
South Water Street east from State Street before 1871.
Magl Helle (Mary Hill) from Valle in Setesdal in Chicago ca. 1906.
A ski jump on Cary Hill at Fox River Grove, Illinois.
An advertisement for Den norske Kafe.
The Norwegian pavilion at the World's Fair in 1893.

Design: Nancy Leeper

Distributed by
University of Illinois Press
54 East Gregory Drive, Champaign, Illinois 61820

For Audrey, Helge, Lynnea, and Ronald

Acknowledgments

A history of the Norwegians in Chicago was one of the early projects adopted by the Norwegian-American Historical Association; it was announced on April 28, 1928, in the Chicago newspaper *Skandinaven*. The completion of this large undertaking — sixty years later — is consequently long overdue. My own interest in this specific project dates from 1980 when I assumed the editorial responsibility for the Association. In the course of the time given to the Chicago history, most especially during two years devoted entirely to research and writing, 1985 to 1987, I became greatly indebted to many people. Indeed, a project such as the present one could not have been undertaken and completed without their generosity and assistance. It behooves me first of all to express my gratitude to St. Olaf College, my academic institution, for its liberal sabbatical leave policy and for extending my leave for a second year. Keith O. Anderson, then the Dean of the College, deserves a special word of thanks for making this arrangement possible. The Norwegian-American Historical Association's president, Lawrence O. Hauge, and its executive secretary, Lloyd Hustvedt, both acted decisively to assure the success of the project. Their warm friendship and sensible advice were a source of comfort and reassurance, as was the ample evidence of support from the Association's executive and publications boards and from the membership at large.

Funding for the project came from many quarters, and a complete list of donors appears at the back of the book. I should, however, like to mention the early and sustained aid, covering both years of the project, from the Lutheran Brotherhood made possible by Arley R. Bjella, then chairman of its board; the grant for a specific aspect of the project relating to Minnesota from the Minnesota Historical Society through Russell W. Fridley, then its president; and an initial grant from the Arthur Andersen Company arranged by Arthur E. Andersen, the Association's treasurer. A generous grant from a fund established at St. Olaf College by E.S. Gandrud of Owatonna, Minnesota, with the balance coming from the Theodore C. Blegen Fellowship Fund, covered my salary during the second year.

No single individual entered more wholeheartedly into the project than the late Helen Fletre. Her residence in the Logan Square community was frequently my home and main headquarters while doing research in Chicago and she tirelessly and with intelligence and imagination assisted in the process. Josefa and J. Harry Andersen, whose affection and hospitality I benefited from on a regular basis, collected valuable information and shared with me precious personal insights into the Norwegian-American community, as well as giving generous financial support. A longtime comrade and fellow worker, Rolf H. Erickson, second vice president of the Association and chairman of the Chicago History Committee, opened his home to me and made it mine. A number of other individuals provided information and were helpful; their names may be found in the notes identifying specific sources or in credits for photographs they located.

It is of course not possible in a brief statement of acknowledgments either to do justice to the value of the assistance received or to include everyone who in some way contributed to the progress of the work, but I should like to mention a few individuals by name, among them Hazel Anderson, who participated eagerly and cordially in the project, Martin W. Reinhart, whose friendship and broad knowledge of Chicago were constant resources, Bert Benson, who contributed liberally of his familiarity with Norwegian Chicago, Florence Van Valkenburgh, who showed warm support and interest, Bergljot Raaen, talented actress of the Norwegian stage in Chicago, whose participation added zest as well as insight, Alf H. Altern, who was an early and faithful supporter, Charlotte Jacobson, the Association's curator, who patiently endured my many queries, my colleague Louis Janus, who possessed the fortitude and endurance to initiate me into the mysteries of computing and word processing, and many other persons who gave encouragement and help in different ways. Among the latter were Karen and P. Rolf Westnes, Magnhild Faland, Ole Besseberg, John and Dorothy Bauer Erland, Lucinda Jondahl, Sister Magdalene Rosene, Connie O'Kieffe, Lawrence M. Nelson, Arthur L. Johnson, Vera Beutlich, Mildred Moe, Elmer E. Abrahamson, Harry J. Williams, Sigurd Olsen, Tella Guttelvik, Marijane Carr, and Ellen Pedersen. Learning to know these people, as well as many others whose names do not appear here, was a greatly rewarding aspect of my research and a lasting benefit.

The Chicago History Committee was formed in 1981 in preparation for a concentrated effort to research and write a history of the Norwegians in Chicago. Its officers are William J. Korsvik, honorary chairman and a member of the Association's executive board, who throughout exhibited a serious and sustained dedication to the project, Darrell F. Treptow, secretary, and L. Charles Brewick, treasurer, whose friendly ministrations were much appreciated. As an untiring and always optimistic chairman Rolf Erickson provided dynamic and amicable leadership. His contributions in all personal as well as professional relations advanced the work immeasurably.

A major portion of the archival and library research was done at the Chicago Historical Society, whose staff was consistently cordial and helpful. Considerable and rewarding time was also spent at the Newberry Library, the University of Chicago, the University of Illinois at Chicago Circle, and the Swedish-American Archives of Greater Chicago at North Park College; I also had access to the archives of the Mt. Olive Cemetery and the Oak Forest Hospital and Infirmary; in Evanston I investigated archival collections at Northwestern University, the Garrett Theological Seminary, and the Frances E. Willard Library. In addition churches, hospitals, nursing homes, and other institutions and societies of Norwegian origin were visited to examine records and conduct personal interviews. Outside the Chicago area research was conducted at the American Lutheran Church archives at Wartburg Seminary, Dubuque, Iowa, the Swenson Research Center at Augustana College, Rock Island, Illinois, the Preus Library at Luther College, Decorah, Iowa, and the Minnesota Historical Society, St. Paul, as well as in the archives of the Norwegian-American Historical Association and in the Rølvaag Library at St. Olaf College. The project benefited from earlier and current research in the University of Oslo Library and in the Norwegian National Archives. In every instance, whichever institution or organization I visited, I was well received and profited from my efforts.

The newspaper *Vinland*, published in Evanston, gave publicity to the project; I wish to thank its editors, first Laurel Neidig and later James M. Erickson, and its publisher Arve Kilen. Johan Fr. Heyerdahl, secretary general of the Norsemen's Federation, announced the endeavor in *Aftenposten* and *The Norseman* in Oslo. These several efforts resulted in valuable responses. The official Norwegian rep-

xii resentatives in Chicago, Consul General Bjarne Solheim and his wife Rutt, and Consul Arnold Svensen and his wife Pat, graciously hosted dinner parties in recognition of the venture. I should also like to thank Charles Fineman, a librarian at Northwestern University, for the many pleasant and intellectually stimulating times we spent together.

I had the good fortune of being assisted by two talented research assistants, Kay J. Carr, a graduate student at the University of Chicago, who patiently worked her way through tedious census manuscripts, and Jostein Molde, a Norwegian graduate student at the University of Trondheim, who with great discipline read files of Norwegian-American newspapers. My competent editorial assistant, Mary R. Hove, worked closely with me in the final editing and her professional skills and knowledge helped to improve the manuscript substantially. As in earlier publications she prepared the index. Alan Ominsky drew the maps and Nancy Leeper is responsible for the book design. Ruth H. Crane, the Association's assistant secretary, was consistently helpful and interested. Finally, I wish to thank my wife Else for her patience and love, and for her enthusiastic interest in every aspect of the project. I dedicate the work to four significant people in my life who made the effort seem all the more worthwhile, my children and children-in-law, Audrey, Helge, Lynnea, and Ronald.

Odd S. Lovoll
St. Olaf College

Contents

A Century of Urban Life

1

A Frontier Community

Waves of immigrants from Europe began arriving in the United States soon after the close of the Napoleonic Wars. The rise of mass migration created awe and wonderment on both sides of the Atlantic Ocean. In 1853 Ludvig Kristensen Daa, editor of *Den norske Tilskuer* (The Norwegian Observer), called the European overseas movement "the most spectacular occurrence in these our peculiar times," predicting that by the end of the century it would transform the rest of the world into a Europe, "with its civilization, its misfortunes, its greatness, and its religion."[1]

Norwegians participated fully in the extension of European civilization to overseas regions. In some ways Norway herself during much of the nineteenth century displayed qualities in her cultural and political life reminiscent of the colonial status of much of the world subjected to European settlement. A quest for a Norwegian cultural identity and complete political autonomy was the red thread in the nation's history. Like the United States, Norway was a child of the French Revolution and its enlightened ideas. The constitution signed at Eidsvoll on May 17, 1814, was based on the same principles as the

Norway in the Nineteenth Century

3

American one. This document signified a rebirth of the Kingdom of Norway following a long period of national decline and the dissolution of the more than four-hundred-year union with Denmark. But in November of the same year the newly established national assembly, the Storting, surrendered Norway's claimed independence to the demands of big-power politics and accepted a union with Sweden under the Swedish king. Full self-government in domestic affairs was, however, secured within the framework of the double monarchy, which itself represented a legal reality with but few common interests to foster a sense of community. There were, of course, the obvious Nordic ethnic bonds and similar language and cultural traditions. A rising Norwegian nationalism which began in the last decades of the union with Denmark was easily redirected against Swedish preeminence in this uneven marriage. Simultaneously there was a striving to break the Danish cultural hegemony—the legacy of the centuries-long union. In these endeavors, however, as public debate revealed, there was not a real national consensus.[2]

The culture of the court, the government institutions, and the university in Copenhagen pervaded the small towns and cities and became the norm for the dominant social classes. Independence did not change the situation; to the contrary, because the inherited common Dano-Norwegian literary language was retained almost unaltered as the official medium, the Danish linguistic influence was strengthened through better education, as well as by a fear of Swedish cultural encroachment. And the official class of civil servants continued to rule as a distant elite. Its most prominent representative in the countryside was the parish priest. The Norwegian Lutheran State Church retained a near monopoly on organized religious life all the way up to 1845. Only then was full religious liberty guaranteed.

The rationalism of the Lutheran clergy, as expressed in cold, utilitarian homiletics, gave rise to lay religious movements. The lack of religious fervor in the congregation opened the way for pietistic lay preachers like Hans Nielsen Hauge, and his adherents called Haugeans, to gather converts. At the beginning of the century Hauge generated a broad religious awakening. His message of repentance and conversion renewed Norwegian Christian life within the framework of the official state church, albeit that zealous ministers had him arrested for violating the Conventicle Act against lay preaching. His activity was, however, more than opposition to a state-church clergy; it represented a growing class consciousness and opposition to authority among the Norwegian peasantry. Local democracy was introduced in the granting of local self-government in 1837. It heralded the end of rule by the elite as the peasantry learned to exercise their rights.[3]

In 1801 more than 91 percent of Norway's 883,487 inhabitants lived in rural communities, and in 1865, when the population had increased to 1,701,756, more than 80 percent still did so. The national romanticists discovered Norway's soul in the rugged beauty of her landscape, in the heroic pre-Danish past, and in the rich peasant folk life with its variety of local vernaculars, thought to be uncontaminated by Danish, and its local traditions in food, dress, music, dance, and the rich lore of tales and legends. This cultural heritage was carried across the Atlantic and became a part of immigrant self-definition. In Norway it inspired romantic painters, composers, and authors to create works in a national spirit.[4]

Social reality conformed only poorly to the idealistic depictions of the national romanticists. An insurmountable social distance existed in East Norway between the wealthy farmer and his cotters; although the same division between landholding and landless farmers existed within West Norwegian peasant society, the smaller independent farms produced greater social equality. Several forces affected Norwegian society and gradually produced a structural change. A high birthrate and a steadily falling death rate gave Norway one of the highest percentages of population growth in Europe. Industrialization and modernization of agricultural production arrived late, but from mid-century, through crises and setbacks, the industrial sector expanded and a gradual mechanization of farming took place. The creation of new jobs, however, fell far short of the rate required to accommodate the accelerated population increase. Labor surpluses were syphoned off through emigration, which became a conspicuous aspect of the national experience. Modernization of economic life owed much to a concomitant growth of the merchant marine. Emigration itself stimulated domestic shipping, in the transportation of passengers as well as commercial freight. But even earlier, based on traditional export commodities such as fish and timber, the number of vessels in the carrying trade grew rapidly in the first decades of the century, making voyages even beyond Europe. A seafaring tradition and shipbuilding capabilities were important national resources. The repeal of the British Navigation Acts in 1849 provided the incentive and opportunity for dramatic expansion, so that by 1860 35,000 sailors manned the Norwegian sailing vessels that plied the oceans of the world with cargoes consigned by larger nations. Cheap ships and low wages and a ready supply of competent skippers and seamen gave Norway an edge in the competition for the carrying trade.[5]

Norwegians were in consequence pulled early into the Atlantic economy and its patterns of trade and migration. The much celebrated Sloopers, the pioneer immigrant group, crossed the Atlantic on the tiny sloop the *Restauration* in 1825, departing from the coastal town of Stavanger on July 4 and landing in New York on October 9. It was a dramatic opening to an important historical development that during the next hundred years would find nearly 800,000 Norwegians seeking America. The Sloopers consisted of only fifty-three people,

**The
Migration**

A full-size replica of the sloop *Restauration* was built for the Norse-American Centennial celebration in Minneapolis in 1925. The vessel was only 39 tons, 54 feet long and 16 feet wide. The group posing in front of the sloop and the people standing on its deck suggest the diminutive size of the *Restauration* and the crowded conditions on board.

crew and passengers, and an infant born en route, all of whom intended to emigrate. They had been encouraged to leave the homeland because of religious intolerance, as they were dissenters, Haugeans and Quaker sympathizers, and by the prospects for freedom and material progress in the New World.[6]

In New York the Sloopers were met by their agent and guide, the enigmatic Cleng Peerson. Peerson had first gone to America in 1821, then returned to Norway in 1824 to inform his compatriots of conditions there. He was back in America in time to prepare for the arrival of the Sloopers and guided most of them to Kendall township, about thirty-five miles from Rochester, New York, on the shores of Lake Ontario. There they struggled through the hardships of pioneer life.

News of better opportunities in the West reached Kendall. It was again the restless wanderer Cleng Peerson who served as pathfinder. In the spring of 1833 he set out on foot from the Kendall settlement, to Ohio, across southern Michigan, through northern Indiana, and to Illinois. He visited the primitive collection of log cabins that then was Chicago, but rejected it as a possible site for Norwegian settlement.[7]

Peerson instead selected an area about seventy miles southwest of Chicago in the Fox River valley in LaSalle county. Existing accounts of how Peerson was guided by benign providence in his selection of land indicated the tendency of a religious people to see a parallel between their own and the Israelites' wanderings. They were also a product of Peerson's vivid imagination. Yet in several regards the Fox River region was a "promised land." The fertile and sparsely wooded prairies were easy to cultivate. Besides, an increase in land values was expected when a projected canal from Lake Michigan would be completed to the Illinois River in LaSalle county.[8]

Immigrants displayed a quick grasp of the basics of American capitalism. Most of the Sloopers hailed from rural communities in Rogaland, with a few from the city of Stavanger. But the largely barter economy of the countryside also gave room for capitalistic activity, such as the sale and purchase of property, and Haugeans promoted ability in business as a means to financial independence. In any case, the Kendall settlers had seen how their small plots appreciated in value through improved communications. The opening of the Erie Canal and other internal improvements gave them a profit on the sale of their property in New York so that they had money to invest in the cheaper land in the West. Most of them moved to the Fox River region during the two years 1834 and 1835.[9]

The Kendall settlers took the water route west from the Atlantic by way of the Great Lakes and the Erie Canal. Multitudes of immigrants arriving in New York would take a steamboat up the Hudson River to Albany, then a canal boat to Buffalo and from there across a thousand miles of water: over Lake Erie, then the Detroit

River to the St. Clair lake and river into Lake Huron and on to Lake Michigan to be set ashore in either Milwaukee or Chicago. It was an ordeal that rivaled the Atlantic crossing. It is estimated that in 1833 alone 100,000 passengers left Buffalo for points on the Great Lakes, about one fifth of them landing in Chicago. Eleven steamboats and numerous sailing craft were in operation that year.[10]

Two brigs, *Den norske klippe* and *Norden*, left Stavanger in the summer of 1836 with a total of 167 people destined for America. This event marked the beginning of annual overseas emigration. It began only after the Kendall settlers had already toiled and suffered through years of privation and hardship and the frontier for Norwegian settlement had moved west to the Fox River in Illinois. When their fortunes had improved they were joined by other Norwegians. In the total movement to America the Sloopers formed a bridgehead. The first crossing was directly related to the exodus that began a decade later. A few individuals had braved the Atlantic in the intervening years and joined the pioneer group in Kendall. Some, like the influential letter writer Gjert Gregoriussen Hovland who had come in 1831, agitated for emigration, praising the virtues of a land with freedom and equality for all citizens. Another emigrant of 1831, Knud Andersen Slogvig, returned to Norway in 1835 carrying a letter from Hovland. Copies of it circulated widely. One might suspect that both the letter and Slogvig's visit represented emigrant recruitment by Norwegians in America. The Kendall settlers needed people to join them to develop the Fox River settlement and to found new ones, and they might have decided to take direct action. Slogvig himself created a great stir; people came from long distances to hear about America. For those who decided to emigrate he served as a leader on board *Norden*. Channels of information about alternative opportunities were thus established. When the time was ripe, people could respond individually and with forethought.[11]

A total of about 200 Norwegians emigrated in 1836. The number had increased to 1,600 by 1843. 6,200 Norwegians moved overseas during the first decade of annual emigration and nearly twice that many left during the following five years. Between 1836 and 1850 18,200 emigrated. Although the exodus displayed a dramatic rise during the 1840s, it was hardly a mass movement, at least not from a national perspective.[12]

The Chicago Setting

Chicago, although still close to its beginnings as a western outpost, had by mid-century become an important commercial and transportation hub. Life there was still crude and the wilderness past was much in evidence. John Lewis Peyton, a lawyer from the East, coming to Chicago in 1848 described the budding metropolis thus: "The city is situated on both sides of the Chicago River, a sluggish, slimy stream too lazy to clean itself, and on both sides of its north and south branches, upon a level piece of ground, half dry and half wet, resembling a salt marsh, and contained a population of about 20,000. There was no pavement, no macadamized streets, no drainage, and three thousand houses in which the people lived were almost entirely small timber buildings, painted white and this white much defaced by mud." Its primitive character reflected the city's rapid growth.[13]

The secret of Chicago's rise to prominence was its strategic location at the mouth of the Chicago River, which flowed across low and swampy land surrounded by seemingly endless prairies. Nearly a mile from Lake Michigan the river divided into a North Branch and a South Branch whose waters mingled as they emptied into the lake. The location of Chicago was at the head of a portage waterway to central Illinois and the Mississippi Valley, which could be eliminated by a canal from the South Branch of the river which would connect Lake Michigan with the Illinois River. The Illinois River was a tributary to the mighty Mississippi and such a canal would create a water route from the Great Lakes to the Gulf of Mexico.[14]

The great advantages to commerce of the projected canal had been envisioned early, and it was precisely to protect the portage, as well as to establish a trading post with the Indians, that the first Fort Dearborn was built in 1803 on the south bank of the Chicago River. In 1812, when war came with Great Britain, the small garrison evacuated this exposed frontier location to seek safety farther east. The bloody Indian massacre which occurred a short distance from the fort was a fearful event in the early history of Chicago. The fort itself was destroyed and there was a great loss of life, including women and children who were accompanying the retreating militia. Among those killed was one Frederick Peterson, a private at the fort who had enlisted in 1808. Surviving accounts of a "Norwegian fiddler" at the fort would lead one to conclude that the fiddler and private Peterson were one and the same. This young man's origins in Norway and the circumstances that brought him to a crude military outpost on the American frontier remain a mystery.[15]

Peace in 1815 placed the United States in a position to assert its power in the region. A military post, a second Fort Dearborn, was erected on the sandy shores of Lake Michigan by the Chicago River. A small village of rough shelters grew up around the fort.[16]

Encouraged by the success of internal improvements in the East and by postwar prosperity, Illinois, admitted to statehood in 1818, launched an elaborate program of road and canal building. The completion of the Erie Canal between the Hudson River and Lake Erie in 1825 created a new avenue for migration and trade, directly benefiting Chicago, and made the desirability of the Illinois and Michigan Canal, as it was to be called, even more obvious. In 1829 the Illinois legislature consequently appointed a commission to plot the canal and dispose of the public lands along the route. In 1830 this commission platted the future town of Chicago.[17]

Top left: The Fort Dearborn monument sculptured in the mid-1890s by the successful Danish-American sculptor Carl Rohl-Smith stood at 18th Street and Calumet Avenue. This was the site of the Fort Dearborn massacre in 1812.

Top right: A replica of the first Fort Dearborn in 1803.

Bottom: Fort Dearborn and surroundings in the early 1830s as depicted in a watercolor by Justin Herriott.

Chicago became an incorporated unit of government, a town of 350 people within Cook county, in the summer of 1833. And with each passing year it looked more and more like a city and less like a frontier settlement. In March, 1837, Chicago was granted its first city charter and elected a mayor and a city council. Its population had expanded to 4,170 in the course of those few years.[18]

In September of 1833 a colorful pageant had taken place at Chicago where six thousand Potawatomi Indians gathered to cede vast land areas west of Lake Michigan. The ceding of land followed the defeat in 1832 of Black Hawk and his roaming bands of warring Indians, which removed the last Indian threat to Chicago and the surrounding countryside. During the next few years the Indians trekked west of the Mississippi to land promised them there. A great westward movement of peoples of European origin, from the eastern states and from overseas, followed closely upon the heels of the relocation of the Indians. [19]

The Genesis of an Urban Colony

The pioneer Norwegian emigration was basically a rural-to-rural movement: in many respects a conservative migration to continue a traditional way of life in America. Chicago was, however, the gateway and the port of entry for most emigrants to the Northwest. It surpassed Milwaukee as the major receiving point. An urban colony of Norwegians had its genesis in 1836 when a few families decided to remain in Chicago rather than continue on to the Fox River settlement, a three-day trek by wagons pulled by oxen.[20]

The first Norwegian to settle permanently in Chicago was, however, a young sailor, David Johnson, who arrived in 1834. It might not be insignificant in a global perspective to note his maritime occupation and the possibilities that Norway's seafaring tradition created for overseas migration. In America, however, Johnson changed careers. His name is entered in the account book of John Calhoun on August 22, 1834. Calhoun had launched Chicago's first newspaper, the *Chicago Democrat*, in late 1833, and had met the young Johnson in New York when he had gone there in 1834 to buy a cylinder press to replace his old hand press. Johnson had gone ashore in New York in 1832 and found employment as a press feeder. At Calhoun's invitation he accompanied the press to Chicago and there installed and operated it.[21]

Johnson's contact with Calhoun appears to have had an impact on immigrant occupational choices. A surprising number of Norwegian newcomers entered the printing trade in the early years. Eric Anderson, for example, in 1839, when he was only twelve years old, worked as a pressman on the same newspaper. He had emigrated from Voss that same year with his parents, Anna and Endre Endreson Rude, young Eric taking the name Anderson. Skills were acquired that would later serve an immigrant press. Anderson was a compositor in the offices of *Nordlyset* (Northern Lights), and in 1847 set the type for the initial number of this first Norwegian-American newspaper. And John Anderson, the successful founder and publisher of *Skandinaven*, the major Norwegian-language organ in Chicago, likewise from 1852 gained experience as a printer on the *Chicago Democrat*. As an immediate benefit the developing Norwegian-American community gained access to a public medium through compatriots in the employ of American newspapers before a separate immigrant press existed. It gave the group visibility and encouraged civic participation.[22]

Most historians consider the colony in Chicago the third permanent Norwegian settlement in America, after that in Kendall and the one in the Fox River valley. The early student of emigration Rasmus B. Anderson identified as the first settlers Halstein Torrison of Fjelberg in Hordaland, with his wife and children, who arrived on October 16, 1836. It is known that Johan Larson, a sailor from Kopervik, was another settler in Chicago in 1836, as were Svein Lothe with his wife and two children from Ullensvang in Hardanger. It is reasonable to assume since Torrison arrived so late in the year that the other settlers had preceded him. The pioneer pastor J. W. C. Dietrichson, on his visit to Chicago in 1844, described Torrison as "an industrious man, orderly and well thought of by the Yankees." He prospered sufficiently to build a simple dwelling for himself and his family just south of the fork in the Chicago River known as Wolf Point, then on the outskirts of town.[23]

It is generally accepted that Nils Knutson Røthe, his wife Torbjørg, and their three children also settled in Chicago in 1836, although some accounts have them staying in Rochester, New York, for a year after their emigration and arriving in Chicago in 1837. They were the first emigrants from Voss, indicating that the urge to go to America had spread north and east from the Stavanger region. By "happy providence," as the amateur historian Knut Rene expressed it, they chose to remain in Chicago, a place they likely first heard of after landing in America. Their residence in Chicago is important, for they were only the first of what became a large colony from the community of Voss. Few from Voss, however, sailed on the bark *Ægir* which left Bergen in April, 1837, with some eighty emigrants from the rural communities in that city's hinterland as the first emigrant vessel from that region. The route by way of Gothenburg was more commonly chosen by the early travelers from Voss. By 1840 about 120 Vossings had emigrated, and enough of them had settled in Chicago that by that year there were more Vossings there than all other Norwegians taken together. They were referred to as the "Voss Circle" (*Vosseringen*). Since most of those who did not come from Voss were from the same general area in western Norway it was from a regional point of view a fairly homogeneous community. The emergence of a specific Vossing group reveals how local loyalties created an intimate sense of

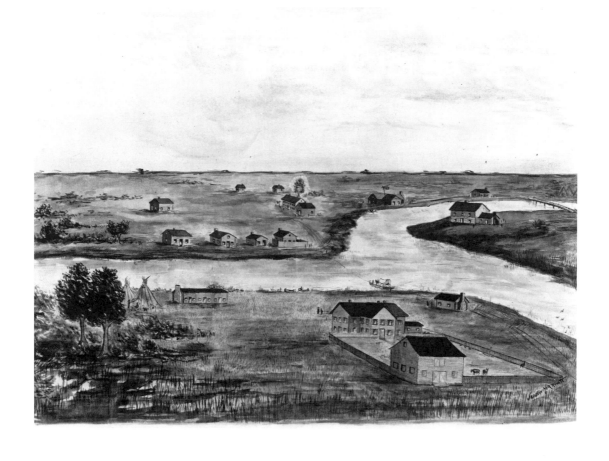

This watercolor was done by Justin Herriott about 1902 of Wolf Point as
he conceived it to have appeared in 1833. Contemporary accounts suggest that it was far from being as pastoral and serene as he portrayed it,
but much closer to becoming an important western commercial center
with attendant chaos, confusion, and the bustling activity of hasty construction and speculation.

identity. It was a common enough pattern in rural settlement but less so in a fast-moving urban environment—a dispersal and then a joining together again in America, the bonds of family and a sense of kinship being the determing factors.[24]

Nils Røthe had decided to emigrate after reading a copy of the Gjert Hovland letter Slogvig brought to Norway in 1835. The well-known lay preacher Elling Eielsen from the farm Sundve at Voss, who himself emigrated in 1839, received the copy on his travels and introduced it to the peasants at Voss. It is a clear example of how information was spread and its role in the resolution to emigrate. "It would greatly please me," Hovland wrote, "if everyone who is needy and has few means would decide to leave Norway and move to America, because here there is employment and livelihood for everyone who is willing to work, so that they can live without lacking anything."[25]

According to Dean M.W. Münster's letter to the county governor (*amtmann*) of Søndre Bergenhus (Hordaland) dated in May, 1837, news had come back to Voss that Røthe and his family had landed safely in New York. In the manner of later emigrants during this initial phase they got passage from Gothenburg on a ship carrying a cargo of iron for America. From information in the city directory of 1839, the total Norwegian population in Chicago that year numbered at least sixty, about two-thirds from Voss. This figure equals less than 7 percent of all those who had left Norway since 1836. It was from this nucleus that a viable and influential urban colony took root and prospered. In contrast to eastern cities such as Boston, the immigrant community did not emerge in a setting full of social, religious, and economic tradition where the immigrants posed a threat to the old society, but instead in an evolving western society with few traditions to lose, where their presence and labor were welcome. The Norwegian colony grew with and adjusted to the shifting demands of the city.[26]

Chicago as a prairie seaport and the port of entry for most immigrants to the Northwest became for most of those who landed there merely a dispersion point or at best a temporary home. But the city did offer immediate income to impecunious newcomers, many of whom stayed only long enough to save enough money to go farther west and purchase or claim the farm of which they had dreamed. Transients and sojourners characterized the Norwegian enclave.

Attractive employment possibilities, even hope for riches in commercial enterprises, special skills best utilized in the city, or in other cases confining poverty kept people in Chicago once they had arrived. Later, when a community of fellow Norwegians stood ready to assist, many immigrants headed directly for Chicago to take up permanent residence. With the passing of years, those who settled on the fertile land in farming communities throughout the Northwest saw their sons and daughters respond to the lure of the city. These were the two major sources for the growth of the Norwegian colony.

Norwegian farmers in the Fox River settlement spoke of "the Chicago mire" in referring to the muddy, occasionally impassable, streets they encountered on arriving in Chicago to market their wheat and other produce. They would sometimes have to hitch five or six yoke of oxen to a single wagon in order to traverse the crude thoroughfares. Chicago was a western boom town, expanding too rapidly to build adequate streets and housing. The great influx of people produced impressive economic growth and a speculative spirit.[27]

Trade with immigrants passing through into the interior and transaction in real estate and western land sales provided an economic base. Easterners, Yankees from the northeastern states, took advantage of these opportunities and made up the majority of citizens. It was a young population and heavily male. Of the close to 4,000 white persons in the city in 1837, more than 45 percent were men twenty-one years of age or older, and there were fewer than half as many women as men. Chicago was thus a frontier settlement without the stability of permanent family life. From the ranks of the Yankees came merchants and early leaders. They tried to transplant eastern social manners onto the prairie frontier and established a fashionable residential area on the north side of the Chicago River.[28]

They were attracted to the city because they envisioned its future importance, but also because they saw a chance to make quick riches on land speculation. The projected Illinois and Michigan Canal was in this regard of inestimable significance. Construction began on July 4, 1836, and after suspension of work in 1842 was completed in 1848. Good wages and steady employment, not only on the Canal, but in harbor and road improvements, produced from 1836 a stream of foreign-born, who increasingly satisfied the need for labor.[29]

The pioneer emigrant from Voss, Nils Røthe, found employment on the Canal, and this opportunity probably explains why he remained in Chicago. It became a common work place for Norwegian newcomers who had been informed about it by earlier immigrants before leaving Norway. Knut Rene states that of the fifty Vossings who emigrated in 1839: "a number of them took work on the Canal thirty miles from town." Halstein Torrison, the emigrant of 1836, was in 1839 in charge of hiring newly arrived Norwegians. Greenhorns who spoke no English could thus find employment and receive guidance in their own language. By 1845 the *Daily Democrat* could report that "the Norwegians are crowding to this country by hundreds to be ready to work on our canal."[30]

The early colony owed much to the Canal. An unofficial and unreliable count in 1844 sets the number of Norwegian-born in Chicago at 531, which would make Norwegians the third-largest immigrant group there, after the Germans and the Irish. It would be difficult to explain the great jump from about sixty in 1839, even if it can be argued that the 1839 city directory only inadequately denoted the size

The drawing illustrates the opening of the Illinois and Michigan Canal in April, 1848. Its construction had attracted many Norwegians and immigrants of other nationalities to the city. It contributed much to making Chicago a center of transportation and commerce.

of the Norwegian population, missing many Norwegian residents.

But in any case the 1844 aggregate figure, not like the 1839 one based
on individual entries, might nevertheless accurately reflect a perceived
as well as an actual strong Norwegian presence during Chicago's for-
mative years. A detailed examination of the population schedules in
the 1850 federal census, the first one to list the immigrant population
by nationality, identified 616 persons as Norwegian. Using the same
source, the Swedish historian Ulf Beijbom identified 214 Swedes.
During the 1840s few Swedes and Danes settled in Chicago; their
emigration was just then getting underway. Until the end of 1850
Norway delivered more than 70 percent of all Scandinavian immigrants to America.[31]

The Irish were also drawn to Chicago to work on the Canal,
some with experience on eastern canals, others fresh off the boat. A
strong emigration tradition to the United States gained mass proportions in the 1840s during the years of potato crop failures, hunger, and
disease. In Chicago the first Irish stronghold became the second ward,
bounded to the north and east by the South Branch of the Chicago
River, where they set up their "shanties" and "rookeries" close to the
source of diverse unskilled employment and brought to the infant city
the beginnings of a slum district. The Germans did not arrive as destitute as the Irish, nor did they come as rapidly. They also were drawn
by the work of building the Canal. But not infrequently they possessed a little capital and often a skill, so that they relatively quickly
established themselves as shopkeepers and artisans, thereby obtaining
economic security and social stability. Their heaviest concentration
was on the north side of the Chicago River, chiefly east of Clark
Street.[32]

"The Panic of 1837," which the growth of speculation on a national scale brought on, deflated the speculative mania in Chicago.
Many easterners left the city. But the depression did not curtail foreign immigration. The depreciated land values made property more
accessible even to immigrants. And there was continued demand for
their labor as the city found a more solid base for urban growth in
trade and commerce. The foreign-born population rose in proportion
to the Yankee element. In 1844 unofficial figures show that 32 percent
of Chicago's 10,000 citizens were foreign-born; the federal census in
1850 documented that as many as 52 percent of the 30,000 people
residing in the city that year had been born outside the United States.
More than half the people encountered were thus immigrants. It is
truly impressive evidence of the role of immigration in the growth of
Chicago from its earliest years.[33]

A careful analysis of the 1839 city directory in a master's thesis by **Settlement**
Mari Lund Wright and the detailed study of early immigrants from **and**
Voss by Knut Rene reveal much about the adjustment of Norwegian **Occupation**

peasants to American urban capitalism. Their resources were family, ethnic cohesion, and individual resourcefulness. The Vossings, constituting a majority in the small immigrant colony, enjoyed a reputation from home for business acumen. Land transactions were especially numerous in Voss, to be sure caused in part by hard times; the farmer sold his property to buy a cheaper farm or to leave the community. It was a part of the economic situation, as were the breeding and sale of horses and the cottage industry which produced simple articles to be sold by local peddlers who carried them along appointed routes all over the country. And Vossings joined men from the coastal communities in seasonal herring fisheries, thereby establishing personal contacts over a wide area and becoming involved in a major commercial venture. Many immigrants consequently arrived in America with entrepreneurial attitudes which were related to their capitalistic and commercial experiences in Norway and could best be utilized in an urban economy. It is therefore not unreasonable to assume that such immigrants favored the city over a farming community. Some of the Vossings, especially, did remarkably well.[34]

The Norwegian colony, which consisted mainly of Vossings and other West Norwegians, was like the population of Chicago in general a young group, but although it included some single men it had a much more pronounced family character. For the most part the immigrants lived close together in an area known as the Sands just north of the Chicago River where it emptied into Lake Michigan. There in the late 1830s and 1840s they squatted on canal ground, owning their primitive huts and shacks but not the ground they stood on. It was an unhealthy and swampy area. In the vicinity, at an appropriate distance from the commercial district on the south side of the Chicago River, there emerged progressively cheap lodging houses, saloons, gambling dens, and brothels.[35]

In their simple homes in this undesirable district Norwegian settlers welcomed arriving kinfolk and former neighbors, who stayed until they found jobs and a place to live or moved out of town. Anders Larson Flage, taking the name Andrew Larson,[36] was one of the prominent men in the Norwegian community. Larson in 1840 wrote back to his home community of Voss to relate that when he, his wife Soffie, and four of their six children and a stepson had come to Chicago in 1839 they had moved in with Baard Johnson Rogne, an emigrant of 1837. The large family then moved in with Per Ivarson Undi whose wife Anna was from Voss. Per Ivarson had emigrated earlier in 1839 from Vik in Sogn, a community north of Voss on the Sognefjord, as the first to do so from that region. The connection to Voss was a decisive factor in his move to America. The Larsons lived with them on condition that Soffie care for the Ivarsons' sick child. Other Norwegian immigrants assisted them in finding work and by the end of the year Larson purchased Ivarson's house for $62.50. Larson was

This crude structure erected by John Amundson (Hefte) might be representative of the simple dwellings of the majority of the early Norwegian settlers north of the Chicago River. Amundson emigrated to Chicago from Voss in 1844.

forty-nine years old when he emigrated, and thus older than most immigrants, and had sold his farm to finance his move. In 1843 he brought over the two daughters who had been left behind. The hospitality extended the Larsons on their arrival was born out of necessity. As Larson's uniquely detailed letter of 1840 shows, most households had bachelors or whole families living with them.[37]

None of the pioneer immigrants attained the prominence of Ivar Larson Bøe, who became Iver Lawson. He reportedly emigrated in 1844 together with his younger brother Steffen, who shortly became Stephan; two elder brothers, Knut and Baard, had gone to America in 1839. The fact that Iver Lawson's name appears in the 1839 city directory, and again in 1843, would strongly suggest that he had actually emigrated together with his brothers Knut and Baard, although other sources indicate 1844 as the correct year.[38] Lawson was twenty-three years old in 1844. Anders Nelson Brekke, assuming the name Andrew Nelson, came to Chicago in 1839 at age twenty-one together with his wife Inger. They were, as was not uncommon, married shortly before going to America, where Andrew Nelson gained prosperity. Andrew B. Johnson, who at age fourteen in 1837 had accompanied his father Baard Johnson (Rogne), also achieved success mainly in the lumber trade.[39]

Those who realized wealth through speculation in property enjoyed the most success. Understanding the future value of Chicago, they "came into wealth effortlessly under this wonder city's fantastic growth," as Knud Langeland, another early immigrant, expressed it. They earned the money to invest in land as common laborers. Andrew Nelson (Brekke) had first worked on the Canal and at whatever else was available. From frugal savings he bought land in central Chicago, which quickly rose in value, and in 1848 he was living in a fine house on a large piece of property on Superior Street, had "several thousand dollars out on interest," and was appointed street commissioner in the North Division. Iver Lawson and his brother Knut met with similar success using the same formula. Iver worked as a day laborer, abandoning his trade as a tailor because of the initial language barrier, and then joining Knut in various investments. Knut Lawson had first bought land at Koshkonong in Wisconsin, which he sold at a profit and settled in Chicago. The two brothers owned half of a lake vessel purchased for $1,500 and bought city lots to the extent resources permitted, simultaneously persisting in their daily humble tasks. Knut held odd jobs as a janitor for half a dozen offices and worked summers in a soft drink factory, while Iver in 1846 had found a clerical position in the Chicago post office, where two years later he was making $25 a month. For Iver Lawson it was a step toward greater social status. Few rigid conventions obstructed social relations in the relatively small and accessible frontier town. Valuable contacts, coupled with driving ambition and entrepreneurial skills, in ensuing years provided Iver Lawson with wealth and prestige.[40]

Although most Norwegian immigrants made a gradual improvement in economic status, the majority continued during the decade of the 1840s to work as day laborers on jobs requiring few skills. Special skills that might have induced them to stay in the city, as was the case with Lawson's tailoring, could only be practiced after the language and the needs of the American market place had been learned. Later a Norwegian-American community could accommodate old-country trades. Norwegian farms or farm communities were in the nineteenth century independent entities and people had special roles to play or trades to practice, from master of ceremonies at weddings, to butchering, or the making of shoes, farm implements, or clothing. They might serve several farms. Endre Endreson Rude, who was forty-three at the time of his emigration in 1839, was a hatmaker, and Svein Lothe, the pioneer emigrant from Hardanger, a carpenter. But at first those who did not work on the Canal found employment on road and bridge construction and in building streets. The increased commerce required better quality. Arne Anderson Vinje, writing back to Voss in 1841, told that his job was to handle a heavy wooden scraper drawn by a pair of oxen to scrape the turf from the sides into the middle of the street. "This is such strenuous work," Vinje wrote, "that Americans do not want to do it, even if they should receive $8.00 a day, while I do it for $16.00 a month and pay my own board." Obviously the lot of the immigrant was hard work at the mercy of employers.[41]

But in one area Norwegians seemed to have an edge. They could compete as seamen. Johan Larson, the sailor who came from Kopervik in 1836, pursued his occupation on the lakes. In the 1839 directory are listed possibly two Norwegian lake captains, George Peterson and Johannes Nicolaisen. Of Peterson nothing more is known. Nicolaisen had emigrated from Trondheim, a part of Norway then almost untouched by emigration, and thus again illustrates the unique position of seafaring men in the overseas movement. Communities in the southwestern and southern coastal districts most affected by emigration naturally delivered more sailors to the lake traffic. The two Agder counties, most especially East Agder, with their long traditions of shipbuilding and sailing, experienced an episodic exodus for about a decade beginning in the mid-1840s, until the expansion in Norwegian shipping made the local economy prosper, halting further emigration until later in the century.

Gabriel Gunderson, born at Farsund in 1831, who came to Chicago in 1848, was a sailor on the lakes, purchased an interest in a schooner, and became its captain. There are numerous other examples, such as Søren Peter Lawrence from Kragerø, who at age twenty-one came to Chicago in 1842, and George A. Wigeland, born in 1822 at nearby Stathelle, who arrived the following year. Both began as sailors, became captains on sailing vessels, and then owners or part-owners of several lake vessels. From the early 1840s grain and other

Top: The first shipment of grain from Chicago was made in 1839. The schooner is docked at the city's first landing pier.

Bottom: A schooner on the Great Lakes.

The lithograph, published in 1842, shows the remains of Fort Dearborn, a lighthouse erected in 1832, and heavy river traffic, suggesting the importance of trade.

The Great Lakes Area

The map shows inland waterways and Norwegian settlements in Illinois and Wisconsin.

agricultural surplus sent east and eastern manufactured goods shipped west, as well as lumber from Michigan, greatly increased shipping on the lakes. Wages on the lakes were high, much higher than in the Norwegian fleet. Before the Civil War they ranged from $1.25 to $2.50 a day, or more, depending on the time of the year, the fall being the season when sailors were most in demand. "I can say," Trond Bakketun declared in a letter back to Voss in 1844, "that a good seaman can do very well"; he added that he himself, coming from an inland community and having sailed only three weeks on the lakes, made only $12 a month because of inexperience. Conditions on the lake were essentially the same as those Norwegian seamen were accustomed to from home, as lake traffic was carried chiefly on small sailing craft, and it attracted a growing number of Norwegians used to life on the sea. Those who rose to captain, frequently on their own modest sailing boat, enjoyed an elevated position in the immigrant community in Chicago.[42]

But whether Norwegians settled permanently or were merely sojourners they made their way in the economic system, staying afloat as best they could. They made an effort to employ all possible means, often holding down several jobs at one time. Even farming skills were not wasted in a city where the open prairie was much in evidence around the modest immigrant dwellings. Endre Endreson Rude and Andrew Larson (Flage) both squatted on canal land; Rude kept two milch cows, and Larson even placed a fence around his plot, where he cultivated potatoes and cabbage, later expanding to garden produce, which he marketed in town.[43]

It was a tight-knit group of people; their existence was based on kinship associations and contacts with people they felt a kindred spirit with. The latter point would, because of a common origin in West Norway, albeit with varying intensity depending on even more restricted local loyalties, as with the Vossings, apply to the entire immigrant community. They all belonged to the peasant class, and traditional social distinctions between independent farmers and the landless cotter, which in any case were less pronounced in West Norway, appear to have had no significance at all in immigrant interaction in Chicago. "Kinship groups proved very responsive to demands of the workplace, the city, and the individual," historian John Bodnar has claimed. The family became an economic unit, for sons, daughters, and wives also worked for the common good and contributed to the family income. Andrew Nelson's (Brekke) wife Inger baked flatbread to sell and used her home as a small restaurant. The unmarried men of the community would be the best customers.[44]

Women became domestic servants on a full-time or part-time basis. In his letter of 1840 Andrew Larson extolled the opportunities for Norwegian women to work in American families. "My two daughters Brithe and Marthe," he wrote, "have been working for men in the city and received their board and clothes as well as schooling since we arrived here." By 1850 about one-fifth of all Norwegian women in Chicago were employed as maids. Synneve B. Fletre wrote back to Voss in 1843 to relate that she had found work as a domestic servant for 50 cents to 75 cents a week, but "when I become more used to the work and understand the language better, then I think I will get $1.00."[45]

Norwegians living on canal land on the Sands could be evicted at any time, as they did not own the property. Concentration near the center of town reflected a need to be close to where unskilled labor was needed. On the docks and wharves and on construction sites they could find work as day laborers. The unsavory and also unsanitary conditions, however, made Norwegians early seek other more permanent residences away from the river to the north and west. Iver Lawson joined Andrew Nelson (Brekke) on Superior Street, and built "a small frame, two-story structure elevated on a high brick basement" on a large piece of land. Lots on the North Side a few blocks from the river sold cheaply in the 1840s in order to attract people to the neighborhood. There in Wards 7 and 8, east of the North Branch of the Chicago River, with the heaviest concentration east of La Salle Street in Ward 8, and centering on such streets as Superior, Erie and Ohio, lived 61 percent of the Norwegian population in 1850. Depending on level of income they lodged mainly in small frame houses and in primitive log cabins, or in rude huts made of rough boards; men like Lawson and Nelson and lake captains could afford to build larger dwellings. The cheap land and the range of options for building explain the rapidity with which Norwegians could list themselves as homeowners. "At present," a letter sent by Chicago Vossings in late 1848 stated, "there are about 75 to 80 families that have built houses on their own lots, and with the exception of 17 families who have no real estate, there are also about 10 individuals who have bought lots and not built on them." Although platted, the North Side was yet to be developed; it was still low and swampy, with pools of stagnant water, open prairie, and here and there stumps or individual trees still standing.

Norwegians shared the area with Germans, who clustered most heavily north of Chicago Avenue and east of Clark Street in what was derogatorily referred to by Americans as the Dutch Settlement. A common neighborhood probably explains why the Norwegians and the Germans in the 1843 city directory were counted as one group. Other Norwegians went farther out when relocating. Andrew Larson (Flage), for instance, moved outside the city where he bought land and cultivated vegetables and fruit for sale in the city. The move west of the North Branch was well underway by 1850, when about 20 percent of the Norwegians resided in the large and sparsely settled sixth ward bounded to the west and north respectively by Western and

North avenues, then the city limit. Most lived close to the river where, as on the North Side, lots could be had "for the mere trouble of sawing a few cords of wood for the owners of the ground," to quote from Ernst W. Olson's *History of the Swedes of Illinois* (1908).

The activities of Kjel Vikingson Gjøastein, later Kiel Williams, who together with his wife Sigrid and their three children was one of the immigrants from Voss in 1839, exemplifies the movement of Norwegians within the city. "Like several other Vossings," writes Knut Rene, "he got himself a small house on canal land, and in 1840 even had saved a little money, working at whatever was available, for a long time sawing wood." "Later," Rene continues, "he put up a house on a valuable piece of property near the cemetery, or where Lincoln Park now is, which he also sold." Rapid rise in property values in central areas in the 1850s and lower prices farther out from the center of town induced people to move. Movement out from the original settlement on the Sands accelerated in the 1840s, but was not completed by the end of the decade, and there and in the near vicinity just north of the Chicago River, Norwegian sailors, newcomers, and also older immigrants still found a convenient and cheap place to live. The main clustering of compatriots was within easy walking distance just to the north, although along streets that were no better than badly kept country roads or paths.[46]

Community Life

The most striking feature of the Norwegian community, a reflection of Chicago's position as a receiving and dispersal point, was its unstable, transitory nature. Only a few of the families identified in the 1839 city directory settled permanently in Chicago, and most of the single young people also left.[47]

The activities of Lars Davidson (Rekve) illustrates the point: mobility and the need to exploit all possibilities. He was born on the farm Rekve in Voss in 1818 and came to Chicago in 1839, where he worked two weeks on the Canal before contracting malaria, which forced him to quit. After he recovered, a fellow immigrant, Peter Davidson (Skjervheim), who had left Voss in 1837, found him work as a day laborer. The following summer he was hired on a steamship on Lake Michigan for five months. In the fall he accompanied other Norwegian settlers to Wisconsin and purchased a quarter section of land in Deerfield township. Having thus invested his money, Davidson saw himself forced to return to Chicago to seek employment. During the winter he made a living sawing wood; the spring of 1841 found him working in a sawmill in Michigan where he labored at $12 a month for five months. The next year Davidson was back on his farm and cleared a piece of land for potatoes, but lack of adequate funds motivated him to seek income as a miner in the lead mines in Wiota, where many Norwegians had settled and were supplementing their earnings from farming by toiling in the mines. Davidson

View of Chicago, from the Prairie.

The engraving titled "View of Chicago, from the Prairie" was made in 1845. It gives evidence of rapid growth through its depiction of church steeples and smoke from steamships and factories, but simultaneously presents Chicago as a "walking city" with close connections to its agricultural hinterland.

returned to his farm in 1844, built a small log cabin, married, and took up farming, for a long time on a modest scale.[48]

Norwegian farming communities in Wisconsin like Jefferson Prairie in Rock county, first settled in 1839, and the fertile Koshkonong in Dane county the year after, where Davidson finally settled, drew people from older settlements such as the Fox River, and also from the pioneer settlement Muskego, dating from 1839, just south of Milwaukee. Others of course came by way of Chicago. Extensive mobility hampered the development of social and religious institutions among Norwegians who remained in the city. Churches, especially, emerged earlier in rural communities, which also experienced great movement in and out, but existed in geographically more confined areas where a sense of permanence could be preserved.

The mobile quality of the immigrant community, however, rather than fragmenting it established a network of personal relations and fostered a sense of broad ethnic unity. In this process Chicago, and consequently the Norwegian colony in the city, assumed a special role. People returned to Chicago to find temporary work and were taken in by friends and relatives, or they shipped out from Chicago to work in lumbering operations in Michigan or to sail on the lakes. Farmers brought their wheat and conducted other business. Peter Davidson (Skjervheim), like Lars Davidson (Rekve), took up farming in Wisconsin. He retained close ties with Norwegians in Chicago, visited the city regularly to sell in winter his wheat and pork, and at other times washboards, axe handles, and brooms he had made. It was not unlike the peddlery engaged in by Vossings in Norway. Chicago gradually emerged as the central point of orientation for the Norwegian-American community.[49]

The Norwegian colony, however, like the city in which it existed received mixed reviews. In August, 1844, the authoritarian J.W.C. Dietrichson, the first university-trained minister among Norwegian immigrants, arrived in the Muskego settlement. He was welcomed by the Danish pastor Claus L. Clausen, who had emigrated the previous year to serve the Norwegian immigrant community at Muskego and had been ordained after his arrival in America. Before Dietrichson moved to Koshkonong to assume his mission there, the two men took a steamboat from Milwaukee to Chicago. In his later account Dietrichson wrote of his meeting with many Norwegian newcomers, most of whom were on their way to settlements in Illinois and Wisconsin. Aside from praising Halstein Torrison, he had little good to say about the small Norwegian colony. He indicted many Norwegians as brawlers and drunkards who had brought all Norwegians into disrepute, making Americans refer to them as "Norwegian Indians."[50]

Dietrichson's sweeping judgment is difficult to reconcile with the evidence of hard work, frugality, and economic progress, although, to be sure, abuse of alcohol was not uncommon among Norwegians whether they lived in Norway or in America. His opinion may of course be seen as an expression of a general critical view toward the peasantry by people of Dietrichson's aristocratic standing and high-church convictions. And like later Norwegian Lutheran ministers in America of all persuasions he was sensitive to how Americans regarded his countrymen. Norwegians also lived near a major vice area where a large population of seamen were catered to by saloons and other establishments of ill repute. Besides, the reputation of Chicago as a wicked city, although national notoriety came only in the 1850s, might have influenced Dietrichson in his judgment. Chicagoans concerned with the city's morals blamed the foreign-born, especially the Irish, for crime and illegal activities. In 1848 the *Daily Democrat* expressed alarm at the multiplication of "drinking shops," numbering one for every 105 inhabitants. The next year the city marshal gave proof of who the transgressors were; of 160 arrests during a thirty-two day period, only twenty-three were identified as "American." On the other hand, there were 9 Germans, 5 Norwegians, 3 Swedes, 1 Dane, a few other nationalities, and 100 Irish. The situation caused the *Chicago Tribune* to ask: "Why do our police reports always average two representatives from Erin, the soft green isle of the sea, to one from almost any other inhabitable land on earth?" Tensions and prejudice easily surfaced in a multi-ethnic environment. On the Canal, confrontations and antagonisms became direct, as in 1845 when, as the *Chicago Democrat* reported, "a party of Norwegians, in an affray, killed Mr. Patrick Fohey on Sunday eve last." The clubbing to death of the Irishman was used by Dietrichson to substantiate his injurious claims.[51]

Chicago newspapers displayed a painful awareness of the city's unfavorable reputation and on many occasions objected defensively to it. The *Chicago Democrat* assured its readers that "the aggregate morals of our people . . . will bear flattering comparison with those of any eastern city of its population." The newspaper extolled the great number of meeting houses, the large church memberships, and the perfect observance of the Sabbath in Chicago. Organized religious life moved into the city from rural communities and tended to reinforce negative impressions of the city as a place in need of moral reform. Dietrichson and Clausen viewed their foray into Chicago as a missionary effort and conducted religious services in an unfinished German Lutheran church. Later in 1844 the less dogmatic Clausen, apparently with the urging and support of Iver Lawson, returned and gathered a small congregation as an annex to the church at Muskego. Distance, however, prevented him from providing regular ministerial functions.[52]

In fact, the Chicago colony had to do without much spiritual leadership during the first decade or more of its existence. The zealous

Haugean lay preacher Elling Eielsen arriving in Chicago from Norway on September 22, 1839, had immediately preached the Gospel to a small flock of Norwegian immigrants. This marked the beginning of organized religious activity. Ole Olson Hetletvedt, one of the Sloopers of 1825 and like Eielsen a Haugean lay preacher as well as a colporteur for the interdenominational American Bible Society, likely deserves credit for being the first to evangelize Norwegians in Chicago, but his mission appears to have had little result. He settled at Middlepoint, later called Norway, on the Chicago Road, acquired a hotel, post office, and stagecoach station, and became known as Ole Middlepoint. Eielsen continued to visit his followers and conducted devotional meetings among them in private homes on Erie and Ohio streets. In the late 1840s he erected a small log meetinghouse on the North Side.[53]

The majority of Norwegians, however, favored a more formal arrangement. In December, 1847, the *Daily Democrat* reported that several Norwegians had entered its offices to voice grievances against their spiritual leader, the Swede John G. Smith, who in a later issue refuted the accusations made against him. This early religious strife was thus aired in English in the American press, because "not having an organ through which to make known their position to the public," as the *Daily Democrat* stated, "they are compelled to resort to the columns of the daily press." The issue was a constitution formulated by Smith—obviously not his name— which would make him pastor for life and give him complete control of the congregation. It was, to be sure, the persistent tension between ecclesiastical authority and congregational freedom, but in this case with a new twist. Coming to Koshkonong in 1841 Smith had gained a following by passing himself off as a former court chaplain in Stockholm, but after the arrival of the forceful Dietrichson, who unmasked him as an impostor, he thought it wisest to move his career to Chicago. There he decided to call himself both a Lutheran minister and a physician, and before his fraudulent claims were exposed he gained the support of about seventy Norwegians, among them Andrew Larson (Flage) and Andrew B. Johnson. These people constituted most of the congregation organized by Clausen. With the aid of Presbyterians they began to build a church on Superior Street between LaSalle and Wells. The unfinished edifice blew down in a storm at about the time Smith was forced to leave town, soon after the exchange in the *Daily Democrat*.[54]

The obvious desire for familiar Lutheran ministerial rituals in baptism, marriage, and burial had motivated the immigrants to take action. When no Norwegian church existed they sought the services of compatible American Protestant pastors, such as Congregationalists and Presbyterians, whose missionary efforts among the immigrants and ability to submerge denominational lines in the interest of advancing Christian work everywhere gave them entry into the

Norwegian-American community. In 1844, for instance, a marriage ceremony was performed by the Reverend Flavel Bascum of the First Presbyterian Church in the home of Nils Knutson Røthe, uniting Randver Lydvo and Lars Knutson Dykesten in matrimony. It was a new experience for the immigrants to have the minister officiate in a private home instead of in church, and they wrote to Norway about it. "It is true," a letter to Voss in 1842 stated, "that weddings are not held in church, and one must fetch the minister home." Immigrants were in this manner brought into contact with American religious life and institutions; it moved them toward assimilation and the acceptance of American Protestant Sabbatarianism, a rigid observance of Sunday. As early as 1842 Knut Lawson (Bøe) boasted in a letter to Voss of how superior America was to Norway in moral standing. "I will let you know," Lawson wrote, "that Sunday is not used here for business, nor for fighting and drinking as in Norway, but here Sunday is honored and observed much better than in Norway, except for the Irish." Clearly Norwegians soon adopted the anti-Irish and anti-Catholic sentiments of the nativists of that day.[55]

Secular leaders such as Iver Lawson and religious ones like Dietrichson identified with the Protestant middle-class ethics of the host society and sought its approval for themselves and their countrymen. This explains the efforts of the leaders to make Norwegians conform to the morals and prejudices of American society. The Norwegian brand of puritanism was also compatible with Yankee Protestant moral reform, work ethic, and philanthropy, which especially characterized the Yankee commercial and political elite. Immigrant leaders who accepted and identified with these values and practices stood forth and made their way into American circles of influence.

Chicago continued during the 1840s, in spite of impressive growth, basically as a "walking city." This made the Norwegian immigrant community visible to local politicians and civic leaders, who fostered ties to the lower classes to assure their own positions of leadership, and took charge of all aspects of public life. In no other decade do the Norwegians seem to have been in a better position to assert their influence; their national identity was recognized and not subsumed under a common Scandinavian one. This fact directly aided the ambitions of men within their ranks. And American political parties were conscious of the potential strength of the immigrant vote as they strove to establish party loyalty through a central, ward, and precinct committee structure. Involvement led to appointments, such as Andrew Nelson's (Brekke) post as street commissioner; Norwegian ethnic merits were accorded praise in the same spirit. George Pilson, whose name in Voss had been Jørgen Pederson Nesthus, fell in 1847 in the bloody battle of Buena Vista in the war with Mexico after showing great valor, thus becoming an early Norwegian-American

The wash drawing pictures a section of Lake Street with tenants of 1843.
The muddy streets and wooden sidewalks as well as the boards laid
across the street to make it possible to cross depict the primitive conditions in a frontier boom town.

hero. The *Daily Democrat* eulogized the "noble private"; for "more patriotic blood does not enrich the field of Buena Vista than that of the Chicago Norwegian volunteer."[56]

As a group Norwegians in Chicago were, however, not greatly active in the civic arena—their energies being invested in survival and material progress—but their support was courted. The *Daily Democrat* was then owned by the influential newspaperman, politician, and United States Congressman "Long John" Wentworth, a strong supporter of the annexation of Mexican land areas and an admirer of Jacksonian democracy. Wentworth apparently had a close relationship to the Norwegian immigrant community, which he promoted, along with other Yankee leaders, in a common purpose of civic duty and, to be sure, of personal gain and power. He had a direct link through the four Norwegians who worked in his newspaper's printing shop.

Norwegians in the 1840s preferred the Democratic party, with its appeal to the common man and its espousal of the principle of equality, to the only alternative national political organization, the strongly upper-class Whig party. The heated municipal election of 1844, which produced hearings on fraud leading to its invalidation, has left a record of Norwegian political involvement. New elections were required for Mayor Augustus Garrett, who was unseated, and two aldermen, one of them Samuel Grier in what until new ward boundaries were drawn in 1847 was the fifth ward, north of the river and west of Clark Street to the North Branch, where the majority of Norwegians lived. At the hearings a Norwegian by the name of Oren Overson admitted having received the sum of one dollar, a day's wages or more, to vote for Garrett, though the only English he recognized was the mayor's name.

The Norwegian Andrew Nielson, not Brekke, who appears as a political leader although little is known about him, testified that the Democrats in Ward 5 had met the night before the election and agreed to open the polls early because, as Alderman Grier said, "great threats had been made to prevent the Norwegians voting . . . so that it was best to have the Norwegians vote before any liquor got about and fighting and quarrelling began." American polling places were not infrequently the scene of drunken brawls. At the meeting, where at least ten Norwegians had been present, transport for Norwegians to the polls and barrels of beer to treat voters were arranged for. At other elections the significance of the Norwegian vote is suggested by the fact that a Norwegian interpreter was hired to assist his countrymen who did not read English.[57]

Services to the party were rewarded through the patronage system, as in the case of Andrew Nelson (Brekke); another example was Endre Nilson Tesdahl, one of the typesetters in Wentworth's newspaper, who became the internal revenue collector on the North Side. From his congressional office in Washington, D.C. Wentworth in

1848 inquired of political friends: "Who is seeing to the German and Norwegian vote?" In the decade before mid-century Norwegians thus appear to have held a viable as well as visible place in the Wentworth Democratic machine in Cook county. It was evidence of a community taking root and moving beyond its pioneer stage, but also of a city where people traveling on foot had access to most economic and public activities.[58]

2

Norwegians in the Great Central City

The year 1848 saw the frontier pass beyond Chicago. It was a year of many firsts, which early historians of the city loved to list, in commerce, communications, and internal improvements. Chicago made a surge toward becoming the great central city of the continent; a metropolitan economy with greater sophistication in many walks of life was emerging. The youthful city bustled with activity; it had an enterprising population. But its adolescent appearance also called forth criticism. The Swedish author and feminist Fredrika Bremer visiting the city at mid-century thought that Chicago was the ugliest and most miserable city she had seen in America. "It is very little deserving of its name, 'Queen of the Lake,'" she wrote, "for, sitting there on the lake in wretched dishabille, she resembles rather a huckstress than a queen."[1]

Commercial enterprise was, to be sure, Chicago's *raison d'etre*. The grain trade, principally wheat and corn, was of prime commercial importance, as it gave profit to buyers and sellers alike, and to those who stored and processed the grain and financed the operations. Farmers' wagons loaded with grain were long such a common sight

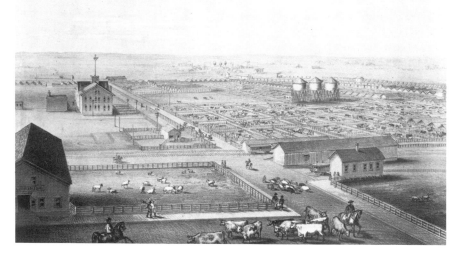

Top: View of the Union Stock Yards, in 1866. This livestock market, which was opened on Christmas Day, 1865, consolidated the several hog and cattle yards scattered over the city.

Bottom: The engraving shows Chicago ca. 1858–1860.

that at times they appeared to be invading the city. Norwegian farmers joined in the trek to the city to market their produce. Writing to Norway in the fall of 1848, Vossings in Chicago related that Erik Knutson (Saue) had just been in town to sell 450 pounds of butter produced on his farm on Queen Ann Prairie in McHenry county, northwest of Chicago, and hoped to deliver 555 bushels of wheat later that year. At about the same time the *Daily Democrat* reported that "farmers' teams blocked up the streets, and the hotels were crowded from morning till night." The farmers were relishing a marketing tour to the city. But these farmers' wagons were being replaced by barges on the Illinois and Michigan Canal; its opening in 1848 brought the rich agricultural areas of the Upper Midwest into the city's orbit. Already in the 1850s meat-packing had become one of Chicago's most important industries.

Railroads gradually surpassed the Canal in the transport of commodities. Between 1848, when the *Daily Democrat* proudly announced that ten miles of track had been laid on the Chicago and Galena Railroad, and 1856 Chicago became the center of a network of railroads connecting the eastern seaboard, the trans-Mississippi West, and all the larger cities of the Ohio and Mississippi valleys. All goods bound in either direction passed through the city. Chicago was becoming the railroad capital of the nation. This was the secret of its unrivalled growth in population, from about 30,000 to nearly 110,000 during the decade of the 1850s.[2]

"The new railroads and canal cooperated with the lake vessels to the benefit of all three agencies," the economist Homer Hoyt stated. The ships on the lakes carried eastward the grain the railroads and the Canal brought to Chicago. In turn these vessels transported back lumber from Wisconsin, Michigan, and Canada which the railroad and the Canal distributed into the interior. Norwegians were attracted to Michigan, which offered immediate income in mining and lumbering, occupations familiar to Norwegians, and they might pursue them seasonally. Lars Davidson (Rekve), mentioned earlier, worked a farm in Wisconsin and sporadically found employment in a sawmill in Michigan as well as on a lake vessel carrying lumber products. Norwegians had, however, been forming permanent colonies in Michigan since 1848 when the first Norwegian settler had arrived in the Muskegon area; their numbers increased in the 1850s in the city of Muskegon, as well as elsewhere in Michigan's lumbering districts, though they still numbered only 384 in 1860. The stacks of plank along the South Branch of the Chicago River bore witness to the diligence of the lumber industry and were almost as impressive as the towering grain elevators. Chicago was quickly becoming the primary corn, wheat, and lumber market of the world.[3]

In the lumber industry one finds Norwegians, not only as laborers in the forests and sawmills and as sailors transporting planks, but in the distribution sector. The robust construction activity and the great demand it created made the lumber business profitable. From the early 1840s the two brothers John B. and Andrew B. Johnson, sons of Baard Johnson (Rogne), ran a prosperous lumberyard by the North Branch on Kingsbury Street. It was destroyed in the Great Fire in 1871. The Johnson brothers were representative of immigrant entrepreneurs who took advantage of opportunities in a rapidly expanding economy.[4]

Chicago's economy, with a minor recession in 1854, prospered until 1857, a year which historian A.T. Andreas stated "was made memorable in the calendar of the city's history by the most serious financial crisis experienced since its founding, twenty years before." Panic swept the country in September of that year when eastern banks failed, closing businesses and curtailing production and fiscal activity. Chicago was severely affected; all but two banks had closed their doors by 1860. Unemployment became rampant, so that by the end of 1857 thousands of workers and their families faced starvation in Chicago alone, while the general rush of people into the city continued and made matters worse. A newly arrived immigrant from Voss in 1859 reported tongue-in-cheek to friends back home that the term "hard times" was the only one understood by all nationalities in Chicago, "Jews and Greeks, Johnny Bulls and Johnny Europas, Yankees and Sauerkrauts, Norwegians and Vossings," the next item in importance in the common vocabulary being "lager beer." The depression lasted with some moderation until the Civil War.[5]

"There are widespread complaints about hard times," wrote the Norwegian-language *Wossingen* in May, 1858; "work is difficult to get and wages are low." A more disturbing insight into the problems many faced during the hard times of the late 1850s was provided in the same monthly's September issue, which related a gruesome incident. In graphic detail it described how poverty had driven a Norwegian in Chicago to madness. He had murdered his own child with an axe rather than see it die of hunger. The *Weekly Democrat* lauded the German and Scandinavian population of Chicago for acting quickly "to take care of its own poor during the coming winter . . . an example against plundering the city government," and accused "the sons of the Emerald Isle" of the latter "for the benefit of the drunken and lazy under the name of public charity." Immigrants were obviously the most vulnerable part of the population during times of depression, facing unemployment as well as prejudice, with insufficient resources to relieve existing wants in their own ranks.[6]

Health Conditions

Arriving in Chicago in 1846 a Norwegian newcomer reported back home that if any nation ought to be praised for an unusual amount of illness, America certainly deserved first prize, "because when we arrived, there were sick people wherever we went." He found health conditions in Chicago particularly deplorable. With its crowded filthy streets, impure drinking water, insufficient drainage, wet swamps, and the polluted Chicago River, the city was in fact an unhealthy place. Deadly epidemics called forth efforts to improve the situation, but although progress was being made, especially in the 1850s, these efforts were inadequate.[7]

Andrew Larson (Flage) in his well-known letter of 1840 claimed that "almost all who come here from Europe become ill." He identified as the most common maladies the fever and ague, or malaria, and cholera, so-called bilious fever, which was frequently fatal. The many illnesses and deaths among Norwegians in Chicago had several causes. In his work of 1850 on the diseases of the Mississippi valley, Daniel Drake wrote that Norwegian immigrants landing in Chicago often sickened under the combined influence of meat and whiskey. Overindulgence in alcohol might well have had adverse effects on the immigrants' well-being. But poor nutrition in general, crowded quarters, and unsanitary conditions that spread bacteria were at least equally culpable. Judging from official medical reports, cleanliness was a nearly unknown virtue in rural Norway in the last century. As late as 1891 the district physician in Voss reported that "in regard to cleanliness the Vossings must be said to be backward . . . and are especially slovenly about their own bodies, as bathing is a rare operation and many women under ordinary circumstances will not wash their face or hands for days."[8]

The city itself presented a dismal picture, with dogs roaming the streets, rotting animal carcasses, and underneath the wooden sidewalks a numerous rat population. Campaigns by the local press to clean up the city had little effect. "In walking through the city," the *Daily Democrat* reported, "the stenches that are met with and pollute the olfactories are both numerous and powerful." The newspaper complained especially about a slaughterhouse on the lake shore, which "when the wind is from the east, emits such disgusting odors that the occupants of some houses on the North Side are often unable to eat."[9]

Working conditions on the Canal and the river caused illness. In an America letter dated December 31, 1839, one reads that "of a party of emigrants, mostly from Voss, that came to Chicago during the hottest part of the summer . . . fourteen or fifteen died." "Most of them were poor people," one reads further, "who had spent more than they possessed to make the journey and had to seek work immediately to survive. Many of them began Canal digging, which is the most steady and favorable, but nonetheless the hardest and most unhealthy work during the summer." Foremen on the Canal might warn newcomers against the grave consequences of getting wet and thus contracting malaria. But Rene thinks that Norwegians ignored such advice, believing that as in Norway they "were able to take it all." One of those who died in 1839 was Andrew Larson's stepson Johannes Olsen.[10]

PHYSICIANS' REPORT.

No. 2 of Deaths

Date 3 June — Name, Edward Walin — Age, 40 — Sex, male

Nation, Irish

Location, Wolcost street North Division

Occupation, Laborer at House moving

Habits, Rather intemperate

SYMPTOMS.

Diarrhoea, Present & Profuse

How long standing, Twelve hours

Vomiting, character of, Present. Fluid

Cramps, where, Present. abdomen & Extremities

Purging, character of, Rice Water & Profuse

Intellectual State, Dull. with tendency to Coma

State of skin and extremities, Cold & Clammy. Profuse perspiration

State of other secretions, No secretion from Kidneys & Salivary glands

Pulse weak & entirely absent at times

Treatment, Sulphur & Charcoal 3 grs. Calomel 10 grs. Quinine 5 grs. Opium ½ gr. Mix. Repeated every 3 hours mustard to extremities and abdomen. All the external heat possible applied to extremities.

Result, Death. 12 hours after the premonitory symptoms and six hours after the first med. was given

Remarks.

This patient had been laboring hard in the open air till 12 o'clock at night previous to the attack at 2 in the morning. Was probably intemperate. Lived in a garret into which 5 or 6 others were crowded. Died; in the opinion of the undersigned on act of neglect in Calling med aid.

W. B. Herrick M.D.

A physician's cholera report dated June 3, 1849.

There was, however, no epidemic illness before May of 1849, when cholera broke out. It had been brought to the city by immigrants arriving by way of the river and canal route from New Orleans, where cholera was raging. "More than any other locality in the city, the disease prevailed on a sandy elevation in the North Division, chiefly inhabited by Norwegians, and many of them recent arrivals," wrote Andreas. It was a district where well water prevailed, and cholera was spread through the drinking water supply. Arne Anderson Vinje told how he and a neighbor made a boat and rowed far out on the lake to fetch pure water. Dr. John Evans, who made a careful study of the epidemic, publishing his findings in 1850, identified forty-four deaths among the 332 Norwegians on the North Side, and described the Norwegians residing there as people in moderate circumstances, who lived as comfortably as the average Americans. One person in every thirty-six in Chicago died during the epidemic; among the Norwegian residents on the North Side it was one in every seven. It was a comfort to the established American element that most of the deaths occurred "among our foreign citizens."[11]

Such statements were also intended to prevent "wonder and alarm," as the *Free West* expressed it. Chicago newspapers criticized those who exaggerated the number of deaths. "Strangers would suppose the whole town is dying off," the *Daily Democrat* complained. There was a fear that people would stay away to the detriment of business. By the end of September, when it was no longer considered an epidemic, the actual number of Chicagoans who had succumbed to the plague was no fewer than 663, among them many prominent citizens. The city directory listed the names of the latter.[12]

Cholera appeared every year after that, with especially many fatalities in 1852, but was not held to be an epidemic until 1854, when the *Free West* explained a shortage of labor and resulting delays in publishing the newspaper by the fact that "the Angel of Death has stretched out his hand over our city. . . . Those who could have left the city for a short sojourn in the country where they might be free from labor and from fear."[13]

Norwegian immigrants bound for Wisconsin who had become infected en route were said to have brought the disease to Chicago on June 29. Six were dead on the train from New York and a seventh died a few minutes after being taken off. This route and the one through New Orleans were the avenues by which the disease was carried inland. The language barrier frequently left Norwegian immigrants who became ill during the overland journey without medical attention. The special immigrant trains were usually wretched, some even having been used to transport cattle. Emigrating in 1854, taking the then common route by way of Quebec, Halle Steensland later, as a prominent businessman in Madison, Wisconsin, recalled how the immigrants were put on freight trains with seats of planks without backs. "Around about us people were dying of cholera which in 1854 was very prevalent," Steensland wrote. The Cook County Medical Society had received a report of a case of cholera in late April, but it was rejected by the health authorities. Not until two months later, when the disease was detected in the Norwegian immigrants, did they act, and then by establishing quarantine grounds along the main routes of immigrant travel.[14]

There were some cases of cholera in 1855, but then the plague did not recur until 1863 and again in 1866, when it took many lives. The Norwegian-language *Skandinaven*, launched in Chicago in early summer 1866, picked up on the many questionable cures that were being advertised and recommended one "The Sunflower Mixture" as good preventive medicine. It was, however, the fright created by the first great epidemic, in 1849, that most severely affected Norwegian attitudes. Its devastating impact among Norwegians in Chicago made people feel more than ever at the mercy of epidemic plagues, and many Norwegians left the city and were joined by emigrants who sought a healthier rural existence.[15]

A Broadening Stream

The scare of the plague notwithstanding, an influx of immigrants swelled Chicago's population. The quickening pace of Norwegian emigration contributed to the increase, although, to be sure, in no dramatic fashion, and fear of the cholera was at least in part responsible. Only during the latter years of the 1850s did Norwegians begin to settle in Chicago in large numbers. An established immigrant community then functioned like a magnet. In 1860 Norwegian-born Chicagoans numbered 1,313, the Swedish–born 816, and the Danish-born 150, for a Scandinavian community equal to a little more than 2 percent of the city's population. [16]

The 1850s were golden years in Norway, with economic growth, employment opportunities in many areas of the nation's economy, and general optimism. But overseas emigration continued to increase. The majority of America travelers came from the inner fjord districts of West Norway and the upper mountain valleys of East Norway; the latter communities had been touched by America fever toward the end of the 1830s. A general cause of migration from these specific parts was acute population pressure in districts which had utilized existing resources to the extent possible at that time. They also had a tradition, even if not a long one, of going to America. In the first half of the decade there was also a sudden surge of emigration overseas from some of Norway's cities, especially from the capital city of Christiania (Oslo). Between 1851 and 1855 756 left from Oslo, among them many craftsmen and artisans. An examination of 210 passport records for these five years shows that 70 percent of the 124 adult men emigrating had a special occupational skill; they were cabinetmakers, bricklayers, bookbinders, tailors, shoemakers, or mates and seamen on sailing ships. A few were office and store clerks; one man listed as "convict" (*tugthusfange*) was obviously starting life over again in America. People in the crafts might have decided to emigrate because they felt the threat of cheaper factory-made products, whether imported or manufactured in Norway. These skilled immigrants were more likely than peasant immigrants to settle in America's great cities. In many instances their names reappear in Chicago city directories in the late 1850s, though their absence need not indicate that they went elsewhere, simply that they were not recorded.[17]

The total exodus, from the sailing of the Sloopers in 1825 to the end of the Civil War—the founding phase in the emigration phenomenon—involved 77,863 people. More than half left in the decade between 1856 and 1865. Some generalizations can be made about these pioneer emigrants. Emigration was a structured and selective process; it was engaged in by individuals who made considered and realistic decisions about their own and their children's lives. These decisions were taken on the basis of social and economic conditions that encouraged people to seek alternative strategies. Capitalistic forces were at work transforming the rural economy from a largely self-sufficient barter system to a money economy. Modernization created surplus labor that had to find gainful employment outside agriculture.[18]

During the entire period under consideration, until the end of the Civil War, most people went to America in family units; it was a permanent move to begin life over in a different part of the world. The early emigrants, men such as Andrew Larson (Flage) and Baard Johnson (Rogne) from Voss, were farm owners. Straitened circumstances induced them to sell their property. They belonged to the category of farmers about to go under financially. But, on the other hand, the profit from the sale gave them the required resources to emigrate. Beginning in the 1850s there was a broadening of the social base; the lower social classes, cotters and agricultural laborers, joined in the emigration in large numbers. Particularly in the movement from the better agricultural districts in East Norway, with their social stratification and increasingly commercial and modernized agricultural production, they were well represented. In the older emigration districts, such as the upland valleys in East Norway, the farm-owning class, farmers and sons of farmers, dominated the overseas movement.

There was, not only in the countryside but also in the cities, a process of impoverishment which made people sink down into lower classes. This process of proletarianization and loss of social status convinced people to go to America; it might be easier to join kinfolk there than to seek a livelihood in some other part of Norway. As has been suggested, the high cost of going to America in the 1830s and 1840s had a selective effect; only those who had saved money, were aided by prosperous kin or friends, or had property to sell were in a position to go. Later, "prepaid tickets" and other assistance from Norwegians in America made it possible for people of modest means to emigrate; a reduction in the price of passage in the 1850s served the same purpose.[19]

Immigrant Self-Assertion

From the late 1830s Norwegian authorities became alarmed at the growing movement overseas. An agitation against leaving the homeland ensued; "stay in the land and support yourself honestly," Bishop Jacob Neumann in Bergen admonished. In their propaganda against emigration the authorities used America letters and other writings sent home by discontented emigrants in America. A letter written by one Sjur Jørgensen Lokrheim and published in *Bergens Stiftstidende* (Bergen Diocese Times) in 1839 was a case in point and of particular interest. The report was published with the aid of Bishop Neumann and is a mournful account of conditions among Norwegians in America and an earnest expression of a desire to return to Norway. Lokrheim accomplished the latter in 1841, and the following year, likely again with Neumann's help, published a ten-page pamphlet titled *Oplysninger om forholdene i Nordamerika* (Information on Conditions in North America), which like the earlier letter discouraged emigration. In this pamphlet he told that he had emigrated from Hardanger in 1836 and together with others in his party was destined for the Fox River settlement, but that when they arrived in Chicago after a long journey some of the emigrants had to remain there because they had no money left. One of those who for this reason settled in Chicago that year with his family was Svein Lothe.[20]

The Lokrheim letter of 1839 came to the attention of the Vossings in Chicago through Lars Nesheim, a bachelor farmer in Voss given to literary pursuits, who acted as their correspondent. Group solidarity in an immigrant population from a common locality, a need to justify their emigration, and a defense of the new society roused the Vossings to action. In an early and notable act of immigrant self-assertion the Vossings mailed a joint letter back. This was the well-known letter penned by Andrew Larson (Flage) referred to previously. It was dated in Chicago on November 23, 1840, and denounced as false statements and allegations made by Lokrheim. "It is not true," the letter declared, "that it is as bad in America as that Sjur Valdres has written. . . . We have enough food and clothes."[21]

Lokrheim hailed from Valdres, and one senses a local bias in how he was identified in the letter; he was an East Norwegian, though he had emigrated from Haaheim in Ulvik in Hardanger. The impact of positive or negative information on the volume of emigration as well as on the choice of specific destination in America cannot be precisely determined, but it is obvious that at a time when letters were the main, if not the only, source on which to make far-reaching personal decisions, they had some impact on overall developments. They were written by people from the peasant community itself, and whether they gave good news or bad, their authors were trusted friends and neighbors. The Norwegian peasants thereby had their own experts on America. Arne Anderson Vinje, who emigrated from Voss in 1840 and settled in Chicago, wrote that that year many Vossings had abandoned plans to go to America after reading the Lokrheim letter. The effect appears, however, to have been temporary, at least partly because of the countermeasures taken by Larson (Flage) and other immigrants in Chicago. In Hardanger, by way of comparison, no letters contradicted the negative reports. Parish priests read Lokrheim's letter from the pulpit to convince people to remain at home.

Other woeful reports from unhappy emigrants from Hardanger arrived as well. On June 11, 1841, *Bergens Stiftstidende* printed a letter from three dissatisfied ones who had left Ulvik in 1839, Brynjulf Lekve and the two brothers Anders and Johan Vik, in a party of twenty emigrants from that community. They arrived in Chicago on August 25 after a journey of about three months, and several of them found jobs on the Canal, some on a schooner on the river, and others as woodcutters in the woods about Chicago. The letter told of trials and hardships and many deaths; it advised people not to come to America. Historian George Flom concluded that the discouraging news in this letter and in Lokrheim's, without rebuttal from other Hardanger emigrants in America, caused a break in the emigration from some parishes until 1846. It also explained why so few of the later emigrants from Hardanger settled in Chicago. [22]

The Vossings were again moved to take action in 1848 to challenge another document. This time it was an official report by the consul general for Sweden and Norway in New York, Adam Løvenskjold, following his visit to "Norwegian settlements in the western districts of the United States" the summer of 1847. His report was published in Bergen the next year. [23]

Løvenskjold's official description of immigrant life was not intentionally distorted or malicious, but it painted a negative picture: the immigrants lived in wretched houses, there was poverty and illness, Norwegians enjoyed little respect, they were slovenly and ignorant. The report was seen by the immigrants as an anti-emigration document and it created great bitterness. There is no evidence that Løvenskjold ever visited Chicago, but the same fall his report was published the Vossings in the city organized the Vossing Correspondence Society (Det vossiske korrespondance Selskab) to give "systematic enlightenment to the Norwegian people concerning the status of their emigrated compatriots and to refute false assertions regarding America and the Norwegian immigrants." They banded together to meet the mailing costs and possibly pay for the postage of correspondence from Norway. The Society may well have been the very first secular organization among Norwegians in America. It is significant that it emerged in a city, where residential concentration encouraged social life, which was an essential factor in its formation.[24]

In their midst the Vossings had a number of capable and talented letter writers, which is clearly evidenced in the eight letters sent back to Norway from September 30, 1848, to May 1, 1849. Active participants in the organization included Iver Lawson, Andrew Nelson (Brekke), and Endre Tesdahl, whose better formal education made him its secretary. The comparison that was drawn between Norway with its confining circumstances and America as the land of freedom and opportunity was perhaps not uncommon, but directly or indirectly the letters give a biting criticism of social conditions in the homeland. There was considerable bitterness against public officials, social injustice, and class differences. This reflected memories from Voss of specific confrontations between the peasant community and the strong-willed Dean Münster, the authoritarian district magistrate (*sorenskriver*) Arnoldus von Western Sydow Koren, and the large estate owner Johan Sechmann Fleischer, "who reigned like a little king over the peasants who sat as tenant farmers on his properties." A careful analysis of the letters would reveal much about attitudes and conditions in the small immigrant community in Chicago. Even in adversity caused by poverty and illness there existed great optimism. The correspondents took pains to show that when given the opportunity, members of the lower classes in Norway had the ability to succeed, and they gave personal information about thirty-two Vossings, probably the members of the Society, emphasizing their material advancement. Lawson's own parents had belonged to the class of tenant farmers, renting the property they farmed. Freedom, equality, and opportunity for everyone — the common man just as much as the educated person — are for the letter writers the basic elements of the American social order; they conclude that "it is high time the civil as well as the religious organizations make justice, freedom, and equality a common measure also in Norway."[25]

In one respect the letters are unique, as they tended to promote a rural to urban migration — not, as in the great number of America letters arriving in Norway in the 1840s, a rural to rural one. The Vossing correspondents instead described life in a city and success in urban occupations and professions. One reads, for example, about one Claus Knutsen Saue, whose work was to build houses as a carpenter, to lay sidewalks, and to load and unload vessels, for which he earned about 75 cents to one dollar daily. His wife did laundry, making from one dollar to one dollar and fifty cents weekly. These were clearly Norwegian peasants entering urban occupational patterns and adjusting to a city environment.[26]

It is obvious from later actions that the broader purpose of the Society's work was not merely to justify the immigrants' existence in

America but just as much to encourage further immigration. Knut Rene thinks that Løvenskjold's negative report merely provided the immediate incentive to organize, as the Vossings were already concerned about a decline in emigration from Voss and the small numbers that came to Chicago. Their motives might have included a strong wish to be joined by kinfolk and neighbors from home; a familiar environment could thereby be recreated, and religious and secular institutions would find support. But also the expanding immigrant farming communities in Illinois and Wisconsin required a steady infusion of new immigrants as the spread of settlement westward reduced their populations; Norwegian-American farmers sought reliable and reasonable labor from home, as immigrant entrepreneurs in Chicago eventually would as well. This is not of course to call into question the sincerity of their expressed opinions about America.[27]

The ultimate purpose of the Society became obvious in the fall of 1849 when three of its members went back to Voss with the clear mission of encouraging Vossings to go to America. The fact that no replies had been received to their correspondence has been given as a partial reason for their visit. Perhaps they hoped through personal testimony to allay fears about the cholera epidemic that year. Cause and effect can of course by no means be established, but one may fairly conclude that their efforts deserve some credit for the sudden jump in emigration from Voss in 1850, when an estimated 300 to 350 Vossings emigrated. Most of them only passed through Chicago, or avoided the city altogether, because of the dreaded disease. Many fearful accounts circulated. Peter Davidson (Skjervheim), who in 1850 went to Chicago from his homestead in Wiota to meet his brother Arne and his family, died of the plague; Arne and his family also caught it, and except for two young sons all succumbed.

The Correspondence Society was in a position, because it emerged among Norwegians in Chicago, to influence the entire movement overseas and to serve the needs of the whole Norwegian-American community. In February, 1848, earlier efforts to organize a Lutheran congregation succeeded, and the Society held its meetings in a small room above the entrance of its church on Superior Street, the same one vacated by the notorious John Smith. Social and religious concerns merged, as the leaders in these various undertakings were the same.[28]

After 1849 the Correspondence Society continued as a discussion group with regular meetings which attracted new members. A debating society that had its genesis in informal meetings in the clothing store of Lewis A. Brown (in Voss Lars Anfinson Bryn) on North Clark Street, a popular place for Norwegians to gather, was organized in 1852 as the Norwegian Debating Society. It assembled leading men and young men on the rise in the Norwegian community, and not only Vossings but men like O. B. Jacobs from the Stavanger area, who

The photograph was taken from the dome of the Court House in 1858
and shows a view of Chicago north on Clark Street and Randolph Street.

later prospered in the lumber business, Kittel Neresen from Skien, who became a successful lathing contractor, and the liberal Dr. Gerhard S.C.H. Paoli from Trondheim, who was active in freethinking circles. Most members were, however, from Voss; Andrew B. Johnson joined, and both Andrew Nelson (Brekke) and Iver Lawson were members. In the spring of 1856 the two last-mentioned men made a trip to Voss and discovered that in their old home community there were many people who wished to emigrate but could not finance the move. An American tourist, Charles L. Brace, who visited Voss that same summer, stayed at the village inn at Vangen where the two men also found lodging. Brace later recorded his impressions and his understanding of their mission. These are worthy of notice. In stark contrast to their simple kinfolk in their peasant garments, they had become urbanized and were well dressed "in blue coats and splendid velvet vests," but "spoke with the most murderous accent and chewed tobacco and spat incessantly." "The two Norwegians," Brace further wrote, "had spent fifteen to sixteen years in our western states and there had acquired a fortune. They had now returned partly to visit friends and relatives, and perhaps partly for the purpose of speculation — in order to bring suitable emigrants to their own claims or to the expanding cities. . . . They [Lawson and Nelson] thought Norway to be intolerably backward."[29]

On returning to Chicago in the fall Lawson and Nelson were instrumental in organizing the Vossing Emigration Society (Det vossiske Emigrationsselskab) on October 23, 1856. The correspondence society must be considered to have merged with the new organization, whose object was "to collect funds through free subscription to be used simply and only to help needy and deserving families to America." Aid was to be given in the form of a loan and repaid to the original fund, which in this manner would perpetuate itself, although direct gifts could be made from it in special cases. Iver Lawson was its president and Andrew Larson (Flage) treasurer; Andrew B. Johnson joined as vice president, with Endre Tesdahl continuing as secretary also in this group. An outgrowth of the new organization's activities was the appearance in December, 1857, of the small monthly, *Wossingen*, published at Leland, in northern La Salle county southwest of Chicago, where many Vossings settled. Its publisher and editor was Nils T. Bakketun, who after emigrating in 1853 had gained experience as a typesetter, working at first for the newspaper *Emigranten*, which had begun publication in Inmansville, Wisconsin, in January, 1852. Copies of *Wossingen*, which came out in America until March, 1860, were sent to Voss, perhaps as an effort to continue the work of the correspondence society, and in it letters from both sides of the Atlantic were printed. The issue of May, 1858, told of the arrival in Voss of Iver Lawson, who had returned to aid in the emigration of Vossings. Lawson remained in Norway for an entire year actively recruiting emigrants and supervising the disposition of funds.[30]

It is difficult to estimate how many were aided by the Emigration Society. The fact, however, that the Chicago group organized chapters in other Norwegian settlements suggests its perceived broader purpose. A chapter founded at Jefferson Prairie in Wisconsin in 1858 sent the considerable amount of $106 to aid impoverished prospective emigrants from Voss. These might of course in turn become laborers for established immigrant farmers. It is reasonable to assume, as this kind of indenture became common, that the newcomers repaid the farmer who had advanced the cost of the ticket by working on his farm. The Society functioned until the Civil War, and Rene thinks that its activities had a significant impact by assisting disadvantaged people who wished to emigrate. It became a model for later similar efforts.[31]

The Place of Immigrant Leaders

In July, 1858, *Wossingen* listed the names of all the Vossings in Chicago. There were that year 200, representing roughly 20 percent of the Norwegian-born population. From the Vossing ranks came many of the original leaders, which reflected not only their early emigration but also a close-knit community that allowed a leadership to emerge, and perhaps even the entrepreneurial local culture in Voss. Men who rose in prominence within a broader setting, and enjoyed the respect of the host society, were in a position to give direction and definition to their own ethnic group, as well as a heightened ethnic awareness and increased visibility.[32]

But the leadership role is ephemeral in nature. The broadening stream of newcomers in the 1850s, bearing a variety of religious persuasions, local loyalties, and cultural interests created tension and strife. There evolved also considerable antagonism against the dominance of the established Vossings. Newly arrived immigrants from Voss shared in this feeling, illustrating an inevitable split between older and newer settlers. The severe depression of the late 1850s added fuel to the tension. It expressed itself most clearly in religious strife and in a bitter challenge to the assimilationist drive of the pioneer community. Early leaders had worked to prepare their countrymen for life in an American urban environment, evidenced not only in the Americanization of names, or in entry into civic life, but in educational efforts as well. An example was the Norwegian Debating Society, which conducted its debates, and one must suspect haltingly so, only in *English*. Topics for discussion at their weekly meetings at the North Market Hall, where Lawson was market clerk and manager, dealt with public issues. In the late 1850s they debated regularly pro and con the institution of slavery, often assuming the identities of public figures of the day, such as Senator Douglas or Lincoln. Annual gala socials identified the members and their wives as a *beau monde* of sorts within the immigrant community.[33]

•
Andrew Nelson (Brekke).

Iver Lawson was undoubtedly one of the most prominent men in this coterie. Making his fortune in the same manner as the early Yankee speculators, though with the difference that he had raised capital to invest through hard labor, he was a genuine immigrant success story. As an ethnic leader he promoted the structural development of the immigrant community.[34]

In Lawson's political ambitions, and in those of other leaders like Andrew B. Johnson and Andrew Nelson (Brekke), societies, clubs, and organized religious life became important in any strategy to rally compatriots around their cause. The strong anti-slavery sentiment in Chicago, which early became a stop on the underground railroad that transported fugitive slaves to Canada and freedom, influenced Norwegian sentiment. Ole Olson Hetletvedt, or Ole Middlepoint, was an abolitionist and his stage station at Norway (then Middlepoint) in La Salle county was a link on the railroad. Most Norwegians, however, in Chicago as elsewhere in the Upper Midwest, embraced the Republican free soil stand of merely keeping slavery out of the territories while leaving it in the old slave states. It was an issue that stimulated interest in public affairs. Norwegians, like other Scandinavians and the Germans, owned enough real property to feel threatened by the prospect of slavery in the territories, and they joined the native-born elite in an anti-Democratic coalition.

The first Norwegian-language newspaper in Chicago, however, *Friheds-Banneret* (The Banner of Freedom) with its programmatic name, began on October 4, 1852, as a free-soil weekly, advocating not only non-extension but the complete abolition of slavery. Its editor, John Mauritzon, was assailed by more conservative elements as a "red Republican." In April, 1853, the Dane George P. Hansen, who here was given an opportunity to establish his credentials in the Republican party, took over and adopted a moderate tone, but the newspaper survived less than a year. Norwegian voters continued to abandon the Democratic party, a flight that was considerably accelerated by the passage of the Kansas-Nebraska Act in 1854 which would leave the decision of slavery to the settlers in the new territories, and much hostility was directed against its author, Senator Stephen A. Douglas of Illinois. His alliance with the Irish in 1855 caused about fifty Scandinavians, half of them Norwegian, in Chicago to give public support to the mayoral candidate of the nativist, and anti-Douglas, Know-Nothing party, later explaining that it was a tactical vote to break the hold of the Germans and the Irish and their Catholicism on local politics. The instigators were apparently the Swedish Episcopalian minister Gustaf Unonius and the Scandinavian Union, a society formed the previous year. Since the Democrats by then were identified with Catholicism and intemperance, the action of this group, "praised by the Americans," suggests the acceptance not only of anti-Irish nativism, but also of other Protestant reforms.

Lawson's position at the North Market Hall gave him an important role in arranging the large gathering there in October, 1854, which heard Lincoln speak against the Kansas-Nebraska measure. In August, 1856, George P. Hansen, later appointed American consul to Helsingör for his services to the Republican party, and Andrew B. Johnson and Dr. Paoli were among the leaders in arranging a mass Scandinavian Republican meeting which made a point of rejecting the Know-Nothings. Reactions to nativist provocations cut across ethnic lines and united immigrant groups. *Emigranten*, then moving toward Republicanism and fearing that the taint of nativism and the Know-Nothing element that existed in the Republican party would alienate Norwegian voters, educated its readers on "the true ideals and nature of Republican ideology." The 1856 meeting rejected the "Douglas Whiskey-Party," and endorsed the Republican party's platform and its presidential candidate, General John C. Fremont, the explorer and

hero of the Mexican War. Nelson (Brekke) and Lawson had not yet
returned from their visit to Voss, and consequently were prevented
from attending. But Lawson had shown his feelings in 1850 when at
the birth of a son he gave him the name Victor Fremont, and he was
not the only Norwegian to so honor the general. The events and issues of the conflict with Mexico, encouraged by John Wentworth and
his *Daily Democrat*, had engaged Norwegian immigrants. Fremont
won Chicago, *Emigranten* attributing the victory to the Scandinavian
vote, even though he lost the national election.[35]

Scandinavian cooperation in local politics evolved from a need
to unite forces in order to gain influence; the leading Swede on the
Chicago scene, Charles Sundell, took part in a Scandinavian, largely
Norwegian, Republican meeting in December, 1856, in Ward 6 on
the Northwest Side, which encouraged the nomination of Andrew B.
Johnson as aldermanic candidate. The meeting resolved that this
would be only fair "in view of the large number of Scandinavians and
their loyalty to the Republican party." Although he did not succeed
on this occasion, Johnson was later a member of the Board of County
Commissioners.[36]

The Swedish-language press, read also by Danes and Norwegians, remained united in its Republican and antislavery stance.
Hemlandet (The Homeland), founded in Galesburg, Illinois, in 1855,
moved to Chicago in 1859; its first editor, the Lutheran minister Tuve
Nilsson Hasselquist, encouraged readers to become American citizens
so that they could vote Republican. To rally the Scandinavian vote
around the Republicans, and perhaps further his own career, Iver
Lawson helped to call a mass meeting in February, 1859, where even
ethnic rivalry was used to rouse Scandinavians. It was pointed out
how much better the Germans were represented in municipal offices.
The following year Lawson was rewarded by being appointed marshal by his friend John Wentworth, who was then mayor and a "reluctant Republican," to quote his biographer. Wentworth, who appeared
to continue to cultivate ties to the Norwegian community, but now
as a Republican, made Dr. Paoli, who twice was president of the Chicago Medical Society, city physician in recognition of his skills, but
obviously just as much because of political services.

As city marshal Lawson had command of the police force and
consequently was in charge of keeping order during the 1860 Republican National Convention, at the famed Republican Wigwam, which
nominated Lincoln. *The Press and Tribune* hailed Lincoln of Illinois as
"The Man of the People." The largest Norwegian-American newspaper, *Emigranten*, with a readership also in Chicago, had with the
editorship of Carl Fredrik Solberg in 1857 completely moved into the
Republican camp, and away from its initial Democratic conviction.
By 1860 its number of subscribers had risen to 4,000, indicating the
acceptance of its political color and advocacy. A Republican campaign

newspaper, *Folkebladet* (People's Gazette), was that year launched in Chicago by Charles M. Reese, a Danish-American editor of three earlier Democratic journals, indicating the change in political allegiance of Scandinavians in general.[37]

The common view of Norwegians and other Scandinavians in Chicago as being politically passive must, as the evidence shows, at least be modified. The political education of the immigrants was facilitated by democratic traditions in Norway, and by their natural and increasing concern for civic affairs and public events in America. Yet Lawson was not able to rally his compatriots behind his personal ambitions in large numbers. Norwegian newcomers who in the late 1850s suffered from unemployment and other hardships were unreceptive, even hostile, to an appeal from people whose speculative ventures only increased their wealth. Lawson became their special target, as he was now blamed for bringing them over. Moreover, the entire group of established individuals referred to as the "Voss Circle" was criticized. A contributor to *Wossingen* in January, 1859, accused the "Voss Circle" of belonging only to politics, and described them as a type of " 'wolf behind the door' to scare small children so that the nursemaids could get the children to bed and have a chance to sleep with their young men."[38]

Before his death in 1872 at age fifty-one, Lawson sat on the city council from 1864 until 1868, elected from what was then the 15th ward, located on the North Side between Division and Huron streets; as a spokesman for the area he enjoyed enthusiastic support from the heavily German population, as he did in 1869 when elected to the state house of representatives. Lawson was closely associated with the establishment of Chicago's excellent system of parks; the creation of Lincoln Park in particular was due in great measure to his efforts.[39].

Lawson's achievements, to be sure, generated ethnic pride, even though jealousy and strife had caused some hostility, and Norwegians tended to exaggerate his influence. They believed in his power to help, whether it was to assist them in problems with the law or in procuring a job, which they thought "he only had to recommend to get." And, indeed, during his tenure in city government Norwegians were helped through his intervention to positions in the police force, the customhouse, and the postal service, where he himself had begun.[40]

The Religious Situation

The involvement of Lawson in the development of organized religion within the immigrant community, with its attendant disharmony and schisms, had alienated sections of the Norwegian electorate. In 1848 he had given leadership to the founding of the First Norwegian Evangelical Lutheran Congregation in Chicago, organized on February 14 of that year. "We have now been able by the blessing of God to get a Norwegian and Swedish church established in Chicago, the metropolis of the west," the *Home Missionary* announced. This magazine was the organ of the American Home Missionary Society, which was sustained by the Presbyterians and the Congregationalists. Their continued concern for Norwegian-American spiritual life was further evidence of their disinterested benevolence and of a general effort by American churches and missionary societies to aid the immigrants. The pastor of the new church, Paul Andersen (Norland), had attended the Presbyterian and Congregationalist Beloit College and had entered the Lutheran ministry at the urging of friends there who were mindful of the religious needs of Scandinavian immigrants. The missionary society gave his ministry financial support for some years.[41]

Andersen was born in Vang in Valdres and emigrated in 1843 at the age of twenty-two. Unlike most immigrants, he arrived with knowledge of English; from the age of twelve he had been in the service of the sheriff (lensmann) at Skjold in Rogaland in West Norway and together with the sheriff's children had been taught by a talented private tutor. There he also learned about America and perhaps also to understand the West Norwegian temperament and regional cultural expressions, which he was to encounter in most of his parishioners. Andersen's contact with the broadminded Protestant educational environment at Beloit greatly influenced his outlook and actions; for more than a decade he was a dynamic leader among Norwegians in Chicago.[42]

On January 6, 1848, Andersen had visited Chicago and begun the work which resulted in the church organization. He was ordained in the Franckean Synod, at that time the most liberal Lutheran body in America, with special concerns for the social issues of the day. Andersen was a reformer, deeply religious, but perhaps with only vague conceptions of Lutheran doctrine, and he harbored a clear anti-clerical and anti-authoritarian attitude. His wishes were to bring immigrants and Americans together in a Lutheran union, and to move his countrymen toward integration. In his religious services he used both Norwegian and English, kept ministerial records in English, and conducted a Sunday school only in English to teach the children the language of the land. The totally inadequate public education of the time made it seem all the more important. Leading Norwegians supported his move toward assimilation, and many of them joined the congregation; besides Lawson, these included such men as Andrew Larson (Flage), Endre Tesdahl, Kittel Neresen, and the lake captain Gabriel Gunderson. Some leading men, like Andrew Nelson (Brekke) and Andrew B. Johnson, however, questioned Andersen's Lutheranism, and became members only later or not at all.[43]

In his letters Andersen described the instability of his congregation: some members were there only a few months of the year, many sailed on the lakes in the summer or secured work on farms, while in winter Scandinavian sailors congregated in the city. Arriving Norwegian and other Scandinavian newcomers sought aid and comfort,

Left: Paul Andersen.

Right: The church of the First Norwegian Evangelical Lutheran Congregation on Superior Street in 1848.

but the majority stayed only temporarily until going farther west. In 1850 when William A. Passavant, a prominent eastern Lutheran leader, visited the congregation he estimated a total membership of 300. In his report to the missionary society that same year, however, Andersen set the membership at only 100. The latter figure still represented close to 20 percent of the Norwegian colony.[44]

In August, 1848, having conducted religious services in the Bethel Chapel, a Methodist seamen's mission on Kinzie Street, the congregation purchased the unfinished church structure on Superior Street begun by Smith and his followers. The First Norwegian Evangelical Lutheran Congregation became known as the North Side or Paul Andersen's church, and was a significant social as well as religious center. In this simple edifice the first marriage ceremony was held on October 14, 1848, uniting in matrimony Neils Christophersen and Sara Gunvalsen; the first ecclesiastical act in the congregation had been the baptism on June 30 of Anne, the baby daughter of Lars and Anne Thornsen. The baptism of Iver and Malinda Lawson's son Victor Fremont was entered into the church records on January 1, 1851. In addition to providing such ministerial services, which earlier had been only sporadically available from visiting clergy or in churches of other nationalities, the congregation, to paraphrase Passavant, extended brotherly love and Christian kindness to the many newcomers, standing as it did at the door by which immigrants entered the West.[45]

A few Swedes and Danes, among the latter George P. Hansen, had joined Andersen's church. Scandinavians abroad, confronted by vastly different cultures, and with similar ethnic, linguistic, and cultural bonds and a sense of a shared past, tended to unite, especially when their numbers were small. Experience would show, however, that nationalistic feelings could not long surrender to a common Scandinavian identity. But when a small party of immigrants from Västergötland in Sweden became stranded in Chicago in the summer of 1852, Norwegian families took them in and Andersen gave pastoral care to the ill. Most of these Swedes became members of his congregation.[46]

It was Andersen who took the initiative to form a Swedish Lutheran congregation which would share the church edifice with the Norwegians. The Methodist mission among the Swedes made this move seem all the more urgent to people who judged the Methodists to be "spiritually blind" as well as "false teachers." The Swedish Methodist Olaf Hedström, who had done missionary work among Swedes in New York since 1845, came to Chicago in November, 1852, together with his brother Jonas. After ten days of revival services at the Bethel Chapel the Scandinavian work was organized in Chicago on Christmas Day, with seventy-five members, mostly Swedish, but also some Danes and Norwegians, and at the end of 1854, the congregation moved from the Bethel Chapel to its own church on Illinois and Market (now Orleans) streets. Samuel Andersen, a converted Norwegian sailor and navigator, served as an assistant pastor, his former occupation suggesting the progress the Methodist mission had made among Scandinavian sailors.[47]

The founding of the Swedish Lutheran Immanuel Congregation on January, 1853, by the Swedes in Andersen's church had, however, attracted many members away from the Methodists, who as a result increased their own organizational efforts among Scandinavians. It was a volatile religious climate and competition for adherents was lively. There was no pastor in the Immanuel congregation until Erland Carlsson arrived from Sweden in August, and then only thirty-six of the original eighty members remained, consisting of eight families and twenty single people, the others having returned to the Methodist church. The dynamic Carlsson served an impoverished immigrant population.

In September, 1854, the expanding Norwegian group laid the cornerstone for a new brick edifice to be built on the corner of Franklin and Erie streets. It cost $18,000 and Andersen solicited funds in American churches in Pennsylvania and Maryland. In 1856 S. W. Harkey, professor of theology at the small Lutheran institution at Springfield which carried the pretentious name of Illinois State University, and H. Curtiss, pastor of the First Presbyterian Church of Chicago, performed the dedication ceremonies. The Swedes then became sole occupants of the Superior Street church. The dedication arrangement revealed a continued link with American Protestantism, but also the fact that in 1851 Andersen's wish for a Lutheran synod in the West had materialized when Scandinavian, German, and American Lutheran congregations formed the Synod of Northern Illinois. The school at Springfield was its seminary.[48]

A confusing array of religious impulses and doctrinal positions confronted the immigrants. All the way up to the Great Fire in 1871 it was a stormy period in the religious life of Norwegians in Chicago as they tried to reconcile old-world traditions with the genuine religious freedom in America. Loyalties to church bodies might easily change, or at times immigrants were merely pragmatic, an attitude stemming perhaps from their early experience when no churches of the homeland existed and they were obliged to seek ministerial services in American churches. But they soon became deeply involved in how best to order their religious life. Strong religious leaders influenced their choice. Gustaf Unonius was one such leader, and Andersen objected to what he considered to be unfair and unchristian proselyting by him. Unonius was the founder of a little colony at Pine Lake, Wisconsin, and had gone through the small Nashotah Episcopal Seminary nearby. He was ordained as an Episcopalian minister in 1845.[49]

Unonius had arrived in Chicago in early 1849 at the invitation of previous followers of John Smith and the later Norwegian and Swedish consul in Chicago Polycarpus von Schneidau, a friend of Unonius, who spoke for the Swedes. Unonius was initially welcomed by Andersen, but antagonism soon developed between the two men. The Episcopalian Unonius, feeling that he better represented the homeland's state-church tradition, accused Andersen and his congregation of being non-Lutheran in confession of faith and in church practices.

Even members of Andersen's own congregation had in 1848 questioned his Lutheranism because of his connection with the confessionally loose Franckeans. The Vossing Correspondence Society had felt compelled in its letter of May 1, 1849, to reassure people at Voss that they were still good Lutherans since they still used "Luther's Little Catechism and Pontoppidan's Explanation," even though, because of the Franckeans, they did not in every respect follow the homeland's church ritual. In September, 1848, H.A. Stub, then pastor in the Muskego congregation, had actually been invited by thirty men in Andersen's church to come to Chicago and determine their pastor's Lutheran credentials. Stub's son, H.G. Stub, has told of a stormy meeting where tempers flared, and where Andersen threatened to call the constables to clear the church of his critics. Stub adjourned the meeting and later met with the dissidents who wanted to organize a new church.[50]

In such a volatile situation converts could obviously be made. Without questioning the sincerity of religious conviction, one might conclude that strife between clergymen was partly based on a simple competition for members. Of those who departed from Andersen's church, there is, however, little evidence that many sought the Episcopal Church, which because of its ordained clergy and high-church ritual and practices Unonius viewed as being nearly identical with the Church of Sweden. The St. Ansgarius congregation which subsequently was founded on March 5, 1849, as a part of the Illinois Episcopal Diocese had by 1850 163 members, men, women, and children, and had established itself in a building erected at the corner of Franklin and Indiana. The celebrated Swedish singer Jenny Lind, at Unonius' solicitation, donated $1,000 and a silver communion set to the congregation.[51]

Andrew B. Johnson joined, as did Andrew Nelson (Brekke), the young John Anderson, and many other Norwegians. Their proportionate number is suggested by the fact that in 1849 about one third of all deaths in the congregation were among the Norwegian-born members. The number of Norwegians compared to Swedes decreased, however, over the years. St. Ansgarius became a central Swedish religious and social center, in the same manner as Andersen's church became the focal point for Norwegians.

A number of the Swedish members bore aristocratic names, von Schneidau being a leader in the church council; successful individuals might seek a church home there attracted by the high social status of the Episcopalians in American society. It might have been a consideration for some upwardly mobile Norwegian members as well. The language of the church was English, but Norwegian and Swedish were also used. Clerical functions such as baptisms or weddings were always conducted in one of these two. Unonius related that he followed "principally the Swedish manual, with a few changes, in order to combine the church rituals and ceremonies of the Swedish and Norwegian churches, which both groups were anxious to retain."

Both Andersen and Unonius thus tried to represent the state-church tradition of the homeland in a form they thought appropriate to the new environment. They both met criticism from strict traditionalists. Norwegian and Swedish ministers attacked Unonius as an impostor disguised as a Lutheran minister and combatted his influence vigorously.[52]

The Social Role of the Church

In many instances the social activities of a congregation might weigh as much as doctrinal position when an individual chose church affiliation. Andersen practiced a selective membership, refusing all who gave no evidence of personal piety; in 1850, for instance, he refused to admit a man who operated his business on the Sabbath. In acute situations or under catastrophic conditions, aid was extended to non-members, but those within the congregational or denominational family were favored. On this same basis, Unonius appealed to the American Episcopalians with great success. The security for oneself and loved ones that church membership gave was an important consideration, and likely made people join, and even bend to unfamiliar practices, who otherwise would not have. Unonius suggested that some calculating immigrants joined more than one church group, Episcopal, Lutheran, Presbyterian, or Methodist, and "supplied with statements from the preachers . . . they would go from house to house, displaying now one, now another certificate of proof of their indigence." This dubious practice was a means of survival at a time when the social program of the churches was a major source of support, but it repelled Unonius, and made him question the immigrants' sincerity.[53]

During the cholera epidemics of 1849–1854 Unonius and Andersen appear frequently to have subjugated religious concerns to their respective congregations' social role. The aid given during the devastating outbreak in 1849 was especially noteworthy. Of forty-seven deaths that year in the St. Ansgarius congregation thirty-seven were from cholera; Andersen's congregation suffered a loss of twenty-five members.[54]

In May, 1849, shortly after cholera struck, the city authorized a pesthouse for indigents to be built. It was a loathsome place, and many of the afflicted were treated in homes or at temporary shelters. The *Daily Democrat* on May 28, 1849, reminded the clergy of their "duty to relieve the suffrage of the poor and sick." In his memoirs Unonius gave graphic accounts of his own contributions. He was better prepared than most, having studied medicine and experienced a cholera epidemic in Stockholm. "A Norwegian," he wrote, "who owned an unfinished building in our neighborhood allowed me to use it as a hospital for the Swedish and Norwegian immigrants." Many children were orphaned among the immigrants and Unonius claimed that most of them were well cared for as foster children or servants in American families. His own ministerial records indicate, however, that many of the orphaned children were actually sent to the Chicago Orphan Asylum. An example from his records is of one Peter Andersson, his wife Christina, and their five children, Maja Stina, Anna Greta, Clara, Johannes, and Carl Johan, who arrived from Sweden in early July, 1852. They became afflicted with cholera, and Peter Andersson died on July 8, Christina and the eleven-year-old Maja Stina on July 11, and four-year-old Johannes on July 18. Anna Greta, age nine, Clara, age seven, and Carl Johan, age three, were all placed in the Chicago Orphan Asylum. Many of those who died were so poor that they were buried "on the expense of the county," as Unonius carefully noted for each case.[55]

Erland Carlsson and the Immanuel congregation gradually took over the central position Unonius had among Chicago Swedes. Social work, as practiced by Carlsson, extended to include many services, from meeting immigrants at the railroad station to finding them a place to live and work, helping them overcome language barriers by being an interpreter, buying money orders, and assisting in many daily affairs. The religious impulse in this manner combined with a social program to form an indispensable immigrant institution.[56]

The National Countermove

Circumstances strengthened Norwegian nationalism as well as Norwegian Lutheranism, the latter exhibiting the divergent emphases and directions embodied in that tradition and also the influence of the complexity of American religious life. Even though Chicago offered many more religious possibilities than was the case in segregated rural communities, and displayed considerable immigrant non-conformity in spiritual affairs, the Norwegian community eventually rejected both Andersen's move toward liberal American Protestantism and the high-churchism of Unonius. The Episcopalian direction perhaps did not founder as much over doctrinal issues as over the fact that in spirit and practice it reminded the immigrants too much of the state-church principle. It violated their sense of congregational freedom and democracy; "any congregation," the Vossing correspondents wrote, "worships the Almighty according to its own conscience," which they thought the people back home would at first find strange. In 1858 Unonius returned to Sweden. One of the American pastors of St. Ansgarius, which by then had been reduced to a mission church, E.B. Tuttle, reported in 1860 that most of the Norwegian and Swedish members "have united with other bodies of Christians." The small congregation had, as listed by Tuttle, twenty-five Swedes and thirteen Norwegians, children and adults. Norwegian nationalistic sentiments and ethnic dissension prevented the Norwegians from joining the Swedes in resuscitating St. Ansgarius, and they withdrew altogether in 1865.[57]

The new arrivals from Norway strengthened the national impulse; and earlier immigrants more secure in their existence in America began to show a greater concern to protect the Norwegian heritage. A nationalistic consciousness strengthened by institutional structures emerged, but not without dissent. In 1846 a low-church pietistic movement led by Elling Eielsen became formalized in a church body known as Eielsen's Synod. Out of this group came Hauge's Synod organized at a meeting in Chicago in 1876. Paul Andersen was at first attracted to Eielsen's brand of Norwegian Lutheranism, but distanced himself from the pietists, whose ultra-Norwegian nationalism, religious emotionalism, and Lutheran orthodoxy were unacceptable to him. Eielsen's followers derived their strength from the fact that they stood for a transfer to American soil of a deep Puritanism rooted in the pietistic Haugean movement in Norway; the American environment reinforced this Puritanism, which became pervasive among Norwegian immigrants and demanded strict adherence to a rigidly moral conduct. The Chicago metropolis offered many sights—dancing, drinking, and other "worldly" practices—which encouraged Eielsen to bring his message of penance and conversion there.[58]

In 1850 Eielsen acquired a new and gifted supporter in young P.A. Rasmussen, who that year emigrated from Stavanger. Their relationship lasted six years, until Rasmussen broke with the frequently obstinate and self-willed older man, but not with the Lutheran direction he represented. In 1857 Rasmussen became the first pastor of the low-church Trinity Lutheran Church, organized that year. Eielsen's religious gatherings and prayer meetings beginning in 1839 were seen as the genesis of the congregation. It built a frame edifice on Grand (then Indiana) and Peoria streets. Socially speaking, the pietistic church had as a general rule less appeal for the upwardly mobile and professionally successful and drew much of its membership from a lower level of immigrant society. Many of these hailed from the southwestern part of Norway, Rasmussen's own place of birth, a district greatly affected by the Haugean revival.[59]

Church boundaries were, however, easily crossed. Rasmussen after a few years seceded from the Haugean pietists and joined forces with the university-trained and ordained pastors from Norway who tried to import as much as possible of the state-church tradition of the Church of Norway. He thereby moved to the other extreme of Norwegian-American Lutheranism. This high-church arrangement gained organizational momentum in the 1850s; in 1853 it expressed itself in a church body commonly known as the Norwegian Synod. In a nation where church and state were constitutionally separated it of course had to accommodate itself to a free-church principle, but within this framework the Norwegian Synod perpetuated familiar modes of worship, with the ritual, ministerial vestments, and teachings of the state church. It preserved a Bible-based principle of pure doctrine, rejected lay preaching, and retained some of the exclusive and aristocratic qualities of the Norwegian clergy. Its emphasis on doctrine rather than conduct did not, however, prevent it from attacking frivolities and vices, but it did practice an open membership that did not require evidence of personal conversion. For several decades the high-church tradition, with its sense of solemnity and security and time-honored forms, attracted the largest number of Norwegians.[60]

Our Savior's Lutheran Church was organized within the liturgical Norwegian Synod on January 18, 1858, at North Market Hall by Pastor Gustav F. Dietrichson, a state-church minister who had emigrated in 1851. He was, like several of his pioneer colleagues, a missionary pastor, and he returned to Norway in 1859. During this time of depression there were voices within the Norwegian community which objected to the founding of yet another Lutheran congregation. These objections were met by accusations against the two existing ones of having "done away with many of the church ceremonies and traditions that our people are accustomed to from Norway." Nevertheless, this nationalistic religious view had to be balanced against the realities of immigrant life. The hard times even dictated ecumenical cooperation. The 110 original members of Our Savior's conducted their services in the Scandinavian Methodist Church on Illinois and Market (now Orleans) streets until they moved in 1859 into their own modest edifice, erected with scarce funds and with aid from rural congregations, on the corner of May and Erie streets. [61]

It can be assumed that the nucleus of Our Savior's was the group that had left the Andersen church since these dissatisfied members had called H.A. Stub, a Norwegian Synod pastor, to sit in judgment between themselves and their minister. But even within the Andersen church there was movement toward nationalism and orthodox Lutheranism, initiated by newcomers rather than the remaining members. In 1858 Abraham Jacobson, who had studied theology at the seminary of the Northern Illinois Synod in Springfield, served the First Norwegian Evangelical Lutheran Congregation while Andersen spent a year in Norway because of ill health. To the surprise of the congregation Jacobson replaced its ritual with that of the Church of Norway; the many newcomers gave impetus to this move toward familiar practices. But the older members met it with strong objections. It was an indication of the strife to come. In the annals of Norwegian church life in Chicago it is known as the "Vossing War"; nationalistic and traditionalist forces were eventually, but only after a bitter and lengthy fight, the victors.[62]

Andersen resumed his ministry in the summer of 1859 and again preached and practiced a broad-church and liberal theology. His second wife was Andrew Larson's (Flage) daughter Marthe. This connection strengthened ties to the pioneer members, who were most of the leading Vossings in the community, men like Andrew Nelson (Brekke), who by then had left the St. Ansgarius congregation, and Iver Lawson. Shortly after his return from Norway Andersen saw his pan-Lutheran prospects dissipate, as ethnic feelings and the high confessionalism of Scandinavian Lutheranism caused the Norwegian and Swedish congregations to depart from the Northern Illinois Synod and form the Scandinavian Augustana Synod. Andersen's church joined the new religious body, which though now obviously more ethnic and stricter on confessional issues, still represented a broad-churchism friendly to lay preaching and in opposition to the principles of church practice adopted by the Norwegian Synod. Andersen himself resigned because of continued poor health and in the spring of 1861 was replaced by C.J.P. Petersen, an ordained minister of the Norwegian state church.[63]

When Petersen, contrary to his promises, immediately donned the ministerial vestments and used the high-church ritual of the state church, a well-documented battle ensued, which on the surface revolved around congregational autonomy. Even the Norwegian Synod leader, A.C. Preus, then serving Our Savior's, in his "wonderful declaration" of 1862 sided with the congregation since it did not involve doctrinal issues. These, however, surfaced as it became a contest between the Scandinavian Augustana Synod and the Norwegian Synod; the latter during that decade showed great organizational strength and an added emphasis on the Norwegian heritage, as the Synod clergy intensified their criticism of the American common school and pushed efforts to emulate the German Missouri Synod and establish a competing parochial school system. The First Norwegian Evangelical Lutheran Congregation split into two warring camps, so that Petersen was at times forced "to make his exit between two hostile lines reaching from the altar to the door."

Leaders in opposition were the established Vossings, men like Iver Lawson and Andrew Nelson, which gave the conflict its name, as well as making some Norwegians antagonistic to their public careers. They found strong support from old friends like Erland Carlsson, and other Swedish ministers in the Augustana Synod, enough so that in confidential letters to the Norwegian Synod clergy Petersen expressed fear of "the Swedes' plans for revenge." In March, 1866, Petersen was formally charged and tried by the Augustana Synod for faithlessness, violations of its constitution, offensive preaching, and unchristian conduct. Not to be outdone, Petersen had through nefarious means, by exclusion and addition of members, gained the support of the majority, and in April he wrote to "My Dear Friend, H.A. Preus," the president of the Norwegian Synod, and asked for a call so that he could bring the congregation into the Synod. When the loaded membership subsequently voted to leave the Augustana, but retain the church property, the minority party took them to court. The civil suit was finally decided by the Illinois Supreme Court in favor of the majority. The Norwegian Synod gained a second congregation in Chicago; Petersen continued to minister to it. The minority party, however, left, many abandoning the Norwegian Lutheran fold altogether.[64]

**Living and
Working in
the City**

The Norwegian Lutheran church, with its contentiousness and diversity, had been formed in a rural environment and its entry into the city was a missionary venture. In this setting it took on new responsibilities and competed more directly with temporal interests than in the immigrant farming communities.

Norwegians enjoyed a general acceptance. "We get no better population," the editors of the *Daily Democratic Press* declared in 1856 about the many Norwegian immigrants arriving in Chicago, "and we most cordially welcome them to the land of 'liberty, equality, and fraternity.'" A growing ethnic self-consciousness was encouraged by such praise. In 1854 Chicagoans were preparing to raise a monument to "the honest little Norwegian boy," Knud Iverson, who had been drowned in the Chicago River on August 9, 1853, according to general belief deliberately by older boys because he refused to join them in stealing apples. An outpouring of admiration, enthusiasm, and also money to raise the monument attracted national attention. The celebrated cause might have had something to do with Chicago's own wish to improve its frayed reputation as a center of vice and crime. The project was, however, abandoned when it was determined that Iverson's death had been accidental and unrelated to the apple pilferage. [65]

Ethnic pride swelled when the renowned Norwegian violin virtuoso Ole Bull visited Chicago in March, 1854. Fresh from the collapse of his grandiose colonization venture Oleana in Potter county, Pennsylvania, and on his way to perform in California, Bull gave concerts as he proceeded westward, including two in Chicago at the fashionable Tremont House. As the *Chicago Daily Tribune* noted, "the great musician displayed his wonderful powers of the violin to the admiration of all present." Though the event obviously was a source of great satisfaction among Norwegians and other Scandinavians in general, it was the emerging ethnic elite that mingled with "the numerous and admiring audience" in the concert hall.[66]

Just before Bull's visit two Scandinavian societies were formed, organized by competing leadership factions. A mixture of benevolence combined with political ambition and a desire for social gatherings was the motivating force in both groups. The immediate cause, however, was reports from Norway and Sweden of crop failures in 1853 and a wish to alleviate resulting need. The Russian embargo on grain exports during the Crimean War aggravated the situation; Lutheran ministers in the two Scandinavian countries, in an early incident of appealing to emigrated countrymen for help, sent petitions directly to brother churchmen in the immigrant community. The clergy consequently became involved in these societies. Early in April, 1854, the group around St. Ansgarius headed by Consul von Schneidau announced their intention to form a society that would transcend national boundaries, but were beaten to the draw and also to the intended name by, according to *Emigranten*, "Norwegians who wished to gain influence in the city," who organized the Scandinavian Society. The St. Ansgarius group then settled on the name Scandinavian Union, but it was to a great extent Swedish, with prominent members like Charles Sundell. It had, however, Norwegian members, men like Andrew B. Johnson, pastor G. F. Dietrichson, then a minister in Wisconsin, and I. Irgens, the corresponding secretary, who wrote to Norway that "it must be said to be very aristocratic." The secretary of the competing Scandinavian Society, B. A. Froiseth, announced in Norwegian newspapers the society's wish "to assist its countrymen with advice and information," and also to sell them tickets for American railroad companies. The profit motive was never far removed from immigrant aid societies.[67]

It was this society that arranged a banquet to honor the great Nordic violinist at the North Market Hall; Bull's response was in his typical "Norse Norwegian from Norway" style. He expressly demanded that no Swedes or Danes could attend; some Swedes reportedly had to return the tickets they had purchased. In a long letter to Dietrichson, printed in *Emigranten*, Unonius complained about this outrageous offense. Before he departed, Bull evidently helped to organize a purely Norwegian society, one that not even in name would claim a Scandinavian identity, giving it the homeland's name, Norge. Activity was minimal, or in the case of Norge non-existent, after that time.[68]

In 1855, however, the Scandinavian Union arranged its annual festival on February 22, Washington's birthday, and unveiled a banner showing the Swedish and Norwegian colors of union. The pastors Dietrichson and Unonius made speeches, the first praising the nation's founding father and the second Scandinavian solidarity, from the Viking Age to life in America. It was in this speech that Unonius encouraged Scandinavians to vote against "the enemy" by supporting the Know-Nothing candidate. Both speeches were warmly applauded. Regardless, in 1857 the Swedes in the Scandinavian Union, representing the economic and social establishment in the Swedish colony, formed the Svea Society, a cultural and benevolent organization which declared itself neutral on political issues. No similar group evolved among the Norwegians for several years, although the Scandinavian Society, which even opened a small Norwegian library in 1857, and curiously the Scandinavian Union, which had moved to the West Side, showed some signs of life. Memberships appear, however, to have been extremely small. Svea's success might be attributed to its support from the Episcopalian St. Ansgarius and its upper class immigrants. Unonius, one of the founders of the Scandinavian Union, gave a warm welcome to Svea. This society's cultural broadmindedness and obvious antipathy to the homeland's state church made it unacceptable to the Lutheran clergy, and its appearance perhaps reflected such differing agenda within the Scandinavian Union. Svea emerged at a time when Norwegians were absorbed in major religious controversy, and secular leaders, who mainly hailed from the peasant class, lacked the self-confidence of the more aristocratic Swedish immigrant elite.[69]

Cultural activities suffered from internal tensions. *Wossingen* carried in its June, 1859, issue a report from Chicago that disagreement had broken up a singing society formed the previous winter. There were, however, social events outside the church; in February, 1859, *Wossingen* related that "during Christmas the Vossing youth have had a couple of parties with eighty to one hundred people attending." An early emigrant, Knud Henderson (Løne), recalled that such pleasant gatherings might be in homes or occasionally at some public hall. Henderson had emigrated from Voss in 1849; later he studied music, played the organ in Andersen's church, and gave regular instruction in singing. The church was nevertheless in the 1850s central to most cultural and social activities. Ole Bull had, for instance, also been entertained in the Andersen church and spoken to the congregation.[70]

Andersen's church sat in the heart of the Norwegian colony, first on Superior Street, then in 1856 just a few blocks farther west and south on Erie and Franklin. St. Ansgarius was only about three blocks farther south again on Franklin. In 1850 the majority of Norwegians lived in this district, near the churches or within walking distance. Of the situation there in 1849 when he purchased the site for the St. Ansgarius Church Unonius wrote that it was located "in what was then a remote part of the city where Swedes and Norwegians had settled . . . the entire region round about had been occupied by Irish laborers who had, as they termed it, 'squatted' and built one miserable shanty after another." The landowner lived in New York and eviction would not be effected until someone else purchased the land on which they lived. In the early 1850s hundreds of Swedes and Norwegians built their modest dwellings in the area, and, generally, as the evidence suggests, on lots they owned.[71]

Norwegians of course constituted a small portion of the 8,000 residents who lived north of the Chicago River in 1850. Within Ward 7 stretching eastward from the North Branch of the river some 167 Swedes formed a visible element, and a few Danes had settled in the area. But more likely than not Scandinavian residents had a German or Irish neighbor rather than a fellow Scandinavian. Some effort, to be sure, to cluster with other Norwegians, Swedes, and Danes was evident. "About a dozen of the more cultured Norwegians in Chicago have bought some lots together . . . and this summer they intend to set up buildings on them side by side, and I am one of them," the proud secretary of the Scandinavian Union, I.Irgens, informed the readers of *Christiania Posten* in Norway in 1854. But residential patterns nevertheless encouraged considerable inter-ethnic communication, in casual encounters, at work, in the marketplace, and in civic life. Thus the forces of assimilation were promoted. A writer to *Christiania Posten* in 1859 complained of indifference "to the old language" among Norwegian Chicagoans, and claimed that "most Scandinavians speak English to each other, as soon as they can," rather than their respective Nordic tongues. This is an obvious exaggeration, even though the urban situation would encourage cultural assimilation. The mutually comprehended Norwegian and Swedish were, for instance, both used, if not consistently, in conducting business and in speeches when the Scandinavian Union met. Such societies were counter-forces to the assimilation process. In the family circle as well as at social gatherings, and in the congregations, the natural speech from home was accepted and strengthened. The immigrants lived in two worlds and experienced a public as well as a private sphere. Institutional growth within the community widened the perimeters of the latter.[72]

Their institutions identified the location of neighborhood clusterings. A desire to be close to other Norwegians and to associate with people with a shared language in the building of community organizations and in religious and social activities influenced the evolution of ethnic neighborhoods. Norwegians, as has been suggested, moved in an almost predictable pattern north and west from the center of the city. The shifts in location were related to such circumstances as occupational preferences and possibilities, available housing, the physical environment, and transportation. The establishment of Trinity Church in 1857 and Our Savior's the following year suggests the growth of the West Side community, in spite of the complaint that Trinity was located way out on the "prairie." The two churches were situated a few blocks apart just south of Milwaukee

Avenue, which was the main thoroughfare on the Northwest Side and in the Norwegian community there, in subsequent years providing the route by which Norwegians continued their trek northwestward. In 1860 Norwegians were congregated in the blocks around Milwaukee Avenue and Kinzie Street; by then Chicago had grown solidly to half a mile west of Halsted Street and as far north as Chicago Avenue, or just to the east of the two churches. About 62 percent of the Norwegians in Chicago that year were to be found in this neighborhood.[73]

Figures employed here differ from the ones in the published federal census, as they are based on a careful, and presumably more accurate, examination of census manuscripts and city directories. In 1850 92 percent of the 616 persons identified as Norwegian were born in Norway. The Norwegian colony, by the same kind of evidence, had increased in 1860 to 1,820; 71 percent of them were immigrants. The demographic composition had changed little during the decade except for a dramatic, and expected, increase in the second generation. In 1850 only 36 of 206 persons under the age of twenty were born in America, while a decade later 522 of 780 individuals in this same category were American-born, a jump from 15 to 40 percent. It remained a typically young family community, and to an overwhelming degree endogamous in the selection of a spouse. The few who ventured outside the group most commonly married a Swede or a Dane. A large percentage of couples were, to be sure, married before emigrating, which is a part of the explanation. The statistics create an impression of a closely knit community of families. It is also a portrait of an ethnic group fairly recently settled in America.[74]

Several large industries developed along Kinzie Street on the north bank of the river. The large McCormick Reaper Factory was located there, and the Galena Railroad built its depot on the corner of Kinzie and Wells. Construction of railroad stations, factories, workshops, and warehouses furnished employment for many men and gave rise to workingmen's houses, boardinghouses, and also slum areas in the vicinity. But as residential areas along the river were converted to industrial use residents were forced to move. Rising land values created by the increased demand encouraged small and large landowners to sell. Squatters were consequently evicted, at times dramatically, as in the raid on the disreputable Sands area on the north bank of the Chicago River, which Mayor Wentworth ordered burned down in 1857.[75]

Norwegians were caused to leave the older settlements by these general developments. Those who owned property increased their wealth and were in a position to invest in lower-priced lots across the North Branch. Newcomers could not afford the expensive property near the lake and joined the older immigrants on the West Side. In the 1850s this section of the city grew rapidly and consequently had an

The Chicago River east from the Rush Street Bridge about 1869. A
steam tugboat is towing a sailing ship into the river; traffic on land is
delayed while the bridges are opened to allow the lake vessels to pass.

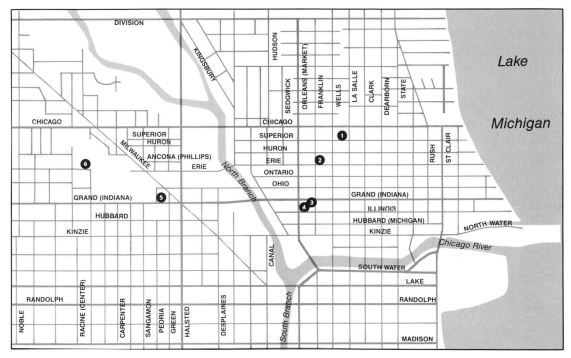

Norwegian areas of settlement around 1860

Current street names are given first with the earlier ones in parentheses

1. First location of the First Norwegian Evangelical Lutheran Congregation
2. Second location of the church of the same congregation
3. St. Ansgarius
4. Scandinavian Methodist Church
5. Trinity Lutheran Church
6. Our Savior's Lutheran Church

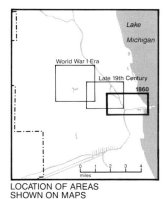

LOCATION OF AREAS
SHOWN ON MAPS

increased demand for labor. Norwegians formed working–class neighborhoods near places of employment.[76]

Many of the prosperous Norwegians and ethnic leaders, men such as Iver Lawson, Andrew Nelson (Brekke), and Andrew Larson (Flage), did not move but established their residences near the lake. There resided also well–to–do lake captains like George A. Wigeland. But status consideration did not prevent prosperous Norwegians from residing among West Side Norwegians, even though they might choose a more exclusive address than their working–class compatriots. A Chicago lawyer, Elmer E. Abrahamson, who grew up half a block from Our Savior's Church, relates that the church had many high-status ship captains as members, among them his maternal grandfather Kittel Johnson, who emigrated from Kragerø in 1854, and his father Martin Abrahamson, who arrived from Farsund toward the end of the century. Andrew B. Johnson, operating his profitable lumber business by the North Branch, lived on Hubbard Street south of Milwaukee Avenue.[77]

A scarcity of labor in the early 1850s at a time of great expansion, especially in the building trades, gave opportunities to Norwegian workers in occupations they favored. "Never since Chicago has been a city was the price of labor so high or laborers so scarce," the *Democratic Press* lamented in 1853. Many adventurous individuals, including a number of Norwegians, were attracted to California by stories of rich gold discoveries in late 1848. "From Chicago many have gone to California, among them Ole Vikingson Gjøastein," a letter in 1849 stated. Gjøastein, like his brother Kiel taking the name Williams, was a blacksmith by trade, and after a few years returned to Chicago, where he operated the Williams Hotel, a modest establishment but a popular place for newcomers and other Norwegians on East Kinzie Street. The rush to the gold fields, however, had made the *Daily Democrat* even express fears that Chicago stood "a fair chance of depopulation." Others were attracted by favorable offers of work on the railroad lines being built into the West.[78]

Norwegian workers were rapidly drawn into the construction field. On the expanding West Side the building of cheap frame houses, which were predominant in that section, employed many. Native experience and background from the peasant community, or, in the emigration of the 1850s, even as an artisan from a Norwegian town, equipped them to enter the crafts as carpenters, painters, and other skilled and semiskilled manual laborers. In Chicago's economic life this became a Norwegian, and in general a Scandinavian, niche. They capitalized on common skills in cabinetmaking and woodworking. By 1860 over half of all Norwegian men were categorized in specialized skilled or semiskilled occupations. Complaints of hard times notwithstanding, Norwegians appear as a group to have fared better during the depression in the late 1850s than other immigrants. The growth of the West Side continued and a fall in the cost of building stimulated new projects. Those in the lake traffic, which in 1860 occupied one-fifth of the Norwegian male labor force, still provided a needed commercial service. Common laborers toiled on dock work, river improvement, and bridge and street construction.[79]

Domestic service gave employment to most women who worked outside the home, in 1860 as in 1850. Many of them, according to census records, resided outside the Norwegian neighborhoods, which indicated their employment in American homes. The latter were obviously the single women thus employed. Writing from Chicago to a friend in Norway in 1855, a newly arrived young man described the transformation that occurred in Norwegian girls as a result. "The first Sunday," he wrote, "when they come to America they wear their old Norwegian garb, the second Sunday it is a new dress, the third Sunday it is a hat, parasol, and silk scarf . . . so that even the plainest girl from Norway is visited by dozens of boys almost every evening." New values and forms of behavior obviously intruded directly into the immigrant community through this contact with American middle-class gentility.

By 1860, however, women were entering other vocations, as Norwegian Americans displayed an increasing occupational variety and an ability to accommodate professional pursuits within the immigrant community itself. There were eight female dressmakers and one midwife, and one woman worked in the Chicago Orphan Asylum. No fewer than eighteen male tailors and forty-seven shoemakers resided in the Norwegian neighborhoods, transferring skills from peasant as well as urban backgrounds. Four Norwegian saloonkeepers and one liquor merchant offered the colony their services; three Norwegian policemen patrolled the Norwegian neighborhood on the West Side. The number of nonmanual workers, store and office clerks, rose considerably during the decade. Only a few Norwegians were, however, to be found in factories, and they avoided Chicago's large butchering industry altogether.[80]

Some structural cohesion existed, especially in congregational life, in the small Norwegian colony in Chicago by the 1860s. The Norwegian journalist Peter Daae suggested that the colony's smallness kept it united, in spite of inner disharmony and strife: the teeming metropolis, with its confusion of voices and nationalities, its tumultuous growth, and its challenges and dangers, made every Norwegian develop a special relationship to every other Norwegian.[81]

3

The Era of the Civil War

The Norwegian Colony Matures

On August 2, 1862, the Norwegian brig *Sleipner* tied up at the Galena railroad dock in the Chicago river harbor. The only earlier ship to arrive directly in Chicago from the ocean had been the *Madeira Pet* on July 14,1857, which had left Liverpool, England, some eighty days earlier. It was welcomed with much fanfare. The *Sleipner* stirred no less interest. "Possibly an arrival from the moon might have created more astonishment than the Norwegian built craft, with Norwegian captain and crew speaking a strange language, and crowded with light-haired Scandinavian farmers, their bouncing wives and children," the *Chicago Tribune* reported. Dr. Gerhard S.C.H. Paoli, as a distinguished citizen of Norwegian birth, led the welcoming ceremony, but, as the *Tribune* noted, "Chicago citizenry of all nationalities were on hand to welcome the newcomers." There was even an eight-gun salute.[1]

The *Sleipner* had left Bergen on May 23, 1862, with 150 emigrants, forty of whom debarked in Detroit, and a cargo of salted herring, dried cod, and anchovies consigned to the wholesale firm of Svanøe and Synnestvedt on South Water Street. It was owned by

●

Top left: Gerhard S.C.H. Paoli.

●

Top right: Plaque erected in 1962 to commemorate the centennial of the
arrival of the *Sleipner*.

●

Bottom: The lithograph by Jevne and Almini is of the Chicago harbor
from the Rush Street Bridge in 1868.

Otto Synnestvedt, who had emigrated from the Osafjord district in Hardanger in 1850, and Peter Svanøe, later Swedish-Norwegian consul in Chicago, who came from Bergen. His ties to the commercial interests in that city, which financed the expedition, were consequently close. The *Sleipner* had sailed by way of Quebec down the St. Lawrence River, through the Welland Canal, and thence across the lakes to Chicago.[2]

Beginning in 1850, when 250 Norwegian emigrants came to the United States through Quebec, this rapidly became the major route. It is estimated that between 1854 and 1865 94 percent of all Norwegian emigrants entered the United States from Quebec. Most emigrants left the lake vessel at Detroit and continued on to Chicago by rail. It was also possible to go by rail from Quebec to Sarnia in Ontario and be ferried across the St. Clair River to Port Huron, where the trip west could be continued either by rail or by steamboat through lakes Huron and Michigan. The lake route might add as much as two days to the trip as compared to going directly by train.[3]

It was the participation by Norwegian shipowners in British commerce that moved the port of debarkation from New York and other American port cities to Quebec. Norwegian sailing vessels transported Canadian lumber to England; from there they continued on to a Norwegian coastal city to return to Quebec with a boatload of emigrants. This profitable triangular trade allowed a reduction in passenger fares.

Extending the route to Chicago would seem to open new trade possibilities. The Norwegian-American community stood ready to consume familiar foodstuffs and buy other products from home, and American grain and flour, as well as other articles, could fill the cargo holds on the return voyage. The *Sleipner* made several crossings during the next few years and other ships joined in. The arrival of the sailing vessel *Skjoldmøen* in 1863 made a great impression especially on the Vossings and people from the Bergen environs where the tiny craft hailed from; they visited the ship in such numbers that it could not unload its cargo the first two days. In 1866 *Skandinaven* reported that the small brig *Vidar* "arrived in the capital of the West" on July 20; "Norwegian hearts beat warmly for the dear old flag waving from the masthead," the newspaper continued, describing how "like the brave Vikings of old" the crew had defied "the dangers of the sea and the Atlantic's stormy billows." It was a contact with the homeland that gave strength to ethnic fervor.[4]

The advantages for Norwegian emigrants in being able to secure passage directly to Chicago were obvious: they did not have to transfer to new modes of transportation, nor fear exploitation or neglect because of language deficiencies. The fearful loss of the steamship *Atlantic* on Lake Erie in August, 1852, with the drowning of over 300 people was a haunting reminder of the risks and hazards emigrants faced after having suffered the hardships of the Atlantic crossing. Sixty-eight of those who drowned were Norwegian emigrants, nearly all from Valdres.[5]

The *Vidar* was the fourth vessel to sail from Norway to the interior of the American continent. This traffic apparently ceased after its voyage in 1866, partly because of stricter Norwegian regulations from 1863 in regard to the transportation of goods and passengers on the same ship, and also because Norwegian sailing vessels were being displaced in the emigrant traffic by British and German steamships.[6]

The increased capacity and security, as well as reliability, offered by the steamship lines made mass migration possible. The transition from sail to steam, however, came late in Norway, so that in 1867 only 10 percent of all Norwegian emigrants crossed the Atlantic by steamship, most continuing to sail on Norwegian brigs and barks. But the change was rapid. In 1871 67 percent chose steamship travel, and in 1875 not a single emigrant ship sailed directly from a Norwegian port. Some Norwegians went to America on German steamships from Bremen or Hamburg, but the most common route was by way of Hull or Newcastle to Liverpool, where the emigrants shipped out on a British liner to New York. From 1853 Castle Garden at the southwest tip of Manhattan had served as a receiving station for immigrants. Thus New York again became the first contact with America for Norwegian emigrants; the Canadian interlude came to an end.[7]

During the years of the Civil War, 1861 to 1865, 23,550 Norwegians arrived in America, an average of 4,710 annually. Then, responding to a post-war economic expansion and increasing knowledge about America, hosts of Norwegians joined in the great European migration overseas. In the following eight years, from 1866 until 1873, 110,896 Norwegians, equaling 63.4 percent of the natural population increase, moved across the Atlantic. The sudden jump in 1866 to 15,455 America travelers ushered in the age of mass migration, and disturbed Norwegian officials. The movement had taken hold all over the country.[8]

Norwegian immigrants continued to exhibit a marked rural preference, but the opportunities and the diversity in an urban environment attracted an increasing number of them. By 1870 there were 8,325 Norwegians in Chicago, a five-fold increase from 1860. Since three quarters of them were born in Norway, the colony obviously had received a share of the post-war immigrants. An urban destination became more common as the cities delivered a larger percentage of the emigrants. Craftsmen from Bergen who intended to settle in Chicago had, for instance, constituted most of the 144 emigrants who sailed directly to Chicago on the *Sleipner*'s voyage in the spring of 1864.

Reflecting a gradual change in the composition of the overseas movement is the smaller proportion of married people in the Chicago

This advertisement by Fleischer & Jurgens in *Skandinaven*, October 6, 1869, offers passage on the steamships of the British Allan Line and on Norwegian sailing ships. It illustrates the transition from sail to steam in the immigrant traffic.

colony, less than 60 percent of those above the age of twenty in 1870 as compared to 70 in 1860. These figures nevertheless represent a higher marriage frequency than in the Norwegian immigrant population in general. This reflects the social and economic importance of the institution of the family in an urban pioneer community. Furthermore, there was no shortage of marriageable women to hamper the formation of families, as was the case in rural pioneer settlements. Inmarriage was encouraged by these same circumstances. The fact that 90 percent of those who were married in 1870 had a Norwegian spouse illustrates a continued ethnic cohesion, even in a bustling urban situation. In Chicago endogamy was even more frequent among Norwegians than among Swedes, who also exhibited a great tendency toward inmarriage. A strong ethnocentric environment that resisted assimilation thus obviously existed in the Norwegian and Swedish enclaves.

Many unattached young women and men had joined the Norwegian exodus, and, of course, young people from Norwegian settlements in nearby areas augmented their numbers as well. The larger number of women than men among Chicago Norwegians, recorded in both the 1860 and the 1870 census, leads one to conclude that employment possibilities, especially in domestic service, represented an attractive alternative for many young single Norwegian women. Announcements advising Scandinavian girls that they "can get good positions with American families, hotels, and shops by applying to their compatriot Mrs. Johnson at 234 East Oak Street" show not only what types of jobs were available but that demand was sufficient to let other women operate a small employment service.[9]

By 1870 the city limits had been moved west from Western Avenue to Crawford, now Pulaski Road. Fullerton was the city's northern boundary from the lake to Western, then moving south on Western to North Avenue and along North to Crawford. In the fifties most ordinary Chicagoans walked to their destination. With growth various means of transportation developed. About 25,000 people were living in the northwest section in 1870. A horsedrawn streetcar line which connected the area with the central business district had been inaugurated in 1859 along Milwaukee Avenue, its main axis. It was a plank road; arriving in 1872, the Danish-American newspaperman Morris Salmonsen described it as "relatively narrow and paved with round wooden blocks made of cedar, plundered from the great forests of neighboring states."[10]

In 1860 Chicago was divided into twenty wards. The heaviest concentration of Norwegians was then in Ward 11, stretching for some blocks west of the North Branch between Randolph and Ohio streets. In this small river ward clustered some 2,847 Norwegians, counting the first and second generations. They represented 18.9 percent of this ward's population and were consequently a visible component. The center of the community was moving north from Kinzie Street, and in the 1870s Grand Avenue, then Indiana, took on its important role as a major thoroughfare in the community, alongside Milwaukee Avenue, which ran diagonally northwestward through this ward and also through the large adjacent Ward 15. Another 1,790 Norwegians lived in that ward, mainly just north of Ohio Street toward Chicago Avenue, and were thus a part of the same neighborhood. 1,057 Norwegians lived just to the west of Ward 11 in Ward 12. In this area, then, lived about 68 percent of the immigrant community.[11]

The emigration of the 1850s and 1860s saw the arrival of people who established businesses and made a living meeting the needs of the expanding Norwegian colony, often, of course, transcending its boundaries to achieve great success in a diverse urban economy. In 1867 *Skandinaven* published a list of eighty-one Norwegian and Danish businessmen and professional people in Chicago. A number identified themselves as *bygmester*, that is, building contractor, a position not infrequently earned by initially organizing a work gang of fellow Norwegians, often newcomers eager for employment and willing to work for low wages, for a special project. When a modicum of capital, a reputation, and contacts were assured, a regular operation could be established. All this evolved naturally from the heavy concentration of Norwegian workers in the building trades. A case in point is perhaps the success in this field of Jens Olsen Kaasa, who emigrated from Upper Telemark in 1843 at the age of nineteen. He learned the trade of mason and bricklayer. He then offered his services to build Our Savior's Church, the second one in 1873, at the same location as the original church, on the corner of Erie and May streets, charging the congregation only for expenditures. Kaasa was a member, residing close to the church on Erie Street, and he cultivated the friendship of leading Lutherans. No doubt the work force he had assembled, his social relations, his position of influence within the congregation, and the personal experience he had gained when erecting the church were factors that he capitalized on to move into a position as a contractor on a large scale.[12]

The career of Christian H. Jevne offers another example of the business opportunities that attracted ambitious young men to Chicago. In a letter sent back to his parents in Hamar in December, 1864, some months after his arrival, Jevne related that he was clerking in a grocery store during the day and evenings attending a commercial school to learn English, bookkeeping, banking, and brokerage. It was a route that many other bright young men arriving in America chose in order to improve their chances for material advancement. Jevne's uncle Otto, who had emigrated earlier, had organized the firm Jevne & Almini on East Kinzie Street in 1855 together with the Swede Peter M. Almini. They became prominent as fresco painters and interior

The Jevne Company, founded by Christian H. Jevne in 1865, was a
major wholesale and retail distributor of fine foods. It gave evidence of
the opportunities Chicago offered for success in business ventures.

decorators. In 1864 they began publishing *Chicago Illustrated*, which printed attractive engravings of the city, and advance copies sent back to Norway convinced Christian Jevne to emigrate. He was then twenty-five years old. He continued as a clerk in the grocery store, having had similar work experience in Norway, until in 1865 he was able to start his own business on East Kinzie Street with a capital of only $200. To his friends Jevne seemed to have an all-absorbing passion for business. He did, however, find time to serve as treasurer of the First Norwegian Evangelical Lutheran Congregation and belonged to C.J.P. Petersen's faction in the "Vossing War." Ultimately he built the largest wholesale and retail grocery concern in Chicago, importing "coffee direct from Sumatra and Arabia; tea from Japan, China, and Ceylon; wine from Europe; cheese, fish, canned goods and aquavit from Norway, Sweden, and Denmark."[13]

The many new ventures following the Civil War appear on the advertising pages of *Skandinaven*. Alongside such modest establishments as the Dane Christian Hansen's hotel and other boarding-houses, Ole Williams operated his small hotel for Scandinavian immigrants on East Kinzie Street, close to the Galena, Milwaukee, and Northwestern railroad depot and the main landing docks for the steamship companies. Near the hotel F. Herfordt opened a bookstore in 1866. On the North Side, mainly in Ward 18 just east of the North Branch, some 1,300 Norwegians lived, and there John Kirkeby and George Eriksen operated one of the several Norwegian shoemaker shops in Chicago. G. Roberg operated a clothing and tailoring business on West Kinzie Street close to the North Branch. Reflecting the growing Norwegian population in the area, many of the new ventures were, however, on the West Side. On Milwaukee Avenue Salmonsen thought there was "a drug store or a saloon in almost every corner house." Sweet's West Side Drug Store offered "Norwegian, Swedish, Danish, and German prescriptions prepared exactly as in the different countries' pharmacies." The Scandinavian Drug Store on 119 (now about 400) Milwaukee Avenue and one calling itself Norwegian close to Milwaukee Avenue on Halsted Street both advertised Norwegian-trained pharmacists and supplies of "the most used Scandinavian health remedies."[14]

Life in the Norwegian community required tailors' workshops, bakeries, butcher and sausage shops, watchmakers, and many other services and products, needs which by the late 1860s were satisfied by people who made an appeal for business on the basis of nationality. Tailoring was the most common Scandinavian craft; tailors, according to a 1874 count, even surpassed the number of Scandinavian carpenters and cabinetmakers. The large number of women engaged in this occupation partly explains the situation; still, one third of the nearly eleven hundred so listed that year were men. Symptomatic of the ethnic environment is A.J. Johannesen's advertisement in 1867 for his Norwegian saloon on Milwaukee Avenue, which in addition to wines, liquor, and beer served "warm coffee and bread all day," and "newspapers from Christiania are available for pleasant perusal." Commercial enterprise added warmth and social ambience and created an environment reminiscent of home.[15]

A Call to Patriotism

Commerce and manufacturing were greatly stimulated by the demands on manpower and supplies made by the Civil War, which gave Chicago a prosperity it had never known before. The dramatic events of the conflict engaged the different immigrant groups and had a decisive impact on their American experience. Politically the conversion to the Republican party and its anti-slavery stand was complete among Germans and Scandinavians, although, to be sure, they still harbored the general prejudice against black Americans of the society in which they lived.[16]

The Irish persisted in their loyalty to the Democratic party, and might have been reluctant to fight a war to free black slaves who could become rivals for jobs, but they nevertheless responded to wartime needs and played a conspicuous role in the Union army, in Chicago as elsewhere. Their hero Stephen Douglas pleaded the cause of the Union following Lincoln's victory in the 1860 presidential race. Irish companies from different areas of Illinois were a part of the Twenty-third Illinois Infantry recruited by Colonel James A. Mulligan, editor of Chicago's first Catholic newspaper, the *Western Tablet*.[17]

The practice of creating military units from specific nationality groups was encouraged by the immigrants themselves, who frequently petitioned state legislatures and governors for approval of their plans to organize in order to fight in the war. Before the Civil War immigrants had not always been welcomed into the American military organizations. They had, however, formed volunteer drilling units, for instance within the fire department, which employed many Irish in Chicago. Many members of such groups would enlist and march off to war together.[18]

Forty German members of the Chicago Turner Society (Turngemeinde) had already signed up for service by the end of March, 1861, although war did not break out until April 12. The celebrated German freedom fighter of the 1848 revolution, Frederick Hecker, organized an exclusively German infantry regiment in Chicago in June, 1861. He later organized the so-called Second Hecker Jaeger Regiment, the Eighty-second Illinois Regiment, which also consisted mainly of Chicago Germans, but with some Scandinavians. It was in this fighting unit that Christian Erickson served. He had arrived in Chicago in 1859 from his native Bergen at the age of twenty. In 1862 he enlisted in Company I and was promoted to first lieutenant and thus commander of the company, which consisted almost exclusively of Scandinavian men from Chicago. The Eighty-second Regiment

10 RECRUITS WANTED!

TO FILL THE QUOTA OF THE
Town of Primrose

$170

CASH IN EXTRA BOUNTY,

The money is deposited in the Bank.

M. GRINAGER,

Capt. 15th Wis. Inf'y, Rec. Officer.

MILLS' BLOCK, KING ST., MADISON.

Madison, Feb. 26th, 1864.

Left: Captain Christian Erickson, Civil War hero.

Right: The public notice promises to pay a generous bounty to men who volunteer to serve in the Fifteenth Wisconsin Regiment.

was known in the army as the "Hecker Boys" and it took part in the 1864 campaign in Georgia and fought in General William Tecumseh Sherman's army on its famous march to the sea. Erickson upon his honorable discharge was given a captain's commission for gallant and meritorious service.[19]

Swedes in Chicago who rose to prominence in the Union army frequently had had military training before emigrating; they reflected Sweden's long military tradition and the aristocratic background of Swedish military officers. Axel Silversparre, a Swedish baron as well as an artillery expert, came to the United States specifically to enlist in the Union army. Another example was Charles John Stolbrand, active in the Swedish community in Chicago, who in 1857 had chaired the meeting organizing the Svea Society. General Sherman said about Stolbrand, who had been an artilleryman in the Swedish army before emigrating, that "a better man and a better artillery officer could not be found in the entire army." He helped to organize a largely Swedish artillery company, although with a few Danish and Norwegian members, in Chicago in 1861 and rose to the rank of brigadier general. Fellow Swedes honored Stolbrand with a sword, sash, and belt, his exploits being a source of extreme pride.[20]

Immigrant regiments from other states recruited among Scandinavians in Chicago, as did the famed Fifteenth Wisconsin Regiment, called the Norwegian regiment, under the command of Colonel Hans C. Heg. Andrew Torkildsen, a Norwegian police officer in Chicago, opened a recruiting office on North Wells Street to enlist Norwegian, Danish, and Swedish volunteers in the Fifteenth Wisconsin. Its broader Scandinavian intent is indicated by its description as "the Scandinavian Regiment," but it remained almost completely Norwegian. Torkildsen was the first captain of Company A, the Chicago company, known as the St. Olaf Rifles.[21]

"The Regiment's officers," Colonel Heg declared in his appeal of October 6, 1861, "will be men who speak the Scandinavian languages. In this way those Scandinavians who do not yet speak English can also enter the military service." Immigrants of all nationalities volunteered or were conscripted in numbers more than commensurate with their percentage in the American population. Patriotic emotions were fortified by bounties to volunteering soldiers, who would substitute for those who could not or would not shoulder arms for the Northern cause. Thus state quotas could be filled and a general draft avoided. *Emigranten* carried an extensive debate that revealed great efforts by some Norwegian immigrants, encouraged and assisted by Swedish-Norwegian diplomats, to avoid military conscription. Such attitudes were harshly condemned by contemporaries, and even more by an admiring later generation that viewed the era of the Civil War with a special reverence.[22]

Admirable services were, however, rendered by the Scandinavian women in Chicago who arranged festivals and fund-raising projects to assist the families of the men serving with the St. Olaf Rifles. In early March, 1862, the Fifteenth Wisconsin stopped briefly in Chicago on its way to Missouri. Events while it was there showed its direct Chicago connection. The Norwegian society Nora entertained the 900 men in the regiment and presented it with a flag, paid for through subscriptions, with the American colors on one side and "on the reverse the American and Norwegian arms united, the Norwegian being the picture of a lion with an axe on a red field." The flag bore the inscription "For Gud og Vort Land" (For God and Our Country). And again in February, 1865, when the last four of the eight regimental companies arrived in Chicago, a delegation from the Nora Society welcomed the men at the railroad depot and treated them to "a little banquet." Several of the veterans were members of Nora, among them Torkildsen.[23]

It was a matter of honor for ethnic groups not to shirk their obligations during periods of national crisis; the host society might easily suspect them of conflicting loyalties or cowardice. Immigrants refuted attacks on their American patriotism and endeavored to establish respect for their commitment to give the supreme sacrifice to "our new fatherland," as Heg expressed it. Heg himself fell in the bloody battle at Chickamauga in September, 1863. Theirs was always the burden of proof. But the conflict also produced ethnic heroes and a record of achievements which not only made the immigrants more acceptable to the Yankee element, but gave them and their children a sense of having made a place for themselves.[24]

Ethnic Organizational Zeal

The Nora Society, so heavily involved in the Norwegian war effort, gave evidence of Norwegian-American social, cultural, and political interests outside the church. It also revealed the limits of pan-Scandinavian sentiment. The Svea Society had emerged on June 22, 1857, and the Danes organized the Dania Society on November 22, 1862. Encouragement in *Emigranten* by leading Norwegian Chicagoans "to be in agreement and act jointly" led to the formation of the purely Norwegian Nora Society on Wednesday, July 18, 1860, when "a few Norwegians met at a blockwright shop at 13 North Wells to organize a Norwegian society," as the minutes recorded it. The few members left in the largely Norwegian Scandinavian Society likely joined, as they gave "all books, pictures, and furniture" of the defunct society to Nora in 1861; some Norwegian names from the Scandinavian Union, men like Andrew Torkildsen and G. Roberg, both members of St. Ansgarius congregation and influenced by its relative tolerance, appear on Nora's membership roster.[25]

All three Scandinavian groups were men's societies. Intimate glimpses are preserved in their minutes, as for instance a notice at Nora's first regular meeting in the "Newberry Block" on the North

Top: The banner given the Fifteenth Wisconsin Regiment by Nora Society in 1862.

Bottom: "An American lodge." Members of Nora Lodge in front of the lodge banner in full regalia and holding the symbols of their degree.

Side on August 6 of the purchase of half a dozen stoneware spittoons. Sixty charter members affixed their signatures to its constitution and bylaws. They obviously represented individuals from the emerging commercial and professional elite in the Norwegian colony, as Svea and Dania did in their respective nationalities. But there were some notable exceptions. John Anderson, in 1860 only twenty-four years old, was the single name from the "Voss Circle" leaders. Missing were the older men like Iver Lawson and Andrew Nelson (Brekke), possibly because they rejected Nora's narrow nationalism or were preoccupied with promoting the Vossing Emigration Society. The new society, as evidenced in its original membership, was connected with Our Savior's Church rather than with the First Norwegian Evangelical Lutheran Congregation, which moved it into a different orbit. Some of Nora's active and prominent members were G.E. Howland, its first president and the blockwright in whose shop it was founded, and Peter Svanøe of the firm to which the *Sleipner*'s cargo was consigned. Direct commercial interest involved several members of Nora in that profitable enterprise. Members were also such prospering people as Jens Olsen Kaasa, the large-scale building contractor, John Kirkeby, the shoe shop owner, J. Reiersen, a distinguished lake captain, and Ole T. Birkeland from Egersund, a coal dealer. Soon to join were Dr. Paoli, who continued his activities in freethought circles, adding an anti-Lutheran taint which was further strengthened in March, 1866, when the self-exiled socialist and labor leader Marcus Thrane was accepted into membership. His contact in the group was obviously Roberg, who had encouraged him to settle in Chicago.[26]

The liberal and secular direction encouraged by leading members alienated the Lutheran clergy, which to begin with had viewed Nora with some sympathy as an educational organization. Pastor A.C. Preus at Our Savior's was among Nora's charter members but removed himself from membership when his motion to prohibit dancing was rejected. A successful masquerade ball on December 26 prompted Preus to take this step. Dances became much favored in some Scandinavian-American circles, Nora for instance exchanging tickets with the Swedish B.B. Society, an educational group, for its Christmas ball. Singing was another popular cultural activity. A small men's chorus, the Norwegian Singing Society (Den norske Sangforening), had entertained at Nora's first meeting in July and was invited to unite with Nora, which shortly arranged a flower festival in the German Hall to mark the singing society's anniversary, perhaps its second, on July 27, if it is identical with the male chorus referred to in *Wossingen* in June, 1859.[27]

Elitist immigrant secular societies engaged in multiple activities and established models of culture and learning for their working-class compatriots based on a strong emphasis on ethnic solidarity. They served a need to mark a social distance and also helped to secure their members positions of prominence within the ethnic group. The Nora Society fit this mold. Its purpose was "by all appropriate means at its disposal to work for the moral and intellectual development of its members." Monthly meetings included lectures, debates, and educational discussions on historical, political, and literary topics, a library of Norwegian and English books was established, and Norwegian newspapers were obtained. Except when a speaker did not know Norwegian "nothing but the Norwegian language shall be spoken," its constitution declared.[28]

The Nora Society gave aid to impoverished immigrants, notably to those arriving on the *Sleipner* in 1862, and gave mutual assistance to members in illness and death. Taking its cue from American fraternal orders it moved toward becoming a secret society. Dr. Paoli and Birkeland were both Freemasons, belonging to American lodges, and they guided developments. In April, 1862, a motion passed to transform Nora into an order along the lines of Masonic lodges. Subsequently, on January 27, 1863, a constitutional meeting created The Order of the Knights of the White Cross (Ordenen af Riddere af det Hvide Kors), with a grand lodge and sublodges, the Nora Society becoming Nora Lodge No. 1. It was an order of three degrees, its purpose to function as a mutual aid society.

The new society was American in its formal organization, but, as the name suggests, it was strongly ethnic in its regalia, rituals, symbols, and terminology. It in fact displayed a remarkable aristocratic strain, seeking its inspiration from the heroic age of Norway's patron saint, St. Olaf; the St. Olaf Rifles of Civil War fame had by its name earlier evinced the Nora Society's strong identification with an exalted past. While the Greeks in America sought identity and acceptance by stressing their Hellenic roots, Norwegians came to cultivate Viking origins and the splendor of the Nordic middle ages. The members of the order became *knights* and on festive occasions appeared with red capes adorned with a white cross over the left shoulder, and depending on degree, held a cross, a halberd — an ancient Nordic weapon — or a spear. The grand lodge was designated Erke Logen, *erke* meaning arch-, and except for this prefix the officers of the sublodges held identical titles. The president was known as *drot* (monarch), the first vice-president as *jarl* (earl), the second vice-president as *lendermand* (feudal lord), and the treasurer as *skatmester*. Sublodges were formed, mainly in the Midwest; the first one outside Chicago was Nora Lodge No. 2, organized in Decorah, Iowa, on September 4, 1866.[29]

The fraternity, with its attention to a Norwegian cultural heritage and consciousness of historical events, played a central role in Norwegian immigrant life in Chicago. Even in the midst of war its concerns were not viewed as a conflict of loyalties. Nora Lodge celebrated the fiftieth anniversary of the Norwegian constitution on May 17, 1864, in the newly completed Turner Hall on Clark Street on the North Side. The highlight of this commemoration of the re-birth of a Norwegian national identity was the presentation of a lodge banner by Norwegian women in Chicago, who for this occasion joined the men. The event further established a social position to which the "knights" might only have aspired at home.

The terse lodge minutes cannot conceal the prevailing elegance and festive spirit: "The ladies assembled in the right side room at the east end of the hall and the society's members in the left side room. The presentation then proceeded in the following order. First a musi-cal group played the national anthem, 'Sons of Norway that Age-old Kingdom,' so well known to all Norwegians.

"The ladies marched into the hall behind their banner from the right and the gentlemen from the left, carrying the flags of Norway and the United States. When the two processions met at the west end of the hall they stopped and Mrs. Christophersen stepped forward on behalf of the ladies and presented the banner with a brief appropriate speech to Mr. A. Torkildsen, who spoke for the society. Mr. [Jacob] Hjorth then recited a poem composed for the occasion. While the mu-sic played 'We Will Rally Round the Flag,' the ladies took their places on the left side of the hall. The gentlemen then marched around the hall in a formation peculiar to their Order, after which the Society's president G. Roberg proposed a salute to the President of the United States to which the audience responded with three loud hurrahs.

"The presentation was over and the gentlemen returned to the side room and removed their capes. They then joined the ladies in the hall to open the ball, which with social pleasure and in good order continued until the sun cast its rays into the hall, reminding the gen-tlemen and the ladies that the celebration of the half-century day of May 17 had ended, and they all betook themselves home harboring unforgettable memories of May 17 and the distant ancestral land."[30]

Ethnic membership qualifications, Norwegian birth or descent, applied in the Knights of the White Cross. Circumstances promoted some joint Scandinavian efforts, however, even among purely na-tional societies like Nora, Svea, and Dania. But Scandinavianism ap-peared at times to be a love-hate relationship, and nearly always it was doomed to fail. It was difficult to assume a new ethnic identity at the expense of a narrow and accustomed nationalistic one; the latter fur-nished a more secure and self-conscious anchor in the immigrant situ-ation. The Scandinavianism of immigrant America was largely un-related to the specific movement by that name in the Nordic countries, though it obviously reflected those sentiments and tradi-tions of the Swedish-Norwegian union that in spite of national differ-ences and tensions between the two peoples promoted a common eth-nic accord. It was expressed in the joint monarch Oscar II's motto "for the good of the sister nations" (*Broderfolkenes vel*). Norwegian-American historians, perhaps prompted by Norwegian historians

Almindeligt skandinavisk

Massemöde

— i —

Aurora Turn Halle paa Milw. Ave.

Lördagen den 12te Juni Kl. 7½ Aften.

———

I Henhold til det foregaaende Mødes Beslut-
ning opfordres herved alle Skandinaver til at
samles til et almindeligt Møde paa ovenan-
førte Tid og Sted for at drøfte med hverandre,
hvad helst bør foretages for at fremkalde større
Samvirken og Enighed mellem de nordiske Brø-
drefolk her paa Pladsen.

Der vil blive forelagt Forsamlingen et fuld-
stændigt Forslag, udarbeidet af den dertil paa
forrige Møde nedsatte Komite med særligt Hen-
syn paa et virksomt Samarbeide mellem Skan-
dinaverne til gjensidig materiel Bistand saavel-
som ogsaa til Oplysning og Sjælsforædling.

Hver og en veltænkende Skandinav opfordres
til at komme did og gjøre Sit til den gode Sags
Fremme.

Chas. J. Sundell,   Jakob Nielsen,
Jens S. Gram,   Chas. Eklund,
C. J. Meyer,   C. E. Ekvall,
Christopher Stange,
Kommitterede.

The notice in *Skandinaven*, October 6, 1869, of "A general Scandinavian
mass meeting" at Aurora Turner Hall on Milwaukee Avenue is an example of appeal to a common Scandinavian heritage in the promotion of political, philanthropic, cultural, and other causes. Prominent men in the
Scandinavian community called the meeting for the purpose of "discuss-
ing with one another how best to encourage joint action and harmony
among the Nordic sister peoples in this place." A committee had been
formed to establish "active cooperation among the Scandinavians for
mutual material aid as well as for enlightenment and the ennoblement of
the spirit."

preoccupied with Norway's move toward complete political independence, have been inattentive to the role of a shared loyalty to the symbols and positive traditions of the double monarchy in explaining the American experience of Swedish and Norwegian immigrants. The cultural legacy of the centuries-long union between Denmark and Norway which encouraged a sense of oneness between those two nations is more easily recognized. Scandinavianism rose in America at mid-century with the establishment of urban colonies of Nordic peoples and after experiencing many fluctuations, with both successes and failures along the way, it declined by the end of the century. It was a means for Scandinavian immigrants to organize and to encounter American urban life, not only in the political sphere, but in a broad array of social, religious, and cultural activities, and it influenced residential and occupational preferences.[31]

Business and Good Works

The Scandinavian-born population grew rapidly during the mass post-war emigration, but it was still small compared to the total foreign-born group: the 13,771 Scandinavian immigrants who lived in Chicago in 1870 equaled only 9.5 percent of all foreign-born, and 4.6 percent of the total population. It was a number sufficiently small to make them feel overwhelmed and to promote a sense of a common Scandinavian heritage. By the end of the 1860s the Swedes were nearly as numerous as the Norwegians, numbering 6,154 to the Norwegians' 6,374 and the Danes' 1,243.

The several Scandinavian organizations that emerged in the late 1860s, whether or not it was directly stated, were united in their common concern to give assistance to immigrants. Athletic clubs and theater groups alongside the immigrant aid societies responded to needs in the Scandinavian-American community. Many of the newcomers in the late 1860s arrived destitute, and whether they remained in Chicago or merely passed through, they were in need of aid and comfort. In 1869 alone, according to the Swedish-Norwegian consulate, 24,260 Swedes and 15,172 Norwegians arrived in Chicago, and most of them, having bought their tickets through to that city, arrived quite penniless and unable to proceed farther inland. Poor people stranded in Quebec, before the British government discontinued the practice, had been sent on to Chicago at the expense of the British emigration office. In 1854 alone some 800 Norwegian immigrants had been assisted in this way. *Emigranten* reported that "many Norwegians fervently wished to be back in Norway, and would have gone, if they only had the needed means."[32]

As the center and receiving point of immigration, Chicago offered a unique opportunity for the army of unscrupulous persons who preyed on the immigrants, taking advantage of their ignorance and misery. *Emigranten* in 1864 had observed two to three hundred Norwegian immigrants stranded outside the Galena railroad depot during the night awaiting transport west. "But the worst of all," the newspaper wrote, "is that some of their own countrymen will try to con them out of their money." The great influx made Chicago a paradise for immigrant racketeers and confidence men. Immigrant "runners" of all kinds descended on the newcomers. These human sharks were frequently in the employ of forwarding establishments or boardinghouses and worked on commission, or they were simply impostors bent on defrauding the unwary. Individuals of their own nationality, easily earning the confidence of the immigrants, had an obvious advantage in victimizing their compatriots.[33]

Some of those who cheated their countrymen hid behind a mask of respectability and legitimacy. For instance, the Swedish Commercial Company systematically swindled the immigrants through dishonest land transactions and the sale of stock in fictitious business ventures. A crusading Swedish editor, Isidor Kjellberg, who in February, 1871, began publishing the newspaper *Justitia*, attacked the exploiters in articles and cartoons, the latter drawn by Marcus Thrane. The company was forced out of business. The immigrant community thus itself took action to correct direct exploitation.[34]

In June, 1866, Scandinavian churches cooperated on an ecumenical basis to form the Scandinavian Emigrant Aid Society (Den skandinaviske Emigranthjælpeforening), the first of its kind, "through combined forces better to assist and protect our countrymen." "Even the hardest heart must bleed at the sight of the masses that steamships and trains bring to our city and then abandon on our streets, hungry, needy, and impoverished," the Society wrote in its appeal for support. The common consular service of Norway and Sweden made cooperation particularly appropriate, and P.L. Hawkinson, the Swedish-Norwegian consul, became the Society's first chairman. Major initiative in the undertaking had come from Paul Andersen, who by then had left the ministry and entered business, Erland Carlsson, and other Swedish, Danish, and Norwegian ministers, including Swedish Methodists. The Danish banker Ferdinand S. Winslow, the Norwegian lawyer A. Jacobsen, and Iver Lawson were on its board. Perhaps the Vossing Emigration Society served as a model, but an existing German immigrant society might equally well have provided an example to emulate.[35]

The Society collected funds through dues and donations, and already on July 11 it was able to hire an agent, the Swede Frederick Nilsson, to meet the immigrants, and, as he stated in his first report, "lend them a helping hand in word and deed." His first act had been to assist sixty Norwegian immigrants to their destination in Wisconsin; dire poverty had stranded them for two weeks in the Northwestern railroad depot. In fact, a large percentage of the 2,240 Swedes, 1,200 Norwegians, and 300 Danes who arrived in the city between mid-July and the end of October had in some way benefited from the Society's services. The Norwegian journalist Paul Hjelm-Hansen, coming to La Crosse in western Wisconsin in 1867, emphasized the wholesomeness of rural life and expressed a common anti-urban idea that the many hapless Norwegian immigrants stranded in Chicago would create a worker's proletariat doomed to poverty. Nothing came of his suggestion that people in the new states cooperate with the Emigrant Aid Society in finding funds to move newcomers out of the city into agricultural work on the fertile soil of Wisconsin and Minnesota. The Society's funds, though never adequate, were nevertheless replenished by gifts from rural Scandinavians, who likely shared Hjelm-Hansen's fear of the city, and also wanted to see their own communities grow. An immigrant settlement in Neenah, Wisconsin, had on direct appeal collected $200 so that "a large party of poor Norwegians . . . twenty-four adults and thirty children," could complete their journey to that settlement.[36]

The services of the Society extended to assisting with hospital care, paying for burials, and finding housing. Immigrants were also exposed to fraud when they visited employment agencies; the Society therefore opened its own employment office. A petition to the Chicago Common Council dated January 12, 1870, for a free license to operate, because "our means is very small," was denied. That spring the Society itself dissolved; it had overextended itself and was heavily in debt. Since July, 1868, it had operated an immigrant hostel on Illinois Street near Wells, which was a heavy drain on resources. Later that year this shelter deteriorated to the level of a common boarding-house with "runners" when it was sold at auction to Henry Hjorth, who operated one of the many labor bureaus. Hjorth, for whatever questionable reasons, retained the name the Scandinavian Emigrant Aid Society for his operation.[37]

Competition from other protection societies had had an adverse impact on the Society's operations as well. The Svea Society, to begin with in cooperation with the Dania Society, worked to establish immigrant shelters. It actually operated two, one close to the Emigration Society's building. Thousands of immigrants made use of these hostels. Rivalry with the church-oriented Society led both Svea and Dania to appoint separate paid agents. Dania advised newcomers that its agent would be wearing the "Dania Emigration Society's sign on his chest, and as he is officially authorized he can protect you against illegal acts."[38]

Historian Ulf Beijbom has pointed to the striking connection between seemingly philanthropic endeavors and businesses backed by American capital, such as steamship companies, railroads, professional immigrant agencies, and land agencies. Many of the same men were active in both kinds of enterprise. These organizations frequently carried a Scandinavian name. Most of them, unlike the Swedish Commercial Company and several Scandinavian "runner" busi-

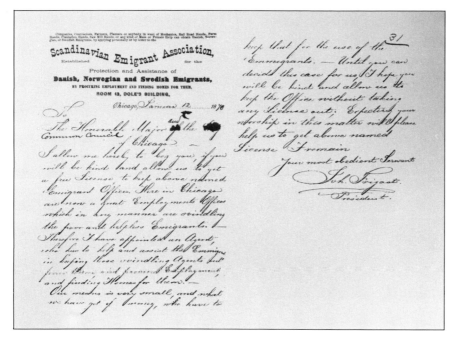

Petition dated January 12, 1870, to the City Council from the Scandinavian Emigrant Association requesting a free license to operate its employment office. The petition, signed by Joh. Frigast, reminds the Council that "in Chicago are now a great Employments Offices which in any manner are swindling the poor and helpless Emigrants."

nesses, were conducted honestly. It was a commercial necessity for American capital to allow Scandinavians to operate among their own. But the relationship seemed to bring the protection societies under the influence of the very groups they were intended to protect the unworldly immigrants from.[39]

Positions of responsibility in the emigrant protection societies, whether religious or secular in their orientation, would give quick contact with the greatest possible number of immigrants, which could be used to personal advantage. Through his private bank on Clark Street Ferdinand Winslow specialized in the transfer of money to Scandinavia and was a general agent for the Montreal Ocean Steamship Company. He advertised his services widely in the existing immigrant journals. Eric Stone, who succeeded Frederick Nilsson as agent for the Emigrant Aid Society, was also employed by Svea, and he combined these two jobs with work for Winslow. Another Norwegian example is the agency that Iver Lawson opened in 1867 at the corner of North Clark and North Water streets, which represented a number of steamship companies and sold bank notes on Scandinavian banks. [40]

The stream of immigrants the aid societies contacted were ready and trusting customers for land sales, for colonization projects, and for a multitude of other business objectives. These were entrepreneurial ventures dependent upon the support of the immigrant community. Without intending to suggest a nefarious design or a conscious manipulation of fellow Scandinavians by these groups, it is nevertheless obvious that immigrant humanitarianism might contain a strong element of commercial self-interest for some of the individuals who engaged in it.

Urban Cultural and Social Life

On February 20, 1868, *Skandinaven* announced the formation of yet another Scandinavian organization, the Scandinavian Society (Skandinavisk Samfund), which since its initial meeting on February 12 had attracted sixty members. It had likely been founded by Winslow, its first president, and it was one of the more successful efforts. The society existed until the Great Fire and devoted itself to musical entertainment, depending exclusively on "the musical talents of resident Swedish, Norwegian, and Danish dilettantes."[41]

In most societies, however, a combination of activities was more common, so that on any one program there might be lectures and a concert, or a dramatic presentation followed by a dance. The social life of the immigrants included popular summer outings, as for instance Nora's "Norwegian basket" picnics arranged as a part of the July Fourth celebration. It all became a part of an important network of support. Concerts and dramatic productions were not infrequently benefit performances. On January 31, 1867, following a play and dance in the German Hall at the corner of Wells and Grand (then Indiana), the Norwegian National Theater (Det norske Nationaltheater) donated its entire profit of $30.30 to the Emigrant Aid Society.[42]

Behind this rather pretentious appellation stood a small theater troupe organized during September-October, 1866, by Marcus Thrane, who had worked in amateur theatrical groups in Norway. It gave its first performance on October 15. Even though Thrane's efforts in Chicago were modest, they may be viewed as a harbinger of a cultural activity that was to flourish to an amazing degree — generally at the amateur level — in independent theater companies, in clubs and lodges, in labor unions and cultural institutions of many kinds. These groups generated and spread culture within the immigrant community and provided inexpensive entertainment in the homeland's language.[43]

From 1866 to 1868 Thrane produced thirty-two plays, seen on twenty-one evenings, five of them his own. Dancing until the wee hours followed each performance; social considerations were as important as cultural ones. The opening performance was a light vaudeville by Thrane himself, *Doktor mod doktor* (Doctor against Doctor). He introduced into the Norwegian community his more serious educational message, as a socialist and reformer, in his two plays *Skydskiftet i Hallingdal* (The Posting Station in Hallingdal) and *Syttende mai* (May Seventeenth). Both were designated as two-act national song pieces and basically deal with social barriers and injustice in Norway.[44]

Mountain scenes, national costumes, and folk tunes were appealing elements. National romantic themes were introduced in Norwegian plays, for instance in Ivar Aasen's *Ervingen* (The Heir), a national romantic ballad, and in C.P. Riis's popular *Til sæters* (To the Mountains), with its splendid medley of folk songs and its nationalistic emphasis.

The Scandinavian-American press in Chicago, both the Norwegian *Skandinaven* and the Swedish *Svenska Amerikanaren*, reviewed the performances seriously. They were thus brought to the attention of a large potential audience. Thrane's son Arthur and daughters Camilla and Wally (Vasilia) performed. Wally Thrane was especially lauded for her acting. But in 1868 Thrane disbanded his troupe.[45]

On March 12, 1868, another formal theater group, the Norwegian Dramatic Society (Den norske dramatiske Forening) organized, and likely included actors from Thrane's troupe. It presented plays until 1872. Its records have been preserved and they provide an insightful entry into the functioning of an artistic group within an immigrant community. It inevitably identified with and gained its strength from the culture native to Norway. Most of the actors stood apart from the peasant society that their performances idealized; they came mainly from the homeland's official and professional classes, and some of them pursued successful careers in the American business world. The number of male actors was limited to ten; no limit was set

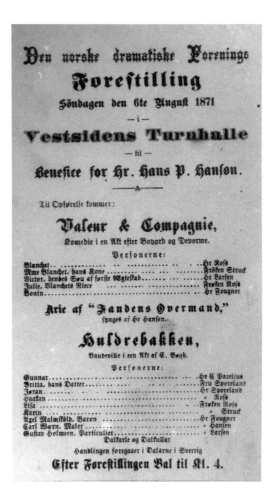

The Norwegian Dramatic Society announces a benefit performance for
Hans P. Hanson, one of the actors in the troupe, on Sunday, August 6,
1871. Following the two one-act plays and an "aria" sung by Hanson
himself, there would be dancing until four o'clock in the morning.

for female actors, although they were fewer. Actresses received $5.00 for each performance, whereas the men would divide equally income in excess of $100. In December, 1868, however, they decided to share the entire treasury of $107.74. Its democratic practice of requiring that "every member must accept whatever role . . . assigned him" was a serious source of tension. The minutes reveal squabbles, rivalry, exclusions, resignations—in short bruised artistic egos—but also warm sociability, camaraderie, and mutual concern for the members' well-being.[46]

During its existence at least thirty-three men and nineteen women participated in the dramatic society's plays. Successful both on the stage and off was Julius Anker-Midling, perhaps the troupe's most colorful actor, who had been one of the founders of a boys' theater in his native Bergen. Carlos Ross, also educated in Bergen, was another leader in the society, as was J.W. Arctander, who later made a career in law and journalism. Those members who did not make a successful transition to American society still clung, while working for a pittance, to their dress suits and silk hats as symbols of their social standing. An artistic clique was emerging in the immigrant community.[47]

The first performance at the German Hall on March 28, 1868, was "only poorly attended," as was the second one on April 6, where the income had been committed to help needy immigrants. Both events actually resulted in deficits. Though constantly short of money the troupe did accrue a profit; the practice of benefit performances for needy individuals and families continued. Here it showed a common concern with the religious institutions. The Lutheran clergy nevertheless condemned the theater as worldly and sinful— if not the plays, then certainly the parties and dancing that followed the performances.[48]

In its repertoire the dramatic society displayed a distinct Norwegian national spirit. It may be likened to the theater Ole Bull had founded in Bergen in 1850 as a center for Norwegian drama and music. Bull was an idolized and not infrequent visitor and performer in Chicago during these years, and his inspiration, as well as the Bergen background of many of the theater's members, made an attempt to recreate Bull's national stage a near certainty. Norwegian determination to shed Danish cultural dominance thus found artistic expression in the charged self-consciousness of the immigrant world. But the limited number of strictly Norwegian dramatic works forced the Chicago players, as it had the theater in Bergen, to rely heavily on Danish plays and continental ones in Danish adaptations. Strong national sentiments were, however, evidenced in the group's May 17th programs, in the singing of national songs by the audience, and in the presentation of folk dances. The actors, much like Thrane's troupe, deliberately chose plays that celebrated Nordic history and romanticized peasant life, *Til sæters* being the most frequently played of the Norwegian pieces. Thus, the plays did not mirror the urban world of the immigrants, although they supplied it with added amenities and injected a feeling for cultural values and a heightened national identity.[49]

Alternatives to social life in a religious setting were offered by several non-church organizations. The Scandinavian Turner Society (Den skandinaviske Turnerforening) was established on August 14, 1867. The purpose of this gymnastic society was "by means of suitable exercises to develop physical strength at the same time as . . . debating general social questions and . . . training the spiritual faculty." It was founded as a joint Scandinavian venture, not in the fervent spirit of nationalism of the dramatic society, and patterned after the German turners, with whom on occasion they had joint outings. The idea had, however, been transferred across the Atlantic from Scandinavia, where the turner movement had reached in the 1850s, and like the theater, bore witness to an exodus of urban immigrants and their practices. In America, Scandinavian turners, like the German, did gymnastics and met in uniform to do military drills.

The West Turner Hall, which in 1868 was built on Milwaukee Avenue and what was then Second Street (now ca. 400 Milwaukee), as well as the North Turner Hall, served as meeting places. But in 1871 the turners moved entirely to the former location, indicating that, in spite of its original pan-Scandinavian appeal it was largely Norwegian. In the 1870 city directory the hall was called Aurora Turner Hall, and it became known as the "old" Aurora Hall when a new Aurora Turner Hall was built farther north in the same area on the corner of Milwaukee Avenue and Huron Street; the first one had been rented and the second one was owned by the German Aurora Turnverein. In September, 1871, the turner society held a fair at the large, wooden, barn-like West Side Turner Hall, which became a center of labor union activity, near the southeast corner of Roosevelt and Halsted; there were "gymnastic exhibitions, pantomimes, a ball, and much much more," the printed program promised. A major enterprise in the 1870s was the financing of a Scandinavian Turner Hall, erected on Halsted Street between Kinzie and Hubbard; the debt it incurred apparently ruined the society.[50]

The Chicago Ethnic Press

The ethnic press had a basic community-building role; it joined the immigrants in churches, clubs, and societies into a unit. Its first modest appearance in Chicago was made in 1845 with the German-language *Chicago Volksfreund* (People's Friend); three years later came the much more influential *Illinois Staatszeitung* (State Times). Like the pioneer Scandinavian-American newspapers they had a distinct political identity and carried political discussions. They were consequently important to the civic education of the immigrants, at the same time serving individual ambitions for election to public office. In the world of Norwegian-American journalism the brief appearance of *Friheds-Banneret* (The Banner of Freedom) in Chicago in 1852–1854 was unique, since until the end of the Civil War Norwegian-American newspapers in general represented rural interests.[51]

Nordlyset (Northern Lights) had inaugurated a Norwegian-American press on July 29, 1847, in the Muskego settlement. The *Daily Democrat*, no doubt influenced by its connections with the Norwegian community, welcomed *Nordlyset* as "a desirable medium for advertising for merchants in this city." Twenty-five of its eventual 280 subscribers resided in Chicago. This was hardly sufficient to lure advertisers and was a cause of *Nordlyset*'s demise after about three years. It had stressed Americanization, printing in its initial issue "the immortal Declaration of Independence," the *Daily Democrat* reported.[52]

To encourage "the process of Americanization" among Norwegian and Danish immigrants was an objective also for *Emigranten*, the major journal in the 1850s. Its mailing address was Inmansville, Wisconsin, until 1857, when it moved to Madison. The weekly was initially sponsored by the Scandinavian Press Association, which was controlled by the conservative clergy of the Norwegian Synod. *Emigranten* circulated among Norwegians in Chicago, and like the Lutheran church itself, moved into the city with a rural perspective. Its first editor was the Danish pastor C.L. Clausen. Under the direction of Carl Fredrik Solberg it continued during the war years as the sole secular Norwegian-American newspaper.[53]

During the second half of the decade of the 1860s, however — a time of breakthrough for many immigrant activities in Chicago — a Norwegian-American press was firmly established there. More than half of all Norwegians in America lived within a triangle formed by LaCrosse, Chicago, and Milwaukee. In this central city with easy railroad transportation to distant Norwegian settlements a newspaper with broad appeal could circulate widely. Indicative of the many interests in the city was the short-lived weekly *Marcus Thrane's Norske Amerikaner*, published by Thrane from May to September, 1866, in defense of the working man. *Skandinaven*, taking advantage of the favorable circumstances to become a major newspaper, espoused a similar democratic spirit and spoke for the rights of the common man. Its first issue is dated June 1, 1866. Norwegians and Danes could also follow the unremitting warfare between the two Republican Swedish newspapers in the city, the clerically dominated *Hemlandet* (The Homeland) and its rival *Svenska Amerikanaren*, launched on September 8 the same year as *Skandinaven*. Its attacks on the Swedish-American Lutheran clergy gained it the favor of the anti-religious element among Swedes in Chicago.[54]

Skandinaven was also Republican and anti-clerical. It was critical of the hierarchy in the Norwegian Synod, but it was not anti-religious; in fact the low-church Haugean Lutherans regarded the newspaper as their organ. The "Vossing War" then raging in the controversy with Petersen in the First Norwegian Evangelical Lutheran Congregation was obviously the immediate cause for *Skandinaven* in its first issue to assail religious dissent as the main hindrance to newspaper publishing, as it splintered the immigrants into warring groups. Political differences could not be blamed, the editorial asserted, because "the Scandinavians in Chicago are numerous and concordant in political conviction." Two of the men who invested in the newspaper enterprise, Andrew Nelson (Brekke) and Iver Lawson, were of course directly involved in both the church feud and Republican politics.[55]

The newspaper described its editorial policy as radical in the sense that "poor and rich, black and white should be punished or rewarded in equal measure according to the same laws." The publishers and editors of *Skandinaven* had themselves come from modest circumstances; they objected to aristocratic tendencies and identified easily with the position of the immigrant. But the newspaper was also a business venture intended to give a profit and a return on investment. John Anderson, *Skandinaven*'s founder, was at the time he began publishing the newspaper head of the composing room of the *Chicago Tribune*. He had worked his way up. As a young boy Anderson had peddled apples on the Chicago streets and delivered newspapers to support his mother and siblings after his father's death in the cholera epidemic in 1849. His newspaper delivery job led Anderson into the printing profession.[56]

Knud Langeland became *Skandinaven*'s first editor and for several years was its co-owner. He was born in Samnanger, trained as a schoolmaster, and in views and actions expressed the class assertiveness of Norwegian peasants. Before going to America in 1843, Langeland had spent six months in England in 1835, which he insisted had given him insights into commerce. In America he worked on several immigrant newspapers, in late 1849, for instance, purchasing *Nordlyset*. Control over immigrant newspapers supplied political credentials. In 1859 Langeland won election to the Wisconsin state assembly.[57]

As editor of *Skandinaven*, Langeland participated vigorously in the long-drawn-out debate regarding human bondage, which the Norwegian Synod insisted had Biblical justification. C. L. Clausen, who had been chaplain for the Fifteenth Wisconsin Regiment and a strong antislavery advocate, resigned from the Synod in 1868 over this question. A second issue, which was revived after the war, was the debate over the American public school system, which the high-church Synod ministers saw as an inherent threat to Lutheranism and the Norwegian language. They therefore desired to supplant it with parochial or congregational schools, as German Lutherans had successfully done. The Synod reaffirmed this position in 1866. Showing sensitivity to assimilationist views, Langeland challenged the Synod clergy editorially, emphasizing how the common school encouraged democracy, indirectly taught religious tolerance, and promoted patriotism and love of freedom.

At great sacrifice, Our Savior's Church in Chicago had established a congregational day school in 1860. Arriving in the 1880s Olaf O. Ray, newspaperman and lawyer, later recalled that "the Norwegians then had their own school at Erie and May." The school operated until 1888 and, to quote from A.T. Andreas, gave instruction "in common English branches, Norwegian language, and Lutheran religion." Struggle and adversity are evident in the records of the school. In 1867 Pastor J.L. Krohn, then serving Our Savior's congregation, contacted his colleague Petersen, who through his own machinations had brought his church into the Synod, to see if the school could be operated jointly by the two congregations. While negotiations were in progress a scandal surfaced in Our Savior's congregation and delayed matters. Rumors were spread that their esteemed teacher since 1863, J.P. Johnson, before leaving Fredrikstad for America in 1860 had "made a child that was both deaf and dumb pregnant." The painful congregational meetings on dismissal, with many curious non-members present although delicate sensibilities excluded women, dragged on for some time. It was finally established through sworn witnesses that the girl in question possessed all her senses, was about nineteen, and "of a nature and character unusually frivolous, rash, and shameless." Johnson was, however, let go and found employment at a German congregational school. In Petersen's congregation legal expenses incurred over the conflict about property rights created a burden, and it was not until May, 1871, that the congregation produced a resolution to open the joint school on September 1, in order to "preserve our nationality and Lutheran faith." Delays in opening the school and then the Great Fire intervened to leave Our Savior's Church again to finance the children's education alone. The heavily Norwegian neighborhood in which the church was situated, however, made the school a feasible undertaking.[58]

It may be that Langeland overstated and misrepresented the opposition of the Synod to the common school. The Synod quite certainly realized that its resources were in no way equal to the task of creating a separate school system. Other Norwegian-American newspapers concerned themselves little with promoting secular education through the medium of the American school. In 1863 Chicago established free public schools, and as most of the Norwegian youth attended these, the argument for separate institutions was weakened. But the debate attracted attention. It obviously reflected a deep conviction on the part of Langeland, whom the Chicago school board rewarded by naming a school in his honor. His contact was very likely

Andrew B. Johnson, who was a member of this body, then as later often the first step toward a political career. The board's formidable responsibility was to educate young people of diverse ethnic backgrounds. An essential factor in this process was the support of all nationalities.[59]

No doubt Anderson's professional background and judicious leadership contributed to *Skandinaven*'s success, but its popular tone, its discussions of burning issues, and its conscious appeal to the ordinary citizen also increased circulation. Revenue from advertising, which sustained and made urban newspapers profitable, eventually secured *Skandinaven* success as well. Its defense of American institutions was balanced by its promotion of Norwegian-American activities and cultural interests. And Langeland was much aware of the value of Scandinavian unity in political affairs. *Skandinaven* was hawked by newspaper boys and given free to Norwegian newcomers at railroad stations. Its influence and its message of urban values and way of life intruded into remote immigrant communities, into farming settlements and small towns and villages, and announced Chicago as a major Norwegian-American center.[60]

4

Coming to Terms
with the City

"What has been assembled and done through many years of restless activity and diligence to make Chicago a world wonder has in one single day been wiped away from the face of the earth," *Skandinaven* declared in its issue dated October 19, 1871.[1] The Great Fire broke out on Sunday evening October 8, and in the course of twenty-four hours lay waste an area two-thirds of a mile wide and four miles long, which included the entire business district. Chicago was by no means a wooden shanty town, as some have thought. The homes and mansions of its wealthy citizens and the buildings in the city's central district were of brick, stone, and iron, albeit often of unsubstantial quality. But with these exceptions wooden structures did dominate: simple cottages, rickety two-story houses, barns, stables, and other outbuildings, warehouses, lumber yards, and grain elevators. Streets paved with pine blocks, wooden sidewalks, and wooden bridges across a river filled with wooden vessels further aided the fire's progress. On the North Side it devoured nearly everything between the river and the lake to Fullerton Avenue. There were no houses farther north.

The Great Fire and Its Aftermath

Top left: The panic produced by the devastating flames is evident in this sketch from 1871 by Alfred R. Waud.

Top right: The remains of the Tremont House, one of the city's fashionable hotels, suggest the destructive force of the fire.

Bottom: One of the first issues of *Skandinaven* after the Great Fire was dated October 18, 1871. It appeared in a much reduced size and dealt exclusively with the fire's impact on the city.

The Great Fire was one of the most spectacular events of the century, and for Chicago it marked the end of an era. It left nearly 100,000 of the city's 334,000 citizens without shelter, killed 300, and caused property damage of $200 million. The fire left a panorama of rubble and ashes, and an incredible amount of human misery and need. "Imagination cannot fathom the horror of the situation," *Skandinaven* cautioned its readers.[2]

Because of their concentration on the North Side the Swedes were among the most hard-pressed. John A. Enander, a leading layman and at that time editor of *Hemlandet*, estimated that at least 5,000 Swedes had been made homeless by the fire. He admired their self-discipline as they left their possessions behind and fled their burning homes. "To no one's loss," the pietistic Enander wrote, "only a few drunken sons of noble families whom highborn relatives had sent here to be 'reformed' perished." Like the Norwegians on the North Side the Swedes took refuge on the West Side. *Skandinaven* reported that many countrymen "left their burning dwellings only with the clothes on their back, while others took with them minor possessions, and have now, as far as we have learned, found temporary shelter among fortunate countrymen on the West Side."[3]

Among the more prominent Norwegians who suffered loss were Christian Jevne, whose large grocery store on Kinzie Street burned down, and Andrew B. Johnson, who lost his profitable lumber business. Andrew Nelson (Brekke) and Iver Lawson also had property destroyed, although Lawson's new residence, "a large frame house with extensive lawns at front and rear" on North Clark Street, was spared. The insolvency of many insurance companies unable to stand the strain rendered policies valueless. Still, Lawson's holdings were considerable at his death the following year, and the other men not only survived their losses but prospered in the rebuilding of the city.[4]

No less than six Swedish newspaper establishments, among them both *Hemlandet* and *Svenska Amerikanaren*, were victims of the fire, and five Norwegian-language publications suffered an equal fate. *Skandinaven*'s offices on the southwest corner of Clark and South Water streets burned down; fortunately the subscription lists were saved. In his typical indefatigable manner, John Anderson borrowed money to go to Madison, where he purchased printing equipment on credit. It was this that permitted him to publish a small four-page edition of *Skandinaven* already on October 14 in a basement on West Erie Street. "With God's help," he assured his readers," it will not be long before *Skandinaven* will pay its regular visit in its usual form."[5]

Six Scandinavian churches, as well as the Svea Society's club house, were swept away. The stately Swedish Immanuel Church on Sedgwick Street, dedicated the previous year, and the old edifice the congregation had occupied on Superior were both lost, as were the St. Ansgarius church and the Norwegian church served by C.J.P. Petersen. "The Norwegian Church on Erie Street, which so long has concerned the courts, exists no longer," *Skandinaven* with its direct ties to the opposing party announced caustically.[6]

Chicago rose from the ashes at an incredible speed; the city retained its position as "the unsurpassed gateway to the middle empire of America."[7] The prevailing spirit of industry and optimism was exemplified by the Norwegian tailor Knud B. Olson, whose tailor shop on Superior Street was destroyed. No insurance payment was available, but his pressers and shop help pitched in to erect a small building, merchandise was purchased in Milwaukee, and on November 1 they were back in business. The most immediate concern following the calamity was, however, assistance to feed and house the needy, made more urgent by an unusually cold winter. The Chicago Relief and Aid Society, responsible for all municipal relief work, and also for the distribution of funds and supplies that poured in from everywhere, reported in December that 18,435 families were being assisted; of these 2,104 were Norwegian or Swedish.[8]

Many Chicago churches set up relief agencies. On the initiative of Erland Carlsson a Swedish relief committee was formed. A mass meeting at Our Savior's Church on October 11 of pastors and lay people from the different Norwegian congregations created a similar Norwegian committee, "like other nationalities," as *Skandinaven* stated. Chairman of the committee was O. T. Birkeland of the Nora Lodge and the secretary was Pastor S. M. Krogness of the recently formed Bethlehem congregation. But purely secular groups were also active, as for instance the persistently poor Norwegian Dramatic Society, which in November sent the considerable amount of $175 to Consul Peter Svanøe, stating in English that it was "for distribution among the by fire norwegian sufferers."[9]

The City Mission Movement

The Scandinavian Methodist Church erected on Illinois Street on the North Side in 1854, known simply as the Illinois Street Church, was one of the buildings laid in ashes. In times of adversity and when death seems imminent, as Bessie Pierce pointed out, converts are more easily made. The Methodists, and then the Baptists, were the largest American Protestant groups in Chicago. They enjoyed a spectacular growth and spread their message of repentance and conversion through mission activity, Sunday schools, tracts, and revival meetings, working tirelessly to save unchristian souls and to convince sinners to mend their ways. In summer there were camp meetings; a common practice was to conduct these in open tents in a wooded section near the DesPlaines Station.[10]

The Baptists and the Methodists had missions among the immigrant population. Until ethnic congregations could be gathered the converted joined American churches. "Here are French Protestants, we have Dutch, Germans, English, and half a township of Norwegians," a Methodist minister reported to the *Home Mission* in 1850,

adding that the "Norwegians have preaching service in their own tongue every three weeks."[11]

Both religious groups condemned the Lutheran way of obtaining members. As recorded in the membership roster, they were admitted through immigration or through confirmation without a conversion experience. The Lutherans on the other hand took no part in Baptist and Methodist revival meetings. This division existed also in Norway, where sectarian groups began appearing in the decade following the law of 1845 granting religious liberties. Norwegian dissenters thereafter gave strength to American denominations. The passengers on board the *Sleipner* on its first voyage in 1862 were followers of the revivalist preacher Gustav Adolph Lammers. Lammers was actually a minister in the Church of Norway who had left his call to form free congregations. Many of the dissenters on the *Sleipner* joined the largely Swedish Methodist church on Illinois Street. One of these, as an example, was Rakel Pedersen, born in Bergen in 1833, who until her death in 1904 was "a faithful and charitable member," first of the Illinois Street congregation then in the one of "her own people."[12]

Revivalism had its day toward the end of the 1860s, when the appeal to religious emotionalism and condemnation of intemperance and sinful practices was carried forward by a number of zealous preachers. In June, 1868, thirty-five Danish and Norwegian members of the Illinois Street church joined by twenty-six other converts formed the First Norwegian-Danish Methodist Church; they had their meeting place on Grand Avenue (Indiana Street) on the West Side. Following the lead of American colleagues, the first resident pastor, John H. Johnson, stirred a great revival. In the course of a few years the congregation increased to 346 members. After the destruction of their church, the Swedes in the Illinois Street congregation worshipped with them. Showing a good understanding of finances, "the few and poor members" traded the North Side lot for four lots on May Street, since a number of Swedes had settled on the West Side after the fire, and reestablished themselves there. Scandinavian Methodism expanded further when as a result of work begun by Christian Treider, editor of the organ of Danish-Norwegian Methodism *Den kristelige Talsmand* (The Christian Advocate), the Immanuel Church came into being in May, 1886, on the West Side; from 1888 it was located on Huron Street a few blocks north of the First Church.[13]

Only after 1880 did the Norwegian-Danish Conference come about as a national body within the Methodist Church. Its major activity was in the volatile religious environment of Chicago, with a separate theological seminary in Evanston, but it never grew very large, nor did the Swedish conference. Some Lutheran commentators have emphasized a Scandinavian dislike of revivals as a cause.

Historian George M. Stephenson instead sees the hierarchical character of Methodism as an obstacle to its broad acceptance, which he believes runs counter to Scandinavian individualism. But also the long subordination of Scandinavian congregations in a church so thoroughly American in its form of worship weakened its appeal.[14]

Demonstrably some Scandinavians did respond positively to Methodism. The pietistic and puritanical, and perhaps often those poor in worldly goods, might here find nurture for body and soul. An anti-intellectual bias was at times expressed by Norwegian Methodists. The preaching did not, as it was said of the Lutheran churches, "move in a high-flying sphere beyond the comprehension of the worshipers," but appealed more to the emotions than the intellect.[15]

Advances among Scandinavians were modest and uneven also for the evangelistic Baptists, who nevertheless attracted a substantial Swedish following. "A new era of missionary activity began in 1866," wrote the Swedish-American Baptist historian J.O. Backlund. The great influx of Scandinavians was considered a fertile field. That year a Swedish Baptist congregation was formed; its church, on Oak Street, perished in the fire. Norwegians baptized by immersion joined groups of Danish and Swedish Baptists or American churches. Two Norwegians in 1864 had joined eighteen Danes to form the First Danish Baptist Church. Permanence was a fleeting goal, however. A small dissenting group, revealing the volatility of immigrant religious life and the tendency toward forming cliques, left this weak congregation and in January, 1870, formed the Danish and Norwegian Nordic Tabernacle Baptist Church.

Disturbed at the slow progress in proselyting compatriots, a group of ten Norwegian Baptists in the Tabernacle congregation, believing that an appeal to nationality and language would help, came together in 1877 in the home of Rudolf Christensen and formed the First Norwegian Baptist Church, the ten in question constituting the original membership. They cited as motives that even though Norwegians were a majority of the Scandinavian population, a questionable claim by that time, there was no Norwegian Baptist church, and holy scriptures taught that it was natural to have most love for one's own nationality. The Danes acted with alarm, as they feared the adverse effect the loss of the Norwegians would have on their own small assembly. Rumors that Christensen "had had brothers and sisters in his home, and with them organized the Norwegian Baptist Church," caused him to be expelled. The Danes at the council called to recognize the Norwegian congregation all as one voted against it, while the Swedes voted in favor, since they thought that "it was not an unchristian act to organize a Norwegian church." In their constitution the Norwegians expressly and pointedly limited the right to hold office to Norwegians. The emphasis on nationality and language would justify the congregation's existence to American Baptists and it was thus a matter of self-preservation.[16]

Economic reality, however, forced a renewed Danish-Norwegian solution. The Baptist Home Mission Society, which gave financial aid to both the Danes and the Norwegians, in 1884 convinced the Danish Baptists to join the Norwegians. In the merger national Danish and Norwegian identification was studiously avoided. The new Danish-Norwegian combination accepted the broader Scandinavian identity and became the Scandinavian Pilgrim Baptist Church, at the corner of Carpenter and Ohio streets. Of the 181 members, only 63 were Norwegian, the remainder Danes, who together labored to pay "for a considerable piece of property [the church] purchased right in the heart of this city."[17]

The weak Norwegian response to the city mission movement, whether Methodist, Baptist, or independent, might to some extent point up a more general circumstance. Immigrants felt alienated from American-dominated religiosity. Because of a special nationalistic fervor Norwegians, more than Swedes or Danes, were likely extra sensitive. Obviously Norwegian immigrants could more easily be convinced of the rightness of Lutheran doctrine and of voluntary membership in Norwegian Lutheran congregations than in non-Lutheran ones. And membership outside the Lutheran fold tended to isolate not only in religious matters. Social life as well was closely associated with the Lutheran tradition. In America this tradition expressed itself in forms that satisfied different religious urges, from the emotional and puritanical church of the laity to the doctrinally pure high church of the clergy.[18]

Evangelists like Dwight L. Moody conducted revival meetings for a largely middle-class Protestant audience, which left out the masses of immigrants. A Norwegian signing himself "born again" who had attended a Moody meeting expressed his pain in *Skandinaven* over how many of his countrymen, because of language barriers and because "no special activity to reach them had occurred," were deprived of experiencing "the conversion of sinners." In his efforts to save and reclaim the thousands of young men who poured into Chicago, Moody invested his energy in The Young Men's Christian Association, organized by him on May 17, 1858. It was open only to members of the evangelical churches and appealed most obviously to young men at the bottom rungs of the middle class, thus leaving out the lower classes, though it engaged in relief work among the needy.

The YMCA gained the support of businessmen and other leading Chicagoans imbued with a Yankee Puritanism which impelled them to devote equal vigor and discipline to business and good works. Among these was the second-generation Norwegian Victor F. Lawson, who through church affiliation, marriage, and friendship with Moody gave evidence of his identification with the Yankee Puritan tradition. This identification had its roots in his early contact with the pioneer Andersen church. From the late 1870s, gaining fame and fortune as publisher of the *Daily News*, Victor Lawson contributed regularly and generously to the YMCA cause. *Skandinaven*, of which his father Iver Lawson was a part owner, in 1868 had praised "this first class society" for its generosity. Reading rooms, libraries, lectures, and in time physical activities in a Christian spirit were seen as a means of moral uplift and a way to keep impressionable youth away from destructive temptations.[19]

In the 1880s a special Scandinavian department was established within the YMCA but concerns among immigrant leaders and moralists about the risks to green newcomers in a large city like Chicago, where "the allurements are many and the temptations great," led them to act sooner and form an independent young men's Christian association. It emerged in strongly evangelical immigrant circles, among the Lutherans the pietistic Haugeans being the most responsive. The first such organization, effected on October 28, 1872, in Trinity Church at the initiative of its forceful evangelistic pastor, John Z. Torgersen, disbanded after a few years.

At a meeting in the Nordic Tabernacle Baptist Church on June 13, 1876, a more successful venture was undertaken. (It was this church that would lose its Norwegian members in 1877). The Scandinavian Young Men's Christian Association (Den skandinaviske unge menns kristelige Forening) formed there in 1876 became a largely Norwegian society. Its constitution admitted to membership "any male person who believes in Jesus Christ and lives in accordance with this faith." A woman could join, but only as a "hjælpende Medlem" (assistant member). It grew very slowly until the 1890s, when it gained the support of such prosperous men as the wealthy butcher and real estate speculator Ole L. Stangeland. In 1893 Iver Olsen, a strong believer in the necessity of a conversion experience, became a force in the society; he was a member of the Lutheran Bethania (Bethany) Free Church, organized by Torgersen when he left Trinity over doctrinal dispute in 1877. In 1899 the Scandinavian Young Men's Christian Association moved into its own building on Erie Street on the West Side in the heart of the Norwegian neighborhood, where it earned a place as a social center, but with a strong evangelical mission "to bring young people under the beneficial influence of the Gospel." Its religious fervor was much in evidence; someone described the society as "a laymen's society, where God's Word was spoken, where they testified, sang and prayed every Sunday afternoon." The extreme loneliness a young person might feel in a large and impersonal city would make him accept the moral restraints imposed by such societies, which also offered comradeship and a warm room.[20]

•
Left: The building of the Scandinavian Young Men's Christian Association on Erie Street.

•
Right: Iver Olsen.

Our Savior's imposing new brick building, its steeple soaring 200 feet above ground, erected on the location of the old edifice and dedicated October 5, 1873, symbolized the strong Lutheran identity of the Norwegian neighborhood. It seated 1,200 worshipers. Pastor O. Juul, coming to the congregation in the fall of 1876, alleged it to be "the largest and costliest church building raised by Norwegians in this country." The expanded facilities were a response to the influx of new members, most of whom settled in the vicinity of the church, in the wake of the post-war emigration wave.[21]

The greater doctrinal discipline in the conservative Our Savior's Church spared it from disruptive splits, at least until the late 1880s, when the church body to which it belonged was itself sundered by internal religious warfare. Not so in the Trinity congregation. Its openness to lay exegesis and religious emotionalism, and its message of a life apart from the world, seemed to make it vulnerable to friction and the formation of factions within the congregation. These were on several occasions moved to leave and form new independent unions. One of the more famous incidents involved Pastor S.M. Krogness, whose ministry in Trinity began shortly after his arrival from Norway in 1866. Its dimensions and consequences had significance not only for the situation in Chicago, but for synodical developments as a whole. In early 1870 a party within Trinity accused their pastor of neglecting his duties and of spreading false teachings. These charges were debated in front of an overflowing crowd and appeared to the uninvolved to be good entertainment. On one occasion Krogness obviously offended temperance sensibilities by insisting that a woman he knew who sold "wine, beer, and food" was also a "good Christian." The ensuing exchange became intensified to the point where four men stood shouting and shaking their fists at each other in the front of the church to the amusement of the onlookers, who "burst out in a storm of laughter, applauded, gave loud encouragement, and stamped their feet so that several pews were broken."[22]

Krogness did not blame the parishioners for such an undignified spectacle, but instead he pointed an accusing finger at August Weenaas, who taught theology at the Scandinavian Augustana Seminary in Paxton, Illinois. Weenaas had contrived, Krogness asserted, to turn Norwegian newcomers against him. Since Krogness also belonged to the Augustana Synod, the synodical affiliation of the two men was not the same as Trinity's. Their differences reflected ethnic dissimilarities within the synod and tensions produced by a move toward a greater national Norwegian emphasis in religious affairs in general. Newly arrived immigrants were evidently receptive. Weenaas, who came to America in 1868, stood for the transfer of a pietistic revivalism within the Norwegian state church associated with the Norwegian professor of theology Gisle Johnson. Weenaas became a major architect of the separation from the Swedes that oc-

Our Savior's church building dedicated October 5, 1873.

curred that year and the creation of the Norwegian Augustana Synod. In the conflict the Swedish pastors in the Scandinavian Augustana had understandably sided with Krogness, reporting in the Swedish-American press about the cowardice of his opponents and how "Pastor Krogness defended himself with noble dignity."

Juridical issues, but even more a move toward nationalistic Norwegian church practices within the Norwegian Augustana, which a minority was not ready for, shortly produced a new split. Under the guidance of Weenaas the majority parted company with the Norwegian Augustana and organized the Lutheran synod known as the Conference, which adopted Norwegian ministerial garments and church ritual. C. L. Clausen became its president. It appealed to the many immigrants who were arriving and filled the middle position in Norwegian-American Lutheranism. With its familiar liturgy and practices it became the major church body alongside the Norwegian Synod.[23]

Only seven ministers, among them Krogness, remained in the Norwegian Augustana. After resigning with "a brief and suitable speech," he left Trinity with ninety-eight members. A number of these appear to have belonged to the "Vossing party" which in 1866 had left the First Norwegian Evangelical Lutheran Congregation in the conflict with Petersen. On March 2, 1870, the departing group organized Bethlehem congregation, which moved into a simple structure "on the corner of N. Sangamon just far enough from Milwaukee Avenue to be nearly invisible." It was a poor congregation in a poor neighborhood, and not particularly a Norwegian one, the church being surrounded by "huts, patched up with pieces of slabs and dry goods boxes." In 1880, however, it was able to move to a location in the Norwegian district at the corner of Racine (then Center) Avenue and Huron Street. The congregation by then held membership in the Conference.[24]

Undoubtedly, theological controversy and confrontations between the congregation and the pastor and between parties within the church could be a lesson on the functioning of a free church system for newcomers from a state-church arrangement. *Skandinaven* in its 1870 end-of-the-year review thought that the church feuds of that year had taught Norwegian Americans about democracy and the positive aspects of clear convictions, not only in the religious sphere but in civic activities as well. The consequence was, however, more often than not split rather than compromise, but all the same religious beliefs and structures were being clarified.[25]

Notwithstanding the drain on Trinity's membership through disharmony, in 1870 it stood at about 1,200 and the congregation saw the need for a new house of worship. It offered to erect a structure sufficiently large to accommodate the long-planned school to train pastors for Eielsen's Synod. This proposal was accepted. On August

27, 1871, the cornerstone of the projected Hauge's College and Eielsen Seminary was formally laid at the location of Trinity Church on Grand (Indiana) and Peoria with the venerable Elling Eielsen himself delivering the main speech. He stressed in an enlightened manner the salutary influence of "a true Christian and civil education for a person who must at the same time be a true Christian and a useful citizen." The school, if realized, would have meant the establishment of institutions of higher learning among Norwegians in Chicago. But it was not to be. Such church schools, with rare exceptions, thrived better in rural and small-town settings where the Lutheran church had a greater say. Another example was the floundering Augustana Seminary, which had been established in Chicago in June, 1860. Classes were conducted in the church basement of the First Norwegian Evangelical Lutheran Congregation with the Swedish theologian Lars Esbjörn, who had left his professorship at the seminary of the Northern Illinois Synod, as president, assisted by Pastor Abraham Jacobson. In 1863 it was moved to the Swedish colony at Paxton, which made Swedish dominance in the Scandinavian Augustana all the more evident.

Eielsen's Synod also after a few years abandoned the Chicago school in favor of Red Wing, Minnesota, as a more fitting site. There had been opposition from the largely rural constituency "throughout the West" to a bustling city as a wholesome environment for the institution. It was yet another evidence of suspicion of the city on the part of the Norwegian immigrant population. The decision to build in Red Wing left Trinity with a large and heavily indebted property. But in 1876 its church building provided a dignified setting for the official formation of the Hauge Synod, the successor to Eielsen's Synod. [26]

For many Norwegians, whether they chose voluntary church membership or merely sought ecclesiastical services without joining, the word Lutheran was of greater consequence than fine juridical and doctrinal distinctions. Many simply attended the nearest Lutheran church. They might not develop a loyalty to any particular congregation. Pastor Amund Mikkelsen, who in the 1870s and 1880s served the First Norwegian Evangelical Lutheran Congregation, complained that "in a large city with many congregations and denominations it is very difficult to convince everyone who in some way wishes to be a Christian of their duty to join the congregation of their faith." Instead they went, Mikkelsen lamented, "one Sunday to one church and the next to a different one." Coming to Bethlehem Church from a rural congregation in Minnesota in 1889, Pastor J.N. Kildahl discovered a disheartening indifference, even sophistication, in his parishioners, who lacked the curiosity, so evident in the rural community, even to inspect the new man in the pulpit. The church was less than half filled at his inaugural sermon. His reluctant flock had to be convinced he was worth listening to.[27]

Available records, though incomplete, would suggest a total Lutheran membership of approximately 3,000 during the mid-1870s, which equaled 36 percent of the Norwegian population in 1870; if accurate, it is a relatively substantial percentage. But it was an unstable membership. Pastor N.C. Brun, serving the Bethlehem congregation from 1877 until Kildahl succeeded him in 1889, complained about "the floating population." As many as 350 of the members received during Brun's tenure had moved away to other parts of the city, or "to the Great Northwest."[28]

The obvious challenge was to move with the population, even to the sparsely populated new neighborhoods in outlying areas. The Norwegian Synod in 1873 entered into a home mission venture when it undertook to give financial aid to the few families that in May of that year organized St. Paul's Lutheran Church and met near Wicker Park. St. Peter's Church, another mission congregation, was formed the following year to gather the scattered Norwegians who had moved farther west toward Humboldt Park. Taking the name St. Paul the two small groups merged in the mid-1880s, and in 1890 moved into the completed basement of their church, dedicated in 1892. It was located midway between the two original churches at 2215 West North Avenue.[29]

A letter from St. Paul's Church in 1881 to the First Norwegian Evangelical Lutheran Congregation is suggestive of the obstacles a city posed to sustaining a viable organized religious life. St. Paul's Church invited "the sister congregation on the North Side," which is how it was addressed, to unite with it so that together they could erect a church "at some convenient place on the West Side." The North Side congregation was suffering the consequences of urban mobility which was robbing it of its membership. Encroaching factory buildings and the destruction caused by the fire accelerated the movement of Norwegians out of the district, which was becoming solidly Irish. Many people, however, retained their membership even after leaving, so that "when the pastor visited the congregational members, he had to make a round trip to Lake View, across the Southwest and South Side, and on the West Side, where most of them lived, and to the Northwest all the way to Humboldt Park." The pastor's tour would encompass all areas of Norwegian settlement. Daniel Kvaase, pastor from 1888, thought that rather than making the long trip to the North Side location, the members "sought whatever Lutheran church was close to their home." Besides, the heated controversy in the Norwegian Synod toward the end of the 1880s concerning the doctrine of predestination removed many members permanently, as it did from Our Savior's and other congregations within the Synod.

In 1890 a solution was agreed upon within the First Norwegian Evangelical Lutheran Congregation. The property was sold and members on the West and South Side were encouraged to transfer to

Our Savior's Church, which Kvaase joined as assistant pastor "to make it easier for West Side members to stay together." These moves were intended to give strength to the conservative camp in the disruptive doctrinal dispute then raging. A later minister in St. Paul's Church thanked God who had allowed the congregation to be "led by conservative pastors throughout all these years." Divisions were deep. Arriving in Chicago in 1888, Peer Strømme, Lutheran minister and author, was offered membership in St. Paul's on condition that he "publicly professed the Synod teaching on Election," to assure that he did not harbor the presumed doctrinal errors of the seceding members and congregations. Not wishing to submit to "an examination of faith," he became one of the many who having left a Synod congregation in Chicago found a church home in Bethlehem Church of the Conference. A weakened Our Savior's Church, having lost such staunch members as Jens Olsen Kaasa, was no longer able to operate its day school.[30]

Divisive forces within the pioneer congregation on the North Side, not over "pure teaching" but over the need to come to terms with the language issue, split it into two parties at the time of the sale. They divided the profits from the sale. The group retaining the name reestablished the church in the rapidly expanding Lake View district to the north. They bought a frame structure and moved it "across the prairie on rollers" to two lots on the corner of Roscoe and Kenmore (then Osgood) streets, and became known as the Lake View Church.[31]

That pioneer church was then forty-two years old, and an English-speaking generation existed which had to be ministered to. The English party, having received half of the profits from the sale, proceeded to organize Christ English Evangelical Lutheran Church. It built a church among its members on the West Side at the corner of Hoyne Avenue and Augusta Boulevard. Its decision to join the German Missouri Synod, closely associated with the orthodox Synod clergy, in all probability only reflected a wish to proselytize among the many German Lutherans residing there. The common language would be English. "The difficult language question" faced all congregations, and the quickened pace of assimilation in an urban area made bilingualism a necessity, not a matter of preference, as "the youth only receive insufficient instruction in their ancestors' tongue . . . and those arriving in this country at a mature age have problems comprehending an English sermon."[32]

In the 1880s, especially, English began to encroach on Norwegian; in 1886, for instance, St. Paul's Church reported two English and four Norwegian services monthly. First the Sunday school, then divine services fell little by little to English; simultaneously the need to preserve Norwegian was reinforced by new waves of immigrants. The formal Norwegian church language continued to be heard for at least another generation. The transition to English represented a painful process and a new source of tension. The rurally-oriented clergy here found the urban environment to pose a special and distinct threat not only to their Lutheran integrity, but also to their ancestral cultural heritage. It was consistently a choice between accommodation and extinction. Few would wish to perish for the sake of the mother tongue.[33]

Pressing Social Issues

The moral challenge of the city was easily recognized, engaging both religious and secular reformers, who denounced specific vices to be corrected through coercive legislation. In their support of temperance evangelicals like the Methodists, Baptists, and Congregationalists advocated both legal moral codes and voluntary means. Their middle-class morality clashed with class and ethnic sensitivities. In 1855 temperance forces succeeded in having the Illinois state legislature pass a "Maine Law" to prohibit sale of liquor in the state. Subsequent developments produced the famed "lager beer riot" in Chicago in which saloonkeepers objecting to the measure, to a large extent German and Irish, confronted the authorities in what a Norwegian immigrant described in a letter home as a little revolution, "uniting the Irish and the Germans against the Americans . . . because liquor was to be banned and all who sold it fined."[34]

In the anti-Democratic coalition of the 1850s nativists and evangelical reformers benefited from each other's activities. The fifty Scandinavians who in the municipal election in March, 1855, broke with the majority of their compatriots to vote for the Know-Nothing candidate reflected not only a departure from the Democrats but a strong Puritan spirit in opposition to the "whiskey party." Embracing reformist programs, large segments of the North Side Norwegian population apparently did not join their Irish and German neighbors in the unruly protest against the Anglo-Saxon Protestant establishment. "People are walking about town to every man's house," the Norwegian correspondent continued, "and asking about nationality, because the Norwegians, Danes, and Swedes are together with the Americans, and the Germans, Irish, and all of Catholicism are against them."

There can be little doubt that a prevailing bent toward anti-Catholic and Protestant pietistic reform sentiments, since these ideas were being encouraged by religious and secular opinion makers in the immigrant community, moved Norwegian Americans toward the acceptance of Anglo-Saxon reformism and leadership. But as was demonstrated on many occasions, counterforces existed in the group, and when ethnic sensitivities and an ethnic way of life were at issue, Norwegians, like other nationalities, were able to transcend ethnic boundaries and join in protests against nativist and reformist onslaughts. It is quite certain that "Norse voices, like grating steel," as

Gilbert Olson,

Lager=Beer Saloon,

No. 39 og 41 Milwaukee Avenue,

Hjørnet af Union og Hubbard St., Chicago, Illinois

p2-1v

•

Skandinaven, September 15, 1869, carried an advertisement for Gilbert Olson's Lager Beer Saloon on Milwaukee Avenue at the corner of Union and Hubbard streets.

one historian described their reaction to the restrictive measures in 1855, were heard together with the German and the Irish, "both calm and wild."[35]

For Scandinavians as well as the Germans drinking was a culturally conditioned practice. The pioneer Norwegian sociologist Eilert Sundt in the 1850s demonstrated how "the bad custom and vice" of alcohol abuse "more than anything has been the misfortune and destruction of our people," indulged in at baptisms, weddings, and funerals. In Chicago the neighborhood saloon was pervasive in Norwegian districts, and it functioned also as a social and charitable institution, with individual saloonkeepers providing support for destitute Norwegian sailors during the slow season on the lakes. It was a part of the working class culture. In 1858 the Hansen & Sorensen brewery, "where Norwegian beer is brewed," was established in Chicago.

A working–class consciousness transcending national divisions was encouraged by joint ethnic protest movements. Another example was the "Revolution of 1873" which represented another smashing victory over the temperance forces. Anton Hessing, owner of the *Illinois Staatszeitung*, organized a German and Irish coalition into the People's party in order to defeat the Sunday closing laws. Though

Skandinaven sided with the "church leaders" and warned its compatriots against "opposing the country's inhabitants on this issue," Norwegians, Danes, and Swedes gave support, most visibly the Danes, who organized a mass meeting. The Scandinavians were perhaps in some cases more attracted to the People's party's agitation for reform in city government than its goal of defeating the temperance forces.

Yet the greater wealth of the Germans than the Irish made them, as it did the Scandinavians, potential political allies of the native born. They could easily see themselves as prosperous Republican citizens. The Republican and reformist *Skandinaven* expressed some incredulity at the ability of Germans and Irish to cooperate. The fact that they did secured certain victory for Hessing's People's party, which the newspaper interpreted mainly as an effort to bring the Germans and other nationalities back to the Democrats to serve the "liquor interests." The Norwegian clergy, whether Lutheran or not, attacked the saloons with a vengeance. Andrew B. Johnson wrote home that his father, Baard Johnson (Rogne), "who at Voss had had some liking for alcohol," had joined a Norwegian temperance society formed in the early 1850s.[36]

Church reformers like A. C. Preus urged the formation of temperance societies within the Norwegian Lutheran congregations and several were formed in the early 1850s. But the Norwegian Synod moved toward a position that "the congregation itself was a completely sufficient temperance society." Notations like "exclusion from the congregation for persistent drunkenness" or "fallen to drink" appear a number of times in the records of the First Norwegian Evangelical Lutheran Congregation, showing both concern and harsh judgment. But the Lutheran clergy no longer found the solution in temperance pledges to independent societies. In March, 1869, Synod president H.A. Preus at the invitation of Pastor Petersen traveled all the way from his parsonage at Spring Grove, Wisconsin, to speak against a temperance society that existed within Petersen's church, because it undermined congregational unity and ministerial authority. In June of the next year he congratulated the congregation for having dissolved it.[37]

In the intervening debate O. B. Jacobs, then the congregation's secretary, defended the temperance society. Its concrete purpose was of course to eliminate the abuse of alcohol. The zealous advocate of temperance Lauritz Carlsen, a member of both the congregation and the society, highlighted this fact by objecting "that if others had felt the pressures of this vice as he had, they would not have suggested to annul the society." It became clear, however, that one of the main objections to its existence was its independent status outside the congregation's control. Non-Lutherans had been admitted, against God's command, it was claimed, which "forbids us to be under the same yoke as the unbelieving." A meeting in February had limited membership to Lutherans, but a petition to the Common Council to enforce Sunday closing of saloons had also been signed. Continued tension caused the temperance society's dissolution. The antebellum prohibition movement failed. However, the reformist spirit of the latter part of the century with its strong moral activism, particularly in its last decade, caused moral uplift campaigns to proliferate and the organizational success of the temperance movement was secured, though not its ultimate goals.[38]

In states like North Dakota and Minnesota with their large rural Scandinavian populations the issues of local option and state and national prohibition became vehicles for Norwegian and Swedish politicians to rally their countrymen behind their candidacies. In Chicago as well, the sale of intoxicating beverages continued to involve political and civic action; reform forces like the Citizens' League, consisting of prominent Chicagoans, pressed for enforcement of all laws and ordinances concerning alcohol distribution. *Skandinaven* and the newspaper *Verdens Gang* (The Way of the World) advocated "public morals" and defeat of the political corruption surrounding the liquor trade.[39]

Civic leaders alarmed at the crime and vice attributable to intemperance joined the churches in the temperance cause. The issue of social control was consequently more in evidence in the metropolis than, for instance, in farming communities in Minnesota. Women became a major element, so much so that in the 1880s the Illinois state house debated whether to grant women the vote in the regulation of intoxicants. This reformist cause pulled women into demanding a greater political say. The Woman's Christian Temperance Union, with its Methodist dominance but also its appeal to other Protestants, established its national headquarters in Evanston in the late 1870s under the vigorous direction of Frances E. Willard. Its strong Anglo-Saxon profile allowed for a few German and Scandinavian members who worked with their own nationalities. Among the latter was Ulrikka Feldtman Bruun from the Kristiansund district on Norway's west coast, who traveled widely for the WCTU, even visiting the Pacific coast, to organize "Unions" of Scandinavian women. The *Union Signal* in 1898 reported her participation in the South Dakota woman suffrage campaign. With equal energy and determination she produced mawkish temperance fiction and poetry and was responsible for the temperance monthly *Det hvide Baand* (The White Ribbon).[40]

Reformed inebriates, whether fictional or real, were important exhibits in the battle against intoxicants. Shortly after a WCTU crusade in 1874, Tallak Ellingsen, who had worked with the Norwegian temperance pioneer Asbjørn Kloster in Stavanger, took the initiative to organize The First Norwegian Total Abstinence Society in Chicago. He was joined by Lauritz Carlsen, who would dramatically wave his hand, missing several fingers lost to frost when in a drunken stupor he had fallen asleep one cold winter's day in a snow bank. While he gestured he recited his standard speech "Carlsen as a slave and Carlsen as free," frequently shouting so that he could be heard for several blocks. Ole Br. Olson entered the temperance cause through conversion to Methodism and in his advocacy appealed to ethnic pride: "to wash the liquor blot off the Norwegian people."[41]

Unlike the temperance cause among Norwegians in Minnesota, which was dominated by the Lutheran clergy, the movement in Chicago was characterized by evangelicals and public-minded—at times unchurched—Norwegian-American businessmen and civic leaders. Motivated by the influences and the needs of a transient Norwegian population and newcomers, their actions fell into the general social control pattern of urban reform activities in Chicago. In their class identities they were also similar to the Yankee civic reformers. The First Norwegian, as it was called, which originally met in the basement of the Haugean Trinity church, split in 1878 over differences in regard to the religious content of their meetings, and the departing group led by Carlsen, and soon to be joined by Olson, formed the Harmony Total Abstinence Society (Harmonien total Afholdsforening). The Norwegian-American reformer and writer Waldemar Ager, who himself had taken the pledge there, later wrote that the membership "consisted mainly of Methodists and liberals." With few exceptions, the Lutheran clergy in the city, abandoning their support of the early 1850s, exhibited their prejudice against secular and non-Lutheran activities and became bitter opponents. During the five years Ager was a member, before he moved to Eau Claire, Wisconsin, to work for the newspaper *Reform*, he could not recall that "a single Norwegian Lutheran minister opened his mouth at a temperance meeting." The "liberals" were such men as the publisher of *Skandinaven* John Anderson, Svein Nilsson, its progressive second editor from 1872, O. B. Jacobs, in the lumber business, and the banker Helge A. Haugan, who had converted to the Congregational faith.[42]

A major characteristic of Norwegian temperance work in Chicago, as the independent temperance societies fell by the wayside, was its strong identification with the Prohibition party, which had been organized by a group of Good Templars in Oswego, New York, in 1869. This third-party affiliation was not, unlike the Republican and Lutheran identity of Minnesota prohibition politicians, likely to result in election to public office, but its support of social issues such as woman suffrage, as well as its clear platform of prohibition of the manufacture and sale of alcohol, appealed to the liberals in Harmony who joined Ole Br. Olson in 1887 in organizing the Scandinavian Prohibition Club. It convened in the offices of *Skandinaven*.

The Norwegian lodges of the International Order of Good Templars naturally fortified that direction, and the WCTU also found

A photograph of the Norrøna Lodge of the International Order of Good Templars from the 1920s. The Lodge was organized in 1903; a major leader in the temperance cause, Henry Weardahl, is seated fifth from the left in the first row.

an appropriate political ally in the Prohibition party, which like the Templars accepted women as members from the beginning. The first Norwegian IOGT lodge, Norden, came into being in November, 1879, organized by the district templar of the Illinois Grand Lodge C.A. Vannatta. The American initiative had been prepared for by Norwegian Good Templar veterans in New York, who corresponded with members of the First Norwegian. These became the charter members of Norden. A Grand Lodge having existed in Norway since 1878, the Good Templar work among the immigrants might be viewed as a Norwegian transplant and not an American intrusion into the immigrant community. Most leaders in America had belonged to the order before emigrating. A good example was Henry Weardahl who already in 1881 at age sixteen had become a templar in Trondheim, and coming to Chicago in 1889 had "the honor of organizing one Swedish and four Norwegian lodges." "The emigrated templars sought each other's company in America," Ager wrote, but they expanded activity to include fellow Scandinavians.

Organizational life, in reform and social activities, thus broadly adopted the pattern of the American lodge system with its rituals and symbols, but retained a strong national identity, even to the extent of forming associated English-speaking lodges, not only because the bond of ethnicity, even after the language was lost, made contact easier, but also to have the second generation join templars of their own nationality. The twelve Norwegian lodges formed before 1900, most of which made their appearance in the 1890s, bore such distinctly Norwegian designations as Nordlyset, Nordkap, Tordenskjold, and Midnatssolen. They assembled Norwegians in the different Norwegian neighborhoods in the city.[43]

In 1900 Ulrikka Bruun saved the clubhouse of the bankrupt Harmony Total Abstinence Society, Harmony Hall, on the corner of Ohio and Noble streets, from becoming a dance hall and saloon by moving her Hope Mission there from Milwaukee Avenue. She received aid from the WCTU, which commended her for working "in the midst of the foreign population . . . in a part of the city that swarms with saloons and every other iniquity." Her gospel temperance mission included a home for Scandinavian working girls.[44]

The purpose of the home, like other similar establishments, was, in the words of the WCTU, "to care for unfortunate girls who have been led astray and to protect the innocent and friendless from being led into the haunts of sin of a great city." The saloon and the brothel were the main targets of moralistic middle-class reformers. They were a visible and ubiquitous aspect of urban life. *Skandinaven* in 1889 gave much space to police raids on disreputable houses, even giving the names of Norwegian girls who had been lured into prostitution. Kristofer Janson in his novel *Sara*, which views Chicago as a monster devouring poor immigrants, let the Norwegian prostitute Lizzie

• *Left:* Ulrikka Feldtman Bruun.

• *Right:* Harmony Hall on the corner of Ohio and Noble streets.

declare in bitter contempt at social injustice that "for sixteen hours' toil and staying awake nights there is no pay, but women's flesh is well paid." In a directory of "sporting and club houses" one Annie Anderson advertised her place of business on South Clark Street "as 'safe' and one of the jolliest houses in Chicago" with rates of $3 to $10 and beer and wine. Raids were merely responses to demands of civic associations for action and did not deter the entrenched, and politically well connected, establishments of prostitution, gambling, and other vices. Throughout the 1870s and 1880s it was claimed, although some like the strong five-times mayor Carter H. Harrison I at least made an effort to supervise games of chance, that "the mayor was no more than a hireling of the town's boss gambler, Mike McDonald." He operated his gambling syndicate with impunity and in a working relationship with the politicians.

Skandinaven urged country girls to think twice before seeking their fortunes in "the great Chicago you hear so much about — and learn about the toil and grief and extremely few pleasures." It cited statistics on illegitimate births showing that the majority of such births occurred in the domestic service occupations favored by Scandinavian women, which exposed them to exploitation by "employers who also in this society harbor the European attitude that servants belong to another race for which they have no responsibility."[45]

Ethnic self-consciousness compelled *Skandinaven* regularly to demonstrate that native Americans were more prone to commit crime than the foreign-born, and yet the "self-satisfied 'natives' would like to lay the crimes at the doors of the immigrants." In 1883, there were only 683 Swedes arrested and 436 Norwegians, but 5,408 Irish and 20,000 Americans. "It is a favorable indication for the Scandinavians," the newspaper concluded. Norwegians, along with such nationalities as the Bohemians and the Greeks, unquestionably had low absolute proportions of the population of violators. Viewed relative to their share of the Chicago citizenry the picture might to some extent change. Political scientist Dianne M. Pinderhughes concluded that between 1880 and 1930 blacks and American-born whites were in that order at the top in the hierarchy of groups arrested, charged, and convicted, then "southern Europeans in the middle of all groups in the city but at the top of white ethnic groups, with northern and western Europeans at the bottom." This descriptive conclusion does not of course address patterns of crime or the question of why these differences existed. The complexity of the latter circumstance may partly, but obviously not fully, as Pinderhughes suggests, be clarified by society's greater sensitivity to violations of social norms and values by some groups than others. Except for the blacks, violation rates declined over time, which tends to support the above contention. Discrimination against blacks continued while white ethnic groups gained gradual acceptance. The general situation fortified a popular

Norwegian, and Scandinavian, self-image, and surely one with some basis in historical fact and contemporary evidence, of being law-abiding and reputable citizens.

Skandinaven admittedly neglected to suggest that perhaps half of the American-born offenders were the children of immigrants. In other connections, however, the newspaper commented on "Scandinavian hoodlum youths" who victimized their own on the West Side, but explained the obvious increase in criminal activity in the second generation by claiming that "they have absorbed the spirit of lawlessness in America." Nativist journalism was thus countered. As the vice district in the late 1890s was extended into the West Side, *Skandinaven* worked to remove gambling agencies and illegal activities, which it claimed "existed galore on Milwaukee Avenue and other streets in the Scandinavian district and robbed poor immigrants."[46]

In 1873 *Skandinaven* shared with its readers insights into immigrant criminal prowess received from "one of Chicago's oldest and most experienced detectives." In short, he had found Irish criminal types to be crafty, the Germans less crafty but better pickpockets than the English, and the Americans fine swindlers and defrauders, while the Scandinavians were inept and like the Bohemians needed to be encouraged by alcohol in order to commit a crime. One of the first lessons Morris Salmonsen learned about Chicago from other Danes in the early 1870s was the necessity to enforce the law for oneself by carrying a weapon.

During that decade, as people streamed into the city to profit from its rebuilding, brazen lawlessness and notorious political corruption became the order of the day. Scandinavians appear to have been frequent victims of crime. Several murders of Scandinavians produced a joint Norwegian, Swedish, and Danish meeting at the West Side Turner Hall in April, 1873. The inefficiency of the police department and the many arrested criminals who escaped prosecution convinced them to organize the Scandinavian Defense and Aid Society (Den skandinaviske Forsvars- og Hjælpeforening). Some of the Norwegian members were Dr. Gerhard Paoli, Ole T. Birkeland, and the lawyer Ingvel Oleson. The broader purpose, as suggested by the presence of Oleson, was to hire an attorney who in cases where a Scandinavian had been the victim of a crime would work for conviction of the perpetrator through the public prosecutor's office. A preventive solution was thus advocated.

Meeting with members of the group Mayor Joseph Medill, then engaged in improving the police department, supported their efforts and promised them "the necessary police authority." He "praised the Scandinavians for standing together in this matter." In promising police authority the mayor likely had in mind the valuable assistance to the police force rendered by the Norwegian Battalion of National Guards consisting of four companies under the command of Major

J.Z. Alstrup. It was raised immediately after the Great Fire, Norwegian volunteers coming forward as the first to do so already on October 9. As a part of the 1st Regiment of Chicago Volunteers authorized on October 11, 1871, they patrolled the streets in the West Division to protect lives and property for a period of about two weeks.[47]

Temporal Matters

Denominational and synodical religious patterns, support of coercive reform measures and moral uplift programs, and benevolent aid to and protection of fellow Norwegians in a spirit of mutual responsibility gave evidence of ways in which the immigrant community came to terms with the urban environment. The decades following the Great Fire were significant in other respects as well. As prelude to an even greater flourishing of Norwegian-American life, the era saw religious institutions attaining permanency, organizational growth, and cultural successes. The attention of visiting Norwegian dignitaries further fueled immigrant self-consciousness.

Norwegians in Chicago were sufficiently proud of their place in America to commemorate the fiftieth anniversary of the sailing of the *Restauration* with a parade and a large open-air folk festival on July 5, 1875. Nora Lodge, which had its own house, Nora Hall, at Green and Ohio streets, took the initiative to mark the half century of the group's history in America; surviving Sloopers who had made the crossing in 1825 were honored guests.[48]

Professor Rasmus B. Anderson, newly appointed to a professorship in Scandinavian languages at the University of Wisconsin in Madison, delivered the main address to an audience estimated at 5,000 in one of the city's parks. Anderson had gained stature as a public figure, at least in Norwegian-American settlements, by his lectures on Leif Ericson, the Viking discoverer of America, and by the publication in 1874 of his *America Not Discovered by Columbus*. A veritable cult was to take shape around the claims of Norse discovery. But that did not prevent Norwegians, at least at this time, from joining the Italians and other nationalities in enthusiastic Columbus Day observances. "The Discovery of America" festivities on October 12, 1870, included a grand parade, watched by "the motley throng of many nationalities," the procession having "gathered Italians, Scandinavians, and American-born—those whose ancestors first discovered America and those who reaped the fruit of that discovery," as the *Chicago Times* recorded the spectacle. Representative of the success of the small Italian community in Chicago was the chief marshal, the prosperous Genoese businessman Antonio Raggio. The idyllic ethnic accord the event demonstrated, even to the point of sharing the honor of discovery, had a strong class basis. The early Italian community, with its pronounced Genoese and North Italian origin, family character, and prosperity, enjoyed a much greater acceptance than the hard-pressed southern Italians arriving at a later date.[49]

Ethnic elites discovered each other in social settings. The "gratifying success" of the Columbus Day observances also featured a ball and a banquet of "macaroni and stufato" arranged by the Chicago Italian Society, where appropriate toasts to the nationalities represented "became the order." In addition to the Italians themselves, they were Danes, Norwegians, Swedes, "native Americans," and the "sons of Erin." Following the close of the feast the Italians met alone to celebrate a reunited Italy.[50]

Chicago Norwegians, "the descendants of Thor and Odin," as the *Chicago Times* reported in July, 1872, vented their enthusiasm for national historical milestones by joining the homeland in its observance of the millennium of Norway's unification under the Viking king Harald Fairhair. "The sturdy and jubilant Northmen and Northwomen," the newspaper continued, "gathered about the Norwegian Hall on North Peoria Street." The "hall" was the first story of Pastor C.J.P. Petersen's home, which his congregation rented while rebuilding. A colorful procession formed and marched to the railroad station to be transported to Haas Park in forty-three railroad cars.[51] Cannon salutes, music, the singing of the new Norwegian national anthem by Bjørnstjerne Bjørnson, "Ja, vi elsker dette landet" (Yes, We Love This Country), and speeches on behalf of Denmark and Sweden prepared the large crowd for Pastor Petersen's main address, which extolled the great significance of the "thousand year festival" in the homeland's heroic history. In what became a common practice on such occasions a congratulatory telegram to Norway, in this instance to the main observance at Haugesund, signified ethnic bonds across the Atlantic.[52]

Divisions were at least as common in secular affairs as in religious ones. Not all Norwegians subscribed to the grand festivities; some assailed them as a celebration of the triumph of despotism, when they ought to have concerned themselves instead with the democracy they found in America. Inevitably some objected to an overly zealous involvement of a group of newcomers in the arrangement of the commemoration. And as in most instances, individual desire for public office split the community. There was also an element of anticlericalism directed against the dominance of Pastor Petersen in the celebration. The lake captain Endre T. Thorson, politically active and courting the coveted appointment as Swedish-Norwegian vice consul, declined a special invitation for this and other reasons and invited "a select company" to a banquet he hosted. Among the guests was the Swede O.G. Lange, billed as "the first Scandinavian in Chicago." Lange had lived in the city since 1838 and been active in Swedish-American affairs; he was a good speaker, but given to strange statements. Uniquely, considering the strong Republican loyalty of most Swedes, Lange remained a staunch Democrat, perhaps in part because his wife was Irish. Thorson's political ambitions aligned him with Lange and the circle around the Danish-Norwegian newspaper

Fremad (Forward), owned by Ferdina[...]v, and also with the Danish Weapon Brothers (De dans[...] rødre), veterans of Denmark's wars with Prussia. Thoug[...] on Brothers did not necessarily follow Lange's lead into [...] ratic party, *Fremad*, which had begun as a Democratic org[...] nen was Republican, and the men associated with it compe[...] *ndinaven* for political influence. Joined by the new editor of [...] *erikanaren* P. A. Sundelius, they called attention to themselves in the summer of 1870, while revealing strong anti-German sentiments, by a cable of support to the "Emperor of the French" in the ongoing Franco-Prussian War, which was duly acknowledged by the emperor.[53]

Regardless of the popularity of the French cause, expressed at an "all-nation mass meeting" in September, the desired diplomatic title, Danish or Swedish-Norwegian, eluded Thorson. Posts in militia companies, which during the Civil War had given honor and recognition, might, however, compensate and give visibility. Military organizations became popular and frequently doubled as mutual aid societies, like the Norwegian National Guard (Den norske National-Garde) organized in September, 1870, whose seventy-five members adopted the uniform of the Norwegian royal guard stationed at the royal palace in Stockholm. This group remained a purely ethnic organization; Thorson was, however, made captain of a Norwegian guard company organized in February, 1871, as Company 4 of the Illinois National Guard. This unit also displayed ethnic colors. In a Norwegian national spirit it adopted the uniforms of Norwegian guard infantrymen (*gardejægere*) but, in order to be issued weapons, conformed to American military rules at its weekly drills. The Norwegian lawyer David Monrad Schøyen was an officer in the unit. He had recently arrived from Norway and was on the editorial staff of *Skandinaven*; its publisher John Anderson generously provided employment for educated newcomers like Schøyen.[54]

Military organizations were intended "to ennoble the spirit" as well as foster physical health, and through arranged debates and discussions Company 4 broadened its appeal. The Civil War experience was glorified in fiction and historical narrative. One of the heroic accounts of the exploits of the Fifteenth Wisconsin was written by P. G. Dietrichson, like Schøyen on *Skandinaven*'s staff. Dietrichson became one of the founders of the Scandinavian Rifle Club (Den skandinaviske Skytterforening) in April, 1882. Practice in marksmanship had long been conducted by a largely German club, but the direct impulse to organize came from Norwegian emigrants who had been involved in the volunteer rifle club movement in Norway, then in its ascendancy and during the constitutional conflict of that decade assuming political significance.

The Chicago group directly rejected any political affiliation and organized "as a means to exercise the body and promote friendship." Political neutrality evidently did not apply to the situation in Norway, as the club did take part in collecting funds for Norwegian rifle

clubs, which might conceivably serve as volunteer units to protect the
Storting should there be open conflict, as widely expected, between
the Storting and King Oscar II and his Norwegian government.
Though tense, the ultimate outcome of the constitutional crisis, an
affirmation of the principle of popular sovereignty, was the introduction of a parliamentary government under Johan Sverdrup in 1884.
The weakened executive power of the joint monarch also meant a
weakening of the bonds of union. It did not appear, however, to have
an adverse effect on immigrant Scandinavianism, as the issue was only
indirectly about union. Such discord in any case was of greater concern to Norwegians than to Swedes, producing anti-Swedish feelings.

Norwegians in Chicago celebrating the victory for the liberal
forces were joined by Swedish sharpshooters and other anti-
monarchical liberals. But even so, the fact that the organizational
meeting of the Scandinavian Rifle Club was held at the new Aurora
Turner Hall on the corner of Milwaukee Avenue and Huron Street
would suggest Norwegian predominance; the three winners in the
first sharpshooter competition were all Norwegian. In September,
1891, Norwegian rifle enthusiasts, many having been active in the
volunteer rifle clubs resulting from the clash between the executive
and legislative branches of the Norwegian government during the
previous decade, organized the purely national Norwegian Sharpshooters (Det norske Skytterlag), which built its own shooting range
at Willow Springs.[55]

The many young Norwegian men who made Chicago their
home gave life to athletic activities. In 1878 The Scandinavian Turner
Brothers (De skandinaviske Turnerbrødre) succeeded the then apparently disbanded gymnastics club formed in 1867 to work for harmony between the two "sister nations" (brødrefolket). It was, however,
more Swedish than Norwegian, even though it in 1879 sponsored a
popular May 17th festival in the spirit of a common Nordic heritage.
Like many of the secular societies, it united people with a liberal and
anti-clerical philosophy. At a large gymnastics meet at Willow
Springs in 1882, the Norwegian-American poet Wilhelm Pettersen,
in the employ of Skandinaven and reflecting the newspaper's liberal
stance, called on the large crowd to give "a long live the speakers" to
Charles Sundell and O.G. Lange, the first speaking in Swedish, the
second in English, both predicting that the republican form of
government would soon "make its entry into all the Scandinavian
lands." Lange's noteworthy proposition that "royal power and clerical
rule were the greatest obstacles to intellectual growth" was warmly
applauded. Such common convictions promoted Scandinavian mutu-
ality in temporal affairs, though it was soon to be put to the test by
events in Norway and Sweden stemming from disagreements over
the conditions of union.[56]

On October 1, 1885, a group of Norwegian gymnasts met at the

Hagbart Hermansen, here seen in the society's uniform, took the initiative in organizing the Norwegian Turner Society in 1885.

invitation of the printer Hagbart Hermansen, later publisher of humor magazines, and organized The Norwegian Turner Society (Den norske Turnforening). Adopting uniforms identical to those of the Norwegian capital's Kristiania Turnforening they were in years to come a colorful element at public events. The troupe was the beginning of a major institutional growth in Norwegian athletic activity in Chicago; in time it became the Norwegian-American Athletic Association, engaging in many sports. The first step was the uniting in 1893 of four Norwegian turner troupes. Clubs from Minneapolis and Brooklyn joined the Chicago turners and a small group, Vikingen, from Pullman, south of Chicago, in The Norwegian-American Gymnastic Union (Det norsk-amerikanske Turnforbund). Fern. A. Kean of Chicago was elected president. In the bitterly cold political climate between Norway and Sweden in the 1890s, when open hostilities seemed a real possibility, "Scandinavianism had no friends," and the idea of Scandinavian cooperation was inconceivable,"as the turners are patriotic Norwegians who do not wish any mixing." It echoed the German nationalism of the *Turnvater* himself, Friedrich Ludwig Jahn, in a Norwegian immigrant context.[57]

Normennenes Singing Society (Normennenes Sangforening) had evolved from the original Scandinavian turner society, as the name suggests, in an earlier instance of Norwegian national affirmation. A group of dissatisfied singers in the male chorus maintained by the turners departed and on October 30, 1870, joined the newly arrived young musician John S. Lindtner, "full of enthusiasm for everything Norwegian," who convinced them to abandon the idea of a Scandinavian chorus and limit it to "Northmen." Lindtner became their first director. Cooperation was a different matter. In June 1871 the callow group of singers joined forces with the Swedish male chorus Freia, both too small to act alone, in serenading the famous Swedish soprano Christina Nilsson then visiting Chicago on a concert tour. Such opportunities gave encouragement and recognition, and in April, 1872, struggling merely to exist after the upheaval caused by the Great Fire, the men, accompanied by a Scandinavian band, marched in procession, with flags, banners, and torches to serenade a deeply moved Ole Bull at the Grand Central Hotel. It was an occasion that "old singers recalled with pride."[58]

The idea of celebrating the millennium of Norwegian unification that year originated in Normennenes Singing Society and it was its youth, and the perceived presumptuousness of some "unknown younger singers" as a self-appointed committee, that riled more established members of the Norwegian community like Endre Thorson and the groups they represented. The society had first come in contact with Pastor Petersen when he gave them free use of the Norwegian Hall in return for their singing at the Sunday church services. Normennenes later moved to Aurora Turner Hall, the site of many cultural activities in the Norwegian colony, and under their able long-time director John W. Colberg became a first-class chorus with regular concerts. Colberg had extensive experience as a director of band and choral groups in Oslo before emigrating in 1870, and from 1874, when he assumed his position with Normennenes, and for a quarter century thereafter he was a major figure in the musical life of the Norwegian colony.[59]

The cultural impact of the Bergen coterie, with their intense local patriotism, and perhaps an urbane exclusiveness, was evidenced in the organization on July 2, 1882, of the Singing Society Bjørgvin (Sang-foreningen Bjørgvin). Only men from Bergen and environs could join. Some of the members were men like Carlos Ross and Julius Anker-Midling from the Norwegian Dramatic Society. In March, 1872, the year this theater troupe disbanded, the Norwegian Society (Det norske Selskab) emerged, in time to display its banner at the millennium festivities. It functioned as a literary society and among its original members were actors from the dramatic society, men like Albert C. Fougner, but also Pastor S. M. Krogness, whose literary and historical interests were well known. Fougner, a cousin of the poet and dramatist Bjørnson, cooperated with Anker-Midling in resurrecting a Norwegian stage in Chicago; they gathered a troupe of actors around them, mainly from the earlier society, and presented plays, commonly at the Aurora Turner Hall. Its dramatic productions in the well-known national romantic tradition offered an identity with the past in the old country, but in plays written by Anker-Midling himself, usually one to three acts, there was evidence of a new immigrant introspection and a solidarity with the common Norwegian. In the genre of "comedy with songs" these plays gave social commentary on current Chicago events and portrayed life among the immigrants. They bore such names as *Paa streik* (On Strike), *Kapital og arbeidere* (Capital and Laborers), and *Under Election* (During an Election). The last-mentioned play has the subtitle *Valglivets mysterier* (The Mystery of Elections), and is centered about the old shoemaker Søren Klaps, a Republican, and his liberated wife Philipine, a Democrat; it satirized the corrupting influences of an aldermanic election. Its setting is recognizably Norwegian-American.[60]

Immigrant realism, as well as contemporary Norwegian dramatic works such as Bjørnson's early effort *De nygifte* (The Newlyweds), found an audience. On his lecture tour of the United States in 1880–1881 the freethinking Bjørnson twice visited his countrymen in Chicago. He arrived the first time on December 23, 1880, and gave a well-attended lecture at McVickers Theater that same day. Following his presentation he was feted at a banquet and praised by Fougner, editor Svein Nilsson of *Skandinaven*, and the attorney Ingolf K. Boyesen, another member of the liberal elite. A song composed in his honor by John Blegen, active in social and fraternal organizations, was sung. At his second lecture at Aurora Turner Hall on "The Old Prophets" he entered on his crusade against the Norwegian Lutheran clergy, whose theology he denounced as "humbug." Following his tour to Norwegian settlements in the Upper Midwest, hampered by an extremely harsh winter, he returned to Chicago for his final lecture on April 9, 1881. The bitter dialogue with the ministers had served to solidify his criticism of them; to his wife Karoline he wrote, "my last lecture here [in America] came off brilliantly and got a storm of applause." *Verdens Gang*, then edited by Schøyen, reported how Bjørnson had walked down into the audience before his lecture to speak to Marcus Thrane, who later in his satirical *Den gamle Wisconsin-biblen* (The Old Wisconsin Bible) described Bjørnson's attacks on orthodoxy. [61]

In an era when public lectures were in vogue other Norwegian celebrities offered themselves to the immigrant community. In April, 1880, Kristofer Janson, later a Unitarian minister in Minneapolis, had spoken to Chicago Norwegians from the same lectern as Bjørnson, with a similar message and thus preparing his way. Bjørnson had introduced the cause of women's liberation as a part of his attack on Lutheran fundamentalism, and left his audience with the thought that he loved his countrymen in America precisely because of their many faults. "But they are strong," he insisted, "as if they were transferred hermetically from Norway." And shortly, on July 10, 1881, the Norwegian pioneer feminist, Aasta Hansteen, then living in America, appeared in the same forum. She was introduced by Dr. Paoli, who initiated her into liberal and progressive Scandinavian circles. Chicago remained Hansteen's home for the next two years, while she strove to make a living as a portrait painter. She became friends with the Norwegian landscape artist John Olson Hammerstad, who then was enjoying a measure of success in Chicago. [62]

Liberal intellectual orientations from the homeland produced debate and were important factors in shaping immigrant cultural life and thinking. Not only formal lectures, but ministers, the press, and other makers of opinion played a role in formulating public attitudes. In 1880 the Chicago Norwegian newspaper *Norden*, edited by the Synod minister Hallvard Hande, carried a heated controversy over the social and moral implications of Ibsen's *A Doll's House*. This debate preceded the first one in English by nine years; the immigrant community was obviously in a better position than American literary circles to keep abreast of European cultural developments. It was in the special immigrant urban environment of Chicago, with its factions, contrasting philosophies, organizations, and newspapers, that Ibsen's even more controversial drama *Ghosts* had its world premiere, produced by Norwegian and Danish actors on May 20, 1882, at the Aurora Turner Hall "before a large audience with a successful outcome," as *Skandinaven* reported. It apparently created no furore. Considering the enormous debate *Ghosts* caused in Scandinavia, *Verdens Gang* suggested that the social criticism of the play, "an accurate depiction of the moral decay of the Norwegian upper classes," was too irrelevant to Norwegian–American audiences to be considered seriously, and besides most ordinary Norwegians in America were untouched by "the higher cultural currents" in Norway. Even though "a decent audience" might object to some of the images of the play, and the clergy, as evidenced in the debate over *A Doll's House*, condemned the realism of modern Norwegian literature, no Lutheran minister or civic leader, conservative or liberal, in Chicago protested its production. The play's "reprimand of vices in certain portions of the upper level of Norwegian society" obviously was, as *Verdens Gang* explained, "no hindrance to its acceptance here in Chicago." Its single performance, in front of a somewhat select audience, may be regarded as a minor episode in a population preoccupied with more pressing and immediate concerns.[63]

5

Norwegians in Industrial America

"In the 1880s, the real Norwegian quarter was bounded by Halsted Street to the east, Noble Street to the west, Kinzie Street to the south, and Chicago Avenue to the north," Olaf Ray, who came to Chicago in 1882, reported. "The wealthier," he continued, "lived north of Indiana Street [Grand Avenue], the poorer south of Indiana, those living on Bismarck Court, Hunt Street, and Paradise Alley being the poorest."[1]

After the new ward boundaries of 1876 divided the city into eighteen wards, this square of blocks—"the heart of the Norwegian colony"—covered parts of wards 10, 11, and 14. The near Northwest Side became a refuge for many workers who wished to build cheap frame homes outside the city fire limits established after the Great Fire. The school census of 1884 showed that of the 18,292 Norwegians counted, the immigrant generation and their children, about 80 percent lived in these three wards on the Northwest Side. Over half lived in the fourteenth ward, the largest in size and population, which stretched west and north to the city limits.

The residential development in the West Town community

showed surprisingly heavy ethnic clusterings as the various nationalities formed their own social worlds. The southernmost canvassing district in Ward 14, number 29, between Ohio and Huron streets was an impressive 77.9 percent Norwegian. District 19 just south of Division Street and west of Ashland to Wood Street was 85.7 percent German. The contiguous Wicker Park neighborhood to the north expanded quickly in the 1880s as Germans and Scandinavians moved in. The canvassing district covering the immediate area of the park in 1884 had 2,526 residents, of whom about half were German and a quarter Norwegian.

The trek to the Humboldt Park area intensified. Young people, the second generation and newcomers to the city, were the most visible. The number of elderly residents declined in proportion to the distance from the center of the city, which is another way of documenting the outward movement. Gert, later George M., Kramer from Bergen was typical of those who could set up their own inexpensive frame houses there on cheaper land. In 1876 he moved to the first two-story building on California Avenue, then in the Town of Jefferson, and claimed to be the first to settle in that subdivision. "The pioneers had to walk almost three miles to the city limits in order to get transportation to work and often waded in mud up to their knees," Kramer later recalled. By 1884 the city limits had been extended to Pulaski Road (then Crawford) and 1,774 people were living in the large district on either side of Humboldt Park west of Western Avenue. More than seventy percent of these were Scandinavian. The Norwegians constituted 31.8 percent, the Danes 21.1, and the Swedes 17.5. This neighborhood thus from its beginning had a clearly documented Scandinavian composition.[2]

Grand Avenue (then Indiana Street) and Milwaukee Avenue formed the center for the Norwegian "Milwaukee Avenue" colony, and also for Norwegians living farther out. Olaf Ray compared Milwaukee Avenue to Oslo's Aker Street, that city's commercial thoroughfare, and Indiana to Karl Johan; like it Indiana Street was the Norwegians' promenade street, "where they walked in their best clothes on Sundays and holidays." After *Skandinaven*'s move to Peoria Street in 1883 its building was among the most imposing there. Captain Christian Erickson, the hero from the Civil War, who married Agnete Jevne, a sister of Christian Jevne, operated a dry goods store on Milwaukee Avenue, close to Erie Street, and along Milwaukee Avenue, near Ohio, Anton Krogh had a well-known cigar and tobacco store. A block farther south Paul O. Stensland, who became one of the best known businessmen and bankers in the community, in 1880 sold real estate and insurance. The civic-minded and popular Dr. Andrew Doe came to America in that year and established his practice farther west at Racine Avenue (then Center Street). "The houses along Milwaukee Avenue were of wood and small," Morris Salmonsen

●

Top: Dr. Andrew Doe.

●

Bottom: Martinius Ager and his wife Mathea are standing in front of their home on West Ohio Street. Their son, Waldemar Ager, is seen to the far left. Martinius Ager was a tailor by profession and his sign may be seen to the far right. Their brick cottage is enclosed with a wooden fence and a board sidewalk runs in front of it.

Ferdinand Johnsen from Oslo and Magl Helle from Valle in Setesdal,
who in America became Mary Hill, are typical of the many young men
and women who came to America after the turn of the century. They
were both photographed in Chicago in their Sunday best, Magl Helle
wearing a Norwegian-embroidered blouse and silver brooch together
with the latest in American fashion.

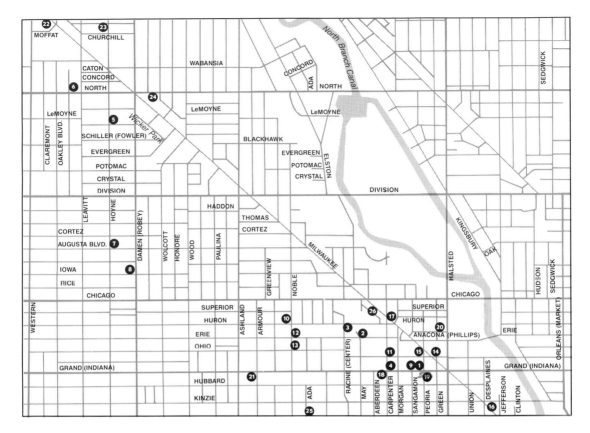

Norwegian Institutions in the Late Nineteenth Century

Lutheran Churches
1. Trinity Church
2. Our Savior's Church
3. Bethlehem Church
4. Lutheran Bethania Free Church
5. Wicker Park Church
6. St. Paul's Church
7. Christ English Church
8. Covenant Church

Methodist
9. First Norwegian-Danish Methodist Church
10. Immanuel Church

Baptist
11. Scandinavian Pilgrim Church

Meeting Places
12. Scandinavian Young Men's Christian Association
13. Harmony Hall
14. Nora Hall
15. Scandia Hall
16. "Old" Aurora Hall
17. Aurora Turner Hall
18. Chicago Commons

Businesses and Major Working Places
19. *Skandinaven*
20. Johnson Chair Company
21. Central Manufacturing Company
22. O.C.S. Olsen & Co.
23. Tobey and Christiansen Cabinet Company
24. The Olson Manufacturing Company
25. The Olson Rug Company
26. John P. Hansen's Cigar Factory

LOCATION OF AREAS
SHOWN ON MAPS

recalled, "and here and there were some of brick which all had been built after the same plan." Churches, like Our Savior's, Trinity, and Bethlehem, lodge halls, and other religious and secular meetinghouses gave ambience to the neighborhood. Ray insisted that English was rarely heard; Norwegian was used unreservedly. In the many saloons, Ray recorded, "nothing but Norwegian and Danish could be heard, and occasionally Swedish as the Swedes began settling among us."[3]

The major Danish colony in Chicago was located in the same district. In 1884 56 percent of the Danish population, or 3,363 first and second generation Danes, lived within the fourteenth ward. Danish store signs and churches were prominent along the same streets as those occupied by the Norwegian ones. This encouraged ethnic cooperation in sustaining such institutions as the small Pilgrim Baptist Church, or in the common Methodist work, and Norwegians and Danes might join Lutheran churches of the other nationality, though on occasion tension surfaced. *Verdens Gang* protested in 1881 when a Chicago correspondent in *Den danske Pioneer*, published in Omaha, Nebraska, insisted that Danes should have nothing to do with Norwegian "religious worship," because as a nation Norwegians were kept in even greater spiritual darkness by the clergy than the Irish; he concluded that "I have never met an Irishman as ignorant as the plurality of Norwegians." Such outbursts, as interpreted also by *Verdens Gang*, were more an effort to mark a special Danish presence, as there was always a risk of simply disappearing in the much larger Norwegian population, than a rejection of "unity and harmony between the two sister nations." The two groups displayed nearly identical patterns of geographic mobility, though the Danes tended to scatter more broadly throughout the city. They gradually formed new neighborhoods in the Wicker Park district and then in the area by Humboldt Park. [4]

Ward 14 also had 2,266 first- and second generation Swedish residents, which made the Scandinavian population equal 19 percent of the total, while the German representation was all of 45 percent. On either side of the North Branch, the river—like the Keel mountain range which separated the two homelands and marked the boundary between their territories—separated Norwegians and Swedes as they moved northward. East of the North Branch in Ward 17 resided 45 percent of the 23,755 Swedes listed in the school census of 1884. Their strong community in Lake View was still outside the Chicago city limits. The Norwegian Lake View church on Roscoe and Kenmore established a few years later manifested the move of some Norwegians north, rather than west, and settlement among the Swedes. Mission churches marked the presence of a few Norwegians who joined the Swedes in their South Side settlement as well. In 1884 2,666 Swedes and 337 Norwegians lived in Ward 5 just east of the South Branch, most heavily concentrated in the neighborhood of 35th Street and Wentworth Avenue.[5]

During the 1880s, however, the major source of new immigrants was quickly changing from northern and western Europe to the eastern and southern parts of the continent. The tide of new workers, speaking their varied languages, created a new ethnic composition and new forms of social interaction. By the 1890s newcomers landing in Chicago were more likely to be Poles, Russian Jews, Bohemians, Hungarians, Lithuanians, or Italians than Scandinavians, or even Germans, Irish, or English.[6]

Over a period of several decades the Norwegians and Danes gradually moved from their old community centered on Milwaukee Avenue and took their businesses with them. In 1891 *Skandinaven* reported that "the section around North and Western avenues is already a nicely developed business district." But their move was by no means a mass flight; the Norwegian community did not willingly or quickly disintegrate. Our Savior's did not in fact leave until the mid-1920s, and societies like the Young Men's Christian Association on Erie Street continued to function with some vigor. Religious institutions were the most resistant. Newcomers found inexpensive housing in the old neighborhood and partly compensated for the population moving out. The latter, however, in time adopted a slightly superior attitude toward those who remained, which indicated the increasing stability and status of the new neighborhoods.[7]

Trinity sold its church to an Italian Catholic congregation in 1899, which defaulted, so it moved back into the church. The Trinity congregation had by then been much depleted through the departure of members from the neighborhood. In 1903 an Eastern Orthodox group purchased the building. The changing ethnic character of the area was reflected in these transactions. Visiting the church building in the 1920s, Pastor K. Seehuus was disturbed by its transformation to a Catholic place of worship, its filth and broken windows, but thought that Lutherans might learn a lesson from the worn-down stairs, which suggested faithful church attendance.[8]

As the Scandinavians moved away they were replaced by Poles and Polish and Russian Jews, who marked their presence by store signs in Polish and Yiddish as the Scandinavian ones were removed. The school census of 1884 listed 15,328 "Polanders" in Ward 14, making it the major Polish ward, with 65 percent of the Polish population. The district between Division Street and North Avenue and east to the river was 74.5 percent Polish. The area of Division and Ashland Avenue became known as the Polish Downtown. The major Norwegian settlement was thus south of the Polish concentration. Later, as the sale of Trinity indicated, Roman Catholic Italians and Slavic and Greek Orthodox Christians moved in numbers to that part of the city. "Around the turn of the century," *Skandinaven* in 1908 wrote, "the southerners in earnest began to invade the old Norwegian settlement west of Milwaukee . . . the Italians from the east and the Poles from the north." By then "the large Norwegian societies had long ago abandoned the West Side as a meeting place."[9]

The dynamics and causes of an urban population succession, whether manifested in class or ethnic dissimilarities, or both, may partly be explained by looking at economic and cultural forces. The expansion of the streetcar system encouraged middle-income Americans to leave central residential areas, and as they left immigrants moved in. Established immigrants followed the lead of the Americans. Working-class immigrants moved in as they left and made their homes in cheap housing in the dirty and smoky industrial districts. In its further commentary on "the great war of conquest," *Skandinaven* explained that the Italians "who also had to exist somewhere" quickly saved enough "with their accustomed frugality and inexpensive way of life" to buy the cheap frame houses west of Milwaukee Avenue. "The old settlers were happy to get whatever they could for their poorly maintained houses," while "among Norwegian youth and the immigrants who had lived there for a while there was a natural wish to seek more desirable living conditions." The immigrant working-class neighborhoods in the river wards were most keenly affected by the crowding and decline in health and morale that an inadequate supply of housing and public services produced. The city, which grew by at least "100 persons a day by birth and immigration," was unable to keep pace with the accelerated demand. Ethnic differences and cultural collision were thereby accentuated.[10]

The arrival of the southern Italians, according to Graham Taylor in his *Pioneering on Social Frontiers* (1930), especially discomfited the Norwegians. Taylor thought that the Norwegians could not reconcile themselves to the demonstrative ways of the southerners whose noisy celebrations disturbed the Sabbath peace. In a sense, Taylor suggested, they were directly crowded out, as the tenements over-filled with Italians were "so different from their own single-family houses." Although, as the city health reports demonstrated, crowding did intensify, most Norwegian working-class districts in wards 10 and 14 in 1880 averaged more than two families per house. Outlying areas, however, had less crowded dwellings. The Danish historian Christian Nielsen called the Humboldt Park neighborhood "a compatible environment for Scandinavians." This district, outside the city fire code limits, encouraged workingmen who could afford to set up inexpensive frame houses to move there. By the beginning of the next century it "was the great Norwegian center."[11]

Developers and real estate speculators appealed to individual nationalities and directed their moves. Stensland, for instance, was active in selling land in the Humboldt Park district to his countrymen in the Milwaukee Avenue colony. The Dane Augustus Jacobsen, who titled himself colonel and avoided direct connection with Scandinavians, having, according to his countryman Morris Salmonsen, decided to be

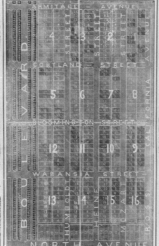

This broadside from the early 1870s advertised real estate in the subdivision just north of Humboldt Park. It made a special appeal to the German population by its printing in both English and German.

Top: A.M. Hanson Meat Market on California Avenue, ca. 1906.

Bottom: Interior of A.M. Hanson Meat Market on Halsted Street, ca. 1890. Adolph Martin Hanson, who had come to Chicago from Farsund, Norway, in 1888 at the age of seventeen, moved his meat market from Halsted Street to California Avenue in 1902. He thus moved with the Norwegian community and made Norwegian meat products to satisfy its needs.

"American," had through his close contact with the banker Winslow acquired large stretches of lots by Humboldt Park. These he offered through an agent to Danish and Norwegian customers in the late 1870s. It was a German developer, a Mr. Greenbaum, who in 1875 had sold George M. Kramer his lot on California Avenue and built his house, even giving him the $50 needed for the down payment. Real estate businesses advertised in different languages. S. E. Gross, for instance, in the 1880s made a special appeal to Germans in bilingual advertisements of his brick cottages near Division and Western.[12]

A Norwegian-American Working Class

There was considerable movement among the neighborhoods occupied by an individual ethnic group, which otherwise retained an outward appearance of permanency that concealed the mobility of persons and households. An attempt was made to sample this circumstance by selecting names, generally distinctive ones to ease later identification, from the 1860, 1870, and 1880 federal censuses and then tracing them in the city directories up to the turn of the century. In this manner residential and occupational patterns were traced for 122 individuals. The two extremes were on the one hand Anton H. Schwartz, identified mostly as a woodturner, who between 1860 and 1900 lived at nine different addresses, and on the other hand Nicholas Tobiason, a common laborer in a lumberyard, who from 1860 until his death in 1895 resided at the same address on Halsted Street. Although conclusions are based on a small sampling, specific skills apparently gave greater freedom of choice than unskilled labor in a factory or other place of business. But mobility was generally confined to a Norwegian or at least Scandinavian immigrant world. Schwartz who moved on the average every third year did so within the West Side Norwegian neighborhood centered on Milwaukee Avenue; others made longer moves, to the South Side or North Side, but predominantly to the West Side. In the 1880s and 1890s especially those first identified in the 1880 census participated in the movement toward Wicker Park and Humboldt Park. As many as 26 percent lived less than three years at the same address, and 34 percent between three and five years. The pattern of movement was encouraged not only by ethnic cohesion, but just as much by employment opportunities in occupations preferred by Norwegians. The latter influenced collective mobility and settlement.[13]

In his *Brogede minder* (Varied Recollections) Salmonsen gives a colorful and illustrative description of Scandinavian workers on Milwaukee Avenue in the 1870s and 1880s. "The Avenue was most characteristic during the early morning hours," Salmonsen related, "between six and seven, when the rush of workers to shops or other places of employment began. They came by the thousands, young and old and of both sexes . . . Their occupations could usually be deter-

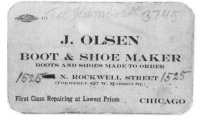

Top: Milwaukee Avenue near Evergreen in the 1890s.

Bottom left: Business card for J. Olsen's shoemaker shop.

Bottom right: The T.J. Olsen shoemaker shop on Madison Street. Johannes Olsen to the far left purchased the shop from T.J. Olsen, standing next to him. Johannes Olsen had emigrated from Biri, Norway, in 1872 when he was twenty-two years old. He operated this shoeshop until about 1900.

mined by how they were dressed. There was the bricklayer in his coarse overalls . . . the carpenter in similar attire, but of finer, blue material, the ditchdigger carrying a shovel over one shoulder, the tailor dressed in clothes of good quality and cut, the shoemaker with polished shoes, barber apprentices with pomaded hair and clean fingernails, waiters in clean linen, coachmen with gloves on to protect their hands . . . Most of the women were young girls on their way to a tailor's workshop . . . hatmaker . . . or cigar factory. But in the crowd one also saw elderly women who carried their work clothes on their way to large establishments where they worked as cleaning women or to the large laundries where the strong heat long ago had given the women their pallid yellow skin color."[14]

In the years after the Great Fire Chicago changed from a city of commerce to a city of manufacturing. By 1890 it was the nation's second manufacturing center and had a population in excess of one million. The labor demands of the city's economy strongly influenced the volume of immigration, so that 41 percent of its residents that year had been born outside the United States. Germans continued to be the largest foreign-born group, but the dramatic rise in Swedish emigration from 1879 on made the 43,032 Swedish-born the third largest group, following the Irish.[15]

Norwegian emigration, like the overseas movement from northern and western Europe in general, culminated in the 1880s. The second wave in the Norwegian crossing began in 1880, following a calmer period after 1873, and lasted until the end of 1893. During these fourteen years an annual average of ten of every thousand Norwegians moved overseas for a total of 256,068. Nearly all, in fact 99.25 percent, came to the United States. A Chicago correspondent in 1879 announced in the Norwegian newspaper *Morgenbladet* (Morning News) in Oslo that while "discouraging reports about bad economic times in Europe" continued, "America has gradually risen from the hard blow suffered during the crisis of 1873." The nation was moving toward prosperity with giant steps and the revitalized economy would produce plentiful employment possibilities. The persistent European depression and economic stagnation during the 1880s made people receptive to news of better times in America.[16]

Morgenbladet enthusiastically presented "The New, Great Wheat Land in North America" in a long descriptive article in 1880. Norwegian peasants continued to be lured by the possibility of becoming American farmers and showed a preference for agricultural pursuits. Their appearance in Chicago sometimes produced comment by established and urbanized compatriots. *Verdens Gang* reported in 1882 that "a party of Norwegian peasants with their wives and children dressed in the customary clothing of the rural population in Numedal created not a little attention yesterday as they waited a few hours here in Chicago on their way to Grand Forks in Dakota Territory." In absolute numbers the Norwegian countryside dominated in the Atlantic crossing, but beginning in 1876 the intensity of the urban exodus surpassed the rural one.[17]

A Norwegian academic thesis in 1979 demonstrates that Oslo, unlike other Norwegian cities, had a high emigration intensity all the way from 1866; the beginning of a general strong urban exodus was marked in 1880 by the departure of more than 2,000 of its citizens. Up until 1895 about one quarter of the thousands who left Norway's capital were destined for Illinois, and "it is," as the study states, "probable that a large part . . . settled in the city [Chicago]." The assumption is that urban emigrants would prefer to settle in a city.[18]

The movement, whether from a city or a rural community, became increasingly more male, and for both men and women younger. At the turn of the century more than 70 percent of all men and 62 percent of all women who left Norway for America were between the ages of 15 and 30. Within that age bracket there were after 1900 twice as many men as women. Nearly 80 percent of the men were single. It was thus a youth movement of people in their most mobile years. Many of those who took part in this labor migration intended to return after a period in the United States. A transition from family to individual migration consequently occurred, although care must be taken not to overemphasize the difference from the earlier family migration, as people continued to move within groups of relatives and friends. It was perhaps family ties in America that made emigration a viable response for young single people to the changing economic circumstances at home.[19]

The proportion of new immigrants from abroad with urban destinations, as David Ward maintained in his *Cities and Immigrants* (1971), was after 1875 no greater than among native-born Americans who migrated. "In some areas," Ward wrote, "a large segment of the latter were the children of immigrants who had settled on the land earlier in the century." Chicago was of course the absolute center for the Great Lakes states. From there and elsewhere in the nation, and from the homeland, Norwegians moved to Chicago. In 1890 the Norwegian population in the city stood at 32,612; of these 21,835 were Norwegian-born. It was an increase of more than 12,000 since the 1880 census.[20]

The young men and women who sought employment in Chicago during the last quarter of the century encountered a much more rigidly fixed social structure than the relatively free intercourse among social classes of the pioneer period. They entered a working class that had emerged among foreign workers earlier in the century and took part in building the city's distinctly working-class culture and institutions. The mass arrival toward the end of the century of new European immigrant groups, frequently poor and unskilled, complicated relationships within the laboring classes as well as the process of industrialization. The working class was now faced, in the words of the labor historian Hermut Keil, with "the decline of artisan crafts, the growth of large factories . . . the establishment of new industries."[21]

Norwegian immigrants were not ignorant of industrial capitalism; they had experience from shops and other places of work. 30.8 percent of the employed who emigrated from Oslo in 1880 were, for instance, engaged in crafts or crafts industries and another 5.5 percent in factories and workshops. Their move to America represented one way of dealing with changes in economic realities, as the expanding Chicago economy provided new opportunities to utilize experiences gained at home. In the general transformation of American industry to employing unskilled labor on a large scale after 1880, however, special skills in crafts were more difficult to transfer. *Skandinaven* reported in its review of Scandinavian sources of income in Chicago for the year 1874 that "the machines are gradually causing the large class of master artisans to disappear," so that "one gets factory owners and workers instead of masters, journeymen, and apprentices." The transition to unskilled labor, as evidenced also by concentrations of Norwegians in the vicinity of such large places of employment as the Johnson Chair Company on Green Street and later on North Avenue, encouraged residential clusterings. Concentrating in certain occupations and finding work in factories operated by entrepreneurs of their own nationality, they settled close to their places of employment.[22]

Vital links in procuring employment were kinship and ethnic ties, which again promoted the creation of ethnic working places. In Chicago German shops, Norwegian shops, and so on, were established. At a later time a worker at the Onsrud Machine Works, a Norwegian workplace, insisted that no one would consider seeking work there except through personal contact, never through an employment agency. This case might also reflect the prestige of working in a highly sophisticated machine shop. Contacts were made through singing societies and other informal gatherings. In this instance the Norsemen's Club, a Norwegian saloon on Fullerton and Spaulding, was the meeting place where news of employment opportunities was passed on.[23]

The Swedish-American building contractor Henry Ericsson recounted in his autobiography that coming to an uncle in Chicago in the early 1880s he made a point of getting acquainted with the many Swedish contractors in the neighborhood "to assure myself of steady work." Within an ethnic network, whether skilled or common labor was sought, employment could thus be found. To be sure, employment agencies also operated among the immigrants, public and private, some specializing in Scandinavian labor, although the latter disappeared by the late 1880s. Labor unions, independently or through union headquarters, sought carpenters, painters, or other skilled workers. Worker solidarity was thereby promoted.[24]

Norwegian carpenters in a factory in Chicago.

"The abundance of carpenters and cabinetmakers is a natural consequence of Chicago being to a large extent a city of wood," *Skandinaven* wrote in 1874 in commenting on Scandinavian occupational preferences. Carpenters, including ship carpenters, constituted 8.8 percent of the 2,757 employed Norwegian-born men residing in wards 10 and 14 in 1880, cabinetmakers and upholsterers, presumably mainly working in the furniture industry, 5.9 percent, and another 7 percent in skilled and semiskilled trades in the building and woodworking industry. One here obviously sees a highly specialized group of workers. Common laborers accounted for 10 percent of the immigrant male labor force, while another 10 percent were listed as "working in" shops and factories. More than 9 percent made a living sailing on the lakes, recruited, as *Skandinaven* stated, from Norwegian sailors and "Norwegians who grew up by the ocean on Norway's west coast."

Tailoring continued to be a typical occupation for urban Norwegian-American men, about 7 percent of the immigrant generation being thus occupied; nearly 3 percent worked as shoemakers, another common craft for Norwegian men. Both crafts were, however, being undermined by factory production. Close to 13 percent of the 2,307 employed Norwegian-born women worked as seamstresses and dressmakers. A contractor or "sweater" located his business among people of his own nationality because, as a 1901 report stated, he was best fitted to be a contractor who "is well acquainted with his neighbors . . . is able to speak the language . . . [and] can easily persuade his neighbors or their wives and children to work for him, and in this way can obtain the cheapest help." This study in 1901, when the situation might be presumed to have improved, disclosed deplorable working conditions and starvation wages, though Scandinavian women fared much better than women from the "new" immigrant populations. In addition, as *Skandinaven* reported in 1874, the system included many married women who took sewing home which "in many a family, especially during the winter months when many men are unemployed, constitutes the main source of income." Activity in the building sector, and also in lake shipping, where a large percentage of Norwegian men made their livelihood, was seasonally determined, and a labor surplus consequently appeared regularly during periods of low demand.

Women, especially single ones, were, however, most often engaged in domestic occupations. In 1880 about three quarters of Norwegian-born women working outside the home were servants, housekeepers, or laundresses. This fact was not lost on American advertisers, the producers of Sapolio scouring soap claiming in *Skandinaven* that "American families learn that Norwegian girls are tidier, cleanlier, and faster than the Irish and German girls," presumably because they used their product. The choice of occupation was of course limited for women, and domestic employment was the most accessible. And housework was decidedly preferred by Norwegian and other Scandinavian women over factory work. In her study of Swedish maids, Stina L. Hirsch quoted one who explained that when it became necessary for her to support herself, the question was: "'What can I do?' The answer was plain—housework. I like it best, was used to it at home, and it seems more natural-like." For the single woman it also afforded a home.

For the second generation in the 1880 census there is a striking 90 percent "no occupation" rate in wards 10 and 14, which suggests the youthfulness of the Norwegian-American population. Only 10 percent of the American-born were old enough to enter specific occupations. The figures are too small to give an accurate picture of second-generation mobility, but they do suggest, as expected, a relative increase in the non-manual labor category as compared to the parent generation, for men a change from 10 to 28 percent in the two groups.[25]

As *Skandinaven* looked back on the year 1879 it predicted continued better times for Scandinavians in Chicago, based on an increased volume of commercial advertising in the immigrant journals and the optimism suggested by the many more marriages that were entered into in the Scandinavian-American population. Endogamy remained the norm. In 1880, of the 2,167 married Norwegians in wards 10 and 14, 91 percent had a Norwegian spouse; 84 percent of all marriages were thus endogamous. Even though lower than ten years earlier, the figure was evidence of persistent ethnocentric forces.[26]

Some idea of the extent of occupational persistence as well as mobility in the Norwegian community can be gained from the 122 case studies referred to earlier. In twenty-four cases the same occupation was engaged in for more than fifteen years, mostly by people in skilled or commercial pursuits. There were extreme examples of occupational change, such as Jacob Birkeland from Sogndal, identified in the 1860 census, who during his working career moved from farmer, to carpenter, to retail grocer, to undertaker, and ended as a cemetery superintendent. Most people who changed jobs, however, did so as a part of upward mobility within the same or related fields or as unskilled laborers. Even Birkeland's career moves, to be sure, had a somewhat logical progression. The restless pursuit of income in whatever work was offered, so characteristic of the pioneer colony, often combining a number of activities, slowly gave way by the 1880s to a more stable occupational identity, in part because of persistent crafts traditions. These were carried over into the next generation and gave evidence of factors other than economic expediency in choosing an occupation. Of the thirty cases identified, five sons entered occupations identical to their fathers', and ten closely related ones. They then commonly, although not consistently, demonstrated upward mobility. An example was B.B. Bolstad, identified in the 1870 census and a carpenter by trade, whose three sons Brengel, Lars, and Henry worked as a tailor, printer, and plater respectively. Henry Bolstad in 1891 formed his own plating company.[27]

The evolving economic structure which affected occupational alternatives had a decisive impact on the nature of Norwegian involvement in the traffic on the lakes. In 1874 a proud Norwegian owner of lake vessels had boasted to *Skandinaven* that "if all ships on the Chicago River hoisted flag according to the nationality of their crew the Norwegian would be more numerous than that of any other." Norwegians had played a significant role in the ascendancy of sailing vessels over steamships, and also as shipbuilders. John Thorson from Stavanger was one of the earliest, but other small Norwegian-operated shipyards built lake vessels in the towns and cities on the western shore of Lake Michigan. George Emerson, arriving in Chicago in 1860, Ole Christophersen from Skien coming three years later, and Gilbert Anderson from near Farsund all transferred skills to the Chicago shipbuilding industry and had their own yards.

In 1870 Knut Gjerset thought that sixty-five percent of all seamen on the sailing vessels on Lake Michigan were first or second generation Norwegians. Many young men took berths on vessels captained by their Norwegian-born fathers. But competition from steamships and railroads in the decade after the Great Fire, as well as a reduction in the transportation of lumber, caused by both lower demand and a depletion of the forests in Michigan and Wisconsin, displaced the sailing vessels. Constant complaints about the lowering of salaries illustrate the dilemma lake sailors found themselves in. "Summer wages for sailors have never been as low as this year," *Skandinaven* complained in 1876, when they fell to $1.00 a day. The crisis came in 1885–1890, when as Olaf Ray explained: "Hundreds of our experienced seamen were laid off and became land crabs and adventurers rather than becoming laborers and stevedores for the steamships." Still, although the proud era of sailing vessels on the lakes, in which Norwegians had played an important part, came to an end and many Norwegians quit the lakes, new men arriving from Norway as well as some of the veterans of the sailing ships found employment on the steamships. Gjerset estimated, though without any hard evidence, that the actual number of Norwegians did not decrease during the transition.[28]

Immigrant Employers

Immigrant entrepreneurs were dependent on the support of the ethnic community. They capitalized on traditions and work experience from home, as clearly illustrated in Norwegian shipbuilding, where both workers and employers had learned the trade before emigrating. Available raw material, an accumulation of capital, and a rising de-

Top: A group of Norwegian lake captains and vessel owners in Chicago about 1885. *Upper row from left:* John Oleson, Arthur N. Nelson, Peter B. Olson, S.M. Peterson, Geo. Gilbertson, John Gjeston. *Lower row from left:* J. Gruda, M.A. Gunderson, J.L. Smith, P.O. Skaaden, M.H. Ryerson, Halvor Michelson.

Bottom: The Johnson Chair Company on Green Street. The Johnson Chair Company lumberyard by the North Branch is depicted in the upper right-hand corner.

mand led to other manufacturing ventures. Out of the long-
established and productive lumber business grew a large woodworking and furniture industry. Norwegians participated at many levels in
that sector of the Chicago economy.[29]

The story of the Johnson Chair Company demonstrates the establishment and functioning of an immigrant company. Andrew P.
Johnson (Gjerager), its organizer, emigrated with his parents from
Voss in 1850 at the age of fifteen and settled on a farm near Beloit,
Wisconsin. He learned carpentry in Beloit and in 1861 moved to Chicago. During the Civil War he put his trade to good use in the army
construction corps, and with the end of hostilities he returned to Chicago and became a contractor and builder. In 1868 Johnson managed
in partnership with other businessmen to raise the money to buy a
small cane-seat factory on Green and Phillips (now Ancona) streets,
then an area being settled by Norwegians, and converted to the
production of wood-seat chairs. In 1877 Johnson became sole owner
and in 1883 incorporated under the name the Johnson Chair Company. Production capacity was expanded by stages at the same location, so that in 1890 the plant consisted of 180,000 square feet, covering an entire street block. Large lumberyards on the North Branch,
where cargo was delivered directly by ship, and the wagons transporting the lumber the fifteen minutes' drive to the factory, created
many jobs.[30]

The company produced between 400 and 500 different styles of
chairs "with seats in wood and cane in walnut, ash, and cherry," as
well as chairs for all kinds of uses, from simple kitchen chairs to large
solid ones in mahogany for offices and clubhouses. The business was
highly successful, and in 1904 expanded production dictated a move
to larger facilities on West North Avenue and North 44th Street.

Around the turn of the century more than 500 people found employment with the firm. The work force was almost exclusively Norwegian. More than 6,000 boys below the age of fifteen worked in
shops and factories in Chicago around 1880, many of them in the furniture industry. The Johnson Chair Company hired a large number
of young boys to work in its factory. Child-labor laws were only
slowly enacted, and the first general one in 1891, which prohibited the
employment of children under the age of thirteen, had exemptions
that made it ineffective. The workers lived in the adjacent neighborhoods and many had been directly recruited from Norway. The firm
gave young men, not infrequently green peasant boys, a ticket to Chicago; they arrived with a sign around their neck with the address of
the factory and an emigrant trunk they had made from boards given
them by Johnson. At the plant on Green Street the newcomers could
stay in one of the production rooms until they began working and had
found a place to live. It was their entry into the American capitalist
system. The Norwegian-speaking place of work eased them into the

Andrew P. Johnson is seated just behind the sign together with the workers in his factory. The photograph, taken about 1890, shows a large number of very young boys in the work force.

new environment. On their side, they provided the Johnson Chair Company with a loyal work force at a reasonable cost.[31]

Much of the early production was by hand; the first test for the workers was the construction of the emigrant trunk. Many were able to put to use crafts learned in Norway. These skills were less important as production gradually became more mechanized and assembly-line procedures were introduced, allowing the company to flood the market with inexpensive but functional chairs.

Andrew P. Johnson based his success on a solidarity with his employees on the grounds of a common nationality. He might be regarded as a paternalistic employer as well as a model for upward mobility. Company picnics allowed "the employer and employees to mingle to the mutual joy of all," as *Skandinaven* reported in 1892, and praised Johnson for "thinking about his workers." It would, the newspaper thought, encourage a sense of family and "honest cooperation." There were also stories of Johnson positioning himself by the factory entrance and tearing up the union cards of workers who had joined organized labor.

Though a part of the Norwegian-American community, Johnson, like many successful immigrants, placed a social distance between himself and the ordinary Norwegian. His residence was in the fashionable part of the Norwegian and German Wicker Park neighborhood, where he lived on Damen (then Robey) Avenue, and belonged to the English-speaking Wicker Park Lutheran Church.[32]

The experience of Nils Arneson, who in the late 1880s built a magnificent home on North Hoyne at Wicker Park, was not unlike Johnson's. Trained as a wagonmaker in Oslo, he emigrated in 1861 at the age of twenty-one. After having served in the St. Olaf Rifles, the Chicago company of the Fifteenth Wisconsin, he practiced his trade until 1868, when he began to manufacture furniture on Canal Street. His factory was lost in the Great Fire but he managed to rebuild. In 1884 Arneson together with partners started the Central Manufacturing Company, which became one of the major producers of office desks in Chicago. The firm, like the Johnson Chair Company, was Norwegian in leadership and presumably also in work force, as it was located on Armour Street in the Norwegian working-class district south of Chicago Avenue. Norwegian workers found employment also with O.C.S. Olsen & Co., another manufacturer of office desks, located on Moffat Street west of Milwaukee Avenue. It was founded in 1890 by Olaf C. S. Olsen, who in 1883 at age twenty had come to Chicago from Stavanger.[33]

The transition from skilled craftsmen to a more automated mode of production in the manufacturing of furniture is evident. But in some branches skills persisted. Firms like the Tobey Furniture Company, founded in the late 1850s by Charles Tobey, continued to excel in producing expensive custom-made parlor furniture. When Charles

•

Top: The Andrew P. Johnson family photographed about 1890 in their middle-class elegance. Left to right: Joseph, Martha, Arthur (standing), Ruth, Andrew, Ole (standing), Anna.

•

Bottom: Wicker Park Lutheran Church.

obey died in 1888, his brother Frank B. Tobey became president of the firm. In order to secure the services of Wilhelm F. Christiansen, an excellent cabinetmaker from Norway, then employed by a rival firm, Tobey formed a subsidiary company and invited Christiansen to become a partner in it. The Tobey and Christiansen Cabinet Company built its factory on Churchill Street. Christiansen had emigrated from Trondheim in 1868 when he was twenty-one years old and had then completed his four-year apprenticeship in a local cabinet shop. Working for manufacturers of fine furniture in Chicago he established a reputation as a master craftsman. Thirty skilled workers were employed under Christiansen's supervision by the factory on Churchill Street, which placed in the top rank of American furniture makers. In the 1890s another Norwegian, Otto Andersen, was the company's chief carver.[34]

In the same decade Carl Bauer worked as a woodcarver and designer in Chicago after emigrating from Ulefoss in Telemark at age twenty in 1893. His German-born father, Valentine Bauer, had come to Norway in his late twenties to work as a builder and had married and settled there. By precept, formal training, and talent Bauer was well prepared for his career as a woodcarver and furniture designer. His daughter Dorothy Bauer Erland has explained how a modest capital could be accumulated: Bauer rented out one of the two flats in the house he purchased. Then pooled resources and partnership with a person having an established company name facilitated upward movement. In 1907 Bauer, together with Joseph Doetsch, a cabinetmaker and furniture manufacturer, and two other men, organized a factory to make furniture frames. When Doetsch died the next year, Bauer bought the interests of the other partners, but retained the name Doetsch & Bauer. It became the second largest producer of wooden frames for upholstered furniture in Chicago. The company employed close to one hundred workers, and after 1914 was located on Altgeld Street in the Logan Square district, by then strongly Norwegian. A crafts tradition persisted well into the present century. Not until the 1920s did new carving inventions simplify production so that craftsmen were largely replaced by semiskilled labor.

Woodworking skills also entered into the large-scale production of the technically advanced pianos produced by A.G. Gulbransen. His father, a furniture manufacturer in Oslo, had moved the family to America in 1869 when Gulbransen was four years old. The Gulbransen Company, which had a modest beginning in 1904, manufactured player pianos that were shipped all over the world. The majority of furniture manufacturers were foreign-born, as were their employees. The Germans were the most prominent in woodworking, but also Scandinavian, Italian, Dutch, and Lithuanian woodworkers were found in that part of the industry in substantial numbers. The Scandinavians increased their percentage of skilled furniture workers from 20 percent in 1880 to 30 percent in 1900.[35]

Transportation of chair frames from the Doetsch & Bauer factory after
the turn of the century.

The strong representation of Norwegians in tailoring gave rise to mass factory production. The Olson Manufacturing Company for the production of men's trousers was founded by Knud B. Olson (Røthe), who emigrated from Voss in 1861. He had been apprenticed to a local tailor in Voss, and after arriving in Chicago he found employment in tailoring shops. On January 1, 1863, he started his own business with one Singer sewing machine and one female assistant. By 1900 the factory, located on Elk Grove Avenue near North Avenue, employed about 150 women and men. The concentration on a single product—trousers—illustrated the value of specialization. The Olson Rug Company, situated in the Norwegian neighborhood south of Grand Avenue, at the same time gave work to from 175 to 200 people. It was begun modestly by Oliver B. Olson, who in 1874 invented what became known as the Olson fluff rug, made from old carpet. It became a distinctive industry. Upon Olson's death in 1890, his Chicago-born son Walter E. Olson, having learned the trade in his father's rug factory, introduced labor-saving devices and increased production.

These major places of employment, alongside numerous small shops and factories, existed in the Norwegian working-class districts, in old as well as in evolving neighborhoods, their presence attracting Norwegian workers to the area. Ivar Doe, for instance, employed seventy men in his furniture factory, Louis Hansen had sixty people working in his "picture, mirror, and frame factory," and in the same Milwaukee Avenue neighborhood John P. Hansen's cigar factory hired nearly one hundred workers. Though of course not only Scandinavians found employment in these shops, immigrant entrepreneurs obviously depended on their countrymen, and in spite of a certain social aloofness, resided in the same districts as the common laborer. Ethnic consciousness made workers prefer "Norwegian" shops and factories to "American" ones of another nationality. When reporting on Scandinavian-American enterprise, the immigrant press took care to note the presence of Scandinavians in the work force.[36]

Working-Class Activism

The Norwegian-language *Scandia* claimed that there were five distinct classes within the Norwegian colony in Chicago: (1) an aristocracy, (2) a middle class, (3) a working class, (4) a very poor class, and (5) a class of the permanently unemployed or shiftless. Somewhat tongue-in-cheek the newspaper expressed the idea that these classes were sharply divided.[37]

In fact of course, as frequently demonstrated, there was considerable interaction, and the social distance could be breached. As the immigrants and their children sifted themselves into any one of these social groupings, however, and the economic disparities between them increased, group identity intensified. Those at the lower levels might view the commercially and professionally successful members of their national group as worthy of emulation, but the wealthy were not the only models for the working-class population. Social activities, such as picnics and lodge meetings, encouraged worker solidarity. In 1878, for instance, the Scandinavian Socialist Singing Society "Internationalen" gathered its "many political party fellows," and the Scandinavian Tailor Society, the Scandinavian Shoemaker Society, and the Scandinavian Workers Association (Den skandinaviske Arbeiderforening) assembled their members to observe July 4th at different locations in the city. To what extent they were affected by appeals to worker solidarity is more difficult to determine, as is the influence of the success ideology of the self-made man. A conflict might easily arise between individuality and group loyalty. The immigration experience innately encouraged the former.[38]

Working-class culture was closely interrelated with the economic and political structures in Chicago and reflected individual and group efforts to protect and advance economic self-interest. It was also related to earlier patterns. The manufacturer Knud B. Olson's wish to have his own tailoring shop was, for instance, in the classic artisan tradition of moving from journeyman to being one's own boss. To promote collective interests he might have joined the Scandinavian Tailor Society (Den skandinaviske Skræder-Forening), founded at about the time he opened his shop in the early 1860s. This early Scandinavian-American trade union concentrated on regulating competition among its members, and like the workers' societies (*arbeidersamfunn*) formed about the same time in Norway under the control of bourgeois philanthropists, it emphasized cultural and entertainment activities, such as lectures, plays, and outings. [39]

The Scandinavian Workers Association (S.W.A.), organized on June 13, 1870, reflected the desire by people outside the laboring class to enlighten and influence the common worker. An appeal for the donation of books to form a workers' library of "appropriate reading" indicated its educational purpose and the social position of its promoters. Donations were to be made to F. Strom, gold- and silversmith, Fritz Frantzen, cigar- and newsdealer, or E. Foss, chemist and apothecary. The society had actually begun some time earlier as the South Side Norwegian Workers Association. A larger membership was sought by making it Scandinavian and moving to the North Side. Dr. Gerhard Paoli was its first president, the Swedish businessman and politician Charles Sundell was vice president, and the Danish architect August C. Hansen secretary. No one from the working class served as officer, or indeed appeared on the initial invitation to the organizing meeting. It met in a hall near the southwestern corner of Halsted Street and Chicago Avenue, which suggests its strong Norwegian and Danish, rather than Swedish, character. Its program, as *Skandinaven* reported, moved "in the customary direction for social organizations: meetings, dances, picnics, fairs." It also had a library, arranged lectures, and set up sick and funeral funds. There was, however, no general agreement as to the Association's specific purpose, some wanting to involve it in politics in order to protect workers' interests in the labor market and likely advance some personal ambitions. Although the Association was to rebound in the 1880s, the immediate consequence of the controversy was a reduction in membership.[40]

Ethnic trade unions emerged in the early 1870s in response to the unique situation created by the rapid pace at which Chicago was being rebuilt after the Great Fire. Both workers and capital streamed into town and, to begin with, labor seemed to have an edge in disputes over salary. There was, as *Skandinaven* later wrote, "an enormous influx of people from all four corners of the world . . . mostly working people with blue overalls and a dinner pail . . . and there was no lack of work at good pay." Scandinavians, concentrating in the building trades, formed unions of carpenters and bricklayers in 1871. An incentive to organize was to protect these crafts against "invasion by inexperienced and incompetent forces," which could cause a lowering of salaries. They joined national bodies and met regularly at the "old" Aurora Hall on Milwaukee Avenue.

That same year a Scandinavian shoemakers' union (Den skandinaviske Skomager-Union) organized as a lodge under the national St. Crispin's Grand Lodge. It was mainly a Norwegian lodge and reflected an effort to safeguard a craft rapidly losing ground to factory production. The Benevolent Scandinavian Painter Society (Den velgjørende skandinaviske Malerforening) was organized, also in 1871, as lodge No. 27 under the national grand lodge in New York. These two lodges operated as secret societies. "Unions are for the workers what stock companies are for capitalists," *Skandinaven* explained, and they encouraged class consciousness. As divisions of national craft unions the local Scandinavian trade organizations took part in strikes and became the victims of lockouts. They declined after the "Panic of 1873" and the depression years that followed; they thereby evidenced the same trend as the American labor movement. "Unemployment is alarmingly high," *Skandinaven* wrote in 1876; a progressive reduction in salaries robbed even those fortunate enough to have work of a living wage.

Social and benevolent activities continued, however, and the unions provided sick and death benefits. The sustained effort by the Benevolent Scandinavian Painter Society in cooperation with the Scandinavian Workers Association to "ennoble and uphold" the profession by establishing a free design and art school for "young Scandinavian artisans" came to naught.[41]

The educational and support function of the early Scandinavian trade unions was obvious; they were little influenced by socialist ideology. Their strong Republicanism, and perhaps sensitivity to the attacks by American newspapers against "foreign communists," appeared to have made Swedes at that point especially immune. In the Swedish community socialist activity appeared to be limited to intellectual debates by salon radicals. A more pronounced social radicalism among Danes and Norwegians must in part be explained by circumstances that brought exiled labor leaders and intellectual liberals to Chicago from Denmark and Norway. On November 23, 1871, Marcus Thrane, joining three German sister clubs, organized Scandinavian Section 4 of the socialist International Workingmen's Association, the famed First International devoted to Marxian socialism, which in 1872 moved its headquarters from London to New York.

The activities of Thrane, the Danish Socialist Louis Pio and the freethinking Dr. Paoli introduced radical thought, though Scandinavian Section 4 did not have any great following. Freethinkers were heavily condemned by the Protestant churches. "No greater reproach could be directed against a man than to call him infidel, agnostic, atheist," wrote Bessie Pierce. Scandinavians as a consequence largely avoided the medical services of Dr. Paoli, according to Marcus Thrane. Before coming to the United States in early 1864, Thrane had spent eight years in Norwegian prisons for "crimes against the security of the state" because of his success, inspired by the revolutions of 1848, in organizing workingmen's societies. Many of his followers emigrated and in 1852 Thranites in America defended Thrane against attacks by the then church-controlled *Emigranten*, which portrayed him as a dangerous agitator. Visiting an old and impoverished man in Chicago in the mid-1870s Pastor Amund Mikkelsen related that the man told him with great bitterness that he had been a part of the failed Thrane movement and had left Norway because he was dissatisfied with its political and economic system. Thrane could of course expect to meet former Thranites after coming to Chicago in 1866, but the number cannot be easily determined. He moved mainly in a circle of Scandinavian socialists and freethinkers, relied on the support of middle-class intellectuals like Dr. Paoli, and published magazines to argue their economic and social philosophy.[42]

His *Marcus Thrane's Norske Amerikaner*, published from May to September, 1866, had according to Thrane himself about two thousand subscribers when *Skandinaven* purchased it. *Dagslyset* (Light of Day), which Thrane launched in 1869, was the organ of the Scandinavian Freethinker Society (Den skandinaviske Fritænkerforening), organized in April of that year by Thrane and Dr. Paoli and a largely Norwegian membership.[43] The Society became the core of the International Section 4, meeting at the "old" Aurora Hall, where Thrane frequently lectured on *Dagslyset*'s stated purpose to spread "free religious inquiry and radical political views." In 1874 the monthly had about 400 subscribers, which suggests the extent of receptiveness to its socialistic and radical message. The Scandinavian freethinkers celebrated the annual Thomas Paine anniversary in 1877, and were able to publish *Dagslyset* until the following year, though with breaks and under difficult circumstances. In strong socialistic terms it indicted the bourgeois-led Scandinavian Workers Association for abusing the name "workers society" since it did not strive "to free labor from the oppression of capital."[44]

In 1878, the year *Dagslyset* ceased publication, Danish Socialists started *Den nye Tid* (The New Age), with Louis Pio as editor; Pio had been bribed to emigrate by Danish officials fearful of his socialistic agitation. For most of its life, however, beginning in that same year, the newspaper was edited apparently with some assistance from Thrane by the popular Norwegian Socialist and violinist Peter Peterson. *Den nye Tid*, which claimed to be the only Scandinavian newspaper in America to "fearlessly and clearly speak the cause of the worker and free thought," existed until 1884. Up to 1881 it spoke for the Workingmen's or Socialist Labor party, then after a split in that group it became the Norwegian and Danish organ of the anarchistic Revolutionary Socialist party. Its offices were on Erie Street close to Milwaukee Avenue and thus highly visible in the Norwegian community. As a premium for taking a year's subscription the newspaper offered a copy of Thrane's blistering satire on the Norwegian Lutheran clergy "The Old Wisconsin Bible." Olaf Ray was associated with *Den nye Tid* during its latter years and has given an example of his, and the journal's, anti-clerical attitude. A Lutheran pastor in "one of the large churches in the area," as Ray told it, "announced that the next Sunday he would preach on the depravity of the Norwegian seamen in Chicago." Ray and two former sailors attended the service and in the middle of "the scarlet sermon" Ray stood up and asked the pastor if the following Sunday, or at any other time, he would be willing to debate the question of "who are most depraved in relationship to their numbers, clergymen or sailors?" The outcome was that no more sermons using sailors as examples of wasted lives were given.[45]

The extent of Socialist influence on the Scandinavian work force is unclear. The election of the German Frank A. Stauber in 1880 on a Socialist ticket as alderman from Ward 14, however, demonstrated Scandinavian, particularly Norwegian and Danish, involvement in the entrenched German Socialist movement. The circle around *Den nye Tid* actively campaigned for Stauber. The attempts by Republicans to defraud Stauber of his victory, which revealed the increasing labor militancy and the fear of its consequences during the hard times of the 1870s, undermined faith in the political system. At the meeting in Chicago of social revolutionary groups in October, 1881, at which the breach in the Socialist ranks occurred, Peterson rejected using the ballot as a means of changing the social order and moved *Den nye Tid* into the Revolutionary Socialist party which was organized at that

Olaf E. Ray.

convention. Running unsuccessfully for alderman from Ward 14 on the Socialist ticket in April of that year he still had garnered nearly 1,000 votes. In contrast to Peterson, August Spies, editor of the *Arbeiter-Zeitung* (Workers' Times), and Albert Parsons, like Spies a future defendant in the Haymarket trial, worked to have the use of the democratic political process included in the Socialist platform. *Den nye Tid* instead trumpeted revolutionary methods and goals.

The boom and bust economy of Chicago produced periods of great unemployment, which most severely affected the vulnerable immigrant workers, and the destitution it caused bred discontent. Tensions between employees and employers and demands of the suffering unemployed produced violence. In May, 1876, *Skandinaven* graphically depicted how 400 policemen had done battle for several hours with unemployed workers bent on "destroying as much as they could" of their former place of employment when the owner hired new workers at a much reduced pay. Police raided union halls and by brute force oppressed the working class.[46]

The labor movement, even though doctrinaire discord existed among its various factions, was united in its protest against the reduction in wages that occurred. After some gains during the economic expansion of the early 1880s, they were again subject to cuts. By 1884 wages for carpenters, joiners, cabinetmakers, and painters—trades heavily engaged in by Norwegians—had been reduced from 12 to 22 percent. In petitioning the Johnson Chair Company to have their wages restored, the employees respectfully asked the employer to view the petition as "an exercise of liberty to maintain and enjoy a true American standard of living."[47]

A major rallying point for labor was the demand for an eight-hour day. Illinois had enacted eight hours as a legal workday as early as 1867, but the law was not enforced. Strikes and protest actions to make employers abide by it had been ineffective. The most notable one was the confrontation that produced the Haymarket Riot in 1886. A general strike was called for May 1, which in Chicago involved 80,000 strikers. They marched through the streets to voice their demands, which gave strong evidence of Chicago as a union town, and many feared revolution. The bomb-throwing incident on May 4, when a mass protest meeting turned violent, horrified the nation. The four "anarchists," Parsons, Spies, Adolph Fischer, and George Engel, who were hanged as convicted instigators, all lived in the working-class neighborhoods in the Wicker Park district. Their funeral cortege wound its way past the worker cottages in this neighborhood where so many Norwegian laborers also resided. Hallvard Hande of *Norden* found that the great number of people who either joined the procession or lined the streets signaled future labor radicalism.[48]

Hostility against the demands of labor following the Haymarket tragedy, and the obvious advantage the employer had in negotiating, as well as the anti-foreign sentiments that engulfed the immigrant workers, lost labor some of its gains. But by the late 1880s, during a period of general prosperity, worker demands again expressed themselves in a growth in crafts unions. Scandinavian locals were formed and some joined the American Federation of Labor. The labor interests of Scandinavian printers were consolidated in April, 1883, with the organization of the Scandinavian Typographical Union. A separate Swedish union of printers was organized in 1893, as the existing one was held to be a Norwegian and Danish organization. The next year it received its charter from the International Typographical Union. The first action of the Swedish printers was against Swedish-American publications, a strike in 1899 against the firm of Engeberg-Holmberg.[49]

One of the largest and most radical unions in Chicago was the Scandinavian Painters Local No. 194, organized on October 9, 1890. It united Danish and Norwegian painters on the Northwest Side who acted with determination within the national brotherhood and had in excess of 800 members at the turn of the century. The Scandinavian Carpenter Local No. 181 with 550 members existed in the same part of the city and was equally radical and influential within Chicago's labor movement. These militant labor organizations represented the interests of the expanding percentage of Scandinavian craftsmen in the Chicago work force.[50]

A Middle-Class Leadership

The Norwegian-American writer Peer Strømme moved to Chicago in January, 1888, to become editor of *Norden*. This weekly had been established in 1874 by I.T. Relling, who operated a Norwegian bookstore and sold steamship tickets and bank notes. In his memoirs Strømme recorded his impressions of upwardly mobile Norwegians like Relling. Strømme and his family rented a house from Dr. Niles T. Quales, originally Nils Kvale, next door to the doctor's own home on Schiller (then Fowler) Street by Wicker Park, "then the city's most fashionable Norwegian district," as Strømme wrote. "On the other side of us," he continued, "there was a large house belonging to Captain Halvor Michelson, and in the part nearest us lived Dr. B. Meyer, while Captain Michelson and his large family resided in the main part of the building on the corner of Fowler Street and Hoyne Avenue. Near us lived Relling, Consul Svanøe, Paul O. Stensland, the rich manufacturer of chairs A. P. Johnson, the political boss Henry Hertz, a Dane, and numerous other such personages. We thus had more genteel, stately, and wealthy neighbors than either earlier or later," Strømme concluded with his characteristic touch of irony. The slightly eccentric Relling, as publisher of *Norden* Strømme's boss, insisted that in consideration of his editorial dignity Strømme should wear a frock coat and silk hat every day.[51]

The Wicker Park community that evolved after the Great Fire within West Town was like most Chicago neighborhoods socially mixed. Professionals and storekeepers lived there, as did common laborers, but, to be sure, in separate sections; workers' cottages identified their area. Germans and Norwegians were the two major groups. Mansions and elegant houses in massive stone conspicuously displayed the wealth of the immigrant elite. Norwegians called the district "Homansbyen," after an exclusive section of Oslo. All of this, as well as Strømme's comments, suggests the attitude and behavior of a parvenu social group eager to establish its position. The upwardly mobile Germans and Norwegians who lived in the fashionable residential area on present-day Schiller (then Fowler), Hoyne, and Pierce streets west of Wicker Park and Caton and Concord north of North Avenue made their wealth as merchants in lumber, building,

Peer O. Strømme.

In this building on Milwaukee Avenue around 1890, I. T. Relling published the newspaper *Norden*, operated Skandinavisk Boghandel (bookstore), and a steamship agency, and sold bank notes on Scandinavian banks. The signs are in Norwegian, suggesting the direct appeal to the Scandinavian community for business.

and wholesale trades, and as successful professional people. Norwegian lake captains as well made their homes there. Whereas Germans built most of the mansions south of North Avenue, many of those farther north were built by Norwegians. The wealthy Norwegian wholesale merchant Ole A. Thorp, for instance, lived on Caton.[52]

The German pastor Edmund Belfour conceived the idea of organizing an English-speaking Lutheran congregation at Wicker Park. After having determined that most residents were Lutherans, he called a meeting in the home of Dr. Quales in August, 1879. Wicker Park Lutheran Church was subsequently organized as a congregation within the Pittsburgh Synod and located on the corner of Le Moyne and Hoyne streets. Quales was one of the many influential men Belfour had interested in the project, and even though the Germans constituted a majority of the members, leadership like his often made the Norwegians appear to play a dominant role in church affairs.[53]

Dr. Quales was born in Kinsarvik in Hardanger in 1831 and educated as a veterinarian, in 1856 taking up residence at Vossevangen in Voss as county veterinarian. When Iver Lawson visited Voss in 1859 to recruit emigrants, he convinced Quales to come to America. After arriving in Chicago, he earned a medical degree at Rush Medical College and established a successful practice. Quales was thus typical of many immigrant leaders who had the advantage of education before they settled in America. His wife Carrie was a cousin of Iver Lawson, which brought Quales into contact with influential people and gave him exposure to American social life. The two settled in Wicker Park in 1873. The obvious move toward assimilation, evidenced as well in the Americanization of his name, did not prevent Quales from being one of the most dynamic leaders in the Norwegian immigrant community. His activities were, however, limited mainly to causes within his own field of medicine and health care.[54]

The middle-class elite to a great extent evolved from the working class as individuals moved into higher levels of income. But even though admission to higher social groupings was common in the social world of the immigrants, a measure of exclusivity and solidarity in an immigrant elite can be seen also in marriage patterns. The three Torrison brothers, born to immigrant parents at Manitowoc, Wisconsin, exemplified the trend. The oldest, I. B. Torrison, who in the 1890s served as pastor of St. Paul's on North Avenue, married Elizabeth Koren, and thus became the son-in-law of Ulrik Vilhelm Koren, an aristocratic and dominant leader in the Norwegian Synod. His brother George A. Torrison, a prominent physician and a member of St. Paul's, married Emma Johnson, an adopted daughter of Andrew P. Johnson. Oscar M. Torrison, the best known of the three, practiced law in Chicago and became judge of the municipal court. In

•

Top: The mansion built by Ole A. Thorp in the 1890s at 2156 West
Caton.

•

Bottom left: The spacious parlor in the home of Carrie and Niles T.
Quales in the Wicker Park neighborhood.

•

Bottom right: Wedding picture of Carrie and Niles Quales, May 26, 1870.

1889 he married Ida Michelson, a daughter of Captain Halvor Michelson. The secular as well as the ecclesiastical elite are identified in these unions.[55]

Individual and group prominence depended on the continuation of a Norwegian-American identity in the large working class. Promotion of things Norwegian, which served the needs of middle-class Norwegian Americans, also pulled the laboring groups into bourgeois activities and created solidarity based on a shared nationality. Ties to the past gave meaning for the common worker in a society in rapid change as well as for those who prospered in the American capitalist order. The Norwegian-American press, expressing diverse agendas and addressing separate audiences, nevertheless promoted a sense of community. Large newspapers like *Skandinaven*, with a readership that represented the whole continuum of the immigrant society, muted differences and encouraged the celebration of a Norwegian heritage.[56]

In 1870 *Skandinaven* launched a tri-weekly edition for its Chicago readers which became a daily the next year alongside its weekly. It was a move by the financially strapped publishers to attract local advertising. Following the death of his father in 1872, Victor F. Lawson joined the firm and moved its offices to a building owned by the Lawson estate. In December, 1875, the later manager of the Associated Press Melville E. Stone and associates began publishing the *Chicago Daily News* in this building. It introduced the penny daily to Chicago. Victor Lawson became the senior proprietor and made it one of the most profitable journalistic enterprises in the country. It benefited from labor unrest when some days it published hourly issues, which were eagerly snatched up by "the anxious, excited questioning throngs" that filled the streets. Lawson was not averse to practicing "yellow journalism," for example sensationalizing events that led to the Haymarket encounter. His friend Dwight L. Moody told the workers to be more interested in their salvation than in an eight-hour day.[57]

Skandinaven, on the other hand, persisted in its democratic spirit and professed a cautious pro-labor stance. It viewed labor unions as a force for much good. John Anderson became sole owner in 1878, Lawson's interest being temporary and as he wrote, "in the nature of care of an investment until it could be sold." *Skandinaven*, like immigrant journals in general, placed itself in the tradition of the penny press, in subject matter as well as in linguistic style. The flood of immigrants in the 1880s swelled the subscription rolls and secured a permanent prosperity for the firm. By 1892 the daily edition, which circulated mainly in the Chicago area, was printed in 10,300 copies. It thus must have entered nearly every Norwegian home. [58]

The Republican *Skandinaven* built its reputation on its wide news coverage and its political involvement, its editorial policy from 1872

Top: John Anderson in his office in *Skandinaven*'s imposing building on Peoria Avenue where the newspaper moved in 1883.

Bottom: The sign on the horsedrawn wagon in front of *Skandinaven*'s offices advertises the firm to be "printers of all languages."

until 1886 being guided by the devoted progressive Svein Nilsson. To capture the newspaper market at all levels Anderson in early 1877 began publishing the smaller and less expensive weekly *Verdens Gang* (The Way of the World) as an "independent political and religious organ." The gifted David Monrad Schøyen edited *Verdens Gang* for many years; the newspaper's masthead indicated a controlling part ownership by people outside the John Anderson publishing firm. It existed until World War I, and though declaring itself politically independent, frequently favored Democratic candidates and like its mother organ found many of labor's demands justified.[59]

Competition for the soul and mind of the immigrant, as well as personal ambition, expressed itself in several other newspaper enterprises. *Norden*, which Strømme described as "more or less a churchly political newspaper," was, with some interruption, edited from its founding in 1874 until 1887 by the Norwegian Synod minister Hallvard Hande. In the disruptive religious warfare of the late 1880s Hande sided with the minority position of the Anti-Missourians in the Synod, a position Strømme continued when he succeeded to the editorial post. This was also the opinion of most of the Norwegian-American press. The conservative majority party in the Synod strongly influenced by the strict Biblical interpretation of the German Missouri Synod, expressed its doctrinal teachings in the newspaper *Amerika*, launched in Chicago in 1884. It was edited by Thrond Bothne, former professor at the Synod's Luther College, who cooperated closely with the pastors Ole Juul and Amund Mikkelsen. In the ongoing labor conflict *Amerika* echoed the moralistic message of much of the American press. *Amerika* saw intemperance as a cause of labor radicalism. When the workers had wasted their money foolishly, the newspaper editorialized during the Haymarket trials, they joined the Socialists and anarchists who told them that "it is right to steal from the rich and give to the poor." The right of property was paramount.[60]

At about the time when the theological strife which split the Synod culminated in 1887 both *Norden* and *Amerika* were, however, moving away from church involvement and entering the civic arena. This change reflected the decreased dominance of religion and church affairs in the life of Norwegian Americans, especially in the urban environment. Temporal interests were increasing as the second generation moved into public life; the many well educated immigrants arriving in Chicago in the 1880s also encouraged a broader vision. These groups became the shapers of opinion as people's ties to the church were loosened. Strømme moved *Norden* toward the Democratic party, whereas O.M. Kalheim, who in 1887 succeeded Bothne as *Amerika*'s editor, retained its Republican affiliation. He and Strømme became fast friends, to the extent, as Strømme related, that they often sat side by side when they wrote their respective editorials. "He attacked me and *Norden*, and I attacked him and *Amerika*," Strømme wrote, "and we did not spare each other. But we read for each other what we had written." Strømme felt that he had converted his competitor, at least to being a "mugwump," i.e. politically independent.[61]

The men who in the 1880s entered Norwegian-American journalism were recruited both from the American-educated second generation and from Norwegian intellectuals and academicians. Sons of immigrants like Victor Lawson abandoned their Norwegian identity to pursue a career outside ethnic bounds, while others became influential ethnic leaders. Many of the latter moved to Chicago from rural settlements. Peer Strømme was born to immigrant parents in Winchester, Wisconsin, in 1856, and grew up in a rural Norwegian church-centered environment. In 1879 he was ordained into the Lutheran ministry, although he was to become primarily a much-traveled lecturer, correspondent, and newspaperman. O.M. Kalheim had come to America at the age of three in 1867, and thus his experience was that of the second generation. His childhood and youth were spent in a Norwegian farming community near Lisbon, Illinois. Kalheim, as Strømme had done, studied at Luther College and for a year taught Latin at St. Olaf College in Northfield, Minnesota, before moving to Chicago. Both men were typical of those whose careers moved within the Norwegian-American environment.[62]

Political office gave social status and influence, frequently attained through the support of one's own compatriots. In the city, with its multitude of career models, it was but one of several means to personal advancement and prestige. The masses of common workers might follow the political lead of middle-class politicians. The lake captain and shipowner S.T. Gunderson, a brother of the lake captain Gabriel Gunderson, served one term in the mid-1870s as alderman from Ward 11, and in 1888 Andrew P. Johnson represented Ward 14 on the city council. Competition among ethnic groups and appeals to national honor rallied compatriots behind a specific candidate. Control of patronage was an important consideration. Andrew B. Johnson as president of the County Board of Commissioners was, for instance, regularly accused by the opposition of appointing Scandinavians to political office and securing his own sons "attractive posts." But the frustration of a small ethnic group is more apparent than its success. *Verdens Gang*'s editorial after the municipal election in 1882 is suggestive of the situation. "Concerning the question of whether the elected candidates will consider the Scandinavian element in appointments to the relatively well paid posts," the newspaper editorialized, "there is at least one comforting thought—the newly elected officials can hardly do less than the departing ones."[63]

Politically Chicago showed a general drift toward the Democratic party in the post-fire decades, thereby reversing the earlier trend, although Republicans and Democrats alternated in governing the city. The popularity of the urbane and worldly Democratic mayor Carter H. Harrison I made him nearly unbeatable; he served four consecutive terms from 1879 and a fifth one later. This was also the period when the Irish overcame many discriminatory barriers and through the Democratic party surged to political strength. They advanced their social position through political office, and dominated in many politically related areas, such as police, fire, and sanitation.[64]

John Allswang in his *A House for All People* (1971) is likely correct in his contention that new immigrants tended to favor the political party in power. No doubt many newly arrived workingmen in the Norwegian group joined the Democrats for this reason and expanded the party's numbers as well as its acceptability by Norwegian immigrants. Allswang also points to reference groups as a strong influence on political behavior: German Americans, for example, voted Republican because German Americans had always done so. Scandinavians as a whole retained a strong loyalty to the Republican party, the Swedes most intensely, the Norwegians and the Danes less so. Gustav Johnson claimed that the story of Swedes in politics in Chicago was the story of loyalty to the Republican party. Even so, as early as 1863, though poorly supported, a Scandinavian Democratic Club was formed under the presidency of the maverick O.G. Lange. Its opposition to the conscription laws made it particularly vulnerable to attack. It was in the Civil War era that Scandinavians in earnest entered party politics, exemplified by Iver Lawson and the Swede John A. Nelson, who in 1864 with a combined German and Swedish Republican vote secured the politically important office of sheriff.[65]

The Dane Henry L. Hertz, son of the Copenhagen police commissioner who had convinced Louis Pio to emigrate, was instrumental in beginning the Danish-language newspaper *Hejmdal* in 1874. He became a leading Republican in Chicago, winning election to important municipal and state posts.[66]

During the 1880s Scandinavians obviously assumed some initiative in political affairs, though perhaps not to a degree commensurate with their potential. Historians have speculated on the causes of a certain political lethargy and pointed to such factors as lack of language facility, antipathy to following a leader, insufficient aggressiveness as office seekers, and a slowness and cautiousness in all relationships. The Irish mastery of these skills, and their racial and religious cohesion, were commented upon with some envy by the Scandinavian immigrant press. The Norwegian-American author Hjalmar Hjorth Boyesen thought that lack of Scandinavian unity rather than a lack of aptitude for public affairs explained the situation, for "the Norwegians and Swedes . . . take as naturally to politics as goslings to water." *Verdens Gang* apparently agreed, stating that "Scandinavian contentiousness, slandering, and jealousy are the main reasons why we have not played the role in city politics that we could and should."[67]

Such criticism was, however, used alongside praise to encourage civic participation. At other times *Verdens Gang* lauded the Scandinavian voters for independence in casting their votes. The political education of the immigrants was conducted in political clubs; these clubs could also promote individual candidacies. There were a number of Republican clubs in Ward 14 in the 1880s, several of them Norwegian or Scandinavian. Politicians like Henry Hertz and S. T. Gundersen were active in these clubs, and such leading men as Ole Birkeland, Kittel Neresen, and Jens Olsen Kaasa found endorsement for political office, though they did not necessarily become their party's candidate. The strong Republican configuration, as has been seen, also included a Socialist element, and Scandinavians in the Democratic party formed similar pressure groups. Returning to the Democrats, Andrew B. Johnson successfully ran for political office in the 1870s on that party's ticket. In 1882 *Verdens Gang* gave its support to a Scandinavian Democratic club, and Peer Strømme, editor of *Norden* until 1890, worked for the Democratic ticket in Chicago, a fact that at times had a chilling effect on some of his compatriots. And a later editor of the same journal, H. O. Oppedale, vigorously advocated the Democratic party. In 1890 Olaf Ray headed the formation of the Scandinavian Jeffersonian Democratic Club to work for the candidacy of Harrison for mayor and John P. Altgeld for governor; both men were popular in liberal circles, Altgeld becoming the first Democratic governor in Illinois after the Civil War. His pardoning of the remaining Haymarket anarchists later branded him as a radical.[68]

In March, 1881, the Scandinavian Republican Club met at Svea Hall to push, though unsuccessfully, the candidacy for city clerk of C.F. Peterson, former editor of *Svenska Tribunen*. A number of notable men spoke, among these the local Republican politician Canute R. Matson, who in 1880 had won election as coroner. He had enjoyed solid support in all the Scandinavian wards and repaid it by appointing the Dane George P. Hansen first deputy, and the Swede Eric Stone clerk, as "he owes the Swedes much gratitude," to quote *Skandinaven*. Matson had emigrated from Voss at age six in 1849. The later so prominent Minnesota politician Knute Nelson, then also six, had come to Chicago the same year. They both grew up in the Norwegian Koshkonong settlement in Wisconsin and together attended Albion Academy, a school started by Seventh-day Baptists.

After establishing his credentials in the Civil War, Matson moved to Chicago in 1868 and made his way in the Republican party. In 1876 he is for instance listed as representing Ward 10 at the Republican county convention. His election as coroner in 1880 was followed by being elected sheriff in 1886. Though accusations by *Den nye Tid* that as coroner he ran the errands of the capitalists by declaring

Sheriff Canute R. Matson.

factory deaths accidental rather than murderous capitalistic abuse
might be unfair, there was no doubt that he was a staunch upholder
of the existing power structure. In his capacity as sheriff he became
involved in the Haymarket proceedings and won wide praise for prohibiting the convicted August Spies from receiving visits from his
fiancée Nina van Zandt, much less marrying her. Finally it was his
duty to arrange for the execution of Spies and the other condemned
men.[69]

Through ward committeemen, or bosses, and the captains of the
several precincts within each ward, the so-called ward heelers, the
major parties built political organizations. The ward bosses chose precinct captains from the predominant ethnic groups in the precincts
and largely from the second generation. Powerful political machines

were thus created. It was within this system that Scandinavians slowly attempted to form cohesive and effective pressure groups to place candidates on the ticket of the major parties. Toward the end of the 1880s the Swedes' numerical strength in state and local politics was evidenced by a multiplication of Swedish Republican clubs. They were mainly naturalization clubs which guided the flood of immigrants to American citizenship as an incidental to becoming good Republicans. Their efforts added energy to the Republican machinery and consequently gave clout to Swedish–American politicians. The many clubs in Chicago were united in a Cook county Swedish Republican League, and in March, 1895, a statewide league was organized, which eventually assumed the name the John Ericsson Republican League of Illinois, thus honoring the inventor of the *Monitor* of naval fame. The Swedish–American press was a major instrument in assembling and wielding might. Swedish power appears, however, to have been destructive to Scandinavian political cooperation. An attempt to have Danes and Norwegians participate in the Cook county organization in March, 1895, faltered, mainly because the latter two groups declined, perhaps fearing that an inevitable Swedish dominance would leave them with little influence. Only in 1909 did a Norwegian Republican club, the Dovre Club, appear for the entire municipality of Chicago. Its program was exclusively political.[70]

The Norwegian–American middle class had many components, as did the working class out of which it had emerged. The latter was not destroyed by the myth of success. In industrial America Norwegians, like other nationalities, sorted themselves out in a variety of social roles, as workers and employers, leaders and followers. In this process the national element was an active part at least until the 1930s.

6

Living in the Second City

The World's Columbian Exposition, the "White City" as the fair was called, opened in Jackson Park on May 1, 1893. It might be seen as a microcosm of the later "city beautiful" movement fathered by the fair's director of works, Daniel H. Burnham, who was responsible for the final appearance of the fairgrounds from landscaping to buildings. The fair represented a Utopian world of glitter and gaiety, a celebration of four centuries of progress, and a demonstration of the limitless possibilities of metropolitan man. Chicago had become the nation's second city in population and had made comparable gains in economic endeavors. Most of the twenty-one million or more who saw the exposition before it closed at the end of October were struck by its grandeur and excitement.[1]

The arrival from Spain on July 7 of replicas of Christopher Columbus's little fleet, the *Santa Maria*, the *Pinta*, and the *Niña*, was one of the highlights. The Spanish caravels were greeted by wild cheering and booming salutes as they were towed to their anchorage. The following week, on July 12, another spectacle again reminded the American public of European discovery. This was the sight of the

• Top: The *Viking* in the Chicago harbor, July 12, 1893.

• Bottom: Captain Magnus Andersen, standing at the rear, and the crew of the *Viking*.

Viking ship the *Viking*, an authentic replica of the famed Gokstad ship from about 900 A.D., which under the command of Captain Magnus Andersen had sailed across the Atlantic, and not been towed as had the Spanish caravels. It was a distinction and an accomplishment not lost on the Norwegian-American community.[2]

On June 14 "the brave Norsemen" — Captain Andersen and his picked crew — had been feted in Newport, Rhode Island. This warm first reception in America was repeated many times as the *Viking* made its way from Newport to New York, through the Hudson River and the Erie Canal, and across the Great Lakes. On July 4th Captain Halvor Michelson, who had braved all kinds of weather on the lakes, met the *Viking* in Cleveland and sailed with it across the lakes. In Milwaukee the inveterate champion of recognition for Norse discovery of America, Rasmus B. Anderson, presented his competing view, claiming that Icelandic might have been the nation's language if the early attempts at Norse settlement had succeeded. The grandest reception was naturally the one in Chicago. Mayor Harrison came on board outside Lincoln Park, and after they had stepped ashore at Van Buren Street the mayor, following a welcome of hurrahs, cannons, and band music, presented the crew the full freedom of Chicago.[3]

The *Viking* then headed for its final destination at Jackson Park. There yet another festive welcome awaited. It was a proud moment in the life of the Norwegian colony in Chicago. Local national committees on arrangements represented many ethnic groups and reflected the cosmopolitan character of Chicago. A Norwegian committee was headed by the lawyer and popular speaker at Norwegian-American affairs Ingolf K. Boyesen. The wealthy businessman Ole A. Thorp was secretary and was also made one of the fair's commissioners by King Oscar II. Other notable Norwegian Americans on the committee were Peter Svanøe, Canute Matson, and the two bankers Helge A. Haugan and Paul Stensland. Proper recognition was thereby assured in all quarters.[4]

Thorp, in 1893 thirty-seven years old, exemplifies the position of prominent ethnic representatives on such occasions as well as an immigrant success story. In an interview in 1890 Thorp related how he had overcome the prejudice suffered because of birth into the lowly cotter class at Eidsberg. Before coming to Chicago in 1880, experience in a wholesale firm in Oslo and a meager capital accumulated at much sacrifice prepared him for a similar venture there. By 1890 he had prospered to the extent of chartering the Norwegian steamship *Wergeland*, which in May of that year transported fish from Norway directly to Chicago and returned with agricultural products. It was, as Thorp proudly announced on his stationery, the first steamship to make the round trip between Europe and the Great Lakes with cargo. His mansion in Wicker Park, where he entertained visiting Norwegian notables, was evidence of his standing in the Chicago com-

Top: A view of the World's Fair north and east from the Liberal Arts
Building and the Manufacturing Building.

Bottom: Norway's pavilion at the World's Fair.

mercial elite. His membership in St. Paul's simultaneously indicated close ties to the immigrant community.[5]

Norway's pavilion at the fair, like the dramatic crossing of the *Viking*, expressed a Norwegian presence through historical recreation. It was modeled on a stave church from the twelfth century, and it became a rendezvous for visiting Norwegians. Norway's day at the fair, May 17, included the dedication of this building and the Norwegian exhibit. There was a colorful procession with E. C. Christensen of Nora Lodge, a wholesale flour dealer, as chief marshal, followed by four bands, units from thirteen Norwegian-American organizations, and carriages carrying dignitaries, which moved to the Festival Hall on the fair grounds for a program of appropriate music and speeches. Throngs of Norwegians from all over the Upper Midwest were in attendance.[6]

The Scandinavian Carpenters' Union and other contingents of workingmen were represented in the parade. But even as they marched, in contrast to the celebration of progress and boisterous ethnic sentiments inside on the fair grounds, the first shock waves of the financial panic of 1893 and a beginning industrial depression were being felt outside. Business failures and bank closings caused a reduction in wages as well as massive unemployment and created a bleak situation for many of Chicago's citizens. The Pullman Strike in May, 1894, threatening the entire nation with social and economic upheaval, was a direct result. A drastic cut in wages by the Pullman Palace Car Company produced the damaging labor conflict and revealed deep social divisions. *Skandinaven* even compared it to the relationship between "master and slave." In 1891 Scandinavians made up about 23 percent, or 1,400 men, of a total work force of 6,000. Only about 150 were Norwegian and 70 Danish, the remainder being Swedish.

The Swedes lived mainly in the model town of Pullman on the western shore of Lake Calumet about twelve miles south of Chicago's business district, a paternalistic experiment by the sleeping-car magnate George Pullman. Like the fair it was another Chicago showpiece. The Swedes lived there in rented homes owned by the company, and thus suffered the intolerable burden of reduced wages but not reduced rent, whereas most Norwegians lived in their own homes in adjacent communities. In June, 1894, *Skandinaven* sent a reporter to Pullman who visited A. Aas, one of the few Norwegians who resided in the town. He paid a monthly rent of $17.71 for a small house with no "modern improvements"; the 71 cents was a water tax. As a wood-carver Aas had earned a daily wage of $3.75, which by stages had been reduced to less than half while the rent to the company had remained unchanged. *Skandinaven*, true to its loyalty to the common laborer, defended the effort to redress grievances through strikes; only the *Chicago Times* of the larger English-language publications expressed a like opinion. The demand of the Pullman workers was in *Skandinaven*'s view merely "to be treated as human beings and to be paid a salary on which they could support themselves and their families." Federal intervention broke the strike during the summer. During the depressed conditions of the 1890s poverty and need reached alarming proportions. Chicago seemed like a "Gray City," which it was quickly dubbed, rather than "White." [7]

**An
Imported
Elite**

The World's Fair attracted talent from abroad, some of it directly engaged in constructing the exposition, and many of those who for one reason or another made the journey to view it remained in Chicago. The social cleavages exposed during the depression were evident also within the Norwegian community and were accentuated by the arrival of immigrants with technical skills. They responded to the shifting needs of the Chicago economy and simultaneously blended with and perhaps partly replaced an established older ethnic leadership. The situation is evident in the membership of the Pioneer Social Club, founded in 1878 with a limited membership of twelve men. The lake captains and prominent merchants who first organized the club were joined by men trained in Norwegian and other European technical institutions. In the context of the immigrant community they were an imported aristocracy. They also formed their own exclusive societies, such as the Arne Garborg Club in November, 1891, a lecture and debate club open to men and women.[8]

The organization the same year in May of the Scandinavian Association of Engineers indicated the growth of this professional group. The migration of skills from Norway, as historian Kenneth O. Bjork described the phenomenon, lasted some fifty years, from about 1880 until the Great Depression. Compared to the total migration, or even to the total movement overseas of technically trained people from Europe as a whole, the Norwegian contribution was of course small. Yet it was a part of a general transfer from the Old to the New World of technical knowledge that had a significant impact on the transformation of America into an industrial giant. Its scope within a national Norwegian context was considerable, and it represented a direct subsidy to American economic growth. As an example, of the 1,290 regular students who graduated from the technical college in Trondheim between 1870 and 1915, no fewer than 27 percent went to America. The Trondheim graduates, calling themselves "Blaalua" (The Blue Cap), had their own society in Chicago, which met at The Tavern, a Norwegian restaurant in Chicago's Loop. The group included graduates of various classes, from 1873 (veterans) to 1911 (greenhorns), according to *Scandia* that year.

A pioneer Norwegian-trained engineer in Chicago was Severin Christian Anker Holth from Oslo, who arrived in 1878. As an engineer at the McCormick Harvester Machinery Company he designed agricultural machines that as the mechanization of farming progressed were used the world over. Many Norwegian engineers, arriving during a period of vigorous development in the steel indus-

A group of Norwegian engineers and businessmen. First row from left: Thomas G. Pihlfeldt, Birger Osland, Isak H. Faleide. Second row from left: Alf Kolflat, J.W. Sinding, J.H. Hille, John O. Batzer, Magnus Gunderson.

Joachim G. Giaver was, as chief structural engineer for the Daniel H. Burnham firm, responsible for the construction of the People's Gas Building on Michigan Avenue in 1911.

try, entered that branch of the economy. One of the first was Julius Aars Dyblie from Alta, who after emigrating in 1879 was for many years chief of the steelworks at Joliet. That same year Leonard Holmboe arrived from Oslo; he spent fifty-one years with the Illinois Steel Company, from 1898 as its chief engineer. Holmboe's technical leadership, illustrative of migrational processes in general, attracted many other Norwegian engineers to Illinois Steel.[9]

The Swiss-trained engineer Karl L. Lehmann, born at Skjolden in inner Sogn, came to Chicago in the late 1880s. He took part in designing the trunnion bascule bridge at Cortland Street, completed in May, 1902. Among Lehmann's gifted disciples was Thomas G. Pihlfeldt, who in a city famous for its bridges established an impressive career in bridge-building, further developing the Chicago-type bascule. Born at Vadsø in 1858 and trained in Norway and in Germany, Pihlfeldt came to Chicago in the fall of 1879. Not until 1894, however, did he find employment in the bridge division of the engineering bureau in Chicago's public works department. But from then on he moved rapidly up, so that in 1901 he was made chief engineer of bridges. He held this position until his death in 1941. During his tenure, which covered the entire era of the development of the Chicago bascule, he supervised the building of no fewer than fifty-five bridges. It was an important chapter in the history of American transportation.[10]

Pihlfeldt's mentor, Lehmann, had served as a structural designer at the World's Fair; his involvement was further evidence of the appeal of the exposition. Richard Mohn from Tønsberg was the most significant Norwegian structural engineer in Chicago, coming there in 1888. Among other buildings for the exposition he worked on structural steel for the fair's Administration Building. Joachim G. Giaver, who won prominence as assistant chief engineer at the fair, and from 1898 as chief structural engineer in Daniel Burnham's architectural firm, was born at Lyngen near Tromsø, emigrated in 1882, and came to Chicago in 1891. He came of a prominent Norwegian family, was tutored at home, and then earned the degree of civil engineer from Trondheim's Technical College. Giaver played an important part in the general development of the modern skyscraper. He was a distinguished and active member of the Norwegian colony.[11]

An early Norwegian architect was Kristian Schneider, who emigrated in 1885 and in Chicago studied under the great architect Louis Sullivan. At the Columbian Exposition he worked on the design of the much discussed golden arch entrance of the Transportation building erected by Sullivan's firm. To many Americans the gilded gateway expressed the crass exploits of the robber barons in the so-called "Gilded Age" in the post-Civil War era. Labor unrest, notably the Pullman Strike, heightened an awareness of its symbolic message. An immigrant professional like Gustav L. Clausen, a graduate from

Jens A. Paasche in the workshop of the company he founded in 1904, the
Jens A. Paasche Airbrush Company.

Trondheim, was another example of Norwegian engineers who found employment in the construction of buildings at the World's Fair. In 1880–1881 he had served as assistant engineer in the building of the model town of Pullman; after the strike it became the foremost reminder of the social injustice perpetrated by great industrialists.[12]

The industrial depression naturally reduced the number of technically trained immigrants until after the turn of the century. Typical of the later arrivals was the architect Christian Ucherman Bagge, who came to Chicago in 1903. There he entered into a long association with the Burnham firm, specializing in perspective drawings, among them the Burnham Chicago Plan of 1909, which had a decisive influence on the growth of Chicago and on city planning throughout the United States. Another influential and productive Norwegian architect with Burnham was Ivar Viehe-Naess, who, coming to Chicago in 1890 at the age of twenty, received his first technical training there. He later studied in France and in 1900 joined the Burnham firm.[13]

Immigrant machinists like Oscar Onsrud also put their mark on industrial developments. Onsrud was the son of a blacksmith in Ullensaker near Oslo. He emigrated in 1893 to see the World's Fair. His rise was more typical of individuals who moved up from the working class than of an imported elite. Finding employment as a machinist, salesman, foreman, and eventually plant superintendent for a Chicago firm, he began his own company in 1912 in the basement of his home. In 1924 he opened his own plant, the Onsrud Machine Works, at 3900 Palmer Street in the Norwegian Logan Square community, and employed seventy-five men. Norwegian engineers found employment in this totally Norwegian operation, and perfected the air-turbine motor, which Onsrud had introduced in 1915. It became renowned as the world's speediest motor. Another precision technique was developed by Jens A. Paasche, who arrived in Chicago from his native Trondheim in 1900. His company, the Paasche Airbrush Company, founded in 1904, improved the airbrush so that the company's equipment became standard for all finishing and coating operations in factories the world over.[14]

These individuals, who in their professional lives moved mainly in American circles, nevertheless entered into ethnic activities and organizations. As an elite within their own nationality, they gained further prominence as hosts for the many Norwegian dignitaries and officials who from the 1880s visited Chicago. The World's Fair was in this respect a gold mine. The Arne Garborg Club entertained a number of noted visitors to the exposition, among them the president of the Storting, Viggo Ullman.

The visit in November, 1897, by the celebrated Norwegian polar explorer Fridtjof Nansen, fresh from his exploits in polar regions, generated not only immense enthusiasm, but sharp competition

●
Top: A family picnic in Chicago in 1893.
●
Bottom: Ole A. Thorp.

among societies and individuals to move in the presence of the great man, and to honor and be honored. The special Norwegian reception committee of seventy-five men identified rather well the immigrant elite whose status on such occasions was enhanced far beyond the Norwegian-American colony. Social and professional aspirations were also aided, and services to the homeland were rewarded with prestigious royal decorations. In 1899 Ole Thorp became the first Norwegian American to be made a knight of the royal order of St. Olaf for his promotion of commerce between Norway and the United States.[15]

Financing the Colony

Intimately associated with the internal workings of the Norwegian-American community were the several immigrant financial institutions. Contrary to the often expressed idea that ethnic banks appeared only with the "new" immigrant groups, evidence as suggested in a previous chapter shows such agencies present much earlier, at least among Scandinavian immigrants. They had generally begun as modest enterprises, selling steamship and railroad tickets, or as real estate and insurance agencies. They provided such basic banking services as making small loans and transmitting money overseas. Immigrants intimidated by large American banks, which might treat them with reluctance and suspicion, sought out these small businesses, which early attained a status in the immigrant community not given any American institution. Some ethnic banks grew strong on accumulated assets from the deposits of their compatriots.

While serving personal ambitions, immigrant bankers financed, not infrequently at a lower rate than American banks, the building of churches, benevolent institutions, and places of business. They were called upon to donate to charitable causes in the immigrant community. At the same time dishonest bankers were in a position to defraud their vulnerable countrymen. Many newcomers lost "their hard-earned savings" when Ferdinand Winslow's Scandinavian National Bank and his West Side Savings Bank on Milwaukee Avenue, both opened after the Great Fire, went bankrupt in the fall of 1872, evidently as a result of fraudulent transactions and speculation by Winslow himself. Winslow's earlier banking activities had been absorbed into his new and short-lived banking firms. Another struggling institution for "Norwegians, Danes, and Swedes," Skow-Petersen, Isberg & Co., offered its banking services from 1873; its owners were the Dane Anton Skow-Petersen and the Swede Axel Isberg, both with banking experience before emigrating. Lack of sufficient capital, a constant problem for immigrant financial institutions and, as rumor would have it, "faithless and deceitful behavior" by the two owners caused its bankruptcy in 1877.

A more successful venture was undertaken in December, 1879, when the private banking firm of Haugan & Lindgren opened its

Paul O. Stensland.

doors. Helge Haugan, the senior partner, was born in Oslo in 1847 and came to Chicago as a young man of sixteen in 1863 after having lived in Canada since 1858. In the 1870s he accumulated capital as a plumbing contractor. His Chicago-born Swedish partner, the twenty-four-year-old John R. Lindgren, had saved money earned as an insurance and ship agent. In its early years their bank on LaSalle and Randolph streets transacted business almost exclusively with Scandinavian customers and functioned as a truly ethnic bank. In 1891 it was incorporated as the State Bank of Chicago, but in the Norwegian community it continued to be referred to as Haugan's Bank.[16]

The active, and in time discredited, banker Paul O. Stensland moved to Chicago just before the Great Fire. In 1880 he established a private bank, engaging mainly in insurance and property sales, which in 1891 became the Milwaukee Avenue State Bank, located on Milwaukee Avenue and Carpenter Street. Stensland had behind him a colorful career as a sailor and cotton dealer in India, and his speculative spirit led him into a multitude of business deals, around 1890 even to ownership of the newspaper *Norden*. He was a respected member of the Norwegian colony and its business community, active in civic and Norwegian-American affairs, and treasurer of Our Savior's Church.

Then on August 6, 1906, his bank closed its doors, and Stensland himself fled the country. The bank had failed because of mismanagement and dishonesty; Stensland was accused of the embezzlement of large amounts of money. Rumor had it that the nearly sixty-year-old widower had squandered fortunes on beautiful women, especially on one Leone Langdon-Key, a former music critic for the *Chicago American*. A five thousand dollar reward brought about Stensland's arrest in October in Tangier, Morocco, where he was hiding. On October 8, only two months after the closing, the Security Bank of Chicago rose on the ruins of the Milwaukee Avenue State Bank. The new name was intended to reassure old and new customers of its solvency, and the bank strove to compensate losses suffered by its depositors, who were, and continued to be, Scandinavian, overwhelmingly Norwegian. Reflecting the changing ethnic composition of the area, many Poles put their money there, a development Stensland had encouraged by hiring Polish employees. An especially popular teller in the Polish community, Frank J. Kowalski, felt so disgraced by the scandal that he committed suicide. Attesting to the vital importance of ethnic banking institutions was the fact that confidence in the bank was restored within a year.[17]

Another profitable bank, this one a joint Swedish, Norwegian, and Danish enterprise, the Union Bank of Chicago, was founded in 1905. It began operations on May 1, at a time when the union between Sweden and Norway was rapidly moving toward dissolution, and the name thus broadcast a message of unity within the Scandinavian-American commercial community. The former treasurer of the Milwaukee Avenue State Bank, Charles E. Schlytern, became president, and Nils Arneson, president of the Central Manufacturing Company, a prominent member of its board. Schlytern had since 1901 operated a real estate, loan, and insurance agency on Milwaukee Avenue, which apparently was his means of accumulating capital for larger ventures. The Union Bank, like the Security Bank and the State Bank, while moving into the general business world of Chicago retained some ethnic ties, reflected in the names of their employees at all levels of their operations, so that "they were well respected among Norwegians in Chicago."[18]

Business enterprise built on an appeal to nationality extended into providing a final resting place for the dead. The pastoral beauty and tranquility of the countryside were recreated in the urban memorial parks. In 1886 "the most beautiful Scandinavian cemetery" was founded on the Northwest Side at North Narragansett Avenue near Irving Park Boulevard, on the outskirts of the city. It took the name Mount Olive and invited people to visit "and admire its lovely paths, tall and stately oak and elm trees and its billowing green lawns." It was organized as a stock company. The enterprising Paul Stensland served as a long-time treasurer; his default in 1906 cut into its profits and his status as a fugitive damaged its reputation. Other prominent men on its board of directors were Ole Stangeland, the major stockholder, S. T. Gunderson, Halvor Michelson, and Charles Schlytern.[19]

The directors were nearly without exception Norwegian, and the cemetery remained Norwegian and to some degree Danish. A special appeal in 1899 to the Swedish community through its Chicago newspapers did little to alter the situation since its location placed it at an inconvenient distance from the major areas of Swedish settlement. It is, however, remarkable how rapidly the Norwegian community responded to the national appeal and purchased lots. Norwegians, like other Chicagoans who did not use the burial ground provided by the city, had been burying their dead at Graceland or Rosehill, especially the former. The burial records of Bethlehem Church showed that of 60 who died in 1886, the year Mount Olive opened, 20 were interred at Graceland and 14 at Mount Olive. Already the following year, however, of the 103 burials from the church 72, or about 70 percent, were at Mount Olive.[20]

Norwegian undertakers bought shares, as did a few Lutheran ministers, though the cemetery corporation mainly consisted of people in commerce. Funeral directors needed the goodwill of the clergy to ply their trade; the congregational minister could influence the place of interment. The earliest Norwegian undertaker, according to the firm itself, was Berent M. Wold, a cabinetmaker who had emigrated on the *Sleipner* from his native Bergen in 1862. Wold opened his funeral business in 1867. The increased demand for such services as the Scandinavian population expanded is evidenced by the regular advertising toward the end of the century by six different Scandinavian funeral homes. The best known was perhaps the one operated by John M. Pedersen, founded in 1898 at Armitage and Nebraska (now Whipple Street); in 1926 it moved to Fullerton Avenue in the Logan Square community. Pedersen was a member of Zion Norwegian Lutheran Church in that district and, according to his obituary, "belonged to more Norwegian societies than anyone else in Chicago." He was a generous benefactor to charitable causes, which by all accounts reflected a true generosity of spirit, but at the same time the contacts he created through his generosity and his social activities represented good business practice.[21]

• *Top left:* This Viking water fountain sculptured out of solid granite by N. Heldt Henriksen stands at the main entrance of Mount Olive Cemetery.

• *Top right:* Monument to Captain Halvor Michelson at Mount Olive Cemetery.

• *Bottom:* Halvor Michelson.

Frequently, however, those who sought burial or other religious functions were not members of any church. In the years between 1910 and 1915, for which statistics are available, the nearly thirty Norwegian Lutheran congregations in Chicago enjoyed a combined membership of less than 8,000. According to the federal census of 1910, the Norwegian-born and their children numbered 47,235, making the Lutheran church membership equal to about 17 percent, and probably even less since the membership statistics included all Norwegian Americans, not only the first and second generations.[22]

The proportion of members decreased from the pioneer period, though it had always been a problem to convince Norwegian immigrants of the need for formal membership. The First Norwegian Evangelical Lutheran Congregation in 1869 even considered, but ultimately rejected, adopting the American practice of renting pews. In this manner all who attended services would contribute to the church. The ministerial report for Trinity Lutheran Church for the year 1884 indicated the important role of the church outside the congregational fold: 43 baptized, of whom 22 were members; 18 confirmed, of whom 9 members; 19 couples married, of whom only 3 couples members; 30 buried, of whom 14 members; last communion to 7, of whom 6 were members. Other Lutheran churches gave similar evidence of a strong commitment to a Lutheran tradition combined with reluctance to assume the responsibility of voluntary membership. It appears to have been a pronounced aspect of urban religious life, though by no means unfamiliar to rural communities.[23]

A detailed analysis of church membership records might have given a more precise idea of who were most likely to seek congregational membership. The Norwegian Lutheran church emerging among impoverished immigrants did not leave out the working class and cannot be claimed to have been an exclusively middle-class institution, yet subjective evidence would suggest that the latter class, ill-defined as it is, and those who aspired to join it, were more likely to fill the immigrant houses of worship than the working class. An incident related by Pastor Amund Mikkelsen from about 1880 even suggests a certain distance between the working class and the church. A woman unknown to him came to the parsonage one day with a baby on her arm to request immediate baptism for her fifth child, which looked quite healthy. She came to Mikkelsen's home to avoid having to find sponsors and other inconveniences. After he had asked the woman if the other four children had been baptized in Norway or in America, the conversation continued as follows:

"Woman: 'The two eldest were baptized at home [Norway], but the two youngest were baptized here.'

"Pastor: 'Were the two baptized in Norway baptized in the home or in the church?'

"Woman: 'Oh, in Norway one had of course to waltz to church

with them otherwise there would be no baptism. The pastor must certainly know how oppressed poor people were in Norway.'

"Pastor: 'What about the other two who were baptized here? Were they also baptized in the church?'

"Woman: 'No, they were baptized in Pastor T's home. He is a decent man who looks out for what is best for the poor. He does not require sponsors and he does not ask if the little kid is a believer, which no one can know. He was not at home today and therefore I came to you. I can't afford to go around and spend so much time.'

"Pastor: 'Do you think that it is a great and important act to baptize your child?'

"Woman: 'Yes, God knows. I only wish to ask the pastor to do it as fast as he can, because I have to get home. Charley (presumably the child's father) will soon be home for dinner and he wants it at the right time.' "[24]

A religious leader might meet the needs of the working-class poor even more dramatically through the congregation's social work. The depression of the 1890s placed heavy demands on this mission. St. Paul's Church placed an alms box at the church entrance. An accounting of the dispensation of the donations and subscriptions received has been preserved in a rare record book. The pastor, who from 1890 to 1898 was I.B. Torrison, or the aid meeting (*hjelpemøde*) paid out the money. Some cases from the record provide a vivid insight. At its meeting on October 29, 1894, it was reported that a Mrs. Fr. Stang had received $10.00 to visit her husband who was sick in St. Paul, Minnesota. On October 23 the pastor had helped Jakob Olsen, an unemployed painter who had seven children, with $6.00. On April 29, 1895, the meeting approved 50 cents as aid to Mrs. Carrie Hanson, who was in poor health, $1.00 to a Mrs. Trosterud whose husband was in the insane asylum, and 25 cents that the pastor had given four times plus a piece of clothing to a young unemployed man, a Mr. Gronbeck. Human tragedy and want are evident and their mitigation would in many instances seem to be beyond the means of the established church.[25]

The Salvation Army, introduced to America from England in the 1880s, adapted the moral and social values of American Protestantism to the urban immigrant population. Its program of aid to the needy and salvation of the soul adjusted to the environment it encountered. A Scandinavian Department was organized in Brooklyn in 1887, at about the same time as the Salvation Army established itself in the Nordic homelands. Emigrating Salvationists became leaders in America. The Swedes dominated the mission among Scandinavian Americans. In such centers as Brooklyn, Minneapolis, and Chicago there were separate Norwegian and Danish corps alongside Swedish and mixed Scandinavian ones. The Scandinavian mother corps in Chicago was the Swedish no. 13 organized in 1891 on the near North

Side. A purely Norwegian corps had its beginning in 1896 on Grand Avenue, and in 1905 an outpost in Humboldt Park was opened by Ensign Maria Edahl, who was trained in Norway. She had joined her six brothers and sisters in Chicago in 1903. This outpost absorbed the initial corps, becoming Humboldt Park Corps no. 15, and located its temple at Wabansia and California. A small Danish corps met at North Avenue and Pulaski Road. Ensign Edahl in 1906 married Colonel Tom Gabrielsen, a major leader in the Scandinavian work in America. He had come to America from Mandal in 1892 as a child of eight. The predominance of the Swedes in the Army in America apparently caused Gabrielsen to abandon the Norwegian language in favor of Swedish in which he became so fluent that "one would think he had come from Sweden rather than Norway."[26]

Some ninety-four Scandinavian corps existed at one time from coast to coast in the large cities of America. Successful Scandinavian businessmen, as well as prosperous Americans, convinced by the Army's social work and fiery brand of evangelism, were major benefactors. An example from a somewhat later period is Gabriel Skrudland, a member of the mixed Scandinavian corps at Irving Park, who contributed generously of money earned from his successful mail order photo business. With their street-corner meetings the Scandinavian corps added to the Nordic flavor of their neighborhoods. A unique Scandinavian contribution appears to have been the string band, but like American corps they also had brass bands. The Norwegian corps no. 15 regularly played in May 17th parades and was thus a visible part of the community which it served.[27]

The established Norwegian Lutheran churches viewed the activities of the Salvation Army with some caution. They felt directly threatened by the many secular charitable efforts that existed. These might easily remove people from Lutheran influence and religious life as a whole. In direct response to their appeal, which would bring "church people into contact with all classes of people and faiths," a number of Lutheran congregations competed by forming their own mutual assistance programs. This is remarkable during a time when most religious leaders viewed insurance as evidence of a lack of faith in God to provide for temporal needs. Trinity, Bethlehem, and Our Savior's churches all operated independent mutual assistance societies within their congregations. On September 10, 1883, the First Norwegian Lutheran Evangelical Congregation formed a similar society which was expanded to become the Norwegian Evangelical Lutheran Sick and Benefit Society of Chicago, open to confirmed Lutherans from all congregations between the ages of 16 and 50. Members received $5.00 weekly as sick benefit and $70 in death benefits. Human needs obviously required a measure of compromise of established principles and theological positions and dictated a pragmatic solution that transcended synodical lines. The Society's chairman,

Pastor Daniel Kvaase, in 1889 strongly encouraged fellow Lutherans to join a society operated in "a Christian spirit." It was one way in which the church met the challenge of the city and made an effort to satisfy the need of its members to protect themselves in a self-reliant manner from the consequences of unemployment and sickness.[28]

But these efforts excluded nominally Lutheran immigrants who only on occasion were brought within the influence of the church, as congregational membership was a prerequisite. Neither did the church invest its scarce resources in recreational facilities or in forming neighborhood clubs. The Sunday school was the one visible instrument at its disposal by which to interact with the neighborhood and gain converts. Congregational youth groups, men's clubs, ladies aid, and church choirs satisfied social needs, to be sure, as did the regular congregational and Sunday school summer outings, but they were mainly a means of edification and a way to secure support for the church. Even the Scandinavian Young Men's Christian Association, with its own building, library, and employment services, as well as its openness to youth not formally members of a Lutheran congregation, was nevertheless parochial and evangelical in its emphasis.[29]

The Settlement House

The settlement house movement on the other hand approached the immigrant neighborhoods on their own terms. But it did so as an outsider and not as an institution emerging from the ethnic community itself. Its program included moral uplift and traditional morality; it was, however, sensitive to the positive qualities of the working classes. The Chicago Commons was a social settlement founded in 1894 by Graham Taylor, a Congregational minister, on the West Side; from 1901 it was located on Grand Avenue and Morgan Street. Like Hull House, which Jane Addams had organized in 1889 some distance farther south, it was intended as a neighborhood social club with a variety of activities for every age.

Growing up close to the Chicago Commons Elmer Abrahamson described it as "the lighthouse of the neighborhood." Its array of boys' clubs, games, plays, Sunday afternoon programs, and summer camps introduced positive activities. Cultural tensions caused by the changing ethnic composition from Norwegian, German, and Irish to Italian and Polish were eased by these circumstances. Victor Lawson, being the friend of moral reform and Americanization that he was, early supported Chicago Commons, which Graham Taylor envisioned as a community center for all residents in the neighborhood, regardless of ethnic, religious, and class background. Cooperation within the framework of the settlement was, for instance, evidenced in the women's adult clubs. An official report from as recently as 1919 listed Norwegian together with Irish, Polish, Italian, and American women in the Chicago Commons mothers' club and in the rug-making club. The ethnic neighborhood succession was, however, suggested by the

Top: The ladies aid at St. Paul's Church.

Bottom: Norwegian boy scouts at Chicago Commons. These boys belonged to Our Savior's Church and attended Sunday school there.

fact that at that time only Italian and Polish women were enrolled in the English class and a special Italian mothers' club had been formed.[30]

In 1899 the Association Home of Chicago was established on West North Avenue, where Norwegians then were settling in numbers. It originated as a "gospel settlement" adapted to women and children. The many young women who worked in the numerous factories, tailor-shops, stores, and laundries in the neighborhood found a place there for social life. By 1905 it was located in its own building at 2150 West North Avenue, and included "boys, young men, and adults." Judge Oscar Torrison sat on its board of directors. In the manner of other settlements its activities were organized around a large number of clubs; it also conducted many classes in such subjects as dressmaking, manual training, and English literature, operated a day care center and a playground, and made available a gymnasium. Its young resident workers carried a religious message to the shops and factories in the area by offering devotional services over the lunch hour to, as they reported, "Scandinavian, German, and Polish, Bohemian, Italian, and Jewish workers."[31]

The work of the settlements was thus clearly an outside element in the life of the immigrants. The settlement staff, however, respected different skills and cultural heritages and introduced progressive reforms into the immigrant communities. Social services otherwise missing might be compensated for by the work of the settlements.

Mutual Assistance

The uncertainties of the urban environment produced a flourishing of mutual aid societies; their connection to the American fraternal movement is obvious. Norwegian members of Court Greeley of the Independent Order of Foresters of Illinois, a fraternal insurance company, met on October 6, 1888, to form a Norwegian-speaking sublodge which took the name Court Normania No. 174. In 1899 this lodge was formally dissolved, and then reconstituted as Tent Normania No. 264 of the Detroit-headquartered order Knights of the Maccabees of the World, which also sold insurance and offered sick benefits, relief for indigent members, and care for the aged. Another Scandinavian lodge, Humboldt Tent No. 26, had been admitted to the same order in 1892 and grew quickly to 500 members, among them Olaf Ray. National sublodges in American orders moved the immigrants into the fraternal movement.[32]

There were also the separate ethnic orders. Nora Lodge No. 1 of the Order of the Knights of the White Cross, "old Nora Lodge" as it was referred to, persisted as a leading secular organization among Norwegians in Chicago. The supreme lodge of the order had in 1881 relinquished its Norwegian membership qualifications and invited Swedes, Danes, and Icelanders to form national or mixed Scandinavian sublodges. From 1886 it operated as a mutual insurance company and moved its headquarters to Milwaukee; its program emulated the

Knights of the Maccabees, and like it from 1911 it introduced women's lodges. Eventually the Knights of the White Cross produced thirty-five men's lodges, and six women's lodges. People too old to become insured, above the age of fifty, were admitted as social members.

The many lodges provided rewarding outlets for social impulses. Nora Lodge made Captain Magnus Andersen and his crew honorary members and served as their host during their stay at the World's Fair. In 1911 it joined the other Chicago lodges, Leif Erikson, the largest, Tordenskjold, and Dovre, in building a common clubhouse at 1733 North Kedvale Avenue, a few blocks west of Pulaski Road. Appropriately it was referred to as Ridderhallen (The Hall of the Knights).[33]

The Dovre Lodge No. 18, taking the name of the mountain by which the constitutional assembly at Eidsvoll in 1814 had sworn solidarity and allegiance, was organized on September 21, 1895. This was the same year the Sons of Norway had its modest beginning in Minneapolis, where it adopted the Eidsvoll motto of "enig og tro til Dovre faller," "united and faithful until Dovre falls." The Dovre Lodge was intended to assemble the many members of Nora Lodge who had moved from the Milwaukee Avenue neighborhood and settled near Humboldt Park. Its preserved minutes record visits to ailing brothers, attendance at funerals, special assessments, criticism of delinquent members, and the initiation of new ones. Its committee on entertainment assumed the name Dovre-Gubben, the troll king of the mountain. Its *lutefisk* banquet, suggested by Brother Christian Johnson in January, 1896, won special favor with the brothers. The women's lodge Aftenstjernen (The Evening Star) No. 4 was organized in June, 1912, with 109 charter members, by the *erkedrott* (arch monarch) Carl Knudsen. It was the largest of the three women's lodges in Chicago. The dignified burial ritual with the sisters wearing long white dresses was one of its more striking ceremonies.[34]

The introduction of women's lodges into fraternal orders, in addition to the usual women's auxiliaries of most men's organizations, manifested the greater independence for women and also the increased leisure time of middle-class married women, who appear to have taken the initiative for separate women's lodges. An earlier organization had united women of more modest means. The First Scandinavian Women's Burial Society of Chicago (Den første skandinaviske kvindelige Begravelses-Forening) had been organized as early as February 12, 1879. Mrs. Christina Christophersen, most active in its formation, consciously set the terms of membership so that any woman, regardless of income, could afford to join. It appealed strongly to the many single women working in domestic service. The weekly dues were set at two cents, making people refer humorously to the society as "to-centen," "the two cent." It consisted mainly of

Top: Ridderhallen—the clubhouse of the Knights of the White Cross at
1733 N. Kedvale Avenue.

Bottom: Members of the Evening Star Lodge wearing their traditional
white dresses.

Norwegian women and gave mutual aid and loans, and guaranteed a respectable burial, the latter, as stated in its bylaws, being the society's major purpose. In 1898 the amount paid was $150 to cover funeral expenses, and "two wagons for the Society's officers who ought to attend dressed in black, and $5 for flowers to be placed on the deceased's coffin." In 1906 the membership stood at 700.[35]

The Scandinavian Workers Association showed renewed vitality as it gained popularity with newcomers and attracted a young leadership. In 1886 when it expanded into offering insurance, it had about 600 members, and began organizing branches in Illinois and Wisconsin. The Scandinavian Women's Society "Thora" was organized on October 9, 1884, by a committee from the Scandinavian Workers Association headed by John Blackstad, a tailor. His wife Olivia was Thora's first president, typifying the process whereby such women's groups emerged. The Workers Association as it expanded lost much of its initial middle-class paternalism. On March 12, 1891, Norwegian Chicago experienced the opening of the fraternity's own building, Scandia Hall, at the corner of Milwaukee Avenue and Ohio Street. *Skandinaven* claimed that the entire Scandinavian colony attended. The versatile and talented Emil Biørn composed a special "Scandia Fest-March" for the occasion.[36]

Scandia Hall was for some time an important social and cultural center, used for theater performances and lodge meetings, and had its own restaurant. But it soon became a victim of the bad times as well as of inner dissent and mismanagement. Indicative of the situation was the withdrawal in 1893 of the S.W.A. branch in Eau Claire, Norden No. 8, founded in 1889. Norden organized the Independent Scandinavian Workers Association and operated as a mutual insurance company with branches throughout the states of the Upper Midwest.[37]

In Chicago the Norwegian Sick Benefit Society "Nordlyset" (Den norske Sygeforening "Nordlyset"), which had been organized on January 22, 1893, as Nordlyset, Branch No. 10 of S.W.A., also withdrew. On July 25, 1895, it organized independently and functioned until it was dissolved on January 1, 1944. Its severance from S.W.A. came in August 1894; until it became independent it was affiliated with another short-lived group, the United Scandinavians of America. Stormy debates and bitter accusations accompanied these moves. A national bias is also clear as immigrant Scandinavianism became a victim of the accelerating tensions between Norway and Sweden. Nordlyset's constitution admitted to membership only men of Norwegian birth or descent who could speak the Norwegian language and were "healthy in body and soul, and did not engage in unseemly business."[38]

The members were solid workers, men in their twenties and thirties, and mostly skilled. Some of the leaders after 1895 were men like Olai Hoitomt, fireman, Jens Hoitomt, pianomaker, Hjalmar M. Fossum, carpenter, and Olaf Oppedale, factory worker. The first death did not occur until August, 1902, when Henry Johnson died at the hospital for the insane at Kankakee after a long illness. The brothers had been regular visitors and had extended extra benefits, and at his funeral and interment at Mount Olive they served as pall-bearers. His widow received $47 in death benefits. Nordlyset's charter was draped in black for a period of three months and a eulogy of the departed brother was inserted in Norwegian-American newspapers. The Society basically functioned in the manner of an extended family to comfort and assist.[39]

The substantial number of burial and mutual aid societies and independent orders that came into being inside as well as outside the Norwegian community were initiated by a few individuals. Their spread, historians have suggested, was evidence of the difficulty for ordinary workers to get life and health insurance. Another example was Nordfælles Supreme Lodge, which had its beginning with five men who met in the home of Andreas Arnesen on Grand Avenue (Indiana Street) in January, 1885. The next month it received its state charter and in May permission to establish sublodges. It remained, however, a local Chicago society.[40]

Into the active organizational life of Chicago the Sons of Norway entered in 1909. Its headquarters in what by then must be considered the new "Norwegian-American capital," Minneapolis, gave it strength. During the decade 1905 to 1914 the fraternal order became a nationwide organization. In Chicago, although several efforts to organize regional fraternal organizations were foundering, the Order of the Knights of the White Cross was moving forward, and the Minneapolis order hesitated to compete.[41]

The initiative that resulted in the formation of the Bjørnstjerne Bjørnson Lodge No. 97 of the Sons of Norway on November 29, 1909, came from Minneapolis members who moved to Chicago. It was also eagerly promoted by such liberals as Olaf Ray, Dr. Andrew Doe, and the lawyer Lasse C. Grundeland, who was associated with Skandinaven. The first president of the new lodge was A. Abrahamsen, who from 1911 directed the employment office of the union of Norwegian-American societies, the Norwegian National League. Repeating the Minneapolis pattern, B.B. Lodge, as it became known, attracted a membership of ordinary workers and frequently a leadership of liberal urban professionals. The latter infused cultural interests and a humanistic spirit into the lodge. Masonic practices with passwords and elaborate rituals added to its appeal.[42]

The Sons of Norway was the result of a grassroots movement among workers in the hard 1890s; the idea had probably come from the Independent Scandinavian Workers Association in Eau Claire. Its arrival in Chicago made Skandinaven declare that "the great order is invading the territory of the Knights." The latter order, of course, had emerged among a more prosperous class of Norwegians. One might speculate that the divergent social origins of the two orders was a factor in the failed attempt by officials of the Sons of Norway to consolidate its lodges with those of the Knights of the White Cross. Instead a second Sons of Norway lodge, Skjold No. 100, was organized in Evanston the following year. And it was only natural that the Sons of Norway's sister organization, the Daughters of Norway, founded in 1897, should shortly follow. In September, 1910, two women's lodges, Anna Kolbjørnsdatter No. 36 and Camilla Collett No. 37, were organized. The strength of fraternalism gave a base for urban Norwegian Americans outside the framework of the churches.[43]

Benevolent Institutions

Those who for some reason, such as poverty, old age, or illness, were unable to care for themselves were beyond the reach of mutual aid societies. They were instead dependent on charitable organizations and the gratuitous help of public and private institutions. The stream of immigrants passing through Chicago called for benevolent measures as well, and protection against the persistent "runner" business and numerous confidence men. Peter M. Balken, who at age twelve in 1849 had emigrated from Stavanger, and was thus a member of the pioneer generation, took the initiative in 1879 to organize the Norwegian Old Settlers Society of Chicago. Its benevolent purpose was "to help needy countrymen in winter and poor immigrants in summer." At well attended annual picnics, much like the later *bygdelag* (old home societies), it gathered old timers and others. The proceeds of the gatherings supported its goals. The requirement for being "an old settler" was set at fifteen years residence. The Norwegian Old Settlers Society paralleled, and perhaps imitated, the social activities of the exclusive Calumet Club, organized the previous year, whose annual old settlers' receptions became a feature of Chicago's social life. Its sole Norwegian member appears to have been Andrew Nelson (Brekke).

In May, 1881, another Scandinavian Emigrant Relief Society, with Ole Stangeland as president, was formed, which appealed for support "to come to the assistance of poor Scandinavian immigrants." It appointed a special agent to meet Scandinavian immigrants, identified with a star on his jacket marked "Special Police, S.E.R. Society." And on November 30, 1886, the Norwegian Relief Association, or "Reliefen" as it was dubbed, was organized to render temporary aid through subscriptions to Scandinavians in distress.[44]

It was of course the well-to-do who could best assume responsibility for social assistance. Women from this level of the immigrant community played an important role, evidenced in the work of the Norwegian Women's Society for Clothing Poor Children (Den norske Kvindeforening til fattige Børns Beklædning), which in December, 1889, gave a glowing report of its accomplishments. The thirty or so women who in this manner displayed a social consciousness were identified as the wives of I.T. Relling, bookstore owner and newspaperman, Peter Svanøe, Swedish and Norwegian consul, Paul O. Stensland, banker, and S. Chr. Bryhn, on *Skandinaven*'s editorial staff, and as wives of other prominent men in the Norwegian community. Many of these men were active members of "Reliefen."[45]

The city physician's responsibility was to provide public assistance to the indigent ill. Dr. Niles Quales, who held that position for a number of years, here confronted the needs of Chicago directly. The county hospital for the poor in Cook county, which also functioned as a poor farm, was from 1855 located at Dunning in Norwood Park twelve miles northwest of downtown Chicago. In 1910 the infirmary, the poor farm, and a consumptive hospital were relocated at Oak Forest south of Chicago. Their records are moving social documents. The aged destitute are the most numerous among the inmates and patients of these institutions, with an overwhelming percentage of men, perhaps suggesting that women were more commonly cared for at home. Grown children may have been more willing to care for their old mothers than their old fathers, according to a director. And perhaps elderly women living alone were more reluctant than men to move into an institution, and likely better able to care for themselves. The many notices in the immigrant press of needy widows and other destitute elderly women living alone would tend to support such an assumption. Death records from Dunning, preserved from 1882, list many Scandinavian names, as do the more complete ones from Oak Forest. Paupers were buried on the hospital grounds. The following is a representative entry for inmates at the poor farm: "George J. Hanson, Lutheran, sixty-eight years old, white male, Norway, carpenter, 14th Street and Ashland, admitted Dec. 1, 1910, died 1915 [added later], thirty-nine years in county."[46]

Norwegian-American organizations and churches sent delegations and gifts to the unfortunate of their own nationality who were on public aid. A common nationality compelled them to act. And within the general framework of the strong charity organization movement, which had its heyday during the last quarter of the century, they established institutions to care for their own. In several issues beginning with October, 1885, *Skandinaven* presented the public and private benevolent institutions in the city of Chicago—from orphan asylums to hospitals and programs for the aged. These could serve as inspiration and as models. *Skandinaven* itself, in common with other immigrant journals, brought individual needs to the attention of its readers. As an example, in 1897 the newspaper described in great detail the dire need in which an aging couple, Aksel and Agathe Vingaard on North Ada Street, found themselves, with no means of subsistence; in later issues gifts were acknowledged and a letter from the grateful couple printed.[47]

Institutions evolved from the social service role of the churches. The immediate needs following the Panic of 1893 produced appeals for help signed by the Norwegian Lutheran pastors of Chicago, and Trinity opened its basement to unemployed men with no place to stay. Charitable efforts were not immune to the religious and other tensions that existed within the immigrant community, but they were nevertheless able to gain its general support. Several of the major undertakings claimed a common origin in the Norwegian Lutheran Tabitha Society (Den norsk lutherske Tabitha Forening). It was founded on November 3, 1885, by twenty-two women. They had been inspired to act by a sermon given at Bethlehem Church by A. Mortensen, a Norwegian seamen's mission pastor in Brooklyn, who during the month of October had preached in several Chicago churches. In his sermons he emphasized the role of the woman diaconate in caring for the sick. In Brooklyn Pastor Mortensen had witnessed the achievements of Sister Elizabeth Fedde of the Deaconess Home in Oslo. In 1883 she had come to Brooklyn as the first Norwegian deaconess in America in response to a call for service to seamen and immigrants and two years later had started a Lutheran deaconess home and hospital there.[48]

The Tabitha Society when it was organized had an identical goal for Chicago. Leading members of the Norwegian community, men like Ole Stangeland and Paul Stensland, Pastor Ole Juul of Our Savior's, and Pastor C.O. Brohaugh of Trinity, had in November, 1886, at the same time as some of them had taken part in the formation of the Norwegian Relief Association, organized the Norwegian Benevolent Society (Det norske Velgjørenheds-Selskab) to work for a Norwegian orphanage. In 1888, when the Tabitha Society was incorporated these men formed its board, the two societies obviously having merged. No woman was elected.[49]

The original founders, all women, seeing their work to build and maintain a deaconess home and hospital lose ground to those who wished a hospital without deaconesses as well as a children's home, departed and organized the Original Norwegian Lutheran Tabitha Society. The other group which retained the corporate name, then, in 1890, made an impassioned appeal to the civic and ethnic consciousness of wealthy Norwegian Americans: "it is astonishing that there has not yet been a Norwegian hospital established in Chicago, where there are so many helpless, sick, and poor countrymen, who struggle and toil in this world, and who sooner or later must resort to the public hospitals or else die in the street."[50]

Six of the eight directors of the seceding "original" Tabitha were women, though the chairman was Pastor N.C. Brun of Bethlehem Church. This congregation then belonged to the United Lutheran Church, formed in June, 1890, of three groups: the Anti-Missourians—who had left the Norwegian Synod over the predestination controversy, the Norwegian Augustana, and the Conference. Under Pastor Brun's guidance a two-story house on Humboldt Street was secured in 1891 by the deaconesses for a home and a hospital. Three sisters were engaged from the deaconess work in Minneapolis and by the end of November, 1892, fifty-three patients had been cared for.[51]

These initial efforts in all their detail provide an insight into the many conflicts and splits which occurred as a consequence of the absence of a central authority in the immigrant world, as well as into the problems caused by limited resources. The latter circumstance overcame differences, at least for a while; the two societies agreed to dissolve and form a new organization to be known by its original name, the Norwegian Lutheran Tabitha Society. Following the destruction by fire of the building on Humboldt Street in August, 1893, these reunited forces were able to raise a considerable amount of money. The cause gained broad support. On June 3, 1894, the cornerstone was laid for a hospital building at Francisco Avenue and Thomas Street by Humboldt Park, and in October the next year the Norwegian Lutheran Tabitha Hospital was formally opened. During the building of the hospital the friends of the deaconess movement felt that their cause had again been defeated and a final split occurred, with various factions reconstituting themselves in new societies.[52]

The Lutheran emphasis of the major institutional benevolences alienated Norwegians outside formal church affiliation or in other denominations, causing one who signed himself "A Non-Lutheran" to declare: "make the organizations Norwegian and not Norwegian-Lutheran." That a broader appeal might be productive was apparent in the strife between the two hospital factions in the Tabitha Society. It had a strong synodical basis. It was a struggle for control between the United Church, which favored the deaconess movement, and the Norwegian Synod. The latter advocated a national rather than a religious hospital and the cornerstone of the hospital had been laid in the name of the Norwegian-American people, not God, as the losing faction that withdrew wanted.[53]

In 1910, under the presidency of Dr. Marie Olsen, the Norwegian Lutheran Tabitha Hospital became a non-sectarian institution, dropping the adjective Lutheran. Bazaars, lawn parties, other fund-raising efforts, donations, and a network of support groups secured its operation and expansion. Growth was especially noteworthy after World War I, when its name was changed to the Norwegian-American Hospital. The Norwegian-American community apparently responded well to its broadly secular and ethnic appeal. Its revised constitution of 1929 still excluded non-Norwegians, with exceptions for those related by marriage, from full membership in the association that operated the hospital.[54]

Those committed to the diaconate in 1896, the year after they had left the Tabitha Society, formed a new organization to realize

- *Top:* A group of deaconesses at the Lutheran Deaconess Home and Hospital. Sister Ingeborg Sponland is seated in the middle of the front row.

- *Bottom left:* The horsedrawn ambulance of the Deaconess Hospital.

- *Bottom right:* The Norwegian Lutheran Deaconess Hospital at Artesian Avenue and LeMoyne Street.

their wish to establish a deaconess home and hospital. Unlike the philosophy behind the Norwegian-American Hospital the deaconess cause was an integral part of an expanded congregational work of the church, which was held to be especially suitable for women. The first Norwegian parish deaconess in Chicago was Sister Caroline Williams from Kristiansand in the Bethlehem Church. In his moralistic novel *When Jesus Enters the Home* (1927), J.L. Kildahl, pastor there from 1889 until 1899, depicted her ministrations, and in the usual manner of such literature showed how her work brought a family made destitute by weakness for beer back to sobriety, prosperity, and church membership. Kildahl was a force in the cause. On May 22, 1897, the Lutheran Deaconess Home and Hospital opened in two small rented buildings on the corner of Artesian Avenue and LeMoyne Street with twenty-five hospital beds. It had the support of men like Andrew P. Johnson and Dr. Niles Quales, who was a leading force in several projects. He served on the medical staff of the deaconess hospital while he also sat on the board of the Norwegian-American Hospital.[55]

The second published report of the Deaconess Home and Hospital, covering the period October 1, 1898, to October 1, 1899, showed that 162 patients had been treated. Of these only 61 had paid the full weekly rate of $7.00; the others were partly or fully charity patients. Care for the impoverished was a constant concern, even though many Norwegians were still being treated free at public institutions. Patients were frequently referred to the hospital by Lutheran ministers. A report dated May 1, 1905, recorded that since October 1, 1903, 611 patients had been treated. It noted their nationality, showing that 502 had been Norwegian, Danish, or Swedish, the Norwegians accounting for 397. Both hospitals, the Deaconess and the Norwegian-American, were thus clearly ethnic. The motherhouse and hospital of the diaconate had by then moved to the corner of Haddon Avenue and Leavitt Street and deeded its property to the United Church. Institutional affiliation gave security.[56]

One of the active members of the original Tabitha Society was Sophie Michaelsen from near Stavanger. There she had taught in an orphan asylum before she moved to Chicago in 1880 together with her husband Christian, a sea captain. She belonged to the faction favoring the orphanage cause, which had deep roots in the Norwegian-American community. At his death in 1883 the pioneer pastor Elling Eielsen, who settled in Chicago in 1872, had left his home on the corner of Paulina and Erie streets for a children's home. The will stipulated, however, that it should be operated jointly by all the Norwegian Lutheran denominations in Chicago, perhaps evidence of a wish for a legacy of harmony by a man whose life had been filled with strife. The gift was prompted by the loss of his eldest son, Elias, in an accident. The Norwegian Benevolent Society of 1886 appears to have been an effort to fulfill the requirements of the will. Pas-

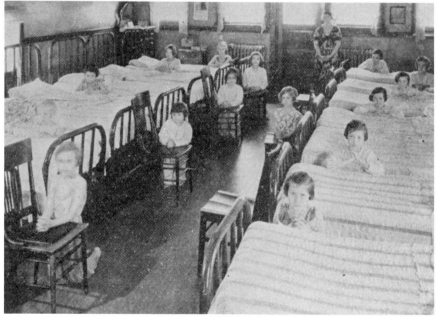

Top: Sophie Michaelsen.

Bottom: Children at evening prayer at the Norwegian Lutheran Children's Home. Strict Christian discipline was the rule.

tor C.O. Brohaugh of the Hauge's Synod Trinity Church, which traced its origin back to Eielsen's pioneer lay activity, played a major role. But no record exists to determine the disposition of these funds.

Sophie Michaelsen, in any case, on January 14, 1892, started a club she called the Little Shepherds Club (De smaa Hyrders Forening), intending it to be only the first of many, for the purpose of building and operating an orphanage for poor and neglected children. The involvement of Pastor John Hetland of the United Church in the project shows the forceful mission of that church body among urban Norwegians. In the broad church tradition it evinced openness to change and compromise, emphasizing Lutheran similarities rather than differences, and thus won the support of Norwegian newcomers who were puzzled by the tradition of Lutheran disharmony in the immigrant commmunity. The Norwegian Lutheran Children's Home Society, formed on September 21, 1896, after the disruption in the Tabitha Society, led on June 18, 1899, to the dedication by Pastor Kildahl of a building bought on Irving Park Boulevard as a home for children.[57]

Ten children moved into the Norwegian Lutheran Children's Home at its opening; by 1915 it accommodated about ninety residents. The published report for 1924 gives information on the nationality and age of the children. Of a total of 127 children cared for that year fifty were Norwegian-born and twenty-nine had at least one Norwegian-born parent. Seventy-five of the children were below the age of five. Indicating the varied callings of a deaconess, Sister Caroline Williams served as matron from 1907 to 1914. Support of an orphanage, as it involved the welfare of children, easily crossed confessional boundaries. When the home was damaged by fire in late December, 1907, one of the first to pledge aid was Pastor Frederick Ring of the First and Immanuel Norwegian Methodist Church. "We as Methodists," Pastor Ring declared, "will do everything we can to assist in the rebuilding of this splendid home, which first and foremost is Norwegian." While such assistance was much welcomed, the pious group operating the children's home in 1908 renounced the "tainted" money willed it by the infamous Norwegian mass murderess Belle Gunness, then presumed to have perished in a fire that destroyed her substantial residence in La Porte, Indiana.[58]

The old building of the children's home was quickly repaired and again occupied, but it was replaced in 1910 by new and larger facilities built on lots purchased in Edison Park. The Norwegian Lutheran Children's Home was a response to specific needs within the immigrant community. In its published reports there are regular complaints about "careless and dissipated parents" and "neglected and abused children." Many children entered through the juvenile court, others came to the home through a congregation, were brought in by a mission worker, or were admitted after private application. In the harsh environment of the city the loss of a spouse, unemployment, or other adversity led to children being placed in the home for longer or shorter periods of time. Orphaned children and those given up by an unwed mother constituted another category. On January 1, 1925, there were eighty-six children, of whom twelve were classified as "full orphans," thirty-six were "half orphans," and the largest number, thirty-eight, had both parents living. Interviews with former residents convey a lack of affection and warmth on one hand and a strict religious discipline on the other. Some children were placed in adoption, as the matron reported in 1922: "A little boy, George, eleven years old, who had lived with us since he was a baby, was adopted by a good Christian family in Wisconsin."[59]

Temporary foster care or adoption would, in the opinion of many, give dependent and neglected children the care and love found in a "normal home," to quote the *Home Finding News*. In order to find substitute parents on this basis, Pastor John R. Birkelund of the Norwegian Synod, struck by the inadequate resources to care for Lutheran children, helped to form the Lutheran Home Finding Society in December, 1905. Its 1913 report showed that the Society that year had cared for thirty children: half were still living in the receiving home it had bought in 1907, and the rest had been placed in private homes or returned to their parents or other relatives. Three of the children had been adopted, in one case "the mother not having visited the child for nearly two years."[60]

The aged presented a different set of problems. In 1915, reporting on its deaconess work, the United Church described its Erie Street Mission on the West Side as being located in a slum. "Formerly this was the great center of our Norwegian population in Chicago," the report stated. The destitute old, whether trapped in such a blighted area or living in neighborhoods heavily inhabited by fellow Norwegians, required the compassion and aid of the community. They were people like Gina Johansen on West Ohio Street and Anna Hansen who lived in a garret near Kinzie Street; both were widows and unable to care for themselves.[61]

A major effort to meet the problem emanated from Bethlehem Church, spearheaded by Hildur Baade. She had come to Chicago from Stavanger in 1892 at the age of seventeen and had become concerned with the welfare of the old and poor, "especially those of Norwegian origin, whom there were so many of in Chicago." According to Baade's own account, her work led to the formation of the Norwegian Lutheran Bethesda Home Association on January 13, 1907, at a meeting in the home of her parents. Its purpose was "to show Christian charity among the Norwegian people" by operating a home "for the old and needy, with free housing, light and heat." In July, 1911, the first home opened with nineteen residents, on Haddon Avenue near the Deaconess Home and Hospital. A new Bethesda Home accommodating seventy-five residents was ready in 1925 at 2833 Nordica Avenue. None but the destitute could be admitted. Entries like the one about the death of Anna Geratine Strom suggest the role of the institution. "She came to the home two years ago," the matron reported, "arthritic and helpless, and with true Christian patience she bore her pain in gratitude toward God and her fellowmen for the home and care she had in her crippled condition."[62]

The Norwegian Old People's Home Society, one of the splinter groups from the Tabitha Society, had operated the Norwood Park Home "according to the principles of the Lutheran Church," since June, 1896, "for deserving indigents and for such other aged persons who are able and willing to pay for a good Christian home." Unlike the Bethesda Home it was thus not a wholly charitable institution. Nevertheless, funds had to be raised for its operation. The Norwegian Old People's Home Society had supporting branch organizations in five Lutheran congregations of Hauge's Synod and the United Church, the latter assuming the main responsibility. Prominent businessmen Helge Haugan and Ole Thorp spoke at the dedication of the home; their presence illustrated a general appeal to the entire Norwegian-American community for aid. Dr. Quales gave initiative, leadership, and recognition also to this care institution. He explained that the Norwood Park Home was intended for the class of persons who had insufficient funds to sustain them through old age, but yet were not paupers, so they could not enter the poorhouse at Oak Forest. "We have admitted old men and old women into the Home," Quales wrote. "We have taken their last dollar and we have agreed to provide for them for the balance of their lives, and to give them a Christian burial."[63]

One Swedish-born and sixteen Norwegian-born persons moved into the home in 1896, a three-story building on property purchased at Norwood Park. Expanded facilities by the mid-1920s housed about one hundred residents. Its appeal was to national sentiments: the comfort of spending one's final years in a Norwegian environment, with a familiar language, food, and religous traditions. Men and women of stature served on the boards of the various benevolent institutions. They rallied the community behind them, and, to be sure, created goodwill for their own personal enterprises. The piano manufacturer A.G. Gulbransen, as an example, was a member of the Old People's Home Society and donated one of his player pianos to the Norwood Home. His generosity was given due publicity. Active in the Society's affairs were manufacturers like Andrew P. Johnson, Carl Bauer, and J.A. Paasche, while Mrs. Paasche, in the manner of many women of her class, headed one of the supporting societies. In the Old People's Home Society's twenty-fifth anniversary report Paasche extended his congratulations "for the splendid work performed for the dear old people of our race." The bond

Dr. Niles T. Quales in his office.

of nationality with its concomitant responsibilities was a constant in the immigrant community's response to the social situation.[64]

Medical Services

Hawkers of patent medicine, quacks, and home-remedy men were common in Norwegian pioneer settlements. Regulation of medical services was for a long time lax, or nearly non-existent. Morris Salmonsen in the 1870s told of three Danish quacks who competed fiercely for the Scandinavian trade on Milwaukee Avenue, Dr. Nebe, Dr. Lund, and Dr. Dybdahl, the last-mentioned name sounding suspiciously Norwegian. They had all purchased the medical diplomas they proudly displayed. Dr. Nebe was apparently adept at "setting leeches that almost always bit, when they . . . were placed on a black eye which the poor patient might have received by walking into an open door in the dark."[65]

Most immigrants had to seek cures for their ills as best they could. Academically trained physicians like Dr. Bernhard I. Madsen from Bergen who opened a practice in Chicago in 1851 and Dr. Gerhard Paoli a few years later were not easily accessible to all who required medical attention. A medical degree from Norway or another Scandinavian country had great credibility among Norwegian Americans and was given much publicity by doctors who sought to build a practice. Dr. Thomas Warloe, an obstetrician and gynecologist who had graduated from the university in Oslo in 1862, recommended himself strongly to his countrymen in the late 1860s on that basis. The Dane Dr. N.P. Petersen with "exams from Copenhagen with best grades" even offered to give poor Scandinavians free medical advice at his office between the hours of 11 and 12.[66]

Through the Rush Medical College, Chicago gave a unique opportunity to ambitious immigrants, especially to those, like Dr. Quales who got his diploma in 1866, with some previous training in related fields. Dr. Paoli was awarded an honorary degree the same year. The growing number of Norwegian graduates from this medical school were proudly noted in newspapers like *Skandinaven*.[67]

Midwifery was a female speciality and a professional service offered early through notices in the immigrant journals. A name that appeared regularly from 1867 on was Anne K. Andersen, a graduate from Christiania Fødselsstiftelse (Christiania Obstetric Institution), who sought the patronage of her fellow Norwegians and promised "a scientific and conscientious treatment." Adoptions could also be arranged. This service would allow children born out of wedlock to be placed with families willing to adopt. Her activities give a further insight into the social situation. Margreta Sehus who for thirty-six years practiced her obstetrical skills among Norwegians in Chicago claimed in 1911 to have delivered 8,000 "human atoms into the world."

In the 1880s *Skandinaven* carried frequent advertising for several small Scandinavian schools of midwifery which offered a six-month course of study. These were located in the Scandinavian neighborhoods, such as Mrs. Brockmann's School of Midwifery (Gjordemoder-Skole), incorporated in 1864, located on May Street near Chicago Avenue. The Swede Dr. Sven Windrow opened in 1889 a similar school on East Huron Street for "a limited number of women of good morals, good comprehension, and a desire for the occupation, between the ages of 20 and 35."[68]

The women thus trained might find a profitable vocation within the Scandinavian-American community. Immigrant benevolent institutions offered career possibilities for men and women with medical knowledge, who might gain recognition beyond these confines as well. Dr. Ludvig Hektoen, born in 1863 on a farm near Westby in western Wisconsin, undoubtedly had the most distinguished career of the Norwegian-American physicians in Chicago. He began his studies at Luther College, a route which many other ambitious and intellectually inclined young Norwegian-American men took. After graduation he entered upon his medical studies. From 1895 Dr. Hektoen was professor of pathology at Rush Medical College, and then at the University of Chicago, with which Rush affiliated. It was his work as research director of the John McCormick Institute of Infectious Diseases that established his national reputation.[69]

Dr. Hektoen was a member of the Scandinavian-American Medical Society of Chicago, organized in October, 1887, on the initiative of Dr. Windrow and patterned after similar medical societies in the Scandinavian homelands. Among the ten charter members were Dr. Paoli and Dr. Andrew Doe from Fjell, who came to Chicago in 1880 after receiving a medical degree from the University of Kristiania. Dr. Doe had a considerable practice among Norwegians in Chicago. 114 Scandinavian-American physicians, surgeons, and medical professors were members by 1912.[70]

The Medical Society fulfilled its professional and social functions through monthly meetings. Its purpose was "to work for the perfection of medical science through mutual communication of knowledge and combined experience, as well as the fellowship between physicians." Papers by members and guest lecturers provided an opportunity for lively discussions. Members held simultaneous appointments at American and specifically ethnic institutions and created an important link to the larger medical community. Dr. George Torrison, for instance, lectured at Rush Medical College on diseases of the chest, throat, and nose and was also an attending physician at the Norwegian Lutheran Deaconess Home and Hospital and for a time the director of the Norwegian-American Hospital.[71]

Though the medical profession continued to be male-dominated, prejudice against female medical education was slowly overcome. Women physicians might still of course have to tolerate

Dr. Ingeborg Rasmussen.

being called "hen medics." In 1870 the founding of the Woman's Medical School in Chicago opened medical training for women in the west. In 1892 it became a department of Northwestern University. Dr. Paoli served on the first teaching staff of the medical college.[72]

No Scandinavian woman graduated before the late 1880s. It must be borne in mind that in Norway women were not admitted to university studies until 1882, though in 1870 nursing had been recognized there as a feminine vocation. Inspired by the American feminist movement and the greater opportunities, in spite of obstacles, for women in America, Dr. Helga Ruud, who came to Chicago from Kongsberg in 1878 when eighteen years old, entered the Women's Medical School in 1882. She had saved money to finance her education by first working as a governess. After her graduation in 1889, she

became, as an American journalist stated, "one of the city's most distinguished 'petticoat surgeons.'" Her social concerns brought her into
contact with Jane Addams at Hull House and they became life-long
friends. For nearly fifty years, from its founding in 1895, Dr. Ruud
was on the staff of the Norwegian-American Hospital. In 1891 Dr.
Marie Olsen from Oslo earned her degree and later joined Dr. Ruud
at the same hospital where she exerted much influence as a member
of its board.[73]

In 1893 Dr. Ingeborg Rasmussen broke the barriers of the
Scandinavian-American Medical Society against female members by
being admitted to this previously all-male organization. She had
graduated from the medical college the year before. Her career exemplifies the expanding vocational roles women could play. Dr. Rasmussen was born in Bergen in 1855. In Norway she had been attracted to the stage and was associated with the Christiania Theater.
At age thirty-two in 1887 she decided to come to America where she
bravely enrolled at the medical college. Like her two women colleagues she was associated with the Norwegian-American Hospital.
Her well-developed cultural interests and her feminist point of view
led her to engage actively in the affairs of the Norwegian-American
community. She edited the "Women's Page" in *Skandinaven*.

Successful female physicians served as role models for other
women. Most Norwegian-American women who sought a medical
career, however, found it in activities society in general considered
more properly feminine. They were nurses, deaconesses, and matrons
at various institutions. Different opinions prevailed even there. As
suggested earlier, the disagreement in the Tabitha Society that led to
the split had partly centered on synodical differences between the
Norwegian Synod and the United Church in regard to the diaconate.
The Norwegian-American Hospital operated a regular school of
nursing from the beginning, graduating its first two nurses in 1896.
The Norwegian Lutheran Deaconess Home and Hospital, on the
other hand, set about to give the medical and religious training required to become a deaconess, graduating its first class in 1900. In
1906 Sister Ingeborg Sponland became Sister Superior of the institution and served until 1936, a period of great growth and change. She
was born at Hevne near Trondheim in 1860, trained in Norway, and
served the deaconess cause in Minneapolis before being called to Chicago. The small and declining number of young women becoming
deaconesses did not, however, nearly satisfy demand and in 1926 a
regular accredited school of nursing was established.

The successful care institutions had emerged modestly in the
difficult 1890s, when needs were intensified. The situation at that time
reinforced negative attitudes to living in the second city harbored by
a rural Norwegian-American population that came to the aid of their
hard-pressed urban countrymen. In March, 1894, after having read in

the newspapers "the many accounts about people in need in Chicago,"

Martin Hanson Highland, a farmer in Lincoln county, South Dakota,
"immediately thought that the farmers ought to do something." He
and his Norwegian neighbors collected eight tons of wheat flour and
corn, and money for "the poor in Chicago." Throughout the decade
rural and small-town Lutheran congregations, school children, and
civic groups took similar action. In spite of the generally depressed
situation, greater resources were nevertheless present to finance the
modestly started institutions; this is evidenced in the financial and
professional progress made by individuals within the ranks of the
Norwegian-American community. They placed themselves in the
new American middle class rapidly gaining strength in the last decade
of the century; as defined by Robert H. Wiebe in his *The Search for Order* (1967), this class consisted of men and women with strong professional aspirations and specialists in business. Both groups were very
conscious of their unique skills and functions, which was reflected in
their professional societies. These not infrequently carried an ethnic
identification.[74]

7

Norwegian Chicago

The New Century In his book *Recollections of a Grandfather* Victor Elting described the amazing transition in communications and transportation that was occurring in Chicago toward the end of the nineteenth century. When he arrived there in 1892 streetcars were pulled by horses, there were cable cars on some main arteries, and for "the well-to-do the one-horse brougham and the hansom cab were the vehicles, and they were everywhere to be seen." But before the turn of the century telephones began to come into general use and "in 1900 horseless carriages were beginning to appear on the streets of Chicago in some numbers."[1]

Even though surface lines were expanded and improved and were fully electrified before World War I, the elevated railroads were perhaps the most spectacular mode of transportation. They began operating the very year Elting came to Chicago, competing with surface transportation. In 1895 trains began running to the Logan Square terminal and on the Humboldt Park branch west to Lawndale Avenue. Two years later the elevated Loop was completed. These two lines, serving the Logan Square and Humboldt Park communities, had the most significant impact on the direction of Norwegian settle-

The great activity and bustle of Chicago's business district is illustrated in
this photograph showing Dearborn Street north across Madison Street in
1892. Buggies, cable cars, and horse cars fill the streets.

•

Top: Lake Shore Drive to Lincoln Park in 1894.

•

Bottom: Painting by the Norwegian-American artist Michael Hoiland titled "The El at California and North Avenue."

ment. They gave the same transportation advantages as the South Side enjoyed to the Northwest Side and stimulated the movement to outlying areas. The Humboldt Park community grew rapidly during the first two decades of the new century, reaching 65,095 by 1920; the same year the Logan Square community had 108,685 inhabitants. Germans and Norwegians were sizable population groups.[2]

Norwegians in Chicago in 1900 were 41,551 strong, counting the first and second generations. Those with one or both parents born in Norway numbered 19,540. Whereas the Norwegian-born category had not increased much since 1890, the second generation had grown by more than 9,000. Few immigrants had come in the depressed 1890s, while the community itself had matured, displaying greater evidence of family life, though many of the American-born were migrants to the city from Chicago's hinterland. The new tide of Norwegian immigrants after 1900 swelled the Norwegian colony, which in 1910 had 24,186 Norwegian-born members and 23,049 of Norwegian or mixed Norwegian parentage. Those with both Norwegian parents numbered 18,156 according to the federal census, which indicated the wards in which they and the immigrant generation resided. In January, 1910, Chicago was divided into thirty-five wards, and about 35 percent of this group resided within wards 27, where the Logan Square community was located, and 35, which contained the Humboldt Park community. If the contiguous Ward 28 encompassing Wicker Park and Ward 15 adjoining it to the south are added, nearly sixty percent of the Norwegian-born and those of unmixed Norwegian parentage are accounted for. About forty percent of the Danish-born and those with two Danish parents, totalling 18,504, lived alongside the Norwegians in wards 27, 28, and 35.[3]

Emigration from Denmark, Norway, and Sweden to the United States exhibited characteristics similar to those of the European overseas movement in general. Following the depression of the 1890s and the severe drop in emigration, it rose again after the turn of the century. The numbers that poured through the doors of Ellis Island, officially opened on January 1, 1892, climbed steadily as new waves of immigrants arrived. Most had to tolerate the indignities and privations of the Atlantic crossing as steerage passengers. The Scandinavian exodus peaked in 1903, but was still high in 1907, when America experienced the climax in its immigration history. Then it dropped in response to the financial crisis of that year, the "Panic of 1907," which caused business failures and unemployment. At the end of 1908 *Skandinaven* wrote of prevailing hard times in all large cities in the country, "but the situation is perhaps worse in Chicago than in any other city because of all the unemployed from the surrounding districts who congregate here." Reports from municipal lodging houses and the Salvation Army indicated an increasing number of homeless and unemployed.[4]

In all, 235,410 Norwegians moved overseas during the first fifteen years after the turn of the century, which, even though it did not match the movement of the 1880s, continued to give Norway the highest emigration intensity of the Scandinavian countries. 95 percent had the United States as their destination and most of the rest Canada; one third left from a Norwegian town or city. The progressively improving economic conditions in Norway could obviously not meet the demand for new jobs, as the third great wave in Norwegian emigration occurred during a period of unparalleled economic growth. The decision to go to America was not based so much on a lack of confidence in prospects at home as on anticipated superior possibilities in America; this is evidenced in the great sensitivity of the total emigration to the needs of the American labor market. In this youthful and male-dominated labor migration the forces that pulled were most important. These included the pressures that Norwegian Americans brought to bear on relatives and friends in Norway. "Everyone who is in good health and has willpower will get ahead here," Dr. Jacob L. Urheim, a Norwegian physician in Chicago, wrote to Norway in 1903, and described the city's dramatic growth, which he insisted was so intense that "there is hardly a house to be rented."[5]

The young and unattached were the most mobile, and they often—like immigrants of that era of other nationalities—saw their stay in America as temporary, to give them resources to pursue personal plans in Norway. Their migration was thus a considered strategy to secure advancement at home after money had been saved in America. They were not dissimilar to guest workers in Norway and other European nations of a more recent time. The Norwegian census for 1920 indicated that about 50,000 Norwegians had returned home after a stay in America. In Chicago the young newcomers gave vitality and vigor to Norwegian-American life. At the same time their youth, their plan to repatriate, and their single status prevented them from establishing commitments to religious and temporal institutions. The institutional structure of the Norwegian-American community suffered as a result.[6]

A study of selected enumeration districts from the 1910 federal census in wards 27 and 28, which had heavy concentrations of Norwegians, nevertheless revealed a high marriage frequency for Norwegian-born women and men above the age of twenty and consequently evidence of community stability. About 64 percent of all members of this group were in fact married. It was, however, a much older population than in the pioneer community of the 1860s, which showed a nearly identical proportion of married people. Pioneer urban conditions obviously made the institution of the family of major significance and encouraged early marriage. In 1910, because of its youthful composition, the second generation had a marriage frequency of only 41 percent for individuals above the age of twenty. If only immigrants between the ages of twenty through thirty are taken into account a similar percentage is achieved, which gives a more accurate impression of a large population of young single people in both the first and the second generations of Norwegians in Chicago. 57 percent of the Norwegian-born in this age category were men, and as many as 64 percent of these were single and were frequently listed in the census as "boarders." Only 37 percent of the women, however, were unmarried, which produced a combined marriage frequency of 47 percent.

When they established a family they continued to prefer a spouse of their own nationality. In 1910 77 percent of the married first-generation Norwegians recorded in the selected enumeration districts had wed another Norwegian. Though lower than the figure for 1880, when 91 percent of all Norwegian-born Chicagoans had a Norwegian spouse, a pronounced ethnocentric environment was still much in evidence. The greater number of marriages outside the group in 1910 than in 1880 also reflected the circumstance that many more people in this later male-dominated migration married only after arriving in America and there encountered a shortage of Scandinavian women. In the second generation endogamy would obviously decline, though it was still high; 46 percent of married persons in this group had found a marriage partner who was born in Norway or who, like themselves, had Norwegian-born parents. This high rate of intragroup marriage was influenced not only by the cultural bonds of nationality but also by a strong Lutheran identity and by the social life of the congregation in both Lutheran and non-Lutheran groups, as well as in secular ones, and by residential propinquity. "Even a smaller proportion than one-half practicing marriage within the nationality group," to quote from Lowry Nelson's study of ten immigrant groups in a rural district in Minnesota west of Minneapolis, "would be sufficient to maintain a 'hard core' of cultural identity."

The annual reports of the employment bureau operated by the Norwegian National League from 1906 until the end of 1917 identify conditions on the labor market and occupations sought by skilled as well as unskilled workers in the Norwegian community. The depressed situation in 1908 caused the bureau to intensify its efforts to place unemployed men as farm laborers; few women would accept such work. Every fall during the busy harvest season Norwegian-American farmers sent money to the bureau for the purchase of railroad tickets in order to enable those who were willing to accept work as farm laborers in healthy rural surroundings to leave the city.

When work was plentiful in Chicago, however, as it was for instance in 1916, according to the bureau's annual report "only those who really preferred farm labor this year went out into the country." Occupational patterns for Norwegian-born men in 1910 revealed the

•

The rapid extension of the built-up areas of the city is suggested by this photograph of real estate development south of Humboldt Park in 1917.

Adventist
1. Humboldt Park Norwegian Adventist Church

Baptist
2. Humboldt Park Norwegian Baptist Church
3. Logan Square Norwegian Baptist Church

Free Church
4. Salem Norwegian Free Church

Lutheran
5. Humboldt Park Mission
6. St. John's Lutheran Church
7. St. Paul's Lutheran Church
8. First Evangelical Lutheran Church
9. Bethel Lutheran Church
10. Bethlehem Lutheran Church
11. Christ Lutheran Church
12. Zion Lutheran Church
13. Hauge Lutheran Church
14. St. Paul's English Lutheran Church
15. Trinity Lutheran Church

Methodist
16. Logan Square Methodist Church (First and Immanuel)
17. Kedzie Avenue Methodist Church
18. Maplewood Methodist Church

Salvation Army
19. Humboldt Park Salvation Army Corps No. 15

Benevolent Institutions
20. Norwegian-American Hospital
21. Lutheran Deaconess Home and Hospital
22. Bethesda Old People's Home
23. The Mission Home for Young Women
24. Salem Mission Home for Young Men and Women

Clubhouses and Halls
25. Scandinavian Young People's Christian Association (The Scandinavian Young Men's Christian Association moved here from its building on Erie Street.)
26. Wicker Park Hall
27. Association Home of Chicago
28. Norwegian Athletic Club Sleipner
29. Norwegian-American Athletic Association
30. Chicago Norske Klub
31. Normennenes Singing Society
32. Bjørgvin Singing Society
33. Bjørnson Singing Society
34. Bjørnstjerne Bjørnson Hall
35. Logan Square Masonic Temple
36. Dania Hall
37. Norwegian Women's Federation (Kvindeheimen)
38. Socialist Workers Lyceum (Folkets Hus)
39. Den norske Kafe
40. Kaffistova

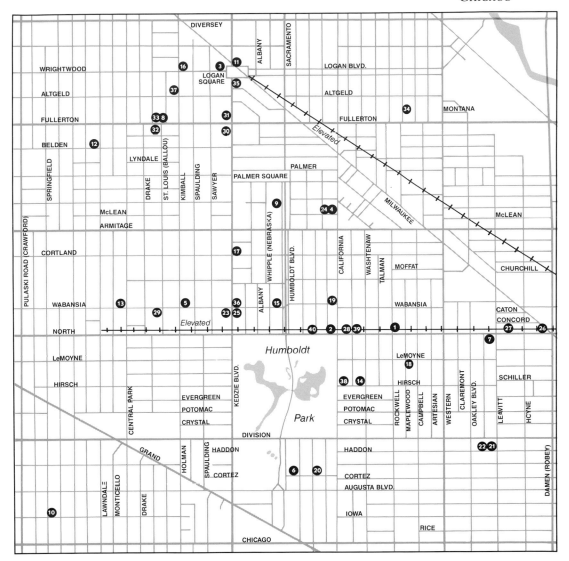

Major Norwegian Institutions around the Time of World War I.

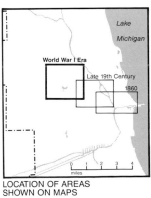

LOCATION OF AREAS
SHOWN ON MAPS

The Norwegian National League Employment Office, managed by A. Abrahamsen.

well established preference for skilled and semiskilled trades in construction and woodworking, as well as in manufacturing. A measure of the changes occurring, both in the educational level of the immigrants then arriving in America and in the upward mobility of the second generation, is suggested by statistics on non-manual occupations, in clerical and professional positions. 15 percent of the employed Norwegian-born men made a living in such pursuits, indicating special skills; the percentage had doubled, increasing to 30 percent, for men in the second generation. There is a distinct increase in both groups when compared to the situation in 1880. The main employment opportunities for immigrant women were still to be found in tailoring and in domestic service, though some female newcomers were able to enter nursing, become matrons in charitable institutions, or find work as store and office clerks. It was, however, the daughters of the immigrants who to an impressive degree moved into the occupations created by an expanding urban economy as stenographers, clerical workers, and telephone operators, and also as teachers in the public school system. In 1910, in the districts examined, as many as 38 percent of second-generation Norwegian women who were listed in specific occupations were engaged in such functions. The remainder continued, like the majority in the immigrant generation, in more traditional female pursuits. Still, the visible progress increased their self-confidence and encouraged a greater role in the affairs of the immigrant community as well as in broader civic concerns.[7]

The Churches and the Neighborhoods

The Norwegian neighborhoods could be located by the steeples of their churches and the symbols that identified other religious meeting houses. Not all of course were Lutheran. From 1910 the Salem Norwegian Free Church was located at the corner of McLean and North California. Social consciousness and concern for the "many young people from across the sea . . . immigrating to our shores" moved the congregation to open small separate mission homes for young women and men, which in 1926 expanded to a large facility, the Salem Mission Home on McLean Avenue. Needy and neglected children were cared for in its Lydia Children's Home founded in 1915.

Salem grew out of the activities of the Dano-Norwegian Department of the Chicago Theological Seminary; the department's establishment in 1884 was a part of the continuing, and increased, missionary zeal of the Congregational Church among the immigrants. Young students could be trained to work among their own nationalities. Helge A. Haugan, who, as has been noted, converted to the Congregationalists, bore much of the early expense of the Dano-Norwegian Department. The immigrant community had thus arrived at a stage where it could finance missionary undertakings by American denominations, and was not, as in the pioneer period, dependent on their support. Christian Trandberg, emigrating from Denmark in 1882, was the first professor in the department; in 1884 he began to lecture to a single student, a Norwegian. Trandberg had been influenced by the pietistic Danish Inner Mission movement, was himself a fiery evangelist, and in Chicago was drawn to the revivalist activities of Dwight L. Moody. Immigrants with his experience were predisposed to embrace American religious convictions. Trandberg's students, holding meetings among Scandinavians, organized Salem Free Church on September 8, 1887, with seventeen Norwegian and Danish members.[8]

Christian T. Dyrness from Fjelberg, a district noted for revival movements and a graduate of the Seminary, became Salem's pastor in 1890. He served for forty-three years. Salem parted company with the Congregationalists in 1895 — "in Christian love" — to join forces with the growing evangelical free-church movement in the West. Dyrness had supposedly given up a business "so as not to lose his faith," but to his own and Salem's benefit cultivated relations with the Norwegian-American commercial elite.[9]

Pastor J. H. Meyer from Vik in Helgeland found the Congregational Church attractive and for five years was a minister in "that branch of God's church." But in 1893 he returned to "his Lutheran mother church," longing for "its doctrine and usage." He became a minister in Zion Lutheran Church, which had begun as a mission in 1891 when Pastor J.N. Kildahl of Bethlehem Church on Huron Street had preached occasionally to Norwegian Lutherans east of Humboldt Park. Pastor Meyer is generally credited with its impressive growth and the erection of a large edifice in 1902 at Artesian and Potomac. In 1905 he gave impetus to organizing Christ Church right in Logan Square on North Kedzie Boulevard, and simultaneously ministered to the two small mission churches among Norwegians on the South Side. Meyer was one of the most active participants in the process that made Lutheran churches relocate or sprout branches in shifting Norwegian neighborhoods.[10]

Indicative of the movement west and north was the relocation of Zion in 1913 to Lawndale and Belden avenues, in the proximity of Christ Church in the Logan Square community. Bethlehem Church itself, of which the Zion Church was an offshoot, sold its property in 1911 to the Catholic Bishop of Chicago and moved to west of Humboldt Park. Pastor Kildahl, then at Bethlehem, had "rendered not a little pastoral service" to the handful of families residing southwest of Humboldt Park at Moreland, in the community of Austin; in 1886 they organized the Moreland Lutheran Church, which in 1890 joined the United Church, then just formed.[11]

The Lutheran organizational urge was strong and its force in community building is obvious. The Bethel Lutheran Church was organized in 1889 north of Humboldt Park within the same broad-church movement. "We the undersigned," the invitation to a meeting at the initiative of Pastor N.C. Brun began, "residents near Humboldt Park believe that it would be beneficial for us that a Lutheran congregation with services mainly in the Norwegian language should be organized and we invite you to a public meeting at Scharlaus Hall next Sunday evening . . . to discuss and if possible come to agreement in this matter." In 1907 Bethel Church moved farther north in the Logan Square community and became a major religious institution. It then had about 1,000 members. St. Timothy Church in the suburb of Hermosa, just west of the Logan Square community, branched off from Bethel; it began as a mission in 1899, and organized five years later. A network of contacts and common concerns existed within the framework of congregational developments.[12]

The tedious, but essential, details of organized religious life among Norwegians in Chicago followed similar patterns regardless of Lutheran stance. The low-church tradition was represented by the Hauge Church, begun as a mission from the so-called "Old Trinity." It was organized in 1900 and set about building a church at Central Park and Wabansia Avenue, and in 1910 the Trinity congregation itself moved, then for the second time, to a location some blocks east of the Hauge Church. Near the Norwegian-American Hospital, the liturgical St. John's, organized within the Norwegian Synod in 1890, pushed its steeple toward the sky. Mergers of congregations too small to survive alone were common. In 1913 St. Matthew and Covenant congregations united to form the First Evangelical Lutheran Church of Logan Square on Fullerton Avenue. Park View Lutheran Church, organized in 1908 at Irving Park farther north, bespoke a Norwegian presence beyond the central Norwegian neighborhoods.[13]

But the religious landscape was even more complicated. The Salvation Army maintained its temple at the corner of Wabansia and California and added its special flavor to religious and charitable observances. And other religious groups gained a foothold in the immigrant community. In 1915 Norwegian and Danish Seventh-day Adventists moved into their Humboldt Park Church on North Avenue; this followed several years of tent meetings and baptism of converts by immersion. Scandinavian Adventists had built a small chapel on West Erie Street as early as 1871. The Dane John G. Matteson, who later introduced Seventh-day Adventism to Denmark and Norway, had organized the small congregation. In 1872 Matteson launched and edited the Danish-Norwegian *Advent Tidende* (Advent Times) in Battle Creek, Michigan. It was the first official non-English publication of the Adventists and gave evidence of zealous missionary work. Locating a chapel in Chicago represented a move to the city of this conservative and predominantly rural Protestant denomination. In the Danish-Norwegian neighborhoods on the Northwest Side colporteurs sold its literature from door to door.[14]

•

Top left: Logan Square Norwegian Baptist Church.

•

Bottom left: Kedzie Avenue Methodist Church.

•

Right: The altar painting in the Bethel Lutheran Church at Humboldt and Dickens by the Norwegian-American artist Anton Reinholtzen.

Baptists and Methodists pursued their Scandinavian work, the Scandinavian Methodists conducting their summer revival meetings at DesPlaines. As city missionary in the Norwegian–Danish Methodist Conference Frederick Ring promoted deaconess work. A Deaconess and Girls Home was established in 1910 in the Humboldt Park neighborhood; it moved to new and enlarged quarters on North Sawyer Avenue in 1922. Pastor Ring had been responsible for the merger which in 1907 formed the First and Immanuel Methodist Church, and for their move from the Milwaukee Avenue neighborhood to Wrightwood and Kimball, close to Logan Square. It became known as the Logan Square Methodist Church. Mission activity emanating from the theological seminary in Evanston in 1892 led to the formation of the Kedzie Avenue Methodist Church; meetings were at first conducted "in a shoemaker's home on the northwestern corner of North and Sawyer avenues." Farther south, east of Humboldt Park, the Maplewood Avenue Methodist Church, which had its origin in the First Church, had in 1891 dedicated an attractive church structure. Though organizational growth was impressive, memberships remained modest. Lutheran leaders nevertheless felt threatened by "Methodists and other sects that sought to come in among the Lutheran church people" as stated by the secretary of the Moreland Lutheran Church.[15]

Logan Square Norwegian Baptist Church was the largest of the Danish and Norwegian Baptist churches in Chicago. At its peak in 1911 it had a baptized membership of 246. The church was founded in 1903 by members of the Scandinavian Pilgrim Baptist Church who had moved to the new Norwegian neighborhood at Logan Square. Pastor C.W. Finwall, who had gathered the congregation, replaced the adjective "Scandinavian" with "Norwegian" to appeal to the large Norwegian population at the new location. Actually, following the withdrawal of the Danish members in 1892, the Pilgrim Church in the old neighborhood was also a Norwegian congregation.

The Dano–Norwegian congregations supported a theological seminary at Morgan Park south of the Chicago business district. It trained pastors for service in America and abroad; missionary activity in Denmark and Norway Americanized religious life there. Finwall, who had emigrated from Bergen in 1883, had through Baptist missionary work been converted and baptized by immersion while still in Norway. He came to Chicago to receive theological training. P. Stiansen, a major leader among Scandinavian Baptists and for some time pastor of the Logan Square Church, was also converted to this faith prior to emigrating. Religious leaders from the homeland reinforced a national attachment but also demonstrated the nature of transatlantic interaction.[16]

In an article in 1904 *Skandinaven* emphasized the practical benefits ethnic cohesion, visibility, and numerical strength gave "in politics and other circumstances . . . not only to the nationality as a whole but to every person who belongs to that nationality." It was therefore beyond the newspaper's comprehension that some Norwegians "deny their nationality" when the city census takers visit their home.[17]

Circumstances were propitious to speak for ethnic pride. National sentiments were being fostered by a new wave of immigration, by occurrences in the homeland, and by the celebration of historic Norwegian events. There was a large Norwegian-speaking population in the United States; in 1910 the combined first and second generations exceeded one million. Consequently, even when considering only what the census describes as the "Norwegian stock," and thereby ignoring the generations beyond the second one, every third Norwegian resided in the United States. The new immigrants went to the cities to a greater extent than earlier ones, yet only 42.2 percent of the Norwegian stock was classified as urban that year, thus retaining its strong rural character. It was not far from the percentage of 46.3 for native-born Americans, but vastly different from the 72.1 percentage of town dwellers when counting the foreign-born as a whole. The 4.7 percent of the total Norwegian-American population, the first and second generations, residing in Chicago, however, because it existed in a central metropolitan area, not only infused the entire subculture with urban values and practices but took the lead in celebrating the merits of a Norwegian identity. [18]

The city gave public space to displaying ethnic enthusiasm and symbols; in the ethnic mosaic that was Chicago such spectacles assumed added significance. They clearly marked a specific national identity and presence. Traditions included foods. The *lutefisk* banquet became common before the turn of the century, and the Scandinavian Old Settlers Herring Society had arranged its herring picnics (*sildepiknik)* since the 1870s. Norwegians found their quintessential hero in Leif Ericson, and even though other Scandinavians were not totally excluded from the worship of the Norse adventurer, it is an interesting comment on the emergence of an ethnic mythology that the Norwegian immigrant community made his recognition as the original European discoverer of the American continent a particularly Norwegian cause. It assumed a unique strength among Norwegians in Chicago. That this idea surfaced with renewed vigor during the preparation for the Columbian Exposition was hardly an accident. Initiative, it appears, came from members of the Leif Erikson Lodge of the Knights of the White Cross. In 1891 it led to the founding of the Leif Erikson Monument Society.

Norwegian Americans in fact arrogated the entire heroic age of the Vikings, not only Leif Ericson, and it was a case where ethnic symbols were a part of the process of assimilation, establishing an admired ancestry and roots back to the very age of discovery, thereby lodging a claim on the early history of the New World. Impetus and support to raise a statue of the Norse discoverer came from prominent men, Nikolay A. Grevstad, from 1892 editor of *Skandinaven*, Ole A. Thorp, and Helge A. Haugan. L. E. Olsen of the Knights of the White Cross pursued the cause with such zeal that he was renamed "Leif Ericson" Olsen, his initials lending themselves to this change. The immigrant elite assured the success of the undertaking. It was also this social class that most eagerly sought acceptance.[19]

The monument committee raised funds and gained visibility by arranging May 17th celebrations. The observance of the day in 1899, a popular festival at the Chicago Auditorium for the benefit of the Norwegian-American Hospital with "the participation of all Norwegian societies in Chicago," led directly to the formation about two months later of the Norwegian National League, a union of member organizations, which from 1900 arranged May 17th festivals and coordinated other concerted actions. On October 12, 1901, a bronze 9 1/2 foot statue was unveiled with great ceremony in Humboldt Park, with high-flying orations by civic leaders and prominent Norwegians like Ole Thorp, Paul Stensland, and L. E. Olson, president of the monument committee. "Leif Erikson in America is now and forever a fact," Stensland declared, "not only in his old Vinland, but in busy Chicago, in our very midst." A large attendance in spite of "a steady downpour" was interpreted by *Skandinaven* as evidence "that the raising of a statue of Leif Erikson was a cause that had taken deeper roots in the Norwegian people in Chicago than . . . one would have thought." The sculptor responsible for the work, Sigvald Asbjørnsen, was already an established artist in Norway when he came to Chicago in 1893.[20]

The ongoing tensions and conflicts that in 1905 led to the dissolution of the union between Norway and Sweden preoccupied Norwegians at home and abroad and fueled nationalistic emotions. Norway's humiliating retreat in 1895 from its demand for a separate foreign consular service, the issue that finally broke the union, had created great anguish in the Norwegian community in Chicago. The conflict impeded cooperation between the "sister nations" in America. Julius E. Olson, professor of Scandinavian at the University of Wisconsin and that year's May 17th orator, cautioned those Norwegian Americans who were raising funds to strengthen Norway's military defenses. A telegram was, however, dispatched to the Storting expressing "warm participation in the fatherland's fight for right."[21]

The unilateral declaration by the Storting on June 7, 1905, that the union with Sweden was dissolved created a new patriotic day of celebration. Few events have had more immediate repercussions in the entire Norwegian community in America. An outpouring of Norwegian national patriotism had been prepared by the visit in late May

The Leif Ericson statue in Humboldt Park. It was sculptured by Sigvald Asbjørnsen.

of the Norwegian Student Singing Society, which hailed its well-attended concerts as "a greeting to countrymen." At a mass meeting at the Chicago Auditorium on June 17 under the auspices of the National League "Four Thousand Men and Women Exalted Norway's Praise," to quote *Skandinaven*'s headline. It was a solemn audience, which consisted mostly of plainly dressed workingmen, many of whom had never before entered the magnificent Auditorium Theater building designed by Louis Sullivan.

Birger Osland, who had emigrated from Stavanger in 1888 at the age of eighteen and became a prominent businessman, read a resolution to be cabled to the Storting in support of Norway's efforts "to defend the proud heritage of Harald, Olaf, Sverre and Haakon." It was again the Viking past that provided appropriate national images. Both Dr. Andrew Doe and Judge Oscar Torrison spoke. Chicago Norwegians took a leading role, involving such other prominent men as Stensland, Olaf C.S. Olsen, and the attorney Andrew Hummeland. They joined the Swedish and Norwegian consul Fredrik Gade, whose Norwegian birth assured his loyalty to the homeland's cause, in a drive to gather signatures on a petition to President Roosevelt for official recognition of Norway's sovereignty. Anticipating a military conflict, they discreetly organized a nationwide relief committee ready to establish branches to give material aid to Norway if needed. The much respected publisher of *Skandinaven* John Anderson was elected chairman, which showed the central position of Chicago Norwegians in the entire Norwegian subculture.[22]

The strained relations with the Swedish-American community, especially as expressed in exchanges between immigrant journals of the two nationalities, subsided quickly after the peaceful resolution of the union crisis. In reality, while regretting the dissolution and blaming Norway for the impasse, such Swedish-American journals as *Svenska Tribunen* and *Svenska Amerikanaren* had shown some understanding of Norway's demands. Their attitude reflected the differing views stated by newspapers in Sweden as well; the Social Democrats were, in fact, sympathetic to the Norwegian cause. The ascension of Haakon VII to the throne of Norway was the ultimate evidence of the homeland's complete sovereignty. The National League sent a select delegation to the coronation ceremonies in the summer of 1906, which was cordially received by the new monarch, whose popularity on both sides of the Atlantic contributed to a sense of ethnic unity. Dr. Andrew Doe headed the Chicago contingent. Olaf Ray, secretary for the combined Norwegian-American coronation delegation, proudly noted this fact in his advertisements for his law practice. The elation of the Norwegian-American populace over the independent status of the homeland obviously made it a valuable selling point.[23]

Official Norway was discovering the immigrant community in America. The Storting in June, 1905, had expressed its gratitude to

Top: The Swedish-Norwegian Consul Fredrik Gade.

Bottom: Skandinaven, June 9, 1905, announces in bold headlines: "King Oscar has ceased to reign in Norway—the government rules. The Storting declares the King removed from office and the Union dissolved."

Norway's "emigrated sons and daughters for their work for the national cause." The slogan of the Norwegian America Line "hands across the ocean" symbolized the strength of ethnic bonds but also, to be sure, commercial considerations reflecting the greater maturity of the Norwegian-American community. This Norwegian passenger line which in 1913 established direct service between Norway and the United States had raised half its capital among Norwegian Americans. Osland and the banker Hauman G. Haugan, a brother of Helge Haugan, took an active part; Osland traveled in Norwegian settlements throughout the United States selling shares. It was the Norwegian consul E.H. Hobe in St. Paul, Minnesota, a member of the steamship line's board of directors, who involved emigrated businessmen. An appeal to nationality promoted commercial enterprise.[24]

The national spirit expressed itself most emphatically in the commemoration of May 17 (Syttende mai). Nonetheless, this festival had evolved slowly. Boisterous public displays were more commonly associated with July 4th celebrations. Nora Lodge frequently took the initiative, in 1866, for instance, arranging a "Norwegian basket picnic" on July 4th by the Calumet River. Processions were at other times a part of the arrangement; the Scandinavian-American societies cooperated "as good citizens to celebrate the 4th of July," as Skandinaven reported in 1878, and "everyone had a good time." And like these, the May 17th observances celebrated the freedom of America as well as a national identity.

Scandinavianism prevailed even at May 17th celebrations, so that in 1876 "all of Milwaukee Avenue was decorated with Norwegian, Danish, Swedish, and American flags." But the different societies celebrated separately. Skandinaven complained in 1882 that efforts to have a folk festival failed, the May 17th commemorations being "of a more private character." Nora Lodge, for instance, had celebrated at Aurora Turner Hall and invited people from the two other nationalities. In 1884, however, perhaps as a result of direct impulses from Norway through the new wave of immigrants, a colorful parade by Norwegian societies and clubs marked the day. Soon a separate children's procession (barnetog) became a distinctive part of the Chicago celebrations, adopted from the practice introduced in Norway by Bjørnson in 1870. Apparently Emil Biørn, always an active force in the Norwegian-American community, transferred the unique exercise to Chicago. In 1890 an observer wrote from "the corner of May and Ohio streets" that 2,000 noisily rejoicing youngsters had passed by "with a flag in their hands, a smile on their lips, and joy in their souls, shouting hurrah and singing." To this central ethnic district many arrived from other parts of the city to participate in the national celebration.[25]

The Norwegian National League had to unite the divergent goals and programs of its nearly forty member societies in a common Norwegian patriotic outpouring. Splits within the community be-

Top left: Children celebrate May 17 in Wicker Park in 1907.

Bottom left: The Norwegian turners march into Humboldt Park in the May 17th parade.

Above: This group photograph of the Norwegian Turner Society was sent to the centennial exhibition in Oslo, Norway, in 1914. The photograph shows an expansion of sports activities and the admission of women athletes.

came obvious. The temperance units were slow in joining, as were the churches. In 1911 the League was forced to cancel its children's parade because some Lutheran ministers had arranged a competing one. The outspoken *Scandia* called this procession "a miserable exhibition, brainlessly planned and arrogantly defended by the ministers." In subsequent years, however, the League took great care to appease the Lutheran clergy. But there was a festive spirit even in 1911. The procession that year was headed by a detachment of twelve police officers, all Norwegian, followed by the Henrik Ibsen Lodge of the Good Templars, marching under its banner and pennants which proclaimed its principles. And along the route of the parade on West North Avenue to the Leif Ericson statue in Humboldt Park "Norwegian flags and other decorations in national colors were prominently displayed . . . from Western Avenue to California and throughout the park."[26]

The year 1914 marked the centennial of the May 17th constitution. The League, headed by George M. Kramer, who because of his Norwegian super-patriotism and promotion of May 17th festivals was called "Syttende mai" Kramer, arranged a grand parade with some 5,000 participants; "women and girls walked the streets in the costume of their mother country," the *Chicago Daily Tribune* reported. The parade marched from Palmer Square to Brands Park, a common setting for the May 17th "folkefest," where, according to the newspaper, "bands played and leading speakers told of the glories of Norway." Judge Oscar Torrison spoke in English and Professor L. M. Gimmestad of Gale College in Norwegian. The main Norwegian-American celebrations of the centennial of the Eidsvoll constitution were, however, in Minneapolis, and ethnic leaders in Chicago, to the disappointment of the entire colony, were often reduced to greeting Norwegian dignitaries at the railroad station as they passed through on their way to the new "Norwegian-American capital."[27]

At the impressive celebrations in Norway of a century of progress and freedom the National League was represented by a delegation of three. One of them was the attorney Lasse Grundeland. He had emigrated from Fresvik in Sogn at age seventeen in 1892, settling first at Koshkonong where he attended Albion Academy, then moving to Chicago. There he studied law while working for *Skandinaven* and participated actively in Norwegian-American affairs. The delegation, the other two members being O.C. Wold and Johanne M. Thye, presented a greeting to the Storting from the Norwegian colony in Chicago.

Relations with Norway were revitalized. The national memorial gift collected by Norwegian Americans gave further evidence of ties across the Atlantic. The idea of assistance and gifts to the homeland had a long tradition, and specific emergencies produced an instantaneous response among the immigrants. In the immediate past Chicago

Norwegians, promoted by the National League, had rendered aid to the survivors of seventy-three fishermen lost at sea in a fearful storm in the fall of 1899 at Rørvær in Rogaland; the destruction by fire of the city of Ålesund in 1904 produced an Ålesund relief committee which vigorously collected funds.[28]

Contemporary heroes like Knute Rockne kindled national pride. Rockne had moved from Voss in 1893 at the age of five to the Logan Square community where he grew up. His father Lars was a wagon-maker who had gone to Chicago to exhibit his prize-winning carriage at the Columbian Exposition. As head football coach at Notre Dame from 1918 and until his death in 1931 Knute Rockne gained celebrity status and became the greatest Norwegian-American figure of his time.[29]

An Ethnic Forte

Many events in the Norwegian colony featured sports and athletic activities. The May 17th observance in 1908 had been especially noteworthy because well-known personalities like Jane Addams had spoken to the children in the morning and the silver-tongued William Jennings Bryan, who in 1906 had attended the coronation of Haakon VII, at the folk festival later in the day, but also because of an especially colorful parade. The strikingly uniformed Norwegian Turner Society, the Norwegian Rifle Club, the Norwegian Athletic Club Sleipner (Den norske Idretts Klub Sleipner), and Norge Ski Club (Skiklubben Norge),the two latter representing Norwegian prowess on snow and ice, all took part in the procession. "In this manner mother Norway's emigrated children ought to celebrate her proudest moment," *Skandinaven* declared.

Sleipner originated on August 15, 1894, among a small group of young men who wished to meet and play ball; they were joined by many turners, who practiced gymnastics. The club distinguished itself, however, as the originator of annual ice-skating races in Chicago. In 1900 it held a speed skating contest for the championship of Illinois. At such events large crowds attended. In 1904 about 50,000 people watched the races conducted on a pond in Humboldt Park. Governor Charles Deneen gave the first prize, a medal bearing his name, which was won by C.L. Christopherson. Sleipner entertained the governor as an honored guest. As the first Norwegian athletic club to have its own house, Sleipner moved into 1620 Fairfield Avenue in 1905. The club was the undertaking of both blue collar and white collar men, carpenters, painters, and salesmen, and was open to a broad spectrum of Norwegian-American society.[30]

The same was true of the Norge Ski Club. Haakon Lehn, identified as a machinist, through *Skandinaven* encouraged ski-lovers to form a society to promote ski sport. In response to Lehn's call eighteen young men, all born in Norway and residing on the Northwest Side, met on November 8, 1905, at Petersen's Hall on California and North

•

Top: Knute Rockne in front of his football team at Notre Dame.

•

Bottom left: Painting of skaters in Humboldt Park by Michael Hoiland.

•

Bottom right: Two soccer teams, Fram and Viking, following a match about 1916.

•

Next page, top left: A jump on Cary Hill at Fox River Grove in the 1920s.

•

Top right: Ragnar Omtvedt, four-time national champion.

•

Bottom: View of scenery around Cary taken from the scaffold on Cary Hill at one of the Norge Day competitions arranged by the Norge Ski Club

avenues, one of the many halls for rent in the area, to make preliminary plans. Four days later, on November 12, Norge Ski Club was officially organized with twenty-eight charter members as a ski-jumping club for the purpose of arranging tournaments. Some found its appearance in the memorable year 1905 significant. *Norden* later interpreted its organization that year as a patriotic act, since skiing was to a special degree a Norwegian national sport.[31]

Skiing was, however, not well known in Chicago, nor in America in general. The National Ski Association had been organized only in 1904, by a small group of Norwegians in Ishpeming, Michigan, an active skiing center. Norge Ski Club became a member. According to early testimony, "ski jumpers" was a new nickname for Norwegians. The sport was carried to the American public in various ways; Carl Howelsen, for instance, who was a charter member of Norge Ski Club, performed daring jumps under the big tent of the Barnum and Bailey Circus. The club itself, in transplanting this spectator sport to American soil, promoted it in a more traditional manner. In 1907 Norge Ski Club arranged its first competition at Fox River Grove, near Cary, about thirty-five miles north of Chicago. A second one was staged in Chicago at Shoot-the-Chutes Park.[32]

Both these tournaments were poorly attended. In 1908, however, when the club staged a ski-jumping competition in Humboldt Park, in the heart of Norwegian Chicago, an estimated 20,000 watched. Norge Ski Club eventually purchased property at Fox River Grove and built a large steel scaffold; trains transported people from Chicago, but distance kept attendance low. Thousands attended in 1912, however, when the club conducted the National Championship Tournament, including the mayor of Chicago, who came "to see the brave Norsemen compete."

It was the acceptance of skiing by the American public that produced large attendances in the 1920s. Norway had, *Norden* explained, its famous Holmenkollen Day, while Chicago had its Norge Day at Fox River Grove. It became an institution alongside May 17, with the same enthusiastic crowds as at meets in Norway, "with lunch packages, and coffee, warm sausages, orange crates [to sit on], and a bottle of spirits in the back pocket." As in Norway, where national pride was associated with international victory on skis, winners in the competitions received proud recognition. Master jumpers like Ragnar Omtvedt, who was national American champion four times and in 1913 set a new world's record, symbolized fortitude and ethnic spirit.[33]

Immigrant industry developed based on the increasing popularity of skiing and skating. Skis for "slalom, downhill, racing, jumping, and touring" were produced by such companies as the Northland Ski Manufacturing Company founded in 1911 in St. Paul, Minnesota. It advertised itself as "the world's largest ski manufacturer," and used as a selling point that "skilled Norwegian craftsmen contribute each his own part toward the perfecting of every ski." National reputation was here obviously the issue. In Chicago two Norwegian-American companies specialized in the production of skates. Before his move from Oslo to Chicago in 1887 at age twenty Nestor Johnson had won a prize in an international skating competition. In Chicago he garnered as a tool and die maker the skills he needed to develop his famous tubular ice skates, which he produced in his own factory. Alfred Johnson was another immigrant entrepreneur to capitalize on Norwegian-American pastimes. Skills acquired while working making skates in Oslo with his father could be directly transferred when he emigrated at age twenty-six in 1901. From 1917 he had his own factory, Alfred's Ice King, on West North Avenue.[34]

Split or Unity?

Special interests, social cliques, and personal ambitions sought expression in a multitude of clubs, societies, and organizations in the years preceding World War I. Within the fluid and occasionally chaotic bounds of the ethnic community a veritable organizational mania existed. Some commentators were concerned about the excessive force of this voluntary association movement. An observer in *Nordvesten* commented critically: "a few people who find that they have somewhat the same interests immediately set out to form a society." The proliferation of societies appeared as an inescapable aspect of immigrant social life.[35]

Regional loyalties and identities surfaced as an organizational force. Representatives of the *bygdelag*, or old-home societies, of Norwegian America in Chicago bore such names as Voss, Søndmøringen, Nordlændingen, and Eikundasund—uniting people from the town of Egersund. These were all founded before 1914. Later they were joined by societies like Nordmørlaget, Karmsund—for people from Haugesund and environs—Oslolaget (Kristianialaget), and Stavangeren. These urban manifestations of a basically rural phenomenon among Norwegians in America shared the piety toward the home community of the general movement, as well as the sense of kinship. Søndmøringen, for instance, took the initiative to organize the relief committee for Ålesund, the main town in that district. In other respects they showed qualities unique to the urban setting. They were secular in nature and did not like the rurally-based societies depend on the Lutheran clergy for leadership. Eikundasund gave colorful masquerade balls, and Oslolaget showed considerable sophistication in its soirees, theater evenings, and other light entertainment. There was less preoccupation with national symbols, especially in the regional groups bearing the names of Norwegian towns and cities. They cultivated an "urban patriotism"; Stavangeren, for example, stated its purpose as "preserving Stavanger's traditions and retaining ties with the home town (*fødeby*)." Responding to the environment in

•

Top: The Society Karmsund in 1922.

•

Bottom: Oscar Frank, a popular entertainer in Oslolaget.

which they existed, they, like other urban immigrant groups, gave assistance "in case of illness and death in our midst," the history of the Karmsund society stated, although they did not become mutual aid societies.[36]

The Bjørgvin Singing Society, which, as has been noted, limited membership to men born in Bergen and vicinity, arranged regular pleasure excursions on Lake Michigan "to be reminded of its native town." Local patriotism, regardless of its intensity, yielded, however, to issues of national honor; all organizations then marched under a common emblem. Nationalism flourished as immigrant Scandinavianism declined. Joint Scandinavian cultivation of male singing under the auspices of the national United Scandinavian Singers of America came to an end in 1892, only six years after its founding. It was yet another victim of the Swedish-Norwegian conflict. Norwegian singers refused to compete for the "Lindblom trophy" given by the Swedish Chicago stockbroker magnate Robert Lindblom because of his disparaging writings about the Norwegian position in the conflict. The Swedes formed their own organization, while the Danish and Norwegian choirs continued as the United Scandinavian Singers and arranged a concert at the Columbian Exposition. Further activity was halted by the depressed times. In October, 1899, encouraged by the efforts that led to the organization of the Norwegian National League, four male singing societies in Chicago formed the Norwegian Singers League (Det norske Sangerforbund). It consisted of Bjørgvin, Normennenes, and the Norwegian Glee Club, organized in 1889 by younger men who left Normennenes, apparently as a result of generational tensions. The fourth society was the Norwegian Quartet Club founded the following year.[37]

Male choral singing flourished in all Norwegian-American communities, directly transplanted from Norway. The visit by the Norwegian student singers in 1905 gave further impetus to male singing. Normennenes and Bjørgvin conducted splendid concerts in their own halls, or when the occasion required it in larger auditoriums like the Wicker Park Hall or the Logan Square Masonic Temple. Celebrated directors gained fame and honor. In 1914 Scandinavian singers in Chicago erected a monument at Mount Olive on the grave of John W. Colberg, the longtime director of Normennenes who died in 1910. Several choirs sang at its unveiling.

Because he wrote the music to such popular patriotic songs as "Når fjordene blåner" (When the fjords are blue) and "Norge, mitt Norge" (Norway, my Norway), Alfred Paulsen was perhaps the best known musical figure. Paulsen was a Norwegian-trained musician from Oslo who came to Chicago in 1888. His compositions were inevitably presented at almost any song festival, as was the hymn "Den store hvite flokk" (The great white host), to Grieg's folk melody. It was first sung in America by the Quartet Club under Paulsen's direc-

Top: The John Colberg monument in Mount Olive Cemetery.

Bottom: The Norwegian Symphony Orchestra in 1903, directed by Fredrik Fredriksen.

tion. During the first decade of the century a Norwegian symphony orchestra existed, directed by the violinist Frederik Fredriksen from Fredrikshald, which contributed to the quality of immigrant cultural life in Chicago.[38]

The fame of Grieg, and the essentially national romantic quality of his music and life, were capitalized on in the immigrant community. In 1915 a group of Norwegian-American businessmen and professionals on the Northwest Side organized the Grieg Male Chorus. That same year, though unrelated to the men's group, the first Norwegian women's choir in Chicago was organized as the Grieg Ladies Singing Society. Mathilde Huseby was its first director, and later the composer Otto Clausen, who composed and arranged music written for women's voices. The group adopted the Norwegian Hardanger peasant costume (*bunad*) as its official dress when performing. This costume, representing the district most idealized by the national romantics, nearly assumed the status of a national dress. It inspired the Daughters of Norway to create an imitation as its official costume. Otto Clausen became a director of Oselia Ladies Chorus, organized within Anna Kolbjørnsdatter Lodge of the Daughters of Norway in 1916. It was the first chorus within the sorority; the initiative was taken by Dr. Susan Ackerman, a medical doctor born at Vadsø.[39]

Literary clubs had of course long been considered appropriate cultural activities for middle-class women. Several existed in the immigrant community "to cultivate the interest in Norwegian literature," as the Norwegian Literary Society (Den norske Læseforening) stated in its constitution when organized in 1898. But the literary heritage posed questions of taste and interest. Initially men were admitted to this group and its predecessor Svava; they appear to have been more conservative in the selection of appropriate reading material than were the women. Svava was the name of the heroine in Bjørnson's play on one sexual standard for men and women *En Hanske* (A Gauntlet), and, according to the literary society's own assessment, Svava failed because "the gentlemen objected to Bjørnson's heroine." Modern literature which the Lutheran clergy might condemn as godless and immoral was purchased and perused.[40]

Many women mainly from the same social segment of immigrant society were active in several clubs. The only civic organization exclusively for these women was, however, the Norwegian Woman's Club, which was formed on April 2, 1914. Solidarity based on sex, and perhaps inadvertently on social class, was further demonstrated when this club took the initative in 1916 in uniting the several women's groups into the Federation of Norwegian Women's Societies. It allied itself with the burgeoning American feminist movement by joining the state federation of women's organizations. The cause of full woman suffrage was a driving force in the Norwegian

Woman's Club; the fact that the franchise had by then been granted
in Illinois at the municipal level strongly influenced its formation. Dr.
Helga Ruud and her sister Marie Ruud, a schoolteacher, both unmarried, represented the role of single professional women who were active in female organizations. There were especially many from the
teaching profession, a common occupation for educated women.
Women like Julia Walther, who together with Helga Ruud originated
the society, and Emilie Beutlich, wife of the painter Anton Beutlich
and an artist in her own right, exemplified the participation of cultured and socially concerned married women. Advances in enfran-
chising women in Norway allowed for ethnic rhetorical boasting.
"Are we [women] less intelligent in this country?" was its slogan in
the suffrage parade in 1919.

The special position of Norway in the world peace movement
after the turn of the century and the first awarding of the Nobel Peace
Prize by the Storting in 1901 gave the country a unique opportunity
to direct the attention of an international community to activities that
promoted peace. Women's groups were especially responsive. Jane
Addams, who was a peace activist, spoke on the topic to the Norwegian Woman's Club, and associated with its members. In 1931 she
received the Nobel Peace Prize.[41]

In urban centers of Norwegian settlement the appellations *det
norske selskab* (the Norwegian society) or *den norske klub* (the Norwegian club), taking their cue from the nationalistic Norwegian society in Copenhagen in the 1770s, identified the immigrant elite. Other
names also appeared. The Norwegian Quartet Club, whose members
formed the male chorus of the same name, in the mid–1890s assumed
the elite role after the Arne Garborg Club ceased to exist. Birger Osland was a member and has given an account of the elegance of the
Quartet Club's annual January banquet and ball "which was always
attended by the Norwegian society folk." Silk hats and white gloves
were obligatory for the men and evening gowns for the women. "The
high point of the evening," Osland wrote, "was reached later when all
members and guests formed a square and danced the française, a formal ceremonious dance full of bows and curtsies."[42] It was a Norwegian high life peculiar to the urban environment and transplanted
from customs in similar social circles in the homeland.

The Quartet Club's exalted position was, however, challenged
in 1905 by a group of young men with technical training, many of
them recent arrivals; an immediate elite, they formed Den norske
Klub i Chicago (The Norwegian Club of Chicago). Both clubs had
sociability and good fellowship as aims; but as Osland stated, "the
Quartet Club was beginning to show its age." It consisted of established older men, such as the lawyer Andrew Hummeland, the physician Thomas Warloe, the piano manufacturer and wholesale dealer
William Gerner, and the famed engineer Joachim G. Giaver. Inter-

The Grieg Ladies Singing Society taking part in the May 17th parade in 1924 dressed in their Hardanger costumes.

locking memberships existed, and it was apparently Gerner, a member of both distinguished groups, who moved them toward the merger that occurred in June, 1911, under the name Chicago Norske Klub. Its clubhouse on Kedzie Boulevard just south of Fullerton Avenue, with its characteristic dragon ornaments and its impressive interior decorative scheme, benefited from the skills of members who were architects, builders, and artists. It was officially opened on July 4, 1917. Men of distinction like Christian U. Bagge, Carl Bauer, Thomas G. Pihlfeldt, and Emil Biørn joined its exclusive circle.[43]

Cultural programs were promoted by special interest groups within Chicago Norske Klub and other organizations. Bjørgvin Singing Society's dramatic troupe, organized and directed by Christian Olsen in 1894, presented romantic song plays. Olsen, born in Stavanger in 1864, had come to Chicago in 1881, and became a leader in many facets of life of the immigrant community. And the Quartet Club male chorus continued as a separate entity in the Chicago Norske Klub; there were also lectures, light entertainment, and balls as well as theater productions. The latter led in 1919 to the formation of an independent dramatic group. On the club's stage Gerner enjoyed success in the main role in a student farce, "Ingvald Enersen," and other members as well found an outlet for a dramatic urge. The Dane Ove Knudsen, a professional actor, entertained in a number of more demanding roles, and did especially well in Holberg's comedy *Jeppe paa Bjerget* (Jeppe on the Hill).

In 1918 a women's auxiliary was permitted. But even before then women, wives and friends of the club members, had entered into the activities of the Norwegian Club, presenting for instance Hulda Garborg's *Rationelt Fjøsstell* (Efficient Barn Chores), with Dr. Ingeborg Rasmussen as director. Eleonora Olson, born in Chicago, played in this piece and gained praise for her mastery of dialogue in peasant vernacular. She and her sister Ethel performed as the Olson Sisters and won fame for their Norwegian dialect stories and portrayal of the difficulty of immigrant adjustment. "Isn't it funny vit people here in America," a Norwegian immigrant woman said in one of their comic monologues, "dey don't talk Norvegian and dey don't talk English."[44]

Few theatrical pieces, however, had their origin in the ethnic community. The many amateur groups preferred imported dramatic works and made ambitious attempts to present serious plays. In 1900 Ibsen's *When We Dead Awaken* was given at Scandia Hall and received high marks from *Skandinaven*'s reviewer. The production of this play, published only the previous year, was again evidence of immigrant contacts with the cultural life of the homeland. During the 1890s, especially, but also later Scandia Hall was the center of Norwegian-American dramatic art. Versatile directors and performers like Emil Biørn held leading positions. Contacts with the professional stage in Norway added to a sense of a shared cultural environment. Visiting

Top: The Norwegian Quartet Club in 1900. Front row from left: Carl Gulbrandsen, William Gerner, Dankert Richter, Alfred Paulsen, Emil Biørn, Carl F. Arnet, Thomas Warloe. Back row from left: Nils Remmen, Birger Osland, Cato Dahl, Sverre Nannestad, Peter W. Stuhr, Fredrik Gade, John A. Ouse, Einar Kling.

Bottom left: Chicago Norske Klub on Kedzie Boulevard.

Bottom right: A performance of the dramatic troupe in Chicago Norske Klub. Left to right: Jon Fürst, Emmy Berbom Larsen, Astri Sundby-Hansen, John Blytt.

Top: A salon evening in the Literary Society of Chicago in the 1920s with a strong Norwegian national-romantic emphasis.

Bottom left: Scandia Hall.

Bottom right: In 1891 L.O. Michelsen, an actor at the National Stage in Bergen, performed at Scandia Hall. Here he plays the title role in the fourth act of Ibsen's play *Brand.*

actors like L.O. Michelsen from the National Stage (Nationale Scene) in Bergen, who appeared there in late 1891, gave, according to *Skandinaven*, "a good and substantial sampling of Norwegian theatrical art." Chicago amateurs performed together with visiting actors from the Norwegian stage. Some of the performers later made a career in Norway, for instance Harald Otto, who became a director at the Central Theater (Centraltheatret) in Oslo, and Harald Stormoen, who made his debut in Scandia Hall and later was a well-known actor at Norway's National Theater (Nationaltheatret).[45]

From 1910 until 1917 a Norwegian-trained actress, Borgny Hammer, and her husband Rolf Hammer, made a career of interpreting Ibsen to a Norwegian-American public in Chicago. Greater frequency of theater productions resulted from the organization in 1913 of Koht's Norske Folketeater (Norwegian Popular Theater) by the Norwegian actor Thorvald Koht and his wife Aagot Koht. It presented dramatic works by Bjørnson, Ibsen, Holberg, and lesser Norwegian dramatists. After the dissolution of the theater in 1919, Thorvald Koht became the director of the Norske Klub's Dramatic Society, exemplifying the merger of elite and cultural interests in an urban Norwegian-American milieu.[46]

The organizations that belonged to the National League in 1912 had a combined membership of about 4,000. They were united in their concern to preserve a Norwegian-American cultural heritage, as symbolized when they marched in step on May 17 under the national Norwegian standard, carrying banners and pennants of their separate organizations. Their activities and causes had an impact far beyond formal membership and their concerted function was to create a familiar and comforting ethnic environment.[47]

The Civic Arena

"Since Mayor [Carter H.] Harrison is not a candidate for reelection next year—at least by his own account—he did not come as promised," *Skandinaven* reported critically in 1886 in writing about the May 17th celebration in Humboldt Park that year. An estimated ten thousand high-spirited Norwegian Americans provided an audience worthy of any ambitious politician's ingratiating remarks. American politicians, hungry for votes, were apparently willing to sit through endless self-congratulatory ethnic speeches delivered in a foreign tongue. In 1889 Mayor Dewitt C. Cregier had attended the May 17th festivities and when his turn came to speak admitted that "he had not understood a single word of what had been said but he knew that it had all been very good," concluding that "Chicago was proud to count so many of Norway's freedom-loving and brave sons among its citizens." "The mayor's powerful speech," *Skandinaven* wrote, "was frequently interrupted by loud approval from the listeners." [48]

A painting by Emil Biørn of a 17th of May parade in Chicago.

Norwegian-American politicians were of course even more concerned about gaining the support of their own nationality. It provided the essential base from which to move into public life. The Republican Lauritz Thoen made frequent appearances at May 17th celebrations to solicit votes. In 1886 Thoen defeated his Democratic opponent to win election as West Town Collector. He had come to Chicago at age five in 1853 from Modum and had taught at Our Savior's parochial school before entering politics. At the end of two terms as town collector he gained patronage appointments through political contacts. It was at that level that most Norwegian-American politicians enjoyed some success. No great political leader emerged.[49]

Thoen's Democratic opponent in 1886 had been none other than the ambitious Paul Stensland. His candidacy, and the move of *Norden*, which Stensland briefly owned, toward the Democrats identified a Democratic minority in the Norwegian community. *Skandinaven* had interpreted it as evidence of great ability and integrity that Andrew B. Johnson had won election in 1875 to the Cook County Board of Commissioners as a Democrat. "Many Republicans voted for him," the newspaper explained. In spite of inroads made by other political movements, Norwegians continued mainly under the Republican banner. "He was born Republican," someone was quoted as saying about a local Norwegian politician. This statement might be applicable to Peter B. Olson, born in Oslo in 1848, who emigrated to Chicago in 1872 and found employment with *Skandinaven*. He became active in Republican politics in Ward 15. In 1898 and again in 1900 he was elected to the general assembly of Illinois on the Republican ticket from the senatorial district comprising the Scandinavian wards on the West and Northwest Side. *Skandinaven*, whose obvious support he enjoyed, commended Olson for working for "laws in which labor unions were interested," which the newspaper saw as the reason for his broad support in the Norwegian community. Membership in a particular ethnic group, as John Allswang has observed, was, however, a greater determinant in voting behavior than socioeconomic issues. Opinion makers like the popular *Skandinaven* and the more exclusive Dovre Club, which according to Osland "had considerable prestige and some influence in the Norwegian wards of the city," worked for the Republican ticket. Paul Kleppner in his study *The Cross of Culture* (1970) considered religious and class components and found that Norwegian Lutherans, and even more so Swedish Lutherans, were strongly anti-Democratic wherever they were found and regardless of degree of economic prosperity. The intensity of anti-Democratic sentiment was greater among the pietistic and evangelical low-church Lutherans than among those of a high-church persuasion. Both groups were, however, strongly Republican.[50]

Newspapers were a major force in political education. In 1916 Senator Knute Nelson of Minnesota, then the foremost Norwegian-

American politician, congratulated *Skandinaven* on its fiftieth anniversary. He credited it with being "largely instrumental in training our people to take active part in the political affairs of this country," and bringing them to the Republican party, thereby, according to Nelson, attaching Norwegians to "a party of culture, intelligence, and progress." In confidential correspondence Nelson and other aspiring Norwegian-American politicians sought the newspaper's endorsement. Its editor-in-chief from 1892 until 1911, Nicolay Grevstad, worked tirelessly to rally all Scandinavians around the Republican party. His reward came in the form of a diplomatic appointment as minister to Uruguay and Paraguay. [51]

Irish dominance of the Democratic party in Chicago further alienated Scandinavians. Because of it the liberal Democrat Olaf Ray abandoned that party in 1897, explaining that even in the strongly Norwegian fifteenth ward "a small band of Irish rule with tyrannical power," leaving the Scandinavians out of consideration. Ray was convinced, as he later stated, that "since the mass of our people vote Republican," this party would give him a more profitable field of action. Idealistic opportunism led him to confront an entrenched Norwegian Republican "machine" element headed by the Norwegian police judge Olaf Seversen in Ward 28, which following new ward divisions in 1890 encompassed much of the Humboldt Park community. By organizing the Norwegian Republican Club of the 28th Ward Ray challenged Seversen and broke his power, which Ray claimed had been such that "no independent Norwegian could be considered for any major office without his consent." Like similar ward clubs it gained new members by assisting newcomers in citizenship proceedings. In close understanding with *Skandinaven* the club in 1902 successfully pushed the election of Adolph Larson, a prosperous Norwegian building contractor, as alderman, and in 1906 Oscar Torrison's election as municipal judge; both were members of the club. The club's achievements, as Ray wrote, demonstrated how Norwegians by acting in unison could acquire the political recognition they deserved.[52]

In 1896 *Skandinaven* had attributed the victory of two Norwegian aldermen on the West Side, Bernhard Anderson and Magnus C. Knudson, to "Scandinavian consensus." Previously, it maintained, even in heavily Norwegian wards "Scandinavians have for many years had little or no influence." Anderson represented Ward 15 and served until his death in 1904. He had come to Chicago from Oslo at the age of five in 1867. Knudson, a well-to-do thirty-three-year-old Norwegian born in Chicago, was elected from Ward 17, the old Norwegian community centering on Milwaukee Avenue. Both men demonstrated the role of the second generation in public service, even though Anderson strictly speaking belonged to the immigrant generation.

Knudson's candidacy and election revealed the reform urges of the social settlement movement and a persistent Norwegian participation in civic reform initiatives, though in this case it was frustrated by Knudson's corruptibility. Shortly after Graham Taylor founded Chicago Commons in 1894, settlement workers aided in the formation of a neighborhood men's club, which called itself the Seventeenth Ward Civic Federation. Many of its members were Norwegian. Such sensational exposés as William T. Stead's *If Christ Came to Chicago* (1894), coming as it did shortly after the assassination of Mayor Harrison I in 1893 by a disappointed office seeker, with its revelation of not only murder, but vice, gambling, police graft, and political bribery, moved leading citizens to organize a reform group called the Civic Federation. Progressive reform came to Chicago through its efforts and those of other reform-minded groups and individuals; these reforms included civic beautification, relief programs for those affected by the industrial depression, and monitoring the activities of aldermen and other public officials. The Seventeenth Ward Civic Federation concerned itself with issues of education and "moral evils," but in this reform-conscious era it was primarily interested in politics. It uncovered gross political irregularities and corruption in the ward and set out, like Ray's political club in Ward 28, to defeat the powerful leader of the Republican organization in Ward 17, James H. Burke, who was responsible for most of the irregularities. Chicago Commons thus became a rallying point for reform.

It was as the Federation's "reform candidate," gaining its endorsement after speaking to the club, that the Republican Knudson won election. When he shortly afterward voted with the "boodlers" on street railway franchises, he was called to a meeting of citizens at the assembly room of the Commons to try to explain his vote. In subsequent elections the Federation abandoned the idea of working through the political parties for better aldermen and nominated candidates from its own members. The Chicago Commons became a real factor in ward politics and the decline of the political boss.[53]

In 1899 a sharper political voice entered Norwegian Chicago when Anton B. Lange moved the newspaper *Scandia* to the city from Duluth, Minnesota, where it had been published since 1888. Lange has been described as "one of Norsedom's most talented and least diplomatic journalists." His editorship was marked by "crass and blunt editorials a fearless critical attitude and a liberal spirit." Lange was born of German parents in Bergen in 1857 and came to the United States in 1880. His liberal views had their roots in the philosophy of the emerging Liberal party (Venstre), whose victory in the constitutional conflict in 1884 introduced parliamentary government in Norway. The chief support of *Scandia* in Chicago was apparently a circle around the Bjørgvin Singing Society, representing Bergen, of which Lange was a member. The singers, to quote from the newspaper's competitor *Skandinaven*, embraced Bergen's "tradition of fearless democratic liberality and urban culture." Stensland belonged, as did men like Carlos Ross from the Norwegian Dramatic Society, another society strongly identified with Bergen. Like it, Bjørgvin made Ole Bull its idol and celebrated his memory on many occasions. Strains of liberalism and nationalism mingled with a transplanted cosmopolitan urban culture associated with Bergen.

Lange's bitter and personal form of polemics alienated many and after his death in 1910 it was discontinued. His successors as editor, Harry Sundby-Hansen and L.H. Lund, who later became sole owner as well as editor, however, preserved *Scandia*'s liberal message. They sharply criticized a move toward cautious and noticeably more conservative policies on social and political issues by *Skandinaven* under the editorship of Grevstad and thereafter. "*Skandinaven*'s policy," *Scandia* insisted, "is to say 'yes' wherever possible, and to please its readers in order to keep them happy." It accused *Skandinaven* of doing this as a matter of "good economic policy," compromising its convictions so as not to offend and lose precious subscribers and advertisers. *Scandia* and *Skandinaven* were, in spite of differences, representatives of a middle-class urge to remove social evils and were inspired by broad efforts to make the city a better place in which to live. Both gave support to the progressive reform issues of the day.[54]

The Cause of Socialism

The working man had the sympathy of both *Skandinaven* and *Scandia*, the latter newspaper even defending aspects of socialistic reform programs, whereas *Skandinaven* gave these a wide berth. It was *Revyen*, founded in 1895 by the Danish socialist Christian Bodtker, which preached a class-based socialism in the Norwegian and Danish wards in Chicago. Scandinavian cooperation was obvious in socialistic circles, based on cultural unity, and reflected the workers' Scandinavianism which was firmly in place in Denmark, Sweden, and Norway. Socialist ideas had been professed earlier by such men as Thrane, Pio, and the radical editor of *Den nye Tid* Peter Peterson. The union movement among Scandinavian workers in America in the 1870s had encouraged a working-class consciousness. The more recent developments were based on these early expressions of worker solidarity.[55]

Though Socialist party organizations never became the political voice of the American labor movement, socialism found many adherents both inside and outside organized labor. It derived strength from the waves of immigrants who arrived after the turn of the century with socialistic ideas and with experience of labor conflicts. These newcomers discovered people in sympathy with their views among countrymen already in America. A causal relationship has been established between the general strike in Sweden in 1909 and an increased volume of emigration; the Swedes because of their larger numbers dominated the Scandinavian socialist movement in America. Newcomers provided leadership. In 1910 Scandinavian socialist clubs from all over the nation met in Chicago and organized the Scandinavian Socialist Union (Skandinaviske Socialistforbund) under the Socialist party of America with Eugene Debs as national leader.

In Chicago the first Scandinavian socialist club was formed by a group of Norwegians in 1904. Located in the district around Halsted and Milwaukee it took the name the 17th Ward's Scandinavian Socialist Society. The later Norwegian labor leader Martin Tranmæl was a member while working as a journeyman painter. His sojourn in America might be seen as an extention of a European tradition of journeyman wanderings which artisans of all trades observed. Like the earlier journeymen he became the carrier of new ideas and impulses. In 1905 he was present when a small group of agitators and socialists met in Chicago to form the militant Industrial Workers of the World; through him its activism and syndicalistic philosophy were to give vitality to Norwegian labor agitation as well. Concerts were presented by the Scandinavian Socialist Singing Society which added its propaganda message to the stirring presentations by traveling speakers. The Scandinavian Socialist Union, in spite of these efforts, grew only slowly; at its height in 1918 it had 3,735 members divided into sixty-eight clubs. These clubs nevertheless gave experience in parliamentary practice and intellectual and cultural stimulation to their members. The Union's headquarters were in Chicago.[56]

The first Scandinavian alderman elected on a straight Socialist ticket was the Norwegian William Johnson in 1903 from Ward 32 south of 39th Street on the South Side. Johnson was born in Oslo in 1875 and came to Chicago in 1888. Here he found employment in the Pullman shops and joined the woodcarvers' union. His motto "drink less beer and buy more books" illustrates the strong temperance sentiment and educational concern of the Scandinavian labor movement. These were also the main matters of interest to the socialist agitator Fridtjof Werenskjold. His fall from family prosperity to relative poverty somewhat paralleled the experience of the pioneer agitator Thrane. Before suffering bankruptcy Werenskjold's father had been a wealthy citizen of Skien; the misfortune sent the younger Werenskjold into the world as a sailor and even a participant in revolutionary movements in South America. Landing in Chicago in 1910, he had already worked in the socialist movements in Norway and Sweden, and he carried his agitation even to the street corners in Scandinavian neighborhoods.

Because of his professional status and active participation in immigrant benevolent efforts Dr. Karl F. M. Sandberg was in a position to present his radical reform message in quarters otherwise insulated from socialist dogma. Sandberg was born at Vestre Aker in 1853, and before emigrating in 1882 he had earned a medical degree. In Chicago he established a medical practice and married Inga Stensland, a step-daughter of Paul Stensland, then busy contending for political office on the Democratic ticket. Sandberg himself joined the Democrats, but shortly after the turn of the century left the Democratic party to speak for the socialist cause. The Socialist party gained strength, and in 1912, when it competed with another third party, the Progressive party, Debs gained nearly six percent of the national vote for the Presidency. In Chicago he did even better with 13 percent of the presidential vote. Sandberg that same year ran, though unsuccessfully, for lieutenant governor of Illinois on the Socialist ticket.[57]

The movement to the Humboldt Park area caused the relocation of the almost totally Norwegian 17th Ward's Scandinavian Socialist Club and a change of name to Scandinavian Socialist Branch No. 1. Danish socialists in the same Humboldt Park neighborhood organized the Scandinavian Socialist Society Karl Marx in May, 1907. It was from these two units in the Socialist party that the initiative was taken which in 1910 produced the Scandinavian Socialist Union. In 1914 the two groups merged as Branch No. 1 Karl Marx; with combined resources they built their own hall in 1918. It was the only Scandinavian socialist club in Chicago to have its own building, Folkets Hus, a workers' lyceum replete with theater, library, reading and meeting rooms. From 100 to 150 Danish and Norwegian socialists were members and partook of the club's educational and political fellowship.[58]

The cause of socialism was considerably damaged by the movement's opposition to American entry into World War I and the antiwar activities of leaders like Debs. Dr. Sandberg was arrested and indicted for "anarchist activities" and sentenced to one year in prison, although he served only two days. Debs, however, spent three years in jail for his socialist agitation. The Russian Revolution in 1917, which caused the Communists in the United States to leave the Socialist party, revealed a strong revolutionary element in the Scandinavian Socialist Union. According to Henry Bengston, an influential Swedish member at its Chicago headquarters, the Union had been on the left wing of the Socialist party, and with "the Bolshevik Revolution in Russia the red wave from the east set the tone." Police raids and threats against workingmen's clubs increased its militancy, while the national hysteria of the Red Scare in 1919 intensified repressive measures. The advances of the Bolsheviks continued to generate excitement and enthusiasm among Scandinavian radicals. At its congress in 1920 at Folkets Hus the Communist wing of the Scandinavian Socialist Union was victorious and voted the Union out of the Socialist party. Moderating voices like Bengston, and earlier Werenskjold, who both assumed a social-democratic position, were not heeded.[59]

Obviously a capitalistic America was challenged by socialism; immigrants who embraced its teachings rejected what they found in

Top: Members of Branch No. 1 Karl Marx in Folkets Hus. The banner on the right has the inscription "The Scandinavian Karl Marx Klub."

Bottom: Folkets Hus, a worker's lyceum built in 1918.

America on idealistic grounds, even though they had left their native lands in order to benefit from the opportunities the new society offered. Most Scandinavians in America, however, opposed the socialist solution, regardless of social class. They instead looked for advancement within the capitalist system. Many pursued it on a temporary basis before returning to the homeland, while others sought the "American dream" by establishing permanent roots. This ideal for most Norwegian Americans appears more often than not to have been embodied in the philosophy and security of a middle-class existence. It was bourgeois values and practices that were on display at public events marking a Norwegian presence in Chicago.

8

The Modern Metropolis

On April 27, 1919, the Foreign Language Division of the Chicago Victory Loan Committee arranged a grand parade on Michigan Avenue. Thirty-three foreign-language units existed, each appealing to a different nationality to purchase "Liberty Bonds." Both ethnic accommodation and a zeal to demonstrate American patriotism were expressed at such events; the pressures these and other activities produced made the various nationalities compete for best results. "Not all of us can serve in the army or navy, but most of us can subscribe to bonds," *Skandinaven* had encouraged its readers in 1917 over the signatures of prominent Norwegian Americans. The Norwegian National League was represented in the procession by "The Viking Float," with Alfred O. Erickson, a lawyer, playing the role of Leif Ericson, and not because of his name. The prosperous Wisconsin-born Erickson was an active and generous member of the Norwegian-American community; he had won a reputation as "an excellent poser for statues representing Leif Ericson and Uncle Sam." Norwegians were proud when the *Daily News* called the float the best one in the entire parade.[1]

The War and Its Aftermath

•

Top: "A Pageant of All Nations" at the United States Government War Exposition in September, 1918.

•

Left: The newspaper *Scandia*, May 5, 1917, announced a mass meeting at Logan Square Auditorium for the purpose of recruiting Norwegian-American members for the Red Cross. "For Our Boys [who] are going to a foreign land to bleed and die for the freedom of the world and our nation's honor and right."

The mixture of ethnic and American symbols was obviously not thought to represent a conflict of loyalties, though the hysterical crusade for "100 percent Americanism" made the hyphen and the traditions it represented suspect. In 1917, May 17, coming only a little more than a month following United States' entry into the war, was observed in Chicago without the traditional children's parade. *Normanden* in Grand Forks, North Dakota, cried "shame" at a decision it insisted would destroy the children's pride in their ancestry. To give further evidence of American patriotism, the Norwegian National League, which arranged a subdued commemoration, sent a cable to President Wilson expressing "our undivided loyalty and devotion to America and the cause of America." On July 4th of the next year, following the President's wishes, Norwegian Americans joined other nationalities in celebrations in various parts of the city, the Norwegians, Danes, and Poles all having festivities in different areas of Humboldt Park, the Swedes in Lincoln Park. These coordinated festivities became, wrote *Skandinaven*, "a demonstration of loyalty unmatched in the nation's history."[2]

Except for the socialist peace movement, in which some Norwegians participated, and the arrest of well-known individual socialists like Dr. Karl Sandberg, the proper patriotic attitude of Norwegian Americans was rarely an issue. Self-consciously they, like other immigrant populations, strove to remove even the slightest suggestion of disloyalty. A debate was generated within the Norwegian-American community, with Pastor I. B. Torrison articulating what can be regarded as an evolving national consciousness on the part of Americans of Norwegian birth or descent by applauding a program of cultural awareness to stimulate pride in ancestry but rejecting the idea of a fixed ethnic identity.[3]

Pluralists like the author Waldemar Ager, however, decried any form of compromise with the goals of the assimilationists, which they were convinced would not only do injustice to American citizens of non-English background but would destroy the nation's creativity. The force of tradition tended to retard the process of Americanization. The May 17th programs, whether for the children or the adults, persisted in a bilingual manner, with one speech in Norwegian and one in English, a practice dating back at least to the turn of the century. This is even more remarkable when it is considered that in 1918 only 5.6 percent of the children enrolled in Norwegian Lutheran Sunday schools in Chicago were taught in Norwegian. The traditionalists withstood an attempt in 1917 to have English supplant Norwegian in the Chicago Norske Klub. The club was, as the victors stated, "to remain a place where Norwegians of the second generation will be able to gain contact with the culture of their ancestors." A countermove to the forces of assimilation was made by the Norwegian Woman's

Club, which had used English from its founding, when it formed a special Norwegian Department in 1918.[4]

Statistics nevertheless reveal an inexorable move toward assimilation. A monolingual generation of Norwegian Americans was clearly emerging. The pace of change was naturally more rapid in an urban environment than in the countryside. It is most easily traced in the decline in the use of Norwegian in Lutheran congregations. In June, 1917, the three major Norwegian Lutheran Church bodies, Hauge's Synod, the Norwegian Synod, and the United Church, formed the Norwegian Lutheran Church in America (Den norsk lutherske kirke i Amerika). Its leaders envisioned a union of all Lutherans, regardless of ethnic origin. This consideration, and the wartime pressures for cultural conformity, hastened the adoption of English. An overly eager clergy was, however, defeated by lay people when it attempted in 1918 to drop the word "Norwegian" from the name of the new Lutheran union. A vocal Norwegian impulse was thus still much in evidence.[5]

Nationwide a dramatic drop in the number of Norwegian divine services from 73.1 percent in 1917 to only 61.2 percent in 1918, with predictably far higher percentages in rural than in urban churches, showed the force of wartime crusades against foreign languages; a reversal in 1918 to 65.7 percent suggests strongly that the decline was an immediate response to the repressive progaganda. In Chicago member congregations of the Norwegian Lutheran Church in America during the first year of its existence conducted 37.8 percent of church services in Norwegian, but paralleling the national development rebounded to 42.1 percent. The Norwegian work in Chicago then declined gradually, but not as rapidly as the national figures, at an annual rate of 1.4 percent compared to a national average of 2.3 percent.

In 1919 28.5 percent of the services were still in Norwegian. The postwar immigration would come to the aid of the traditionalists. Many more newcomers settled in the cities than earlier. Some strong religious spokesmen embraced the Norwegian work; they became the spiritual leaders of separate Norwegian departments maintained by some large congregations. H.P. Ausan of Our Savior's was enthusiastically called to that position in 1925 by the United Lutheran Church in the suburb of Oak Park, which that year united Our Savior's, Bethlehem, and St. Paul's English Lutheran congregations. But even though these circumstances preserved Norwegian services in the congregations, their mere numbers are an imperfect measure of the strength of the language. Attendance is a much better indicator. "Norwegian services were held every Sunday until the attendance fell to 15 or 16," wrote the historian of St. Timothy Church of the 1920s; yet according to the 1929 parochial report for St. Timothy about 37 percent of all services were that year conducted in the Norwegian language. Not until 1947 did Zion Church vote to discontinue Norwegian services, and then only after a heated debate and opposition by a small minority. Individuals tenaciously resisted the tide of change.[6]

In the 1920s the war and subsequent restrictions on immigration altered the composition of Chicago's population. The percentage of foreign-born whites decreased from nearly 36 percent of the population in 1910 to less than a quarter in 1930. This drop had significance for the retention of subcultures of European background. The place of European immigrants in the work force and in residential ghettos was increasingly being taken by unskilled blacks from the South and by Mexican peasants who migrated in large numbers during those two decades, moving into the central areas of the city as these were vacated by earlier immigrant groups in favor of outlying neighborhoods.[7]

The very restrictions on immigration that were bringing about the ethnic and racial transformation of Chicago, however, produced opposition in all immigrant groups, a part of the postwar reaction to wartime repressions. The Norwegian National League through its representatives in the Immigrants' Protective League of Chicago, an organization originally created by the founders of Hull House in 1908 to assist immigrants already in this country, worked to liberalize the restrictive measures, especially in efforts to reunite families separated as a result of the new legislation. In its first annual report the League told of its efforts to protect immigrant girls arriving in Chicago. Girls destined for the city, whose names were received from the port of entry, were met at the railroad station by women speaking their language, among them Norwegian. Conditions at the receiving point had been much improved, and runners and other exploiters of immigrants were denied access to the newcomers, but en route to the interior the risks were many, especially for the ignorant immigrant girl. In addition to such humanitarian responses, Norwegian-American organizations and individuals joined in efforts to raise the limits set on immigration from the "old" immigrant groups. The Immigration Act of 1924, which set quotas for each nationality which greatly favored these same groups, gave when fully operative in 1929 a quota of 2,377 to Norway, as compared to 2,784 to Russia and 5,802 to Italy. In spite of the favored treatment evidenced in these figures, Scandinavians, Germans, and Irish arranged a mass meeting in Chicago to protest the restrictions on their nationalities, describing the law as "unfair, unworkable, and un-American," with among others Alfred Erickson giving eloquent though intolerant voice to the Norwegian position.[8]

The intent and effect of the skewed immigration law of 1924 was to increase immigration from northern and western Europe at the expense of eastern and southern Europe. Because of a general decrease in emigration from the former regions and the Great Depression, the

The Chicago skyline in the 1920s. The photograph shows North Lake Shore Drive at Oak Street Beach.

increase was much less than those who enacted the law had anticipated. In the decade of the 1920s close to 65,000 Norwegians
emigrated to the United States; the top year was 1923, following the
brief postwar depression of the early 1920s, with recovery beginning
already in 1922. The emigration thus showed great sensitivity to conditions on the American labor market, and would have been larger
without the later restrictions on immigration. In part in response to
the new legislation nearly 21,000 Norwegians went to Canada during
the decade.

Norwegians in Chicago continued throughout the 1920s to con-
stitute "the third largest Norwegian city in the world," after Oslo and
Bergen. The Norwegian-born, however, increased by only a little
more than one thousand between the two censuses, from 20,481 in
1920 to 21,740 in 1930. The second generation showed a more substantial growth, numbering 24,748 at the beginning of the decade and
31,190 at its close. In that year the "city," if only these two generations
are considered, had 55,948 residents.[9]

Taking Part in Chicago's Growth

Modern Chicago took shape in the 1920s, symbolized by the new
skyline that rose above the Loop. The Chicago Plan of 1909 provided
vision for major public works and the lake front development was the
most striking aspect of its realization. It was the large-scale migration
into Chicago, whose population grew by 35 percent from 1918 to
1926, that produced a building boom and expansion in the central
business district as well as in outlying areas. In 1930 the city's population was approaching 3.4 million. Distant neighborhoods became accessible through the explosion in automobile sales; radio and motion
pictures also showed spectacular gains. The rapid spread of electrical
appliances created an increased consumption of electric power.
Prosperity and higher wages shaped the consumer society of the post-
war era. Though the years after World War I saw setbacks, unemployment, and a persistent crisis in the agricultural sector of the economy, economic historian George Soule nevertheless found cause to
label the period *Prosperity Decade*. Increased consumer buying and the
revival in residential construction, which employed many Norwegians, pushed up the average annual income of employed wage
earners in terms of constant purchasing power. By 1923 it was 19 percent above the base year of 1914, and by 1928 32 percent above the
1914 level.

Economic activity was a boon to banking establishments; such
Scandinavian banks as the Union Bank and the State Bank greatly increased their deposits and capital to make them large financial institutions. Illinois law prohibiting branch banking stimulated the formation of many small banks; in Chicago many of these banking agencies
were located in communities on the outskirts of the city. People associated with the State Bank opened banking establishments in the

•

Top: A gas-filling station in Chicago in the late 1920s.

•

Bottom two: These advertisements translated into Norwegian appeared in *Skandinaven* in the 1920s. They advertised Essex automobiles with "free selection of color without additional cost" and Camel cigarettes "made from the choicest tobacco grown" and are striking examples of consumerism in the Norwegian-American community.

Scandinavian districts which continued to be regarded as ethnic places of business. Banks sought the neighborhood savings for investment and financed the many community centers that were being built; there motion picture palaces and shopping streets offering a variety of merchandise competed with the Loop as entertainment and commercial centers. Consumer purchasing supported local stores and other businesses and created self-contained communities. An entire lifetime could be spent there without wandering beyond the community's bounds or feeling deprived for not doing so.[10]

A number of individual careers were launched or substantially advanced in the postwar boom. It was in the 1920s that Andrew E. Wigeland, a grandson of the pioneer lake captain George A. Wigeland, laid the foundation for a prosperous career in banking and investment. In the same decade the Arthur Andersen accounting firm expanded beyond the Midwest to become one of the largest companies of its kind. Andersen was born in 1885 to immigrant parents who just after his birth went back to Norway for a time and then returned to America settling in the Norwegian neighborhood on the West Side. Orphaned in his mid-teens, Arthur Andersen sought advancement through education, and his studies and experience — involving much struggle and sacrifice — led him to an academic position as professor of accounting at Northwestern University. On December 1, 1913, he cooperated with partners to found the company that bore his name. Expansion soon resulted from tax business for large companies. Birger Osland, also an investment banker, said of Andersen that "he prizes more than most men the spiritual heritage of his race." It might be symptomatic of the heightened ethnic fervor of the times and the desire of successful individuals to establish acceptable ethnic credentials that all three men, Wigeland, Andersen, and Osland, became heavily involved in the recording of their own group's history through their support of the Norwegian-American Historical Association founded in 1925.[11]

A common national origin continued as a viable organizational basis within professional and commercial elites. It gave both cultural and material rewards. The Chicago Norwegian Technical Society, founded in 1923 with thirty-nine charter members, was a case in point. Joachim Giaver was president, and another prominent member was Thomas Pihlfeldt, who during the 1920s directed the construction of some of the most spectacular bridges of his career, such as the Michigan Avenue Bridge over the Chicago River, which implemented a significant expansion of the central business district to the North Side. The Society nurtured sociability and gave professional stimulus through regular meetings with lectures and discussions. By 1929 membership consisted of about 150 Norwegian men with technical training.[12]

The members of the Norwegian Technical Society possessed

•
Top: The Michigan Avenue Bridge in operation from 1920.

•
Bottom: The Wabash Avenue Bridge was completed in 1930.

Many Norwegian workers found employment on such construction sites
as the improvements on Chicago's South Water Street photographed
above on September 22, 1920.

skills much in demand as architects and engineers. The latter group comprised individual specializations such as civil, electrical, structural, and mechanical. They found positions of responsibility as consultants and directors in the building of bridges, streets, skyscrapers, and apartment buildings. Isak H. Faleide from Nordfjord, a graduate of Bergen's Technical College, was, for example, chief engineer at the Folwell Engineering Company, and Alfred Alsaker, a graduate of the same college, was chief engineer at the Delta Star Electric Company. Other persons took advantage of the bustling economic activity to work their way up. Torbjørn O. Hope, who arrived in Chicago in 1923 from near Trondheim as a young man of nineteen to begin an apprenticeship in construction, within eight years established his own successful firm, the Hope Construction Company, and Nils J. Johnson from Bamble worked his way up from carpenter to owning his own company, which specialized in iron and steel buildings. Success stories abounded in that optimistic decade.[13]

Logan Square

The Logan Square community experienced a rapid and extensive growth in the 1920s. Large apartment buildings, smaller stone dwellings with two or three flats, mansions, and modest frame houses in the industrial district along the railroads accommodated people from all social levels and several nationalities. Scandinavians clustered most heavily in the western part of the community. " 'Little Norway' is the district from California Avenue west to Crawford Avenue, and from Armitage Avenue north to Diversey," *Scandia* wrote in 1928. "In that territory," the newspaper continued, "we find the Norske Klub, Bjørgvin Singing Society, the Norwegian Theater, *Scandia* Publishing Company, Normennenes Singing Society, the Norwegian Turner Society, Bjørnstjerne Bjørnson Hall, and several Norwegian churches. In or near that territory we find the Scandinavian banks, the First Humboldt and the Second Humboldt. There are three hospitals, two Norwegian and one Danish." *Scandia* then proceeded to list the Danish societies, halls, churches, and other institutions located, as the newspaper described it, "on the outskirts of 'Little Norway,' " concluding that "the Norwegians are around Fullerton Avenue and the Danes around North Avenue."[14]

By 1930 more than 8,000 first and second generation Norwegians and 2,500 Danes lived in what the federal census defined as the Logan Square community. It became a natural ethnic center. Statistics support *Scandia*'s impressions, showing that there were nearly as many Danes in the Humboldt Park community as in Logan Square, whereas the Norwegians were twice as numerous in Logan Square as in the Humboldt Park district. Both nationalities were, however, obviously moving north and west. Indicative of the pattern of mobility was the Arntzen Bakery, built in 1907 on North Avenue at Kimball Avenue, which later moved to Fullerton Avenue west of

The plaque placed in 1937 at the original site of the Andersonville School at the southwestern corner of Foster and Clark.

Humboldt Boulevard. Fullerton Avenue became an important Norwegian shopping street, running east-west through the district described by *Scandia* as "Little Norway"; Milwaukee Avenue ran diagonally northwest through the community and was the main business center. If adjacent communities are considered, 63 percent of the Norwegian and 43 percent of the Danish population in Chicago centered on Logan Square. Within that community the Scandinavian population was augmented by 3,500 first and second generation Swedes.

The main centers of the Swedish-American community in Chicago were, however, on the North Side in the old Swedish settlement in the Lake View section around Belmont Avenue, and the more recent "Andersonville" settlement north of Lawrence Avenue, some distance farther north, between Halsted and Damen avenues. From the early 1920s the lofty Immanuel Church, with its proud history back to the pioneer era, identified the "Andersonville" neighborhood. The inescapable Scandinavian patronymic "Anderson"—the Danish and Norwegian form -sen, regularly being spelled -son—gives no clue to the true identity of the person for whom it was named. "Andersonville owes its name to Rev. Paul Andersen Norland, a Norwegian who came to Chicago in 1843," *Svenska Amerikanaren Tribunen* stated in its issue of October 7, 1964. Andersen owned land in this subdivision, worked as a farmer, taught school, and had a school named in his honor here. The original name was spelled Andersenville School with -sen. If it is indeed the person for whom the Swedish settlement is named, which the evidence seems to support, it would be a striking as well as a reverent link to the Swedish and Norwegian pioneer community in Chicago. The Swedish Immanuel congregation itself had sprung from the First Norwegian Evangelical Lutheran Congregation, started by Andersen in 1848 on Superior Street. Another Swedish clustering existed due west between Pulaski Road and California Avenue. On the South Side many Swedes lived in the Englewood district south of 59th Street.[15]

The Danish-American landscape architect and urban planner Jens Jensen, who had come to Chicago from his native South Jutland in 1884, lived for many years in the Humboldt Park neighborhood. As superintendent of Humboldt Park he transformed it into a social center, as evidenced in May 17th and other celebrations, athletic competitions, and family outings. His ideas were perhaps, as commentators have suggested, a reflection of a Scandinavian love of nature which encouraged him to bring the Illinois landscape into the heart of the commercial city. In 1905 Jensen became superintendent of the whole West Chicago park system and in that capacity designed the boulevards which connected Logan Square to the city parks by way of Logan Boulevard, Kedzie Boulevard, Palmer Square, and Humboldt Boulevard. Along these wide and shaded boulevards mansions were built to show the status of the residents. In 1918 Governor Frank Lowden dedicated the eagle-topped marble monument in Logan Square that commemorates the centennial of statehood for Illinois. It became an identifying symbol of the community.[16]

The Chicago Norske Klub with its elegant quarters on Kedzie Boulevard in sight of the centennial monument had 141 members between 1917 and 1930. Seventy-two of these lived in the Logan Square community, but even so, they showed a surprising degree of mobility. Many of them moved several times during the period, but generally—though there was some movement to the outlying areas—within the community, and nearly always to increasingly better addresses, not uncommonly in one of the brick mansions on the boulevards. The Norwegian undertaker N.B. Wold, for instance, in 1917 lived on North Avenue, in 1922 he had moved to Humboldt Avenue, the following year his residence was at Palmer Square, and

Top: The home of Tomas Øien and his family before 1906; it was on Nebraska, now Whipple, Avenue near Humboldt Park.

Bottom: North Avenue Businessmen's Parade on North Avenue in 1914. Members of the Arntzen family and bakers are photographed in front of the A.N. Arntzen Bakery.

Den norske Kafe

2738 W. NORTH AVE., När California Ave.

Et pent, hyggeligt Lokale, hjemligt og rensligt Stel.

JULEKAGE, FATTIGMANDSBAKKELSER, PERSESYLTE
RULLEPØLSE, LUDEFISK M. M.

DELIKATE SMØRREBRØD   GODE VAFLER

Varm Aftensmad hver Dag fra Kl. 5.30 til Kl. 7.30
Söndagsmiddag Kl. 12.30 til 2.30

MUSIK!   JULETRÄ!   AVISER!

•

Top two: Den norske Kafe at 2738 West North Avenue and an advertisement in *Skandinaven*, December 22, 1917, for traditional Norwegian
Christmas fare served in "nice and pleasant facilities."

•

Bottom: After she was widowed in 1913, Maren T. Hennes, born in Oslo,
first operated a rooming house and then this grocery store at Maplewood
and Diversey. In this photograph from 1923 she is seen together with
her nephew Ollie Lagerholm, who worked in her store.

by 1928 he had established himself on Logan Boulevard. Such other distinguished club members as Carl Bauer, Dr. Nils E. Remmen, a prominent eye surgeon, and Dr. Andrew Doe also lived on that boulevard, while Judge John Sonsteby, a well-known Democratic politician, Dr. George A. Torrison, and A.A. Krabol, president of the Colonial Chair Company, found appropriate residences on Kedzie Boulevard. The Norwegian-American congressman Magne Alfred Michaelson lived on Palmer Square, and others had fine dwellings in good residential districts, like Jens Paasche, president of the Paasche Airbrush Company, who lived just north of Fullerton on Kimball Avenue. A visible resident elite existed in the Logan Square community.[17]

Yet Scandinavians in 1930 made up only 12 percent of that community's 114,000 residents, the Germans nearly 16 percent, the Russians, mainly Jews, 6.4 percent, and the Poles as much as 28 percent. Avondale to the north of Logan Square was even more heavily Polish, and it was from there that Polish Americans in the postwar period moved into Logan Square. An ethnic neighborhood succession was under way.[18]

But Norwegians who grew up in the Logan Square community had a sense of living in a Norwegian social world. Walking down any main street one would encounter people who spoke Norwegian. Perhaps it reflected a certain occupational stability that depending on how they made a living people were addressed as Carpenter Pedersen, Plasterer Abrahamsen, Housemover Andersen, or Shoemaker Olsen. Also this practice was an old-world transplant. The heavy traffic on Fullerton made it an unsafe place for children to be outdoors alone, as the newly arrived Bergljot Anker-Nilssen wrote back to Norway in 1923. Together with their young son Jens she had joined her husband Karl who had emigrated earlier, and lived in an apartment above a store on Fullerton Avenue. They took in three roomers, all "fine young men," as she wrote. The many single young men arriving from Norway roomed with families and were a distinctive social group in the immigrant community.[19]

North Avenue in the Humboldt Park district persisted, however, throughout the 1920s as a major Norwegian, and Danish, commercial thoroughfare and gathering place on the Northwest Side. Norwegians might refer to it as Karl Johan, as they previously had Indiana Street, and the Danes just as vigorously thought of North Avenue as Nörrebro, a major street in Copenhagen. People promenaded, Saturday being an especially lively time. In the evening one might observe the Salvation Army marching from its temple to take up its place on a specific street corner; other religious groups competed, as did political agitators, most often of a leftist leaning, and peddlers, each occupying a street corner. There were many saloons, some bearing such names as Midnight Sun; Norwegian drunks and bums mixed with the more respectable crowd. Competing with the saloons were Norwegian restaurants and coffeehouses. Kaffistova, which opened for business in 1908 on West North Avenue was owned from 1922 by Olav Fidje from the Mandal area, and Edward Hansen from the same district was from 1921 the sole owner of Den norske Kafe, opened in 1915, located close by. Both men were driven by deep religious concerns to offer an alternative to the saloons, though Hansen operated his establishment in a more liberal manner than the pietistic Fidje. Den norske Kafe opened its spacious banquet rooms for cultural and political arrangements and provided a relaxed environment where traditional Norwegian dishes were enjoyed and good company could be found. Both restaurants prohibited any use of liquor. They were especially busy on the maids' day off on Thursday when young people of both sexes congregated. In the multi-ethnic setting of Chicago it was possible to retain a vision of a specific Norwegian-American environment.[20]

The Politics of Prohibition

The unparalleled prosperity of the "new economic era" of most of the 1920s until the stock-market crash in 1929 was marred by social tensions. The flow into Chicago of poor black migrants who did not enter into the social structure with the same ease and acceptance as the European immigrants they were replacing in the work force produced race riots against the black ghetto, notably in 1919, and demonstrated deep-seated and lasting issues. There were, historian Donald R. McCoy has said of American life in the 1920s, "severe antagonisms among the various groups that composed the nation's people." The debate over immigration restrictions revealed the tight social class system based on ancestry that was at the root of the existing ethnic and racial tensions. The blacks, along with new immigrant groups, were, however, to play an important part in shaping Chicago's political culture. The 1920s has been described as the heyday of ethnic politics. Following the America First movement during the war, which made ethnic politics unfeasible, Jews, Czechs, Poles, and Italians, having become citizens in large numbers, joined the Germans, Irish, and Scandinavians, the major ethnic voters before the war, to create new alignments and coalitions. Reform impulses, honesty in government, and opposition to criminal influence aggravated by the issue of prohibition became major forces for change.[21]

The Volstead Act, prohibiting the manufacture and sale of intoxicating beverages, passed under the hysteria of war and becoming effective in January, 1920, encouraged disregard for the law and produced a rapid rise in the crime rate. Illegal sale of liquor was rampant. Arriving in Chicago in the late 1920s as a recent immigrant from Lyngdal, Bert Benson recalls how he made his way on the elevated train to California and North avenues and wondered indeed if he had arrived at the Norwegian neighborhood. His fears were dispelled when, as he walked by a building under the elevated tracks, he saw a man being kicked out the door of the building accompanied with the unmistakably Norwegian: "Dra til helvete!" (Go to hell!). This was the disreputable Norwegian-operated Børnehjemmet (The Orphanage), a gambling den and speakeasy dispensing illegal liquor. It was located in the center of a small mob territory on the Northwest Side controlled by a subsidiary syndicate in Al Capone's vast empire. Fifty salesmen and persuaders under the streamlined direction of the mobster Martin Guilfoyle ran a brisk booze trade by serving the saloons in this outlying corner of the business.[22]

In 1920 *Skandinaven* showed its distaste for the link between Chicago politics and the rising organized crime. At the funeral in May of that year of the gangster boss "Big Jim" Colosimo, a predecessor of Al Capone, the newspaper editorially noted that his cortege "should disrupt the complacent thoughts of Chicago." For behind the funeral car moved "three judges, eight aldermen, an assistant state attorney, a congressman, and a state representative, and leading artists of the Chicago Opera Company are listed as honorary pallbearers along with gamblers, ex-gamblers, divekeepers and ex-divekeepers." "How much can power derived from the life of the underworld influence institutions of law and order?" *Skandinaven* asked its readers. The growing influence of gangsters in city politics was on this occasion made visible.[23]

Lutheraneren, the Norwegian-language organ of The Norwegian Lutheran Church in America, published in Minneapolis, heralded prohibition as "a great victory." Its opinion represented the rural mind of much of Norwegian America and might be further evidence that national prohibition was in the judgment of an historian of this reform, Andrew Sinclair, "a measure passed by village America against urban America." Not all Norwegian Americans, even if Lutheran, agreed with *Lutheraneren*, especially as the dire consequences of the measure became obvious. By 1926 prohibition was seen to be a failure and was quickly losing support in all segments of society. It doomed the efforts of drys like Waldemar Ager, who in his newspaper *Reform* stubbornly countered the evidence of unfortunate developments mustered by *Skandinaven*. Distressed by the apparent increase in the consumption of alcohol and the ease with which it was available throughout Chicago, Pastor C.T. Dyrness in 1927 called a mass meeting at Salem Free Church of Norwegian groups who supported prohibition: temperance lodges, Methodist and Baptist church groups, free churches, and also Lutheran clerical representation. A strong resolution to enforce the laws was sent to the city fathers.

Representatives from these same bodies constituted a Scandinavian Temperance Council (Det skandinaviske Ædruelighetsraad) to promote compliance with the prohibition laws; disagreements with the Norwegian National League and polemic exchanges with oppo-

Norwegian-born policeman Anthony Halvorsen from Oslo established a
reputation for bravery and the effective use of firearms against "bandits."

nents of prohibition revealed the divided opinion in the Norwegian-American community. *Scandia* vigorously advocated the dissolution of the Council, "which never has gotten much support." Scandinavians and blacks, both Protestant groups, might be less opposed to prohibition than Germans in general, and Catholics and Jews, but a majority of them did vote against it in all four opinion referenda between 1919 and 1930. In one instance a representative of the Anti-Saloon League, after he had spoken to the congregation, left Our Savior's Church without a single donation and irate communicants surrounded Pastor H.P. Ausan to protest the League's presence. Old-stock Americans also voted wet, and newer immigrant groups saw prohibition as a violation of their rights. These circumstances created large majorities in favor of repeal.[24]

Locally the opposition to prohibition strengthened the national trend toward the Democratic party; urban ethnic groups played a significant part in the revival of the Democratic party, bringing it to national prominence. It was gradually seen as the voice of the anti-prohibitionists. The strong emotional ties of Norwegian-American opinion makers to the Republican party were also loosened, though their loyalty to Republicanism remained a political factor. Chicago Norske Klub in 1916 feted the Republican congressman Niels Juul, a Danish American who had established himself as a book dealer in the Chicago Scandinavian community. The Republicanism of middle and upper class Norwegian Americans and other Scandinavians reflected American concerns at the same class levels—protection of their economic position and emulation of the leaders of society, who were, in Chicago as elsewhere, strongly Republican.[25]

Objections to corruption and zeal for reform, though secular, drew their strength from Protestant morality; they overrode both ethnic and political loyalties. The entanglement of local Republicans with crime was important here. The Republican Mayor William Hale "Big Bill" Thompson became the target of opposition by all reformers because of his connection with such crime figures as Colosimo, over-lord of prostitution, and then with Capone. And there was also immigrant resentment of his strong black alliance. It was the Swedish-American Fred Lundin—whom "no Irishman could beat"—who in 1915 built the Republican organization that elected Thompson mayor. Although known as "The Poor Swede," Lundin had risen to a position of popularity and wealth in the Swedish community as the producer of a nonalcoholic Juniper Ade.[26]

The Norwegian Republican Club of the 28th Ward, organized by Olaf Ray, worked for the election to the City Council of Magne Michaelson from Kristiansand. He served two terms as alderman and was Mayor Thompson's floor leader. In this manner he made his way up the Republican political ladder. In 1920, however, his association with the Thompson faction lost him the endorsement of the Republican Dovre Club when he successfully ran for election to the United States Congress. He was the first Norwegian from Chicago to be elected to such high office. The reformist tendencies of his countrymen and their objection to corruption, however, progressively deprived him of much of their support. Opponents cast aspersions on him for his rapid accumulation of wealth, moving as he did from a lowly salaried schoolteacher to a major bank investor with a stately residence at Palmer Square.

In later elections, municipal and state, Birger Osland and other prominent men in the Dovre Club, as well as influential persons in the Norwegian National League, endorsed Democratic candidates in order to beat Thompson. Osland's son-in-law Judge John J. Sonsteby represented the group of leading Norwegian Americans who by conviction had already joined forces with the Democratic party. Most Norwegian leaders might, however, be seen more as leaving the Republicans than as joining the Democrats. The three mayoral elections, 1923, 1927, and 1931, reveal the change. Following indictments for fraud against his crony Fred Lundin, Thompson withdrew his candidacy in 1923. The election that year of the Democratic William E. Dever was applauded by *Skandinaven*. In 1927, when Thompson ran for mayor, Osland and other Norwegians gave their support to the Republican League for Dever's Reelection. In order to convince fellow Norwegians to vote for "Dever and Decency" many of the members of Chicago Norske Klub joined the Norwegian Nonpartisan Dever League, headed by Einar Graff, journalist on the *Chicago Herald* and a member of the Norske Klub. Lundin after he parted company with Thompson following the legal scandal in 1923 directed such scorching attacks against him that the *Chicago Daily Tribune* described Lundin as his "Nordic Nemesis"; Lundin accused Thompson of involving himself with "gangsters, gunmen, hoodlums, and disreputable characters." Thompson nevertheless won and *Skandinaven* attributed his victory to black support and alluded to large financial campaign contributions by Al Capone.

Prohibition brought the gangsters center stage and provided a target for reformers to attack. The swing away from Thompson continued among leading Norwegian Americans. Though the issue of socioeconomic class in the 1920s does not appear to have been a dominant determinant in voting behavior among Norwegian Americans, working-class political loyalties were developing which caused this class to move more readily into the Democratic party than those at a higher social level. The major switch from the Republicans to the Democrats in Chicago occurred during the final years of the 1920s.

The successful Czech-American politician Anton J. Cermak was able to exploit the prohibition issue to form a large ethnic coalition and become the Democratic boss. He thereby broke the dominance of the Irish in the local Democractic party and made it more acceptable to non-Catholic immigrants, and even to some Catholics who objected to the strong controlling influence of the Irish. The Norwegian American Democratic Club of Chicago, organized to support Cermak, worked for his candidacy in 1931 against Thompson in large political advertisements in the Norwegian-American press signed by 151 men, representing Norwegian Americans at many social levels. *Scandia* officially endorsed Cermak, and Grevstad, having returned to edit *Skandinaven* in 1930, praised Cermak's great victory in the election as a sign that the Chicago electorate wanted "to clean house" and rid the city of an administration "in league with gangsters." The circumstance that "Chicago's new mayor belongs to the foreign-language group, as he was born in Bohemia," further facilitated Norwegian-American identification with his cause. Endorsement by solid Republican middle-class organizations of Democratic candidates revealed that the overriding concern was for good government. This factor coupled with the greater attraction of the Democratic party for working-class Norwegians as it rose nationally combined to give Cermak about 75 percent of the vote compared to 25 perecnt for Thompson in the precincts roughly covering "Little Norway." In 1927 these same precincts had voted 51 percent for Thompson. Cermak's election as mayor in 1931 established the supremacy of the Democratic party in Chicago politics.[27]

Ethnicity on Parade

Political horsetrading was employed as a means to advance Norwegian-American honor and standing. The greatest victory for those who sought to establish a Norwegian presence in the city came in 1927 when they succeeded in having the new outer drive on the South Side named the Leif Eriksen Drive, from Jackson Park, north, according to Osland, to Monroe Street, though it may have extended only to Achsah Bond Drive close to the northern boundary of Grant Park. The cause of Leif Ericson played a significant part in a continuing and insistent demand by Chicago Norwegians for recognition in the life of the metropolis; it was reinforced by the general postwar ethnic self-assertion. A small ethnic group had in this regard fewer options than those with greater clout through numerical strength. In the volatile ethnic political environment of Chicago in the 1920s, the naming of the drive became a tangible symbol of Norwegian protest against the homogenizing influence of the American consumer society. The Norwegian National League took the lead in the matter energetically directed by Christian Olsen, its president, and Berthe C. Petersen, first vice president, who bombarded officials with petitions requesting that "the boulevard closest to the open water should be called Leif Ericson in honor of America's discoverer, the fearless courageous explorer of the unknown lands." She enlisted the support of Victor Lawson whose *Daily News* announced that "Chicago Norwegians Demand Recognition for Ericson." Splendid annual public

Above: A May 17th parade in the late 1920s as it turns off North Avenue onto California Avenue to enter Humboldt Park. Norwegian places of business, the offices of Norwegian lawyers, physicians, and artists, and popular meeting places such as Den norske Kafe, as well as moving picture theaters and large American stores, can be identified along North Avenue. It gave evidence of being a self-contained community.

Next page: Officers of the Norwegian National League in 1926 with portraits of Christian Olsen, president, Berthe C. Petersen, first vice president, Knute Nelson, second vice president, Emma Hjelkrem, third vice president, Erwin Larsen, treasurer, and Sig. Huseby, recording secretary.

festivals arranged in *English* by the National League to communicate the group's wishes attracted wide attention; in 1925 the League arranged the visit of Magnus Andersen, the celebrated captain of the *Viking* in 1893, which made, as a later commentator wrote, "the Leif Ericson movement spread its sails."

But already in 1922 Osland had joined men like Olsen, Sonsteby, Andrew Hummeland, and Louis M. Anderson, publisher of *Skandinaven*, to move the immodest quest to mark a Norwegian presence into the political arena. A deal was eventually struck with Edward J. Kelly, president of the South Park Board and later mayor, who was then serving as campaign manager for George Brennan, Democratic candidate for the United States Senate, to form a Norwegian-American committee to work for his election in exchange for giving the boulevard the name of the Norse discoverer. Since the Republican candidate had discredited himself in the eyes of most Norwegian voters by his close ties to Samuel Insull, the public utility magnate, it was apparently easy to set up a committee. This action benefited other Democratic candidates as well. During the mayoral election campaign of 1927 Kelly appeared together with Mayor William Dever at mass meetings arranged by the Norwegian National League and told of plans for the opening of the drive. He was the hero of the day, and at the opening ceremonies, after claiming Norse-Irish ancestry, "accepted as a Norwegian."[28]

The Norwegian National League was, however, because of insufficient funds forced to drop its grandiose plans for a magnificent monument to Leif Ericson in Grant Park by Lake Michigan. The theme of Norse discovery had been prominently injected into the Norse-American Centennial in 1925 commemorating the arrival of the sloop the *Restauration*. Speaking at the main celebrations in Minneapolis in early June, Calvin Coolidge had endorsed the claim that Leif Ericson had been the first European to discover America. "It has to fill Americans of Norwegian descent with enthusiasm when they hear the nation's President assert this claim," Congressman O.J. Kvale of Minnesota stated in his speech at the local celebrations in Chicago at the end of the month.

Much of the restless parading of Norwegian ethnicity during the 1920s seemingly had the double purpose of convincing the American-born to take pride in their heritage and making a Norwegian existence visible to Americans of all nationalities. Ethnic tensions during the decade heightened self-awareness and encouraged a larger view of the group's future. It sought recognition and respectability within Protestant America. The centennial festival did not express faith in the continuation of a Norwegian subculture, as the 1914 festivities had done, but became a celebration of a record of past achievements of a successful and secure ethnic group. Nicolay Grevstad, who spoke in Minneapolis for the governor of Illinois, traced "the unique position of Norwegian Americans in war and peace . . . during their history of one hundred years," and emphasized "the wonderful heritage Norway has given her children." The festival in Minneapolis included a pageant in twenty-four scenes depicting their historical experience. *Skandinaven* found most scenes "effective," especially those from the Civil War portraying Colonel Hans Christian Heg, which were warmly applauded, but thought the one representing the arrival of the pioneer immigrants in 1825 "unfortunately selected." It had depicted the Sloopers smoking a peace pipe with the Indians and then breaking out into song, intoning the much later Norwegian national anthem "Yes, We Love this Country."[29]

High-flown rhetoric was heard as well by a crowd of about 6,000 who attended the centennial festival at the Auditorium on the

Municipal Pier (later Navy Pier) in Chicago. Bishop Johan Peter Lunde of Oslo was the only one of the Norwegian dignitaries in attendance who represented Norway at the main celebrations in Minneapolis. Eloquently he lauded Norwegian Americans as "an exemplary immigrant population that had cast honor and luster on the homeland," with whose "spiritual and cultural values they were endowed." Among the several speakers were Alfred Erickson who praised his countrymen as law-abiding citizens who did not, like some nationalities, "prowl about in the darkness of the night, plundering the homes and blasting vaults"; Congressman Michaelson spoke in the same vein, but mildly reproached his countrymen for their "kindness, which lets another nation take the honor of America's discovery," and their "modesty, which is inappropriate . . . [because] we are building the nation in the right way." An ethnic self-perception was defined by these orations.[30]

A Peak in Immigrant Culture

During the 1920s, in the midst of the escape of a second generation receptive to agitation for Americanization, Norwegian-American cultural expressions reached a new height. In literature the success of Ole E. Rølvaag's minor classic *Giants in the Earth* in 1927, a translation of his *I de dage* and *Riket grundlægges*, exemplified the coming of age of immigrant creative writing. It presupposed, as did other cultural activities, an established tradition and thus flourished toward the end of a distinct Norwegian-American cultural world. Some of its attributes were more resistant to assimilationist contravention than others, with those dependent on a Norwegian-speaking audience being least able to survive.

Academically trained and culturally interested young people from Norway gave impetus to the intellectual and cultural life of the community. They convened in halls and meeting rooms such as Den norske Kafe on North Avenue, which provided a convenient and relaxed setting. In 1926 recent as well as older graduates of Norwegian educational institutions organized the Chicago Norwegian Student Society (Chicago norske Studenterforening), patterned after the one in Oslo. It advertised itself as "a torchbearer for everything Norwegian," but went beyond that parochial concern to listen to lectures on historical and current issues. More restricted in its interests was the Literary Society of Chicago (Det litterære Samfund), formed in January of the previous year. In April, 1927, the student organization invited the literary society's members to hear Professor Julius E. Olson of the University of Wisconsin interpret the place of Norwegian literature in America; his sanguine "message that our literature is held in high regard" received their plaudits. The Literary Society joined the older Norwegian Reading Society, organized in 1898, in an enthusiastic promotion of Norwegian literary art, though the former adopted a broader cultural focus. Its popular "salon evenings"

•

Left: Bergljot Raaen reciting poetry at a meeting of the Literary Society.

•

Right: The high seat on festive occasions in the clubhouse of Chicago Norske Klub, which was the site of numerous social and cultural events in the Norwegian community.

provided an outlet for dramatic and literary talent. There were plays, musical numbers, and declamations. In this circle Bergljot Raaen, who had studied drama in Oslo before coming to Chicago in 1922, gained wide recognition for her acting and readings. A Norwegian artistic life could thus be cultivated in the Norwegian-American community. These nationally inspired societies enhanced its intellectual and cultural status.[31]

The elegant clubhouse of the Chicago Norske Klub on fashionable Kedzie Boulevard was the center of an array of cultural activities. The Dramatic Society of the club and the Chicago Norske Klub Ladies Auxiliary entertained with plays and musical performances on the club's stage. The Dramatic Society ambitiously staged demanding productions of works by Bjørnson and Ibsen. The members of Chicago Norske Klub provided an appreciative audience for the community's talent. In this elite group cultural interests mixed with social functions in a typical middle-class manner. Card parties were popular, as were dances and informal gatherings. In March, 1919, for instance, there were four card parties for the men, one for the members of the women's auxiliary, and one "Ladies'and Men's Card Night." There were "Music and Dancing" evenings three times, one billed as "Young People's Dance Night," one vaudeville, and two educational lectures.[32]

In 1920 the Chicago Norske Klub held the first of a series of annual juried commercial shows of the works of Norwegian-American artists. These exhibitions made visible an urbane taste and attracted participation on a national scale. They revealed the artistic activity stimulated by the ethnic community. Several of these Norwegian-American artists were members of the prestigious Palette & Chisel Club, as painters, lithographers and sculptors; the Chicago-born Fred T. Larson, an established woodcut artist, had been a charter member in 1895. Norwegian and American subjects inspired artistic depiction, the latter including the Chicago scene. Among the elder artists exhibiting in 1920, most of them trained at art institutes in Norway, were Emil Biørn, Sigvald Asbjørnsen, and Svend Svendsen. Svendsen's creative powers had by the 1920s been greatly reduced through poverty and alcohol abuse; when he came to Chicago in the early 1880s no Norwegian patrons of the arts had stood ready to assist. He was representative of the several gifted and sensitive souls who could not reconcile themselves to the reality of immigrant life, and indeed had no marketable skill. The brief sojourn in Chicago in 1891 of the high-strung and impractical young Norwegian poet Sigbjørn Obstfelder ended in defeat as well. He thought Chicago to be "a loathsome city," the adversity he suffered making him critical of the people he met: the Norwegians were "uncultured and boring," and the Germans "lack the faintest ability to understand a man like me." Svendsen had studied under the Norwegian city and landscape painter Fritz

Thaulow before emigrating and had been a promising landscape artist.[33]

The greater flourishing of artistic endeavors in the 1920s gave evidence of a responsive audience and the general prosperity of the decade. Art was a commodity that appealed to middle-class consumer tastes in the Norwegian-American community. Like the purchase of automobiles and homes in the suburbs it represented an identification with American consumerism; simultaneously the promotion of Norwegian cultural expressions was a protest against assimilation. The popularity of romantic paintings of Norwegian landscapes not only gave evidence of a desire to escape back to an idealized way of life but the pastoral scenes depicted in these paintings also denoted anti-urban sentiments. Few immigrant artists, however, could survive on commissions and sales of art alone; most had to make a living in related professions, as illustrators and commercial artists, or even as housepainters. Like Svendsen, Gulbrand Saether was a student of Thaulow; he came to Chicago at the time of the World's Fair in 1893 and worked at numerous odd jobs, as waiter, dishwasher, and even train conductor. After 1900 he could afford his own studio and devoted himself to artistic pursuits, writing, painting, and sculpting; he "dressed the part of the artist, wearing flowing silk ties and broad-brimmed hats." To this circle of artists belonged also Lars Haukaness from Hardanger, attracted like many others by "the promise of America's World's Fair," after having studied under Thaulow and such other artists as Christian Krohg and Erik Werenskjold at the royal academy in Oslo. In 1913 Haukaness had a one-man show in Chicago offering some forty paintings produced during a four-year sojourn "among the fjords and mountains of his loved Hardanger," as the catalog stated. His romantic Norwegian landscapes appealed strongly to immigrant nostalgia.[34]

Many of the artists who made their debut later received their training in America, being American-born or having emigrated at a young age. But inspiration was still found in a romantic concept of an ancestral homeland. Ben Blessum from Romsdalen emigrated at age ten in 1888; he learned art in evening courses at the fine arts academy of the Art Institute in Chicago. His commission to decorate the building exhibiting "the emigrated Norway" at the Centennial Exposition in Oslo in 1914 resulted in his best known works. The large canvas depicting the departure of the *Restauration* from Stavanger in 1825 was purchased by the Norwegian America Line, and his "Hjemlængsel," (Longing for Home) touched a sentimental nerve in the Norwegian-American community and was eventually reproduced in several thousand copies.[35]

It would, however, be unfair to dismiss Norwegian-American artists as peddlers of nostalgia. Though their romantic portrayals of Norwegian scenery, folk life, and historical events and figures, in

A historical national–romantic painting by Ben Blessum of a *røykstove*
(dwelling with open fireplace and smoke hole directly above) in Setesdal
with peasants in festive dress.

Self-portrait of Karl Ouren.

paintings as well as in sculpture and carvings, would appeal most directly to the majority of their compatriots, a number of them also involved themselves in the broader cultural life of Chicago and showed their works at exhibitions of the Art Institute. Karl Ouren from Fredrikshald was undoubtedly the most gifted of the Norwegian Chicago artists and won many awards and prizes, including the Palette and Chisel Club gold medal in 1919; he exhibited regularly at the Chicago Norske Klub as well as at the Art Institute. He painted uplifting pictures, often winter scenes, of Chicago's parks and environs and striking Norwegian landscapes. [36]

The exhibitions at the Chicago Norske Klub followed the general move toward professionalism in the fine arts, but they were uniquely ethnic and a stimulus to artistic development. In the

Artists and friends in the studio of Anton Beutlich. From left to right: Signe Hansen Kirkeby, who was model for the evening, B. Falk, Marie Løkke, Lars Haukaness, Anton Beutlich, and Sigvald Asbjørnsen.

Norwegian-American community they heightened appreciation of esthetics; they also expressed and strengthened cultural ties to Norway. Other forms of artistic expression worked to the same end. Traditional choral singing achieved new heights in these years. A major participant stated that it was then in its heyday, and attributed this to the existence of closely knit immigrant communities and continued emigration, and "there was money." Under the direction of Otto Clausen, Normennenes Singing Society toured Norway in 1924; the reunion with the homeland created lasting images. "As the 'America boat' adorned with flags slowly approached the dock," a local newspaper in Bergen reported, "the melody of 'Yes, We Love this Country' sounded from the Chicago singers on board the ship and on the dock the Bergen choir responded with 'Singers' Greeting.' " Well received

The painter and sculptor Lars Fletre, born in Voss, Norway, in his studio
on North Avenue about 1930.

Normennenes Singing Society at its fiftieth anniversary concert in 1920.
The director was Otto Clausen.

and critically acclaimed concerts were given all over Norway. A
newspaper in Trondheim saw in the "American choir's visit . . . a
devotion and love for the fatherland and its traditions that should ad-
monish us [Norwegians in Norway] to serious reflection." The approval of Norwegian critics, whether in literature, art, or musical performance, was eagerly sought by immigrant practitioners. It reflected
an immigrant inferiority complex, but there was also an element of
defiance and self-confidence and a sense of cultural independence. A
deep-rooted yearning to prove individual and group success to the
homeland was intrinsic to the immigrant experience.[37]

It became a common occurrence for visiting Norwegian-
American singing societies to sing their "love throughout our old and
dear land," as the program of the Norwegian Singers' Association ex-

Knute Hansen.

pressed it in 1926. That year the Association arranged its biennial *sangerfest* in Chicago. In 1914 Emil Biørn had directed its combined choir, chosen from member societies which visited Norway for the centennial festivities; at the convention in 1926 Biørn directed the orchestra. The *sangerfest* was arranged under the auspices of the Norwegian Singers' League of Chicago, which had a new member society, the Bjørnson Male Chorus. It had been organized on March 21, 1924, on the initiative of members of the Bjørnstjerne Bjørnson lodge of the Sons of Norway and met in its own club house on Fullerton Avenue. Knute Hansen, a talented musician from Fredrikstad, played an active and significant role in Norwegian–American musical life. In 1926 he was director for the two venerable male choruses, Normennenes and Bjørgvin, and in years to come he cut a handsome figure as he conducted joint and individual concerts by the Norwegian and also Swedish singing societies.[38]

As the social world of Norwegian America gradually dissolved during the 1920s, and the second generation escaped into American society, its symbols and cultural expressions acquired added importance in the definition of ethnic identity. In the context of the urban environment of Chicago a forceful nationalism and, to be sure, one expressed with an appreciation for esthetic values, was displayed at public festivals and appeared in the cultural program of the community. A final Norwegian-American rally which drew sustenance from both the homeland's culture and the Norwegian-American community itself as it sought to establish a permanent place in the American ethnic mosaic was the red thread that can be discerned throughout the decade.

In its review of "Norwegian Chicago in 1930" *Skandinaven* concluded that "Norwegian congregations and organizations have had a good year." Convincingly the newspaper enumerated divine services, meetings of societies and lodges, theater evenings and concerts, athletic and sporting events, anniversaries, and celebrations. "One gets," *Skandinaven* commented, "a vivid picture of life in Norwegian Chicago and the activity shown by that group which still believes there is fertile soil in Chicago for that which is Norwegian."[39]

A Decade of Transition

The conclusion expresses a bittersweet sentiment rather than a firm conviction. A Norwegian-American cultural tradition had, however, as *Skandinaven* pointed out, attained a respectable age. That year Nora Lodge celebrated its seventieth anniversary and Normennenes its sixtieth. Besides commemorative festivities for Bjørnson, Ole Bull, and Leif Ericson, Chicago Norwegians celebrated "the most Norwegian and most festive May 17 outside of Norway." And sports retained a strong following. The Norwegian American Athletic Association, located in its own large clubhouse at Wabansia and St. Louis (then Ballou) avenues just northwest of Humboldt Park, boasted that it was the largest athletic society outside the homeland. It represented the merger of several Norwegian-American athletic clubs, dating its origin from the organization of the Norwegian Turner Society in 1885. It was formally organized in 1919 when it consolidated with the Football Club Fram and promoted a number of sports and athletic activities for men and women in team competitions on turf and cinder track, gymnastics, boxing and wrestling, skiing and skating. Alongside the Norge Ski Club, with its spectacular jumping competitions at Cary, the Norwegian American Athletic Association was a significant ethnic institution. The group also thought of itself as a major promoter of "Norsedom" among the young; second and third generation youth were attracted to its program, and Norwegian continued to be the official language, though its use obviously could not be en-

• *Across top:* The Norwegian-American Athletic Association at its fiftieth anniversary in 1935. It had started as the Norwegian Turner Society in 1885, and the original banner is seen at the back of the photograph. Many new activities were, however, introduced through the years.

• *Bottom next page:* Members of the Norge Ski Club in the 1920s.

forced. Still, such institutions, because of their appeal on non-ethnic grounds and their survivability, paradoxically could provide a later age the means and symbols to identify with a specific transplanted national heritage.[40]

In 1930 the Norwegian American Athletic Association sponsored the Norwegian "skating princess" Sonja Henie and her figure skating show. She was welcomed and feted by an enthusiastic audience. Looking back on the accumulated evidence of a Norwegian-American presence, *Skandinaven* might in 1930 easily find grounds for optimism. The Norwegian National League included about fifty member organizations, and there were another twenty-five groups, including mission and benevolent societies, that did not belong. As the Great Depression deepened the Norwegian-American community pulled together to come to the aid of compatriots in need. Benefit performances and fund raising efforts stimulated the cultural and social life of the community. In November, 1931, the aid committee of the Norwegian National League engaged member societies in a "Benefit Festival" at the Logan Square Masonic Temple.[41]

The Logan Square community persisted as a central ethnic district; those who moved out returned to it to participate in Norwegian-American affairs. Upward mobility facilitated by the general prosperity of the 1920s accelerated the movement out of the community as people left the city for new homes in nearby suburbs and outlying districts. But, as Christian Nielsen wrote of the Danes moving out of the Humboldt Park community, "there was no joint departure, and . . . a thousand Danish homes are now widely spread." There was a gradual dispersion through the residential districts of the city. No new Norwegian-American residential enclaves or ethnic neighborhoods took shape. Movement by more prosperous Norwegian Americans from Wicker Park, Humboldt Park, and Logan Square accelerated to Oak Park, a western suburb which Andreas already in the 1880s described as "a pleasant suburban town." There Norwegian women, both single and married, while still living in Logan Square, could find work in domestic service in some of the large residences; streetcars and buses provided transportation. The location of the United Lutheran Church of Oak Park in that suburb in 1925 gave evidence of the pattern of mobility. More ordinary as well as more exclusive residential neighborhoods existed elsewhere in the city and eventually in the suburbs beyond its boundaries. The pattern of movement north and west still prevailed. To be sure, not all Norwegians had ever lived in a relative concentration with other Norwegians; many had lived dispersed and interspersed with other nationalities. Common ancestry does not automatically translate into ethnic cohesiveness, yet it is equally true that clustering with other Norwegian Americans was not a pre-condition for ethnic fervor and participation in Norwegian-American affairs. A lasting sense of belonging to a specific nationality survived the dissolution of distinct Norwegian-American neighborhoods. A detailed investigation on an individual basis might, however, disclose a different manner of regarding ethnic membership in later generations. It might be seen as only one component of self-identification. The strength of ethnic impulses is, however, frequently underrated. In the 1960s, for instance, Norwegians in Chicago ceased their aid to the large public institution the Oak Forest Infirmary when the last Norwegian inmate died because "there was no longer anyone to give to." National ties still conditioned a charitable response. But the suburban experience affected how individuals defined and redefined their Norwegian identity, some perhaps, especially as the generations shifted, giving it little thought.[42]

Notes

Notes

[1]Quoted in Ingrid Semmingsen, *Veien mot vest*, 2 vols. (Oslo, 1941, 1950), 1:216; **Chapter 1**
Maldwyn Allen Jones, *American Immigration* (Chicago, 1960), 92–94.

[2]T. K. Derry, *A History of Modern Norway, 1814–1972* (Oxford, 1973), 1–16.

[3]Derry, *Modern Norway*, 17–40; Magnus Nodtvedt, *Rebirth of Norway's Peasantry: Folk Leader Hans Nielsen Hauge* (Tacoma, Washington, 1965), 98–122, 214–231. See also Einar Molland, *Church Life in Norway, 1800–1950*, trans. by Harris Kaasa (Minneapolis, 1957).

[4]Kåre Ofstad, ed., *Historisk statistikk 1978* (Oslo, 1978), 33. See O.J. Falnes, *National Romanticism in Norway* (New York, 1933).

[5]Derry, *Modern Norway*, 116–118; Sima Lieberman, *The Industrialization of Norway, 1800–1920* (Oslo, 1970), 48–53; Jacob S. Worm-Müller, *Den norske sjøfarts historie. Fra de ældste tider til vore dage*, 2 (Oslo, 1935), 219–231, 321–409. See also Bernt Lorentzen, *Norsk næringsliv gjennom tidene* (Oslo, 1969).

[6]Semmingsen, *Veien mot vest*, 1:9–32; Theodore C. Blegen, *Norwegian Migration to America, 1825–1860* (Northfield, 1931), 24–56; Odd S. Lovoll,*The Promise of America: A History of the Norwegian-American People* (Minneapolis, 1984), chapter one.

[7]See Hjalmar Rued Holand, *De norske settlementers historie* (Ephraim, Wisconsin, 1908), 40–46. Holand makes the ridiculous suggestion that Peerson was offered the opportunity to purchase large land areas where Chicago was to be located.

[8]Holand, *Norske settlementer*, 44–45; Lovoll, *Promise of America*, 33; Homer Hoyt, *One Hundred Years of Land Values in Chicago* (Chicago, 1933), 23–44.

[9]Carlton C. Qualey, *Norwegian Settlement in the United States* (Northfield, 1938), 17–39.

[10]Bessie Louise Pierce, *Beginnings of a City, 1673–1848*, vol. 1 of *A History of Chicago* (Chicago, 1937), 75–76; J. Hart Rosdail, *The Sloopers: Their Ancestry and Posterity* (Broadview, Illinois, 1961), 66–67.

[11]Lovoll, "A Pioneer Chicago Colony of Immigrants from Voss: Its Impact on the Overseas Migration," a paper delivered at an international conference A Century of European Migrations, held in Minneapolis, November 6–9, 1986, and published in its proceedings; Nils Kolle, "Den tidlegaste utvandringa frå Hordaland," in Ståle Dyrvik and Kolle, eds., *Eit blidare tilvere?* (Voss, Norway, 1986), 15–61.

[12]Andres A. Svalestuen, "Om den regionale spreiinga av norsk utvandring før 1865," in Arnfinn Engen, ed., *Utvandringa—det store oppbrotet* (Oslo, 1978), 57–85. The article traces statistically the spread of emigration from southwestern Norway north and east and shows its varying intensity. The urge to emigrate reached East Norway in 1837 when the first group left from Numedal and Upper Telemark.

[13]Pierce, comp. and ed., *As Others See Us: Impressions of Visitors, 1673–1933* (Chicago, 1933), 100.

[14]Pierce, *Beginnings of a City*, 5; James William Putnam, *The Illinois and Michigan Canal: A Study in Economic History* (Chicago, 1918), 1–29, 92–125.

[15]Pierce, *Beginnings of a City*, 14–24; Holand, *Norske settlementer*, 42; Fort Dearborn Muster Rolls, 1808 and 1810, in Heald Papers, Chicago Historical Society.

[16]Pierce, *Beginnings of a City*, 24–31.

[17]Pierce, *Beginnings of a City*, 30–33; Putnam, *Illinois and Michigan Canal*, 23–24, 154–158; Harold M. Mayer and Richard C. Wade, *Chicago: Growth of a Metropolis* (Chicago, 1969), 3–31.

[18]Pierce, *Beginnings of a City*, 43–44.

[19]James A. Clifton, "Chicago, September 14, 1833: The Last Great Indian Treaty in the Old Northwest," in *Chicago History*, Summer, 1980, 86–97.

[20]Rasmus B. Anderson, *The First Chapter of Norwegian Immigration, 1821–1840* (Madison, Wisconsin, 1895), 102–103; George T. Flom, *A History of Norwegian Immigration to the United States. From the Earliest Beginning Down to the Year 1848* (Iowa City, Iowa, 1909), 230–240.

[21]John Calhoun, Account Book, in Calhoun Papers, Chicago Historical Society; A.T. Andreas, *History of Chicago. From the Earliest Period to the Present Time*, 3 vols. (Chicago, 1884–1886), 1:232, 360, 365, 371; Flom, *Norwegian Immigration*, 232–233; Holand, *Norske settlementer*, 100.

[22]Flom, *Norwegian Immigration*, 232, 348–350; A.E. Strand, comp. and ed., *A History of the Norwegians in Illinois* (Chicago, 1905), 187; K.A. Rene, *Historie om udvandringen fra Voss og vossingerne i Amerika* (Madison, Wisconsin, 1930), 135–136.

[23]Holand, *Norske settlementer*, 100–101; Anderson, *First Chapter*, 194–195; Flom, *Norwegian Immigration*, 95–96; E. Clifford Nelson, ed., *A Pioneer Churchman: J.W.C. Dietrichson in Wisconsin*, trans. by Malcolm Rosholt and Harris E. Kaasa (New York, 1973), 116–117.

[24]Rene, *Historie om udvandringen*, 110–112; Holand, *Norske settlementer*, 100–101; Anderson, *Bygdejævning* (Madison, Wisconsin, 1903), 42.

[25]Kolle, "Den tidlegaste utvandringa frå Hordaland," 24–27; Flom, *Norwegian Immigration*, 62; Blegen, *Amerikabrev* (Oslo, 1958), 14–15.

[26]Rene, *Historie om udvandringen*, 99–100; Oscar Handlin, *Boston's Immigrants: A Study in Acculturation* (Rev. ed., Cambridge, Massachusetts, 1959), 1–24. See Robert Fergus, comp., *Directory of the City of Chicago* (Chicago, 1839).

[27]Anderson, *First Chapter*, 228; Hoyt, *Land Values*, 14, 24–36; Pierce, *Beginnings of a City*, 171.

[28]Pierce, *Beginnings of a City*, 171–172; Harriet Martineau, *Society in America* (London, 1837), 351–352.

[29]Hoyt, *Land Values*, 14, 24–39; Putnam, *Illinois and Michigan Canal*, 3–65.

[30]Rene, *Historie om udvandringen*, 43; *Vossingen*, 3/1922, 4–11; *Daily Democrat*, July 16, 1845.

[31]J.W. Norris, *A Business Advertiser and General Directory of the City of Chicago 1845–1846* (Chicago, 1845), 152–153; Federal Population Schedules of the Seventh Census of the United States, 1850, for Cook County, Illinois, Roll 102; Svalestuen, "Tidlig norsk utvandring sett i nordisk perspektiv," in Dyrvik and Kolle, *Eit blidare*

tilvere? 142–143; Ulf Beijbom, *Swedes in Chicago: A Demographic and Social Study of the 1846–1880 Immigration* (Uppsala, 1971), 58.

[32]Pierce, *Beginnings of a City*, 179–180, 181–182; David Ward, *Cities and Immigrants* (New York, 1971), 106; Michael F. Funchion, "Irish Chicago," in Peter d'A. Jones and Melvin G. Holli, eds., *Ethnic Chicago* (Grand Rapids, Michigan, 1981), 9–10; Rudolf A. Hofmeister, *The Germans of Chicago* (Champaign, Illinois, 1976), 1–12. Justin B. Galford, "The Foreign Born and Urban Growth in Chicago, 1850–1950," 100, manuscript at Chicago Historical Society, shows that the Irish constituted the largest foreign-born group in 1850 and the Germans the second largest, but after that the Germans held first place and the Irish second in all censuses from 1860 until 1900.

[33]Norris, *Directory of the City of Chicago*, 152–153; Galford, "The Foreign Born and Urban Growth," 96, 98.

[34]Mari Lund Wright, "The Pioneer Norwegian Community in Chicago before the Great Fire (1836–1871)" (M.A. thesis, University of Wisconsin, 1958), 6–35; Rene, *Historie om udvandringen*, 101–103; Lovoll, "A Pioneer Chicago Colony of Immigrants from Voss."

[35]Lund Wright, "Pioneer Norwegian Community," 15–21; Emmett Dedmon, *Fabulous Chicago* (New York, 1953), 28.

[36]Immigrants frequently chose their patronymic in America, regularly giving it an American form, but among fellow Norwegians continued to be known by their farm names. The American form will be used as far as possible, but in order to aid identification the Norwegian original or the farm name will be given in parentheses. Not only the adoption of the patronymic, but such changes as Lars Knutsen Kvernhaugen becoming Lewis Newton, Lars Brynildsen Bryn becoming Lewis Brown, Kjel Vikingson Gjøastein becoming Kiel Williams, or Bakkethun becoming Baker, Prestegaarden becoming Prescott and Vike becoming Wicker obscure the Norwegian origin and complicate the process of identification. A strong wish to assimilate and to identify with the established Anglo-Saxon tradition are evident in these changes.

[37]*Skandinaven*, June 8, 1917; Rene, *Historie om udvandringen*, 136–137; Rasmus Sunde, "Emigration from the District of Sogn, 1839–1915," trans. by C.A. Clausen, in *Norwegian-American Studies*, 29 (Northfield, Minnesota, 1982), 122.

[38]Rene, *Historie om udvandringen*, 260 and 262, and Flom, *Norwegian Immigration*, 113, both state that Iver Lawson emigrated in 1844.

[39]Rene, *Historie om udvandringen*, 112–114, 138–139, 260–262.

[40]Rene, *Historie om udvandringen*, 138–139, 260–262, 368–369; Knud Langeland, *Nordmændene i Amerika* (Chicago, 1889), 41; Charles H. Dennis, *Victor Lawson: His Time and His Work* (Chicago, 1935), 20–23.

[41]Rene, *Historie om udvandringen*, 135–136, 177–178. See also Sverre Steen, *Det gamle samfunn*, vol. 4 of *Det frie Norge* (Oslo, 1957).

[42]Lund Wright, "Pioneer Norwegian Community," 18–19, 21–22; Rene, *Historie om udvandringen*, 257; Knut Gjerset, *Norwegian Sailors on the Great Lakes* (Northfield, 1928), 5, 18–19, 20; biographical information on George A. Wigeland in Wigeland Papers at the Norwegian-American Historical Association; Helge Ove Tveiten, "En utvandring blusser opp—og slokner. Sørlandsk emigrasjon på 1800-tallet"(cand. philol. thesis, University of Oslo, 1974).

[43]Rene, *Historie om udvandringen*, 135, 136, 243.

[44]Rene, *Historie om udvandringen*, 138–139; John Bodnar, *The Transplanted: A History of Immigrants in Urban America* (Bloomington, Indiana, 1985), 71, 74.

[45]Lund Wright, "Pioneer Norwegian Community," 50; *Skandinaven*, June 8, 1917; *Vossingen*, 3/1922, 10–11, 1–2/1925, 11–12.

[46]Dennis, *Victor Lawson*, 20–23; Rene, *Historie om udvandringen*, 132, 136–138, 139, 140, 365; Pierce, *Beginnings of a City*, 182; Hofmeister, *Germans of Chicago*, 53–54; Federal Population Schedules in the Seventh Census; Ernst W. Olson, ed., *History of the Swedes of Illinois*, 1 (Chicago, 1908), 309–310.

[47]Lund Wright, "Pioneer Norwegian Community," 20–21.

[48]Rene, *Historie om udvandringen*, 243.

[49]Rene, *Historie om udvandringen*, 179–180; Hoyt, *Land Values*, 57.

[50]Nelson, *Pioneer Churchman*, 116–117.

[51]*Chicago Tribune*, December 23, 1853; *Chicago Democrat*, April 9, 1845; *Daily Democrat*, December 27, 1848, September 25, 1849; Henry Justin Smith, *Chicago's Great Century, 1833-1933* (Chicago, 1933), 42-43. See also Lloyd Lewis and Henry Justin Smith, *Chicago: A History of its Reputation* (New York, 1929).

[52]*Chicago Morning Democrat*, September 15, 1841; Nelson, *Pioneer Churchman*, 117; Holand, *Norske settlementer*, 102; O. M. Norlie, *Norsk lutherske menigheter i Amerika 1843-1916*, 1 (Minneapolis, 1918), 53; Th. S. Haukenæs, *Gammelt og nyt fra Voss og Vossestranden* (Bergen, Norway, 1896), 196.

[53]Strand, *Norwegians in Illinois*, 142; Lund Wright, "Pioneer Norwegian Community," 27; Rene, *Historie om udvandringen*, 376-377; Blegen, *Norwegian Migration to America: The American Transition* (Northfield, 1940), 134-135; information on Ole Olson Hetletvedt is in the J.J. Wang Collection at the Garrett Theological Seminary in Evanston.

[54]*Daily Democrat*, December 1, 3, 1847; Nils William Olsson, ed., *A Pioneer in Northwest America 1841-1858*, trans. by Jonas Oscar Backlund, 2 (Minneapolis, 1960), 102-104, 165-167; C.A.Clausen, trans., *A Chronicler of Immigrant Life: Svein Nilsson's Articles in* Billed-Magazin, *1868-1870* (Northfield, 1982), 118-119; Nelson, *Pioneer Churchman*, 81, 93-94.

[55]Flom, *Norwegian Immigration*, 236; Rene, *Historie om udvandringen*, 264, 371, 764; *Vossingen*, 1-2/1925, 16.

[56]Rene, *Historie om udvandringen*, 138, 325, 351-355; *Daily Democrat*, July 15, 1847.

[57]Andreas, *History of Chicago*, 1:360-371; Pierce, *Beginnings of a City*, 380, note; *Chicago Daily Journal*, March 31, 1845. I am indebted to Robin L. Einhorn for information about the hearings on vote fraud in the Chicago City Clerk Papers held by the Illinois State Archives in Springfield. *Emigranten*, March 14, 1856, reports that Andrew Nielson, active in the Democratic party, in an attack of insanity committed suicide and blamed the "whiskey party" for it. Scandinavians joined the anti-Democratic coalition of the 1850s.

[58]Rene, *Historie om udvandringen*, 380; John Wentworth to Edmund S. Kimberly, July 17, 1848, in Kimberly Papers at Chicago Historical Society.

Chapter 2

[1]Pierce, *As Others See Us*, 129; William J. Cronon, "To Be the Central City: Chicago, 1848-1857," in *Chicago History*, Fall,1981, 130-140; "Chicago in 1856," in *Chicago History*, Fall, 1956, 257-285.

[2]Rene, *Historie om udvandringen*, 267, 372; *Daily Democrat*, October 12, November 21, 1848; "Chicago in 1856," 266-269; Pierce, *From Town to City, 1848- 1871*, vol. 2 of *A History of Chicago* (New York, 1940), 35-76, 95; Mayer and Wade, *Chicago*, 48-52; Hoyt, *Land Values*, 279-294.

[3]Rene, *Historie om udvandringen*, 243; Qualey, *Norwegian Settlement*, 172-186, 247; Hoyt, *Land Values*, 58.

[4]Rene, *Historie om udvandringen*, 112-114.

[5]Andreas, *History of Chicago*, 1:preface; *Democratic Press*, June 16, 1853; letter to *Aftenbladet* (Oslo), April 8, 1859, in NAHA archives; Pierce, *From Town to City*, 118, 126-128; Hoyt, *Land Values*, 74-76.

[6]*Weekly Democrat*, November 21, 1857; *Wossingen*, May, September, 1858.

[7]Letter from Niels Nielsen to relatives and friends, September 21, 1846, printed in *Bergens Stiftstidende*, January 21, 1847, in NAHA archives.

[8]*Vossingen*, 3/1922, 5; *Skandinaven*, June 8, 1917; Rene, *Historie om udvandringen*, 134; Gjerset and Ludvig Hektoen, "Health Conditions and the Practice of Medicine Among the Early Norwegian Settlers, 1825-1865," in *Norwegian-American Studies and Records*, 1 (1926), 12-16, 28-29; *Medisinalberetning for Søndre Bergenhus Amt*, in *Norges Offisielle Statistikk*, 1891, 146.

[9]*Daily Democrat*, June 2, 1849.

[10]Rene, *Historie om udvandringen*, 134; letter from Johannes Johansen and Søren Bache to relatives, dated December 31, 1839, printed in *Tiden* (Drammen), March 3, 1840, in NAHA archives.

[11]Andreas, *History of Chicago*, 1:595; Rene, *Historie om udvandringen*, 177-178; Gjerset and Hektoen, "Health Conditions," 15; William K. Beatty, "When Cholera

Scourged Chicago," in *Chicago History*, Spring, 1982, 2–13; *Daily Democrat*, May 14, 1849.

[12]*Free West*, July 20, 1854; *Daily Democrat*, June 30, September 8, 1849; *Chicago City Directory*, 1849, 261.

[13]*Free West*, July 20, 1854.

[14]Halle Steensland, "Erindringer," in *Symra*, 2/1909, 7; protocol for Cook County Medical Society, entry for meeting of June 13, 1854, in Chicago Historical Society archives; Andreas, *History of Chicago*, 1:596–597; letter from Johannes C. Spillum, dated January 25, 1850, printed in *Stavanger Amtstidende og Adresseavis*, May 3, 1850, in NAHA archives.

[15]*Skandinaven*, October 18, 1866.

[16]Galford, "The Foreign Born and Urban Growth," 102.

[17]Semmingsen, *Veien mot vest*, 1:416–463; Passport Protocols, 1850–1855, in the Norwegian National Archives (Riksarkivet), Oslo; Chicago city directories for selected years, 1850–1860.

[18]Julie E. Backer, *Ekteskap, fødsler og vandringer i Norge 1856–1960* (Oslo, 1965), 157–163.

[19]Rene, *Historie om udvandringen*, 112, 137; Backer, *Ekteskap*, 166–167, 172–173. See also discussion of social background in Lovoll, *Promise of America*, 16–18, 27–29.

[20]Albert O. Barton, "Norwegian-American Emigration Societies of the Forties and Fifties," in *Norwegian-American Studies and Records*, 3 (1928), 24–25. Sjur Jørgensen Lokrheim was also known as Sjur Jørgensen Haaeim.

[21]Gunnar J. Malmin, "The Disillusionment of an Immigrant: Sjur Jørgensen Haaeim's 'Information on Conditions in North America,' " in *Norwegian-American Studies and Records*, 3 (1928), 3; *Skandinaven*, June 8, 1917, printed the letter by Andrew Larson (Flage) under the heading "Et gammelt Brev" (An Old Letter). It is a unique historical document.

[22]Flom, *Norwegian Immigration*, 234–235; Rene, *Historie om udvandringen*, 172–173; *Vossingen*, 4/1924, 4–9.

[23]Gjerset, trans. "An Account of the Norwegian Settlers in North America," in *Wisconsin Magazine of History*, September, 1924, 77–88.

[24]Barton, "Norwegian-American Emigration Societies," 34; Rene, *Historie om udvandringen*, 437–438.

[25]Lars Fletre, trans., "The Vossing Correspondence Society and the Report of Adam Løvenskjold," in *Norwegian-American Studies*, 28 (1979), 245–272; Rene, *Historie om udvandringen*, 262, 363. Arne Sunde gave information on Koren and Fleischer. Fleischer, born in 1788, reigned as estate owner from 1810 until his death in 1863; Sechmann is a name from the Danish nobility; Fleischer is German.

[26]Rene, *Historie om udvandringen*, 371.

[27]Rene, *Historie om udvandringen*, 362–363.

[28]Barton, "Norwegian-American Emigration Societies," 34; Rene, *Historie om udvandringen*, 179, 239, 437–430.

[29]*Skandinaven*, October 4, 1899, contains a valuable article by Rognald Henderson (Løne), older brother of the better known Knut Henderson (Løne), about Norwegians in Chicago in the 1850s. *Skandinaven*, April 18, 1900; Rene, *Historie om udvandringen*, 322, 384–389; Barton, "Norwegian-American Emigration Societies," 35–39; Haukenæs, *Natur, folkeliv og folketro paa Voss og Vossestranden* (Hardanger, 1887), 66–72.

[30]Barton, "Norwegian-American Emigration Societies," 35–40. The State Historical Society of Wisconsin has a nearly complete file of *Wossingen*. *Wossingen* appeared irregularly for a little more than two years, when, having been removed to Milwaukee, it suspended publication in March, 1860, to be resumed in Voss, Norway, under the same title in 1871.

[31]Rene, *Historie om udvandringen*, 499.

[32]*Wossingen*, July, 1858. See John Higham, ed., *Ethnic Leadership in America* (Baltimore, 1978).

[33]*Skandinaven*, October 4, 1899.

[34]See Craig Buettinger, "Economic Inequality in Early Chicago 1840–1850," in *Journal of Social History*, Spring, 1978, 413–418.

[35]*Emigranten*, March 23, April 27, December 14, 1855, September 5, 12, November 28, 1856; *Friheds-Banneret*, October 4, November 20, 1852; "Chicago in 1856," 265–266; Erik Helmer Pedersen, *Drømmen om Amerika* (Copenhagen, 1985), 128; Arlow W. Andersen, *The Immigrant Takes His Stand: The Norwegian-American Press and Public Affairs, 1847–1872* (Northfield,1953), 19–20. See also John B. Jentz and Richard Schneirov, "Class and Politics in an Antebellum Commercial Boom Town, Chicago 1848 to 1861," a paper delivered in January, 1987, to the Chicago Area Labor History Group, the Newberry Library.

[36]*Emigranten*, February 17, 1858; *Skandinaven* (daily), July 13, 1890.

[37]Beijbom, *Swedes in Chicago*, 315–318; Andersen, *The Immigrant Takes His Stand*, 23–25, 30, 69–70; the Knut Gjerset Papers in NAHA archives; Gustav Elwood Johnson, "The Swedes of Chicago," (Ph.D. dissertation, University of Chicago, 1940), 30–31. See also Don E. Fehrenbacher, *Chicago Giant: A Biography of "Long John" Wentworth* (Madison, Wisconsin, 1957), and *Lincoln in Chicago*, a booklet prepared by the Chicago Historical Society.

[38]Quoted in Lund Wright, "Pioneer Norwegian Community," 80; Haukenæs, *Gammelt og nyt*, 191–199.

[39]*Skandinaven*, May 14, 1868, carries a translation from "one of the dailies in Chicago," which stated that "the completion of this project, which is so beneficial to the public, is almost entirely the work of Mr. Iver Lawson, the recently retired alderman from the 15th ward." See Frederick Rex, comp., "Centennial List of Mayors, City Clerks, City Treasurers and Aldermen, Elected by the People of Chicago, from its Incorporation of the City on March 4, 1837 to March 4, 1937, Arranged in Alphabetical Order Showing the Years During which Each Official Held Office," typescript in the Chicago Historical Society.

[40]Haukenæs, *Gammelt og nyt*, 193.

[41]Quoted in the *Missionary Advocate*, 1854, 14; Kendrick Charles Babcock, *The Scandinavian Element in the United States* (Urbana, Illinois, 1914), 116–117. Paul Andersen quite probably holds the honor of being the first Norwegian matriculated at an American college. The initial name of the congregation was the First Scandinavian Evangelical Lutheran Church in Chicago.

[42]O.J. Hatlestad, *Historiske meddelelser om Den norske Augustana Synode samt nogle oplysninger om andre samfund i Amerika* (Decorah, Iowa, 1887), 95–96.

[43]Blegen, *The American Transition*, 148–154; George M. Stephenson, *The Founding of the Augustana Synod 1850–1860* (Rock Island, Illinois), 15–17; J. Magnus Rohne, *Norwegian American Lutheranism up to 1872* (New York, 1926),96.

[44]*Home Missionary*, March, 1850, 154; G.H. Gerberdinger, *Life and Letters of W.A. Passavant, D.D.* (Greenville, Pennsylvania, 1906), 211–212.

[45]Andreas, *History of Chicago*, 1:349; Gerberdinger, *Life and Letters of W.A. Passavant*, 211–212; Parish Register for Lake View Church in the American Lutheran Church Archives, Wartburg Seminary, Dubuque, Iowa.

[46]*Minnesskrift, illustreradt album, utgifvet af Svenska ev. lutherska Immanuelsförsamlingen i Chicago med anledning af dess femtioårsjubileum den 16–18 januari 1903* (Rock Island, 1903), 9–10; Eric Norelius, *The Pioneer Swedish Settlements and Swedish Lutheran Churches in America 1845–1860*, trans. by Conrad Bergendoff (Rock Island, 1984), 14.

[47]*Evangelisk Luthersk Kirketidende*, 1876, 143, 206–207, 394–397. The Norwegian Synod organ here discusses what it considers Methodist fallacies. Information on the early Scandinavian Methodists in Chicago is found in the J.J. Wang Collection at the Garrett Theological Seminary in Evanston.

[48]Beijbom, *Swedes in Chicago*, 237–239; *Minnesskrift . . . Immanuel*, 10–12; Stephenson, *Founding of the Augustana Synod*, 17–18; Andreas, *History of Chicago*, 1:349; *Daily Tribune*, September 5, 1854.

[49]Stephenson, *Founding of the Augustana*, 16.

[50]Olsson, trans., *A Pioneer in Northwest America 1841–1859: The Memoirs of Gustaf Unonius*, 2 (Minneapolis, 1960), 165–188; Fletre, "Vossing Correspondence Society," 270–271; H.G. Stub, "Fra mors og fars liv," in *Symra*,1907, 14–42.

[51]Olsson, *Memoirs of Gustaf Unonius*, 169–174.

[52]Olsson, *Memoirs of Gustaf Unonius*, 173–174; Parish Register for St. Ansgarius

Church in the American Lutheran Church Archives; Stephenson, *The Religious Aspects of Swedish Immigration* (Minneapolis,1932), 200–203.

[53]Blegen, *The American Transition*, 153; Olsson, *Memoirs of Gustaf Unonius*, 196–197, 202.

[54]*Home Missionary*, March, 1850, 26; Parish Register for St. Ansgarius Church.

[55]Andreas, *History of Chicago*, 1:595; Beijbom, *Swedes in Chicago*, 253; Olsson, *Memoirs of Gustaf Unonius*, 192, 197; Parish Register for St. Ansgarius Church.

[56]Beijbom, *Swedes in Chicago*, 253–254.

[57]Andreas, *History of Chicago*, 2:443; Beijbom, *Swedes in Chicago*, 239–240; Parish Register for St. Ansgarius Church.

[58]Chr. O. Brohaugh and I. Eisteinsen, *Kortfattet beretning om Elling Eielsens liv og virksomhet* (Chicago, 1883), 80–81; Blegen, *The American Transition*, 150–151, 222–223. See also Marcus L. Hansen, "Immigration and Puritanism," in *Norwegian-American Studies and Records*, 9 (1936), 1–28.

[59]Brohaugh and Eisteinsen, *Kortfattet*, 85–89; S. S. Gjerde and P. Ljostvedt, *The Hauge Movement in America* (Minneapolis, 1941), 142–143. The full name of the church body referred to as Eielsen's Synod was The Evangelical Lutheran Church in America.

[60]The standard work on Norwegian Lutheranism in America is the two volumes by E. Clifford Nelson and Eugene L. Fevold, *The Lutheran Church Among Norwegian-Americans* (Minneapolis, 1960). The full name of the Norwegian Synod was The Synod of the Norwegian Evangelical Lutheran Church in America.

[61]Strand, *Norwegians in Illinois*, 102; *"Festskrift" Published in Commemoration of the Jubilee Celebrated by Our Savior's Norwegian Evangelical Lutheran Church of Chicago, Illinois, October 19th, 1912* (Chicago, 1913), 16.

[62]Blegen, *The American Transition*, 158; "Brief Historical Sketch of the Lake View Congregation" in its *80th Anniversary Program*.

[63]In her M.A. thesis, 101–107, Mari Lund Wright has a good discussion of these developments. See also broad treatment in Stephenson, *Founding of the Augustana Synod*.

[64]For the treatment of the Petersen case, letters and other documents, including published statements and accounts, in the extensive files on the matter in the Archives Collection in the Preus Library at Luther College, Decorah, Iowa, have been consulted. The bitter controversy over exclusion of members and the resignation of others is clearly illustrated. Included in this collection is the opinion of the Illinois Supreme Court, dated September 9, 1873.

[65]*Daily Democratic Press*, June 21, 1856; *Free West*, June 29, 1854; Andreas, *History of Chicago*, 2:444. In all, $1,579 was collected. An indication of the lingering interest is the fact that *Skandinaven*, June 13, 1867, contained an article by Paul Andersen discussing the final disposal of these funds.

[66]*Chicago Daily Tribune*, March 23, 24, 1854; Mortimer Smith, *The Life of Ole Bull* (New York, 1947), 124–127.

[67]*Morgenbladet* (Oslo), June 18, 1855; *Christiania-Posten*, April 7, 1856; *Emigranten*, March 31, April 28, June 30, 1854, March 8, 1855.

[68]*Emigranten*, March 31, April 28, June 30, November 24, 1854; Johannes B. Wist, ed., *Norsk-amerikanernes festskrift 1914* (Decorah, Iowa,1914), 22. The banquet for Ole Bull had an attendance of 400; all were Norwegian men and women, except for some invited American guests such as the publisher of the *Democratic Press*. B.A. Froiseth spoke, as did Paul Andersen, who gave the main address.

[69]*Emigranten*, March 8, 1855, March 20, 1857, July 11, August 8, 1859; Beijbom, *Swedes in Chicago*, 39–44, 267–268; Johnson, "The Swedes of Chicago," 99–100; Stephenson, "The Stormy Years of the Swedish Colony in Chicago Before the Great Fire," in *Transactions of the Illinois State Historical Society* (Springfield, 1929), 173.

[70]*Vossingen*, 4/1922. 3–4; *Vossingen*, February, 1859; Barton, "Norwegian Emigration Societies," 40–41.

[71]Beijbom, *Swedes in Chicago*, 61; Olsson, *Memoirs of Gustaf Unonius*, 285–286.

[72]Beijbom, *Swedes in Chicago*, 167; Johnson, "The Swedes of Chicago," 5–6; Philip S. Friedman, "The Danish Community of Chicago," in *The Bridge*, 1/1985, 33–52. Letters in *Christiania Posten*, dated April 7, 1854, and June 3, 1859, in NAHA

archives. The letter of April 7, 1854, is not signed, but the letter writer identifies himself as correspondence secretary. *Emigranten* for March 8, 1855, lists I. Irgens as holding that position.

[73]Beijbom, *Swedes in Chicago*, 62; Lund Wright, "Pioneer Norwegian Community," 40–41, 84–85; Hoyt, *Land Values*, 66. For an insightful discussion of the formation of ethnic communities, see Kathleen Neils Conzen, "Immigrants, Immigrant Neighborhoods, and Ethnic Identity: Historical Issues," in *The Journal of American History*, December, 1979, 603–615, and her incisive study *Immigrant Milwaukee, 1836–1860* (Cambridge, Massachusetts, 1976), 136–153.

[74]Lund Wright, "Pioneer Norwegian Community," 49–50, 94–95.

[75]Hoyt, *Land Values*, 65–66; Dedmon, *Fabulous Chicago*, 33–36.

[76]Hoyt, *Land Values*, 65, 66.

[77]Rene, *Historie om udvandringen*, 114; *Chicago City Directory*, 1861, 186; interview with Elmer E. Abrahamson, February 21, 1986.

[78]*Democratic Press*, June 16, 1853; Pierce, *From Town to City*, 29–30; Rene, *Historie om udvandringen*, 326, 432.

[79]Hoyt, *Land Values*, 74–75; Lund Wright, "Pioneer Norwegian Community," 45; Gjerset, *Sailors on the Great Lakes*, 73–76.

[80]Lund Wright, "Pioneer Norwegian Community," 45, 89, 90; letter from Enewald J. Grude to S.T. Haaland in Stavanger, Norway, dated April, 27, 1855, in NAHA archives.

[81]Peter Daae, *Amerikas mest amerikanske by og den tredie største norske by i verden* (Kristiania, Norway, 1903), 135.

Chapter 3

[1]*Chicago Tribune*, August 2, 1862; "Direct to Europe," in *Chicago History*, Spring, 1959, 197–200; Blegen, *The American Transition*, 403; Semmingsen, *Veien mot vest*, 1:133–134. The captain of the *Sleipner* was Hans Jacob Waage. On August 2, 1962, Norwegians in Chicago placed a memorial plaque on the State Street Bridge, the approximate site of the landing of the *Sleipner*.

[2]*Skandinaven*, March 22, 1893; *Emigranten*, August 9, 11, 1862. The Welland Canal between Lake Ontario and Lake Erie was completed in 1829. See Pierce, *Beginnings of a City*, 89.

[3]John A. Johnson, "Om udvandringen," in *Billed-Magazin*, 1869, 123–124; Henrietta Larson, trans. and ed., "An Immigration Journey to America," in *Norwegian-American Studies and Records*, 3 (1928), 61–62; Blegen, *Norwegian Migration to America, 1825–1860* (Northfield, 1931), 351.

[4]Semmingsen, *Veien mot vest*, 1:134–135; *Skandinaven*, July 26, 1866.

[5]*Christiania Posten*, October 18, 1852. *Skandinaven* (New York), October 27, 1852, listed the names of the Norwegians known to have perished in the disaster. See Larson, trans. and ed., "The Sinking of the 'Atlantic' on Lake Erie: An Immigrant Journey from Quebec to Wisconsin in 1852," in *Norwegian-American Studies and Records*, 4 (1929), 92–98.

[6]Semmingsen, *Veien mot vest*, 1:134; *Skandinaven*, July 26, 1866. *Emigranten*, June 19, 1865, carried a report from Bergen of the hindrance to this traffic of such requirements as "double herring barrels" on passenger vessels, and efforts to prevail upon the Storting to remove them.

[7]Semmingsen, *Veien mot vest*, 2:141; Ann Novotny, *Strangers at the Door: Ellis Island, Castle Garden, and the Great Migration to America* (New York, 1974), 79–89.

[8]Hoyt, *Land Values*, 88–89; Backer, *Ekteskap*, 158, 165.

[9]Lund Wright, "Pioneer Norwegian Community," 138–140; Beijbom, *Swedes in Chicago*, 125–127, 136–138; Lowry Nelson, *Rural Sociology* (New York, 1948), 295–299; *Emigranten*, May 23, June 20, 1864; *Skandinaven*, September 14, 1871.

[10]Hoyt, *Land Values*, 77–78; Pierce, *From Town to City*, 323; Morris Salmonsen, *Brogede minder fra fyrretyve aars ophold i Chicago* (Chicago, 1913), 21.

[11]Lund Wright, "Pioneer Norwegian Community," 128, 129, 130; Federal Population Schedules, *Eighth Census of the United States*, 1860.

[12]*Skandinaven*, August 29, 1867; Strand, *Norwegians in Illinois*, 216; Flom, *Norwegian Immigration*, 235–236.

[13]Brynjolf J. Hovde, trans. and ed., "Chicago as Viewed by a Norwegian in

1864," in *Norwegian-American Studies and Records*, 3 (1928), 65–72; Blegen, *The American Transition*, 283–284; Strand, *Norwegians in Illinois*, 244–245; "Jevne and Almini," in *Chicago History*, Spring, 1948, 313–321. Christian Jevne's obituary in *Skandinaven*, March 18, 1898, contains a number of factual errors.

[14]Lund Wright, "Pioneer Norwegian Community," 128, 129, 130; Salmonsen, *Brogede minder*, 22; *Skandinaven*, June 1, 28, 1866, January 31, 1867, September 14, December 19, 1871.

[15]*Skandinaven*, January 31, 1867, February 17, 1874.

[16]Pierce, *From Town to City*, 157, 272.

[17]Carl Wittke, *The Irish in America* (New York, 1956), 130, 135, 141; Paul Michael Green, "The Irish in Nineteenth-Century Politics: A Battle for Acceptance and Legitimacy," in d'A. Jones and Holli, *Ethnic Chicago*, 216; Pierce, *From Town to City*, 260–261.

[18]Green, "The Irish in Nineteenth-Century Politics," 213–214.

[19]Hofmeister, *Germans of Chicago*, 87–90; Strand, *Norwegians in Illinois*, 218.

[20]Johnson, "Swedes of Chicago," 33–34; Allan Kastrup, *The Swedish Heritage in America* (St. Paul, 1975), 280–281, 285–286.

[21]Blegen, ed., *The Civil War Letters of Colonel Hans Christian Heg* (Northfield, 1936), 22–25, 52–53; Johnson, "Swedes of Chicago," 33; Babcock, *Scandinavian Element*, 76.

[22]Pierce, *From Town to City*, 256–258, 272–273; Wist, *Norsk-amerikanernes festskrift*, 33.

[23]Blegen, *Civil War Letters*, 26. See Nora Record Book, 1860–1871, minutes of meetings, February 24, 1862, January 31, February 14, 1865, in NAHA archives.

[24]Blegen, *Civil War Letters*, 37–43.

[25]*Emigranten*, February 20, 1860; *Skandinaven*, November 18, 1873. See Nora Record Book, minutes for meetings, July 18, 1860, February 4, 1861. *Emigranten*, March 31, 1858, carried a letter signed by Norwegian members of St. Ansgarius denying the correctness of a claim by *Kirketidende* that they intended to form a Norwegian Lutheran congregation.

[26]Nora Record Book, minutes for meeting, August 6, 1860; *Skandinaven* (daily), November 22, 1876; Terje I. Leiren, *Marcus Thrane: A Norwegian Radical in America* (Northfield, 1987), 21. Ole T. Birkeland is identified in the 1880 federal census as a government official and in the 1900 census as a coal dealer. City directories do not give his occupation.

[27]Nora Record Book, minutes for meetings, July 18, December 17, 1860, February 4, 1861; Beijbom, *Swedes in Chicago*, 270; *Wossingen*, June, 1859.

[28]Bodnar, *The Transplanted*, 138–141, discusses the role of elitist secular groups within the immigrant community. The minutes for August 4, 1860, in the Nora Record Book, include the constitution and bylaws, and the signatures of the charter members.

[29]Nora Record Book, minutes for meeting, January 30, 1863; *Ritual for Ordenen Riddere af det Hvide Kors*, in the NAHA archives. The Order established itself in Norway in 1902 when Hans Hansen, one of Nora's members, returned to Norway. A history was published in 1977 for its 75th anniversary, which also contains information on the American Order. Lucinda Jondahl, active in Nora Lodge, has provided information about it and the Order.

[30]Nora Record Book, minutes for meeting, May 17, 1864.

[31]*Skandinaven* (daily) for August 15, 1876, gives an extensive report of "en stor pic-nic" at Washington Heights arranged jointly by Nora, Svea, and Dania. For a good discussion of immigrant Scandinavianism see John R. Jenswold, "The Rise and Fall of Pan-Scandinavianism in Urban America," in Lovoll, ed., *Scandinavians and Other Immigrants in Urban America: The Proceedings of a Research Conference October 26–27, 1984* (Northfield, 1985), 159–170.

[32]Galford, "The Foreign Born and Urban Growth," 99–100; *Emigranten*, December 8, 1854, October 17, 1864, October 30, 1865; Semmingsen, *Veien mot vest*, 2:50, 100; Charlotte Erickson, *American Industry and the European Immigrant 1860- 1885* (Cambridge, Massachusetts, 1957), 89.

[33]*Emigranten*, June 27, 1864; *Skandinaven*, June 10, July 29, 1873; Hofmeister,

Germans of Chicago, 41–44; Johnson, "Swedes in Chicago," 7–10.

[34]Johnson, "Swedes of Chicago," 8–9.

[35]*Skandinaven*, August 30, 1866; Beijbom, *Swedes in Chicago*, 302–303; Hofmeister, *Germans of Chicago*, 15–17.

[36]*Skandinaven*, November 1, 1866; Lars Ljungmark, *For Sale—Minnesota: Organized Promotion of Scandinavian Immigration 1866- 1873* (Stockholm, 1971), 61; Beijbom, *Swedes in Chicago*, 302–303.

[37]Beijbom, *Swedes in Chicago*, 304–305; Erickson, *American Industry*, 90; documents in Chicago City Council Proceedings Files in Illinois State Archives, Springfield, Illinois.

[38]Johnson, "Swedes of Chicago," 10–11; *Skandinaven*, May 30, 1867.

[39]Beijbom, *Swedes in Chicago*, 303, 305–306.

[40]Beijbom, *Swedes in Chicago*, 303; *Skandinaven*, May 30, October 24, 1867. *Nordisk Folkeblad*, published in Minneapolis, in November 17, 1869, carried a detailed description of Winslow's broad financial activities.

[41]*Skandinaven*, February 20, March 12, 1868.

[42]*Skandinaven*, June 28, 1866, February 14, 1867.

[43]*Skandinaven*, September 13, October 4, 1866; Napier Wilt and Henriette C. Koren Naeseth, "Two Early Norwegian Dramatic Societies in Chicago," in *Norwegian-American Studies and Records*, 10 (1938), 44–50.

[44]Wilt and Naeseth, "Two Early Norwegian Dramatic Societies," 47; Leiren, *Marcus Thrane*, 55, 73.

[45]Wilt and Naeseth, "Two Early Norwegian Dramatic Societies," 50; Leiren, *Marcus Thrane*, 61, 62.

[46]The NAHA archives possesses the carefully kept Protocol of the dramatic society, titled "Den norske dramatiske Forening i Chicago. Stiftet den 12te Martz 1868. Motto: 'Ei blot til Lyst,' " i.e. "Not for Pleasure Alone." This was the motto of the Royal Theater in Copenhagen.

[47]Reports of performances in the society's Protocol. See also Wilt and Naeseth, "Two Early Norwegian Dramatic Societies," 50–75.

[48]The dramatic society's Protocol; *Skandinaven*, March 19, April 23, 30, 1868. The ethnic theater is treated in Maxine Schwartz Seller, *Ethnic Theatre in the United States* (Westport, Connecticut, 1983), which includes an article on the Danish-American theater by Clinton M. Hyde and appendices listing Danish and Norwegian dramatic groups.

[49]The dramatic society's Protocol; Wilt and Naeseth, "Two Early Norwegian Dramatic Societies," 59, 63–65; *Skandinaven*, January 16, May 21, 1868.

[50]Quoted from *Svenska Amerikanaren*, September 20, 1870, in Beijbom, *Swedes in Chicago*, 270. See also *Skandinaven*, April 23, May 14, 21, 1868, January 20, February 3, 1869, February 8, 15, March 29, April 5, August 9, September 14, 1871. *Skandinaven*, August 19, 1873, encourages people to attend a concert to support the building fund, and in March 17, 1874, gives an account of a lottery to raise funds. The West Turner Hall, or "old" Aurora Hall, was located at 113 Milwaukee Avenue, which now would be approximately 400, though that address does not exist. William J. Adelman, *Pilsen and the West Side* (Chicago, 1983), 46–48; *Marquis' Handbook of Chicago* (Chicago, 1885), 144.

[51]Hofmeister, *Germans of Chicago*, 152–156; Wist, *Norsk-amerikanernes festskrift*, 14; Andersen, *Immigrant Takes His Stand*, 19–20. *Skandinaven*, in October 22, 1878, estimated that *Friheds-Banneret* had had close to 400 subscribers.

[52]*Daily Democrat*, August 6, 1847; Langeland, *Nordmændene i Amerika*, 99–106; Andersen, *Immigrant Takes His Stand*, 10.

[53]Andersen, *Immigrant Takes His Stand*, 69–70.

[54]Andersen, *Immigrant Takes His Stand*, 13–31; Johnson, "Swedes of Chicago," 76–78. The first issue of *Skandinaven* is dated June 1, 1866. In *Norsk-amerikanernes festskrift*, 45, Wist gives the incorrect date of May 2.

[55]*Skandinaven*, June 1, 1866.

[56]*Skandinaven*, June 1, 1866; Wist, *Norsk-amerikanernes festskrift*, 48–49.

Chapter 4

[57]Wist, *Norsk-amerikanernes festskrift*, 17, 45–46; Langeland, *Nordmændene i Amerika*, 94–99; Andersen, *Immigrant Takes His Stand*, 126.

[58]*Scandia*, December 27, 1934; Andreas, *History of Chicago*, 1:350. Information pertaining to the efforts to establish a joint school, the Johnson case, and the financial burden of legal proceedings are in the church records of Our Savior's Lutheran Church and of the First Norwegian Evangelical Lutheran Congregation (identified as Lake View Church) in the American Lutheran Church Archives in Wartburg Seminary. Letters, the declarations of sworn witnesses, and other pertinent documents on the Johnson case are in the collection dealing with the Petersen controversy in the Archives Collection in the Preus Library at Luther College.

[59]Pierce, *From Town to City*, 339; Rene, *Historie om udvandringen*, 113. *Skandinaven* (daily), July 13, 1890, carries Andrew B. Johnson's obituary.

[60]Langeland, *Nordmændene i Amerika*, 111; Andersen, *Immigrant Takes His Stand*, 140; *Skandinaven*, September 13, 1866.

[1]This was the second weekly issue of *Skandinaven* published after the fire. The first one appeared on October 14. It was incorrectly dated October 24, indicating the confusion and haste that existed, and was corrected by pen before distribution. A tri-weekly, begun in 1867 for the Chicago market, appeared on October 18.

[2]*Skandinaven* (tri-weekly), October 18, 1871; David Lowe, comp. and ed., *The Great Chicago Fire* (New York, 1979), 1–5; Pierce, *The Rise of a Modern City, 1871–1893*, vol. 3 of *A History of Chicago* (Chicago, 1957), 3–8; Robert Cromie, *A Short History of Chicago* (San Francisco, 1984), 79–88; Mayer and Wade, *Chicago*, 106–115.

[3]*Skandinaven* (tri-weekly), October 18, 1871; John A. Enander, "Chicago-branden. Ett trettioårs-minne," in *Illustrerade kalendern "Vintersol 1901"*(Stockholm, 1901), copy in the Swenson Archives, Augustana College, Rock Island, Illinois; Kastrup, *Swedish Heritage*, 376–377; Pierce, *Rise of a Modern City*, 12.

[4]Dennis, *Victor Lawson*, 23; Strand, *Norwegians in Illinois*, 215, 217; *Skandinaven*, July 13, 1896, March 18, 1898.

[5]*Skandinaven*, October 19, 1871, May 1, 1916.

[6]*Skandinaven*, October 19, 1871.

[7] Quoted in Pierce, *Rise of a Modern City*, 17.

[8]Strand, *Norwegians in Illinois*, 440; Pierce, *Rise of a Modern City*, 8; *Skandinaven*, December 27, 1871.

[9]Enander, "Chicago-branden"; Beijbom, *Swedes in Chicago*, 255; *Skandinaven*, October 19, 1871; letter from Carlos Ross, President of the Norwegian Dramatic Society, to Consul P. Svanøe, dated November 20, 1871, in the Norwegian Dramatic Society Papers in NAHA archives.

[10]Pierce, *From Town to City*, 375–378; *Den kristelige Talsmand*, August 2, 1906, tells of the dedication of the Norwegian-Danish Tabernacle built at DesPlaines, where Norwegian, Danish, and Swedish Methodists had conducted "camp meetings" every summer since about 1870.

[11]*Home Mission*, September, 1850, 119, in J.J. Wang Collection at the Garrett Theological Seminary in Evanston. Kevin Leonard assisted in identifying material in the collection, which is only partly catalogued.

[12]*Missionary Advocate*, October, 1862, 53; this and other information from the J.J. Wang Collection.

[13]*Kvartalskrift*, October 6, 1869, in J.J. Wang Collection; A. Haagensen, *Den norsk-danske Methodismes historie* (Chicago, 1894), 55, 158–159; N.M. Liljegren et al., *Svenska Metodismen i Amerika* (Chicago, 1895), 208–225; Strand, *Norwegians in Illinois*, 154.

[14]The Norwegian-Danish department at Garrett Theological Seminary was the central theological training institute. See Andersen, *The Salt of the Earth: A History of Norwegian-Danish Methodism in America* (Nashville, Tennessee, 1962). See also Stephenson, *Religious Aspects*, 256–257.

[15]H.P. Bergh, *Femtiaarsskrift. Udgivet ianledningaf Den norsk-danske Methodismes femtiaarsjubilæum, 1901* (Chicago, 1901), 10–11.

[16]Stephenson, *Religious Aspects*, 248, 255; J.O. Backlund, *Swedish Baptists in*

America: A History (Chicago, 1933), 54–56; P. Stiansen, *A History of the Norwegian Baptists in America* (Wheaton, Illinois, 1939), 76–78. The biblical passage quoted was Romans 9:1–4.

[17]N. S. Lawdahl, *De danske Baptisters historie i Amerika* (Morgan Park, Illinois, 1909), 228–237; Stiansen, *Norwegian Baptists*, 76–77, 79.

[18]See for instance Stephenson, "The Mind of the Scandinavian Immigrant," in *Norwegian-American Studies and Records*, 4 (1929), 63–73.

[19]Dedmon, *Great Enterprises: 100 Years of the YMCA of Metropolitan Chicago* (Chicago, 1957), 38–39, 94, 163–164, 241–248; Board of Managers, *Fifty-Five Years: The Young Men's Christian Association of Chicago* (Chicago, 1913), 1–2; Boyer, *Urban Masses*, 108–112, 132–142; Pierce, *From Town to City*, 372–373; *Skandinaven*, September 26, 1867, November 17, 1870.

[20]Dedmon, *Great Enterprises*, 141; Strand, *Norwegians in Illinois*, 199–201, 538–539; Boyer, *Urban Masses*, 117–118; Gjerde and Ljostvedt, *The Hauge Movement in America*, 490–492; *Skandinaven*, June 10, 20, July 21, 1876, November 8, 1899, July 6, 1904, June 10, 1906, August 20, 1910; protocols for both 1872 and 1876 organizations in NAHA archives, given by Sigrid Thompson, and brought to the archives by Bert Benson and Thor R. Benson. According to *Skandinaven*, March 6, 1877, a Scandinavian Young Men's Christian Association with Swedish and Norwegian members was that year organized on the South Side.

[21]*"Festskrift"* . . . *Our Savior's*, 8–10, 37–38.

[22]In *Luthersk Kirketidende*, December 24, 1882, S. M. Krogness defended the consistency of his beliefs and practices. In the Krogness Papers in the NAHA archives there is full documentation of the conflict, from church records, letters, and newspaper accounts. Much of the material is in a scrapbook assembled by Krogness himself.

[23]*Svenska Amerikanaren*, February–March, 1870, in Krogness Papers. See also Nelson and Fevold, *The Lutheran Church Among Norwegian-Americans*, 1:Chapter 11. The Norwegian names of the two church bodies were Den norske Augustana-synode and Konferensen for Den norsk-danske evangeliske lutherske kirke i Amerika.

[24]When the small structure on Sangamon was dedicated February 12, 1871, the prominent churchman W.A. Passavant preached, and such leaders in the Scandinavian Augustana, then entirely Swedish, as Erland Carlsson and T.W. Hasselquist showed their friendship for Krogness and his congregation by taking part in the dedication ceremonies. See report in *Skandinaven*, February 15, 1871. See also *Skandinaven*, November 2, 1870; Andreas, *History of Chicago*, 1:349; and *Jubilate*, a large unpaged booklet produced by the Bethlehem congregation in 1912.

[25]*Skandinaven*, December 28, 1870.

[26]Rohne, *Norwegian American Lutheranism*, 188–189; Emil Erpestad, "A History of Augustana College" (Sioux Falls, South Dakota, 1955), typescript, 27–32, 38. Eielsen's Synod did not dissolve, as a few congregations led by Eielsen himself continued.

[27]See *Jubilate* and also Amund Mikkelsen, *Nogle af en prests erfaringer* (Decorah, Iowa, 1894), 39.

[28]Norlie, *Norsk lutherske menigheter*, 1:45–63, lists Norwegian Lutheran churches in Cook county, Illinois, and gives approximate membership for the early years. See also *Jubilate* for N.C. Brun's observations.

[29]*Skandinaven*, January 13, 1886. Extensive church records exist for St. Paul's Church preserved at the church and made available through the courtesy of the Reverend Hubert E. Davis. In 1928 Pastor G.A. Gullixson of St. Paul's Church from 1902 until 1928 prepared a sketch of the congregation's history, printed in its fifty-fifth anniversary commemorative program.

[30]Congregational records of Lake View in the American Lutheran Church archives at Wartburg Seminary; congregational records of St. Paul's. See *"Festskrift"* . . . *Our Savior's*, 41–42; *Skandinaven*, May 8, 1889; Peer Strømme, *Erindringer* (Minneapolis, 1923), 239–243; Hoyt, *Land Values*, 195; Johnson, "Swedes of Chicago," 114.

[31]Hoyt, *Land Values*, 195; Johnson, "Swedes of Chicago," 114; Lake View Congregational Records.

[32]*"Festskrift"* . . . *Our Savior's*, 11.

[33]St. Paul's Congregational Records; Lake View Congregational Records; *Kirketidende*, 1891, 515–517.

[34]Boyer, *Urban Masses*, 77–78; Jentz and Schneirov, "Class and Politics"; Enewald J. Grude to S.T. Haaland, April 27, 1855, in NAHA archives; J.C. Furnas, *The Life and Times of the Late Demon Rum* (New York, 1965), 161–185. See also Richard Wilson Renner, "In a Perfect Ferment: Chicago, the Know-Nothings, and the Riot for Lager Beer," in *Chicago History*, Fall, 1976, 161–170.

[35]*Emigranten*, March 23, April 27, 1855; *Skandinaven*, August 5, October 14, 1873; Grude to Haaland, April 27, 1855; Lewis and Smith, *Chicago: A History of Its Reputation*, 72–73.

[36]See Eilert Sundt, *Om ædrueligheds-tilstanden i Norge* (Oslo, 1976; first ed. 1859), 1. In *Scandia*, April 7, 1938, Olaf Ray writes of the 1880s: "We had many generous [Norwegian] saloonkeepers who kept unemployed sailors going for months with free beer and lunch." Waldemar Ager, *Afholdsfolkets festskrift 1914* (Eau Claire, Wisconsin, 1914), 6; Rene, *Historie om udvandringen*, 113; Johnson, "Swedes of Chicago," 36–37; *Skandinaven og Amerika*, August 5, October 4, 14, 28, November 5, 1873; *Emigranten*, March 24, 1858.

[37]Boyer, *Urban Masses*, 163; Blegen, *The American Transition*, 153; J. L. Nydahl, *Afholdssagens historie* (Minneapolis, 1896), 249–253; copy of protocol for congregational meeting of the First Norwegian Evangelical Lutheran Congregation, March 20, 1869, and letter from H.A. Preus to the Deacons and Trustees dated August 22, 1870, in the Archives Collection at Luther College.

[38]Parish Register for Lake View Church in the American Lutheran Church Archives.

[39]Blegen, *The American Transition*, 556; Ager, *Afholdsfolkets festskrift*, 5; Pierce, *Rise of a Modern City*, 455–460; *Verdens Gang*, February 17, 1881.

[40]Ruth Borden, *Woman and Temperance: The Quest for Power and Liberty, 1873–1900* (Philadelphia, 1981),3–14, 170–171; Pierce, *Rise of the Modern City*, 459; *Verdens Gang*, February 17, 1881; *Union Signal*, August 14, 1890, January 15, 1891, November 3, 1898, February 8, 1899, August 29, 1901. Marilyn T. Staples at the Frances E. Willard Library of the WCTU in Evanston was most helpful.

[41]Nydahl, *Afholdssagens historie*, 254–255; Ager, *Afholdsfolkets festskrift*, 10, 11; Strand, *Norwegians in Illinois*, 196–197; Henry Weardahl, *Illinois norske Goodtemplars historie til minde om 30-aars dagen for I.O.G.T.'s virksomhed blandt de norske i staten Illinois* (Chicago, 1909), 10–11. The lodge books of the Illinois IOGT were given to the author by Toby and Bjarne Hillervik.

[42]Strand, *Norwegians in Illinois*, 196–197; Ager, *Afholdsfolkets festskrift*, 10, 13. Ole Br. Olson was the driving force in establishing *Reform*, which appeared with that name in 1890 in Eau Claire, Wisconsin, based on a merger of earlier publications in Chicago and in Eau Claire. It became the primary Norwegian-American temperance organ.

[43]Ager, *Afholdsfolkets festskrift*, 13, 14; Borden, *Woman and Temperance*, 123–124. In 1907 a Scandinavian Grand Lodge of Illinois united the Scandinavian IOGT lodges in the state. See Weardal, *Illinois norske Goodtemplars historie*, 19–20, 27–28. See also *Festskrift vid Illinois skandinaviska Storloge I.O.G.T. tjugoårs-jubileum* (n.p., n.d.).

[44]Strand, *Norwegians in Illinois*, 195, 285–286; *The Union Signal*, April 14, 1898, October 10, 1901; *Skandinaven*, April 15, 1896. The Harmony Total Abstinence Society dissolved in 1902.

[45]Quoted in Pierce, *Rise of a Modern City*, 460, see also the same work, 305; Dedmon, *Fabulous Chicago*, 138–140, 142–144; Kristofer Janson, *Sara* (Christiania, 1891), 244; *Skandinaven* (daily), January 30, 1889, January 22, 1893; *Skandinaven*, April 15, 1891. Walter C. Reckless, *Vice in Chicago* (Chicago, 1933), is the classic study of prostitution in Chicago. Justice was unevenly dispensed, *Verdens Gang*, May 10, 1882, found, as it related the death of the young Norwegian newcomer Betsy Olsen as a result of an abortion being performed on her after she became pregnant by a Mr. L. Bush in her place of employment as a maid. The midwife responsible for the illegal operation was arrested, but Mr. Bush, *Verdens Gang* commented acidly, "the Coroner's Jury saw no cause to proceed against." In 1876, *Skandinaven*, on August 8, reported a case against a Norwegian, Andrew Anderson, and his wife who attempted

to force their daughter to work in a house of prostitution on Washington Street on the West Side, even accompanying her to the establishment. The daughter reported her parents to the authorities, resulting in their arrest.

[46]*Skandinaven*, March 8, 1881, October 6, 1907; *Skandinaven* (daily), January 28, 1884, March 14, 1897; Dianne M. Pinderhughes, *Race and Ethnicity in Chicago Politics: A Reexamination of Pluralist Theory* (Urbana, Illinois, 1987), 154–155, 160, 180; Louise C. Wade, *Graham Taylor: Pioneer for Social Justice 1851–1938* (Chicago, 1964), 197; Pierce, *Rise of a Modern City*, 304–305, cites reports from the Chicago Board of Inspectors of the House of Correction. In its issue of April 26, 1882, *Verdens Gang* remarked in reporting on the arrest of delinquent young people by the Chicago Avenue Station on the West Side that "it pains us to note that many of those arrested are Americans of Scandinavian descent."

[47]*Skandinaven*, October 30, 1872, February 11, April 8, 15, May 20, October 30, 1873; Pierce, *Rise of the Modern City*, 303–304; Salmonsen, *Brogede minder*, 19–20. There is much information about the Norwegian Battalion in the John J. Sonsteby Papers in the NAHA archives. Sonsteby made considerable efforts, using his prestige as Chief Justice of the Chicago Municipal Court, to identify the volunteers. A petition to the Common Council for compensation for services rendered carried their names.

[48]*Skandinaven*, June 1, July 13, 1875. July 4th, the actual day of *Restauration*'s departure, being on a Sunday, the celebration was postponed so as not to break the Sabbath.

[49]Lloyd Hustvedt, *Rasmus Bjørn Anderson: Pioneer Scholar* (Northfield, 1966), 57, 89–102; Rudolph J. Vecoli, "Chicago's Italians Prior to World War I: A Study of Their Social and Economic Adjustment" (Ph.D. dissertation, University of Wisconsin, 1962), 10, 13, 26–29; *Skandinaven*, July 13, 1875; *Chicago Times*, October 5, 13, 1870.

[50]*Chicago Times*, October 13, 1870.

[51]Haas Park is now Concordia Cemetery in Forest Park.

[52]*Chicago Times*, July 19, 1872; *Skandinaven*, July 17, 19, 24, 1872; Parish Register for Lake View Church. A monument, Haraldstøtten, was raised in 1872 north of Haugesund where Harald Fairhair's burial mound was presumed located.

[53]*Chicago Times*, July 19, 1872; *Skandinaven*, July 27, August 3, November 16, 30, December 7, 1870, August 23, 1871, July 17, 24, 31, August 14, 23, 1872, February 14, 1894; Salmonsen, *Brogede minder*, 136–138; Wist, *Norsk-amerikanernes festskrift*, 81; Gjerset, *Norwegian Sailors*, 171; Kastrup, *Swedish Heritage*, 192; Beijbom, *Swedes in Chicago*, 320–321; Stephenson, "The Stormy Years of the Swedish Colony in Chicago Before the Great Fire," 173. The group meeting in 1870 called itself the Scandinavian Aid and Sanitary Society, formed to collect money for returning Civil War veterans. The earlier Danish vice-consul George Hansen was its president, O.G. Lange, vice president, and the Dane S. Beder, editor of *Fremad*, P.A. Sundelius, then editor of *Svenska Amerikanaren*, and Endre Thorson, all active in political affairs, filled the position of "secretary." The sole Norwegian member of the Danish Weapon Brothers was Theodor Mork from Bergen, a volunteer in the conflict of 1848–1849, who ran a small stationery store on the West Side.

[54]*Skandinaven*, September 28, October 5, 1870, February 15, June 14, 1871, January 3, 1873, August 13, 1876; Wist, *Norsk-amerikanernes festskrift*, 52.

[55]Det norske Skytterlag Papers in NAHA archives; Wist, *Norsk-amerikanernes festskrift*, 145; program for Det norske Skytterlags Stiftelses-Ball in Emil Biørn scrapbook in NAHA. The Norwegian-American composer Emil Biørn wrote a march for the inaugural event. See also *Marquis' Handbook of Chicago*, 152; *Skandinaven*, April 4, 1882, March 4, 25, May 20, July 22, 1884, May 26, 1899; *Verdens Gang*, March 29, April 26, May 3, 1882.

[56]*Skandinaven*, April 2, May 20, 1879; *Verdens Gang*, July 5, 1882; Wist, *Norsk-amerikanernes festskrift*, 47.

[57]*Souvenir Program for the 75th Anniversary of the Norwegian-American Athletic Association, October 1, 1960* (Chicago, 1960), n.p.; Wist, *Norsk-amerikanernes festskrift*, 168, 171; *Skandinaven*, September 6, 1893, March 20, April 10, July 24, October 2, 1895, August 1, 1900; Einar S. Ween, *Oslo Turnforenings historie 1855–1930* (Oslo, 1930). Jo-

hanna Barstad, librarian at the University of Oslo Library, has provided information on Norwegian sports history.

[58]*Skravla*, 1918, a copy in the possession of Rolf H. Erickson; Hans L. Oftedahl, *Normændenes Sangforening af Chicago. Historisk beretning 1870–1920* (Minneapolis, 1920), 7–10. The name of the singing society was originally spelled Nordmændenes, then Normændenes, and finally Normennenes. The latter form is consistently used here.

[59]*Skandinaven*, July 17, 1872; Oftedal, *Normændenes Sangforening*, 10–13; Strand, *Norwegians in Illinois*, 291–292.

[60]*Souvenir-Program. Forty Years Anniversary Celebrated by Singing Society Bjørgvin, Sunday Evening, March 26, 1922*; Wist, *Norsk-amerikanernes festskrift*, 91; Eva Lund Haugen and Einar Haugen, *Land of the Free: Bjørnstjerne Bjørnson's America Letters, 1880–1881* (Northfield, 1978), 183; Strand, *Norwegians in Illinois*, 283–284; *Skandinaven*, January 14, 21, April 22, 1873, January 13, 1874, September 30, December 4, 1876, February 19, 1878; Julius Anker-Midling, *Under Election eller valglivets mysterier* (Chicago, 1875).

[61]*Skandinavian*, January 4, 1876, April 5, 12, 19, 1881; *Verdens Gang*, April 14, 1881; Lund Haugen and Haugen, *Land of the Free*, 152–157, 241, 276. I.K. Boyesen was a brother of the author Hjalmar Hjorth Boyesen.

[62]Nina Draxten, *Kristofer Janson in America* (Northfield, 1976), 30–31; Janet Rasmussen, "The Best Place on Earth for Women': The American Experience of Aasta Hansteen," in *Norwegian-American Studies*, 31 (1986), 245–267; *Verdens Gang*, April 14, June 23, July 7, 14, 1881.

[63]*Skandinaven*, May 30, 1882; Arthur C. Paulson and Kenneth O. Bjork, "A Doll's House on the Prairie: The First Ibsen Controversy in America," in *Norwegian-American Studies and Records*, 11 (1940), 1–16; *Verdens Gang*, May 17, 24, 1882.

Chapter 5

[1]*Scandia*, December 27, 1934.

[2]*Scandia*, December 27, 1934, April 7, 1938; *School Census of the City of Chicago Taken May, 1884*, 11, 24–25; Louis Wirth and Eleanor H. Bernert, *Local Community Fact Book of Chicago* (Chicago, 1949), 62; *Tenth Census of the United States*, 1880, rolls 192, 195, and 196 for Cook county.

[3]*Scandia*, December 27, 1934; Salmonsen, *Brogede minder*, 22; Strand, *Norwegians in Illinois*, 218, 296, 306–307.

[4]*Verdens Gang*, March 17, 31, 1881; *Scandia*, April 7, 1938; *School Census 1884*, 11, 24–25; Christian Nielsen, "Halvfems aar i Chicagos danske koloni 1837–1927," typescript, a copy at Northwestern University library, 41–44.

[5]*School Census 1884*, 11, 24–25; Reuel Gustav Hemdahl, "The Swedes in Illinois Politics: An Immigrant Group in an American Political Setting" (Ph.D. dissertation, Northwestern University, 1932), 168.

[6]Vecoli, "Chicago's Italians," 73; Dedmon, *Fabulous Chicago*, 148–149.

[7]*Skandinaven*, December 21, 1891.

[8]*Skandinaven*, January 7, 1925; *Sixtieth Anniversary . . . Trinity*.

[9]Wirth and Bernert, *Community Fact Book*, 62; Humbert S. Nelli, *Italians in Chicago, 1880–1930: A Study in Ethnic Mobility* (New York, 1979), 22–54; *School Census 1884*, 11, 24–25; *Skandinaven*, September 9, 1908.

[10]Vecoli, "Chicago's Italians," 129–130; *Report of the Department of Health, City of Chicago, for the Years 1881 and 1882* (Chicago, 1883), 15, 46–48; *Skandinaven*, September 9, 1908. See also discussion in David Ward, *Cities and Immigrants* (New York, 1971), 120–121, 123.

[11]Graham Taylor, *Pioneering on Social Frontiers* (Chicago, 1930), 191–193; Taylor, *Chicago Commons Through Forty Years* (Chicago, 1936), 91–92; Wirth and Bernert, *Community Fact Book*, 59; Nielsen, "Halvfems aar," 41–42; *Tenth Census of the United States*, 1880, rolls 192, 195, 196 for Cook county; *Skandinaven*, September 9, 1908.

[12]Salmonsen, *Brogede minder*, 77–78; *Scandia*, April 7, 1938; Mayer and Wade, *Chicago*, 155.

[13]Ward, *Cities and Immigrants*, 148–149; Chicago city directories, 1860–1900; Cook county census schedules from the Eighth Federal Census, 1860, Ninth Federal Census, 1870, and Tenth Federal Census, 1880.

[14]Salmonsen, *Brogede minder*, 22–24.

[15]Ward, *Cities and Immigrants*, 51; Pierce, *Rise of a Modern City*, 145–149; Galford, "The Foreign Born and Urban Growth," 101; Sten Carlsson, "Chronology and Composition of Swedish Emigration to America," in Harald Runblom and Hans Norman, eds., *From Sweden to America: A History of the Migration* (Minneapolis, 1976), 123–126.

[16]Backer, *Ekteskap*, 158–159; *Morgenbladet*, December 14, 1879; Rolf Kåre Østrem and Peter Rinnan, "Utvandringen fra Kristiania 1880–1907. En studie i urban utvandring" (cand. philol. thesis, University of Oslo, 1979), 99.

[17]*Morgenbladet*, September 27, 1880; *Verdens Gang*, May 31, 1882; Backer, *Ekteskap*, 164.

[18]Østrem and Rinnan, "Utvandringen fra Kristiania," 14, 15, 222.

[19]Backer, *Ekteskap*, 167, 171, 172.

[20]Ward, *Cities and Immigrants*, 58; *The People of Chicago: Who We Are and Who We Have Been* (Chicago, 1976), 21.

[21]Jentz and Schneirov, "Class and Politics," 19; Hartmut Keil, "Chicago's German Working Class in 1900," in Keil and Jentz,eds., *German Workers in Industrial Chicago, 1850–1910: A Comparative Perspective* (DeKalb, Illinois, 1983), 24–25.

[22]Østrem and Rinnan, "Utvandringen fra Kristiania," 101.

[23]*Skandinaven*, February 17, 1874, February 5, 1900; interview with Louis Berge, November 22, 1985.

[24]Henry Ericsson, *Sixty Years a Builder: The Autobiography of Henry Ericsson* (Chicago, 1942), 57; Erickson, *American Industry*, 90–91, 93–94. Charlotte Erickson identified no fewer than eleven agencies dealing in Scandinavian labor. *Skandinaven*, October 25, 1866, carried a typical advertisement from one of them, the Christian & Linn agency: "We need 200 railroad workers, 1,000 men to go south, 200 sawmill workers, 200 common laborers, 50 miners, and everyone else wishing employment."

[25]*Skandinaven*, February 3, 17, 1874, March 1, 1881, March 30, 1901; Stina L. Hirsch, "The Swedish Maid: 1900–1915" (M.A. thesis, De Paul University, 1985), 34; *Tenth Census of the United States*, 1880, Federal Population Schedules for Cook County, Rolls 192, 195, 196; "Reports of the United States Industrial Commission on Immigration and on Education, XV (Washington, D.C., 1901), pp. 319–22," in Stanley Feldstein and Lawrence Costello, eds., *The Ordeal of Assimilation* (Garden City, New York, 1974), 301.

[26]*Skandinaven*, January 6, 1880; Federal Census Schedules, *Tenth Census of the United States*, 1880, Cook county, Illinois, Rolls 192, 195, 196.

[27]*Skandinaven*, October 21, 1896; study of Census Schedules 1860, 1870, and 1880, and City Directories 1860–1900.

[28]*Skandinaven*, February 3, 1874, June 29, 1875; *Scandia*, April 7, 1938; Gjerset, *Norwegian Sailors*, 61–68, 93–95.

[29]Pierce, *Rise of a Modern City*, 164–165.

[30]Strand, *Norwegians in Illinois*, 241–242; Johs. Wong, *Norske utvandrere og forretningsdrivende i Amerika* (Oslo, [1925]), 190–191.

[31]Pierce, *Rise of a Modern City*, 294–295; Sharon Darling, *Chicago Furniture: Art, Craft, & Industry 1833–1983* (New York, 1984), 110–112; *Skandinaven*, March 1, 1881. Also interview with Arthur L. Johnson, November 16, 1985. Several respondents in the Norwegian community in Chicago claimed that the Johnson Chair Company was popularly referred to as "fattighuset," "the poor house," to indicate the low salaries paid. It has, however, not been possible to confirm that the company actually paid lower wages than other similar employers. There was obviously an element of exploitation in the company's policy of hiring young boys at a certain time in its history, though it was perhaps not much different from that of nineteenth-century entrepreneurs in general.

[32]*Skandinaven*, August 17, 1892; Strand, *Norwegians in Illinois*, 368–369; interview with Mrs. Mary Johnson Frey, February 1, 1987. See also *Wicker Park Evangelical Lutheran Church's 100th Anniversary Commemorative Book 1879–1979*. In memory of A.P. Johnson the family donated a magnificently carved altar to the Wicker Park Church, a replica in wood of Leonardo Da Vinci's painting "The Last Supper."

[33]Strand, *Norwegians in Illinois*, 245, 269–270; Wong, *Norske utvandrere*, 195;

Nicholas H. Sommers, *The Historic Homes of Old Wicker Park: A Tour Guide and Sampler* (Chicago, 1979), n.p.; *Who's Who in Chicago*, 761.

[34]Darling, *Chicago Furniture*, 23, 186–189, 236; Strand, *Norwegians in Illinois*, 288–289.

[35]Darling, *Chicago Furniture*, 295, 299; Wong, *Norske utvandrere*, 210; *Viking*, August 15, 1946, March 20, 1947; interview with Grace K. Gulbransen, September 27, 1985; Jentz, "Skilled Workers and Industrialization: Chicago's German Cabinet-makers and Machinists," in Keil and Jentz, *German Workers in Industrial Chicago*, 77.

[36]Strand, *Norwegians in Illinois*, 440, 441–442; *Skandinaven*, October 28, 1878, May 18, August 24, December 7, 1880, June 7, July 5, 1881.

[37]*Scandia*, January 8, 1921.

[38]*Skandinaven*, July 9, 1878; Jenswold, "In Search of a Norwegian-American Working Class," in *Minnesota History*, Summer, 1986, 63–70; Keil and Jentz, "German Working-Class Culture in Chicago: A Problem of Definition, Method, and Analysis," in *Gulliver German-English Yearbook*, 9:128–147.

[39]Strand, *Norwegians in Illinois*, 440; Beijbom, *Swedes in Chicago*, 330.

[40]Beijbom, *Swedes in Chicago*, 330; Pierce, *Rise of a Modern City*, 30; *Skandinaven*, June 22, 29, July 6, August 10, 24, 1870, June 19, 1872, December 16, 1873.

[41]*Skandinaven*, December 23, 1873, February 17, September 8, 1874, September 28, 1875, March 10, May 9, 16, 1876.

[42]Beijbom, *Swedes in Chicago*, 331; Pierce, *Rise of a Modern City*, 28, 434–436; Wist, *Norsk-amerikanernes festskrift*, 20; Mikkelsen, *Nogle af en prests erfaringer*, 104–105; *Dagslyset*, January, 1872; Leiren, *Marcus Thrane*, 22; Waldemar Westergaard, trans. and ed., "Marcus Thrane in America: Some Unpublished Letters from 1880–1884," in *Norwegian-American Studies and Records*, 9 (1936), 67–76.

[43]It was organized as Den skandinaviske Fremskridts-Forening, i.e. The Scandinavian Society of Progress. A number of men associated with *Skandinaven* were members. It later altered its name to The Scandinavian Freethinker Society.

[44]*Skandinaven*, September 13, 1866, January 13, 1874, January 18, March 18, 1876; *Dagslyset*, November, 1869, June, 1875; Pierce, *From Town to City*, 381, *Rise of a Modern City*, 28.

[45]Wist, *Norsk-amerikanernes festskrift*, 93, 280; *Skandinaven*, July 9, 1879; *Scandia*, April 7, 1938; Paul Avrich, *The Haymarket Tragedy* (Princeton, New Jersey, 1984), 49, 60, 133; Morris Hillquit, *History of Socialism in the United States* (New York, 1971), 236–249.

[46]*Skandinaven*, May 16, 1876, November 1, 1881; *Verdens Gang*, April 7, 1881; Adelman, *Haymarket Revisited* (Chicago, 1976), 4–6; Avrich, *Haymarket Tragedy*, 58–61, 133; Henry David, *The History of the Haymarket: A Study in the American Social-Revolutionary and Labor Movements* (New York, 1958), 60, 71; Philip S. Foner, *From the Founding of the American Federation of Labor to the Emergence of American Imperialism*, vol. 2 of *History of the Labor Movement in the United States* (2nd ed., New York, 1975), 37–44. In *Scandia*, April 14, 1938, Olaf Ray commented on the importance to Norwegian liberals and radicals in 1880–1881 of securing the election of Stauber.

[47]A copy of the petition from the workers received from Arthur L. Johnson; Pierce, *Rise of a Modern City*, 269; Keil and Jentz, "German Working-Class Culture," 135.

[48]Andersen, "The Haymarket Affair and the Norwegian Immigrant Press," in *Norwegian-American Studies*, 31 (1986), 109; Adelman, *Haymarket Revisited*, 14–24; Avrich, *Haymarket Tragedy*, 381–398.

[49]Pierce, *Rise of a Modern City*, 297; Strand, *Norwegians in Illinois*, 187. See *Svenska typografföreningen i Chicago, Illinois, U.S.A. 1893–1913*.

[50]In a letter dated April 22, 1985, Steven Sapolsky shared some of his research into Scandinavian labor unions, especially the Scandinavian Carpenters Union; *Skandinaven*, September 6, 1899; *Local Union No. 194 Souvenir Program of Fiftieth Anniversary Celebration, October 4, 1940*; Foner, *The Policies and Practices of the American Federation of Labor*, vol. 3 of *History of the Labor Movement in the United States* (New York, 1964), 256–281.

[51]Wist, *Norsk-amerikanernes festskrift*, 86–87; Strømme, *Erindringer*, 236–238.

[52]Strømme, *Erindringer*, 238; Sommers, *Historic Homes of Old Wicker Park*.

[53]Parish Register of Wicker Park Evangelical Lutheran Church; *Wicker Park Evangelical Lutheran Church's 100th Anniversary Commemorative Book, 1879–1979.* A new church structure was dedicated in 1907 on the same site as the first.

[54]Strand, *Norwegians in Illinois*, 453–455; Eunice, Myles, and Eric Stenshoel, eds., *Rokne Root & Branch: The Families of Martha Bardsdatter Osgjerd and Lars Mikkelson Rokne.*

[55]Strand, *Norwegians in Illinois*, 504–505; Strømme, *Erindringer*, 240; Norlie, *Norsk lutherske prester i Amerika 1843–1913* (Minneapolis, 1914), 99, 216; Parish Register for St. Paul's Church.

[56]See Bodnar, *The Transplanted*, 141–142.

[57]Andreas, *History of Chicago*, 3: 700–702; Joseph Kirkland, *The Story of Chicago*, 2 vols. (Chicago, 1892–1894), 2:281; Dennis, *Victor Lawson*, 1; Adelman, *Haymarket Revisited*, 56. See *Chicago Daily News*, May 1, 5, 1886, for examples of its "extras" on the Haymarket riot.

[58]Quoted in Dennis, *Victor Lawson*, 19; Wist, *Norsk-amerikanernes festskrift*, 46; Jean Skogerboe Hansen, "*Skandinaven* and the John Anderson Publishing Company," in *Norwegian-American Studies*, 28 (1979), 48. Information on *Skandinaven* has also come from Marijane Carr.

[59]Norlie, *Norwegian-American Papers, 1847–1945* (Northfield, 1946), 14; Wist, *Norsk-amerikanernes festskrift*, 47; *Verdens Gang*, January 13, May 5, 1881.

[60]Strømme, *Erindringer*, 234; *Amerika*, November 3, 1886.

[61]Strømme, *Erindringer*, 235; Wist, *Norsk-amerikanernes festskrift*, 86–89, 110–114.

[62]Wist, *Norsk-amerikanernes festskrift*, 113–114; Gerald Thorson, "The Novels of Peer Strømme," in *Norwegian-American Studies and Records*, 18 (1954), 144–147.

[63]*Skandinaven* (daily), January 29, 1876; *Skandinaven*, June 8, 1875, January 25, 1876, March 11, 1908; *Verdens Gang*, November 15, 1882.

[64]Pierce, *Rise of a Modern City*, 379–380; Holli, *Ethnic Chicago*, 213–220; Cromie, *Chicago*, 98.

[65]John Allswang, *A House for All People: Ethnic Politics in Chicago 1890–1936* (Lexington, Kentucky, 1971), 6, 23; Hemdahl, "Swedes in Illinois Politics," 203; Pierce, *Rise of a Modern City*, 30; Beijbom, *Swedes in Chicago*, 317; Johnson, "Swedes of Chicago," 54.

[66]Nielsen, "Halvfems aar," 15; George R. Nielsen, *The Danish Americans* (Boston, 1981), 188.

[67]*Verdens Gang*, February 15, 1882; Hjalmar Hjorth Boyesen, "The Scandinavians in the United States," in *North American Review*, June, 1892, 531.

[68]*Skandinaven*, December 14, 1875, December 4, 1876; *Verdens Gang*, June 23, 1881, April 5, 1882; *Scandia*, April 14, 1938; Wist, *Norsk-amerikanernes festskrift*, 85–86; P. Groth, "Nordmænd," in Henrik Cavling, *Fra Amerika*, 2 (Copenhagen, 1897), 244–246.

[69]Beijbom, *Swedes in Chicago*, 291; Rene, *Historie om udvandringen*, 389–390; Strand, *Norwegians in Illinois*, 540; *Skandinaven* (daily), October 12, 1876; *Skandinaven*, November 9, December 7, 1880.

[70]Harold F. Gosnell, *Machine Politics Chicago Model* (2nd ed., Chicago, 1968), 51, 63–64; Birger Osland, *A Long Pull from Stavanger* (Northfield, 1945), 48–53; Hemdahl, "Swedes in Illinois Politics," 206–212; Johnson, "Swedes of Chicago," 137–139; *Skandinaven*, January 21, 1896.

Chapter 6

[1]Pierce, *Rise of a Modern City*, 501–512; Cromie, *Chicago*, 104–105; Mayer and Wade, *Chicago*, 143–194; Thomas S. Hines, *Burnham of Chicago: Architect and Planner* (2nd. ed., Chicago, 1979), 73–74. See also R. Reid Badger, *The Great American Fair: The World's Columbian Exposition & American Culture* (Chicago, 1979).

[2]"The Columbus Caravels," in *Chicago History*, Fall, 1968, 257–269; Rasmus Elias Rasmussen, Viking: *From Norway to America*, Helen Fletre, trans., Darrell F. Treptow *et al.*, eds. (Chicago, 1984); Magnus Andersen, *Vikingfærden. En illustrert beskrivelse af "Vikings" reise i 1893* (Kristiania, 1895), 267–421. The *Viking* is today in Lincoln Park.

[3]Andersen, *Vikingfærden*, 422–448. A misunderstanding had led to many of the

crew being arrested in New York when they inadvertently got involved in a street altercation. Mayor Harrison's permission "to paint the city red" without fear of arrest "as you were in the East" was in direct response and an exercise in outdoing New York.

[4]*Skandinaven*, August 17, 1892.

[5]Strand, *Norwegians in Illinois*, 223–224, 543–544; *Skandinaven*, February 19, 1890, April 20, 1893, January 25, 1899; letter dated April 23, 1893, to Colonel Rice in NAHA archives.

[6]Strand, *Norwegians in Illinois*, 234–235, 288; Moses P. Handy, ed., *The Official Directory of the World's Columbian Exposition, May 1st to October 30th, 1893* (Chicago, 1893), 136. The stave church is now a part of the outdoor museum Little Norway at Blue Mounds, Wisconsin.

[7]Almot Lindsey, *The Pullman Strike: The Story of a Unique Experiment and a Great Labor Upheaval* (New ed., Chicago, 1964), 38–60, 92–93; Kirkland, *The Story of Chicago*, 1:396; *Skandinaven*, June 6, 13, 1894; Mayer and Wade, *Chicago*, 193–194.

[8]*The Pioneer Social Club—Founded 1878*, a booklet published in 1966, contains the biographies of sixty pioneers. Rolf Erickson provided a copy of it. See also the records of the Arne Garborg Club in the NAHA archives, especially its "Referat Protokol."

[9]*Illinois Staats Zeitung*, May 22, 1891; Bjork, *Saga in Steel and Concrete* (Northfield, 1947), 3, 45; Bjork, "A Migration of Skills," in *Norwegian-American Studies and Records*, 14 (1944), 25; *Scandia*, November 11, 1911.

[10]Bjork, *Saga in Steel and Concrete*, 49–51, 121–138; interview with Betty Cotsonas, granddaughter of Thomas Pihlfeldt, by Helen Fletre, February 27, 1986.

[11]Bjork, *Saga in Steel and Concrete*, 50, 221–225; Strand, *Norwegians in Illinois*, 319–320.

[12]Bjork, *Saga in Steel and Concrete*, 359–360, 406–407; Badger, *The Great American Fair*, 116–117; Martin W. Reinhart, "Norwegian-born Sculptor, Kristian Schneider: His Essential Contribution to the Development of Louis Sullivan's Ornamental Style," paper read at the Norwegian-American Life of Chicago Symposium, October 23, 1982.

[13]Bjork, *Saga in Steel and Concrete*, 408; Hines, *Burnham of Chicago*, 312–345.

[14]*Viking*, October 16, 1947; *Onsrud Machine Works*, promotional booklet; interview with Sigurd Olsen and Louis Berge, November 22, 1985; Bjork, *Saga in Steel and Concrete*, 366–367; Wong, *Norske utvandrere*, 211.

[15]Osland, *Long Pull from Stavanger*, 37–39; Strand, *Norwegians in Illinois*, 228–231; *Skandinaven*, October 20, 1897, January 12, 1898, January 29, 1899.

[16]*Skandinaven*, January 15, February 21, May 15, December 18, 1872, January 14, 28, May 13, June 17, August 12, 1873, July 29, 1875, March 27, April 3, 1877, February 17, November 30, 1880, March 6, 1889, May 12, 1897, May 18, 1909; *Verdens Gang*, July 12, 1882; *Scandia*, January 7, 1911, January 10, 1914; Strand, *Norwegians in Illinois*, 342–343; Nielsen, "Halvfems aar," 85–86; Olson, *History of the Swedes of Illinois*, 2 (Chicago, 1908), 7.

[17]*Skandinaven*, August 5, 1873, January 20, October 5, 1880; *Skandinaven* (daily), October 8, 1910, January 12, 1911; *Svenska-Tribunen*, August 14, October 23, 30, 1906. The Norwegian-American writer Lars A. Stenholt has treated the bank scandal in an exposé titled *Paul O. Stensland og hans hjælpere, eller milliontyvene i Chicago* (1906) (Paul O. Stensland and his Helpers, or the Millionaire Thieves in Chicago).

[18]*Skandinaven*, October 5, 1901, April 19, 1905; *Skandinaven* (daily), June 10, 1911; *Scandia*, January 13, 1906; Wong, *Norske utvandrere*, 192.

[19]Minutes of Meetings of Board of Directors of the Scandinavian Lutheran Cemetery Association, August 14, December 1, 1906, May 7, 1907, in archives of Mount Olive Cemetery; list of stockholders of Mount Olive Cemetery Association, in archives of Mount Olive Cemetery; publicity flyer for Mount Olive Cemetery in NAHA archives; *Skandinaven*, May 21, 1890, August 31, 1898; Strand, *Norwegians in Illinois*, 327–328.

[20]Parish Register of Bethlehem Lutheran Church in the American Lutheran Church archives at Wartburg Seminary; Minutes of Meeting of Board of Directors of the Scandinavian Lutheran Cemetery Association, July 18, 1899; list of stock-

holders of Mount Olive Cemetery Association; record of interments at Mount Olive Cemetery, April, 1886, to July, 1900, in archives of Mount Olive Cemetery.

[21]Strand, *Norwegians in Illinois*, 227; *Viking*, March 29, 1945; *Scandia*, October 21, 1937; *Skandinaven*, August 15. 1926.

[22]*The People of Chicago*, 27; Norlie, *Norsk lutherske menigheter*, 1: 53–63.

[23]Parish Register for Trinity Lutheran Church in the Hauge Lutheran Church in Chicago; Parish Register for Lake View Church, meeting of January 1, 1869, in the American Lutheran Church archives at Wartburg Seminary.

[24]Mikkelsen, *Nogle af en prests erfaringer*, 48–49.

[25]Parish Register and minutes for the aid society in St. Paul's Church.

[26]Boyer, *Urban Masses*, 138–141; interview with Violet Nelson, February 26, 1986; *Vinland*, February 12, 1976; Edward O. Nelson, "Recollections of the Scandinavian Army's Scandinavian Corps," in *Swedish Pioneer Historical Quarterly*, October, 1978, 257–276.

[27]Nelson "Recollections of the Salvation Army Scandinavian Work in the United States 1887–1965," a typescript on which the article in the *Swedish Pioneer Historical Quarterly* is based, identified by Helen Fletre. See also Tom Gabrielsen, *Återblick över Frälsningsarmens skandinaviska arbete i Amerika, 1887–1933* (Chicago, 1933).

[28]*Skandinaven*, January 8, 1890, September 23, December 4, 1908; Strand, *Norwegians in Illinois*, 213; *"Festskrift"* . . . *Our Savior's*, 36; *Sixtieth Anniversary Souvenir of Trinity Evangelical Lutheran Church, Chicago, Illinois, September 30th to October 7th, 1917*, n.p.

[29]Strand, *Norwegians in Illinois*, 200–201.

[30]Interview with Elmer E. Abrahamson, February 1, 1987; report on adult clubs, March, 1919, in the Chicago Commons Papers in the Chicago Historical Society; Taylor, *Pioneering*, 187–202; Guy Szuberia, "The Chicago Settlements: Their Architectural Form and Social Meaning," in *Journal of the Illinois State Historical Society*, May 1977, 114–129. See also Taylor, *Chicago Commons Through Forty Years* (Chicago, 1936).

[31]*Association House (Settlement) of Chicago 474 West North Avenue, 1900–1901*, and similarly titled annual reports for 1904–1905 and 1911–1912, in the collection of the Chicago Historical Society.

[32]Strand, *Norwegians in Illinois*, 209–211; *Det norske Nationalforbunds Adressekalender 1913* (Chicago, 1913), 36; *Statistics Fraternal Societies 1933. 39th Annual Edition* (Rochester, N.Y., 1933), 125–127.

[33]*Scandia*, April 7, 1938; *Verdens Gang*, February 17, 1881; *Skandinaven Almanak 1930*, 128–129; *Riddere av Det hvite Kors 75 år, 1902–1977* (Halden, Norway, 1978), 32–35, 39–41; Constitution, Instrument of Incorporation, and other documents in NAHA archives. In 1938 Nora Lodge No. 1, R.H.K. joined the Sons of Norway as Lodge No. 415.

[34]Record Book for Dovre Lodge in NAHA archives; *Scandia*, April 7, 1938.

[35]*Skandinaven*, September 29, 1899, February 9, 1900, February 17, 1904; Strand, *Norwegians in Illinois*, 211–212; *1912–1937 Twenty-Fifth Anniversary Aftenstjernen Lodge No. 4 D.R.H.K.* (Chicago, June 26, 1937) in NAHA archives. A rare document, *Bi-love for Den første skandinaviske kvindelige Begravelses-Forening*, was located by Rolf Erickson.

[36]Emil Biørn Scrapbook in NAHA archives; Daae, *Om Chicago*, 137–139; *Skandinaven* (daily), March 13, 1891; *Skandinaven*, March 1, 1899, October 12, 1904; *NNL Adressekalender*, 32.

[37]Wist, *Norsk-amerikanernes festskrift*, 284.

[38]Record Book of Den norske Sygeforening "Nordlyset" in NAHA archives; also Instrument of Dissolution and other documents are in the same collection.

[39]Record Book of Den norske Sygeforening "Nordlyset."

[40]*Scandia*, April 7, 1938; *Viking*, December 25, 1941; *Vinland*, February 5, 1959. Nordfælles was dissolved on December 26, 1958.

[41]Sverre Norborg, *An American Saga* (Minneapolis, 1970), 57–86.

[42]*Skandinaven* (daily), March 1, 1914; *Viking*, February 5, 1946; Strand, *Norwegians in Illinois*, 532–533; Norborg, *An American Saga*, 71.

[43]*Skandinaven* (daily), June 12, 1909; *Scandia*, April 7, 1938; Norborg, *An American Saga*, 71; Carl G.O. Hansen, *History of the Sons of Norway* (Minneapolis, 1945), 75.

[44]*Skandinaven*, August 26, 1879, July 27, December 21, 1880, March 22, April 29, May 10, 31, September 6, 1881, September 19, 1882, March 16, 1892, January 22, March 1, 1893; *Skandinaven* (daily), January 26, September 16, 1893; *Verdens Gang*, May 26, 1881; Strand, *Norwegians in Illinois*, 273; Pierce, *Rise of a Modern City*, 483–484; Andreas, *History of Chicago*, 3:399.

[45]*Skandinaven*, June 12, December 25, 1889. S. Chr. Bryhn died June 10, 1889.

[46]*Skandinaven*, October 24, 1867; James Brown, *The History of Public Assistance in Chicago, 1833–1893* (Chicago, 1941), 58–61; Charles B. Johnson, *Growth of Cook County*, 1 (Chicago, 1960), 252–274; Death Records for Dunning, 1882; Record of Inmates at Cook County Oak Forest Infirmary, at the Oak Forest Hospital. The director of medical records, Jean Skeen, was of great assistance. Magnhild Faland has provided additional information.

[47]*Skandinaven*, series of articles throughout October to December, 1885, also August 11, 18, September 1, 1897.

[48]*Skandinaven*, October 28, November 11, 1885, January 6, 1886. See N.N. Rønning, *Fiftieth Anniversary of the Lutheran Deaconess Home and Hospital, 1897–1947*, a booklet published for the occasion. See also Frederick S. Weiser, "Serving Love: Chapters in the Early History of the Diaconate in American Lutheranism" (Bachelor of Divinity thesis, Lutheran Theological Seminary, Gettysburg, Pennsylvania, May, 1960).

[49]*Skandinaven*, December 15, 22, 1886. See also issues of *Skandinaven*, March–April, 1888.

[50]*Skandinaven*, December 17, 1890.

[51]H.B. Kildahl, "History of the Lutheran Deaconess Home and Hospital, Chicago, Illinois," typescript in NAHA archives.

[52]Kildahl, "Lutheran Deaconess Home and Hospital."

[53]*Skandinaven*, December 22, 1886; Strand, *Norwegians in Illinois*, 525.

[54]Minutes of the Board of Directors of the Tabitha Hospital Society at the Norwegian-American Hospital, examined through the courtesy of Mr. Elmer Abrahamson.

[55]Minutes . . . Tabitha Society; *Den anden aarsberetning for Den norsk-lutherske diakonisse- forening*, 1899, in NAHA archives.

[56]*Den anden aarsberetning*; *Den syvende aarsberetning for Det norsk-lutherske diakonissehjem og hospital*, 1905, in NAHA archives. Records of the Deaconess Hospital, stored at the Lutheran General Hospital at Park Ridge, were made available through the courtesy and assistance of Ruth Bengtsen on its staff.

[57]Strand, *Norwegians in Illinois*, 417–418; *Vinland*, November 15, 1956; *Skandinaven*, December 22, 1886; *Sixtieth Anniversary. History and 1955 Annual Report of the Norwegian Lutheran Home Society, 1896–1956*, in NAHA archives.

[58]*Skandinaven*, January 1, 10, 15, May 6, 1908; *Annual Report of the Norwegian Lutheran Children's Home Society* (Chicago, 1924), 11. A copy of Belle Gunness' will and many other documents relating to her life and activities are in the La Porte County Historical Society. The associate curator Dorothy Rowley was of much help. Belle Gunness was born Brynhild Paulsdatter Størset in Selbu in 1859 and came to Chicago in 1881, where she discovered the opportunities for easy money in life and fire insurance policies. These encouraged her grizzly, and long undetected, career of murder and arson. It is generally thought that she did not die in the fire in 1908, though her whereabouts thereafter are open to speculation. See Janet Louise Langlois, "Belle Gunness, the Lady Bluebeard, Community Legend as Metaphor"(Ph.D. dissertation, Indiana University, 1977).

[59]*Skandinaven*, January 22, 1908; *Annual Report of the Norwegian Lutheran Children's Home* (Chicago, 1915), 3; *Annual Report of the Norwegian Lutheran Children's Home* (Chicago, 1922), 12; interview with Marybelle Cassidy, February 26, 1986; interviews conducted by Hazel Anderson and Helen Fletre November 15, 1986, of five former residents, Leonard Anderson, Russel Oyen, Joyce Oyen, June Wylie, and Mary Lundegard. Hazel Anderson has also collected additional information on the

Home, and on September 22, 1986, interviewed Leroy Carlson, who entered the home at age five when his father abandoned his mother and seven small children.

[60]*Home Finding News*, December, 1955; *Church Messenger*, February 8, 1914.

[61]*Annual Report, 1915*, 19–20.

[62]*Betesdaforeningens niende aarsmøde og rapporter* (Chicago, 1916), n.p.; *1907- 1937 Thirtieth Anniversary of the Norwegian Lutheran Bethesda Home Association of Chicago* (Chicago, 1937), 8–9; *Vinland*, September 4, 1952.

[63]*Seventh Annual Report of the Norwegian Old People's Home Society* (Chicago, 1903), 4–8, 33–41.

[64]*Twenty-fifth Anniversary of the Norwegian Old People's Home Society* (Chicago, 1921), 14, 20; *Thirtieth Annual Report of the Norwegian Old Peoples' Home Society* (Chicago, 1926), 11, 17–19.

[65]Salmonsen, *Brogede minder*, 88–105.

[66]*Skandinaven*, November 22, December 13, 1866; Rolf H. Erickson and Olsson, "Scandinavian Physicians in Chicago 1887-1912," in *Swedish American Genealogist*, March, 1986, n.p.; Gjerset and Hektoen, "Health Conditions," 49.

[67]Rush Medical College was founded in 1837, although not finally organized until 1843, and it gave early impetus to medical training in Chicago. See Pierce, *Beginnings of a City*, 192, 284; Andreas, *History of Chicago*, 1:464–466; *Scandia*, January 11, 1911.

[68]*Skandinaven*, July 4, 1867, March 13, 1889; *Scandia*, May 27, 1911.

[69]Strand, *Norwegians in Illinois*, 348–349; Beatty, "Medical Care for Norwegian Immigrants in the Chicago Area," in *The Proceedings of The Institute of Medicine of Chicago*, October/December, 1983, 147–150.

[70]Strand, *Norwegians in Illinois*, 296; Baltazar Meyer, *A History of the Scandinavian-American Medical Society of Chicago on the Occasion of Its Twenty-fifth Anniversary* (Chicago, 1913). This booklet was located by Rolf Erickson.

[71]Meyer, *Scandinavian-American Medical Society*, 6–11; Strand, *Norwegians in Illinois*, 504.

[72]Arthur Herbert Wilde, *Northwestern University 1855–1905: A History*, 4 (New York, 1905), 367–389.

[73]*Scandia*, May 5, 1938; *Chicago Tribune*, May 16, 1951; *Viking*, February 2, 1956; Alumni Records of the Women's Medical School in the archives of Northwestern University.

[74]*Skandinaven*, March 28, May 23, 1894, July 21, 1897, February 2, 1898, May 10, 1900; Robert H. Wiebe, *The Search for Order, 1877–1920* (New York, 1967), 111–112. See also Ingeborg Sponland, *My Reasonable Service* (Minneapolis, 1938).

Chapter 7

[1]Victor Elting, *Recollections of a Grandfather* (Chicago, 1940), 59–60, 102, 104.

[2]James Leslie Davis, *The Elevated System and the Growth of Northern Chicago* (Evanston, Illinois, 1965), 13–17, 54–59; Wirth and Bernert, *Community Fact Book*, 55, 59; Hoyt, *Land Values*, 208–210.

[3]*Thirteenth Census of the United States, 1910: Population*, 1:912, 942–943, 2:512–514. There were 2,268 of mixed Danish parentage, making the Danish stock number 20,772. The Swedish stock, first and second generation, numbered 116,740 and the Norwegian stock 47,235. The Scandinavian population thus was 184,747.

[4]*Skandinaven*, January 29, 1908; Backer, *Ekteskap*, 158; Carlsson, "Chronology . . . Swedish Emigration," 126–127; Kristian Hvidt, *Flight to America: The Social Background of 300,000 Danish Emigrants* (New York, 1975), 9–14, 89–90; Philip Taylor, *The Distant Magnet: European Emigration to the U.S.A.* (New York, 1971), 103, 105–106; Ann Novotny, *Strangers at the Door: Ellis Island, Castle Garden, and the Great Migration to America* (New York, 1971), 8, 102–104. See also "'Steerage Conditions,' Reports of the United States Immigration Commission, XXXVII (1911)," in Feldstein and Costello, *The Ordeal of Assimilation*, 38–50.

[5]Strand, *Norwegians in Illinois*, 509; letter from Dr. Jacob L. Urheim to Lars T. Kinsarvik, April 10, 1903, in Lars Kinsarvik archives, Lofthus, Norway, copy in NAHA archives; Backer, *Ekteskap*, 158–159.

[6]Backer, *Ekteskap*, 182–185.

[7]Federal Population Schedules of the *Thirteenth Census of the United States*, 1910,

Cook County, Illinois, reels 270, 271, 273. The enumeration districts cover an area bounded on the north by Diversey Avenue, on the east by California Avenue, on the south by North Avenue, and on the west by Kimball Avenue. Within this district resided 2,680 Norwegians of the first generation and 2,760 of the second. The percentages are based on an analysis of these figures. The quotation is from Lowry Nelson, "Intermarriage among Nationality Groups in a Rural Area of Minnesota," in *The American Journal of Sociology*, 48 (March, 1943), 591. See also *Skandinaven*, September 13, 1906, and *Aarsberetning for Det norske Nationalforbund i Chicago* for the years 1908, 1912, 1916, 1917, in the NAHA archives, for detailed reports of the activities of the employment office.

[8]*Salems Budbærer*, October, 1962; *Skandinaven*, June 2, 1911; R. Arlo Odegaard, *With Singleness of Heart* (Minneapolis, [1971]), 78–90, 138.

[9]*Salems Budbærer*, October, 1962; Odegaard, *Singleness of Heart*, 135–190, 461; interview with Bert Benson, September 29, 1985.

[10]Addresses for the churches are found in the *Chicago City Directory*, 1914, 14–17; Strand, *Norwegians in Illinois*, 114–115, 127–128. Christ Church is now the Norwegian Memorial Church, the only Norwegian-speaking Lutheran congregation in Chicago.

[11]*Fifty Years for Christ, 1886–1936*, a commemorative booklet of the Moreland Lutheran Church, was provided by Josefa and J. Harry Andersen; additional information from Bert Benson.

[12]Strand, *Norwegians in Illinois*, 115–116; Norlie, *Norsk lutherske menigheter*, 1:55; *St. Timothy Lutheran Church 75th Year of Faith, 1904–1979*; the quotation is from the original congregational minutes of Bethel Lutheran Church, which, together with other original documents, were made available through the courtesy of Eunice Engebretsen.

[13]*Sixtieth Anniversary, October 9–16, 1960, Hauge Evangelical Lutheran Church*; *Trinity Fiftieth Anniversary*.

[14]Information on Adventists in Dyre Dyresen Papers in NAHA archives; *Lake Union Herald*, December 12, 1978.

[15]*Viking*, October 16, 1952; *Sunday Tribune*, June 26, 1937; *Talsmanden*, December 6, 19, 1907; Andersen, *Salt of the Earth*, 260; Strand, *Norwegians in Illinois*, 152–153, 160–165. Carol E. Sundby gave information on the Methodist deaconess movement.

[16]Stiansen, *Norwegian Baptists*, 142–143; Strand, *Norwegians in Illinois*, 313–314; Parish Register of the Logan Square Norwegian Baptist Church was made available by Karen and P. Rolf Westnes. Bert Benson gave information on the seminary in Morgan Park.

[17]*Skandinaven*, May 18, 1904. *Skandinaven* as well as the Norwegian National League had a continuous disagreement with the school board census, which they claimed undercounted the Norwegian population.

[18]*Thirteenth Census of the United States, 1910: Population*, 2:512–514.

[19]*Skandinaven*, February 21, 1894; Osland, *Long Pull from Stavanger*, 65; Hustvedt, *Pioneer Scholar*, 222–223; *Riddere av Det hvite Kors*, 33.

[20]*Skandinaven*, May 22, 1895, May 20, 1896, May 19, 1897, October 16, 1901; Osland, *Long Pull from Stavanger*, 56–58; *Centennial Celebration of Norway's Independence under the Auspices of the Norwegian National League*, May 16 and 17, 1914, 4–6; *Souvenir Program Folke-Fest*, May 17, 1899.

[21]*Skandinaven*, May 22, 1895.

[22]*Skandinaven*, May 24, 1905; Osland, *Long Pull from Stavanger*, 1–6, 58–61.

[23]*Centennial Celebration*, 1914, 5–6; *Skandinaven*, June 14, 16, 21, 23, August 18, 1905. In its September 8, 1905, issue *Skandinaven* bitterly condemned a lecture by a visiting member of the Swedish parliament (Riksdag), P. Waldenström, who gave the conservative Swedish view that the newspaper described as "an ignorant, hateful, openly dishonest and untrue attack on the Norwegian people."

[24]*Skandinaven*, June 23, 1905; Osland, *Long Pull from Stavanger*, 70–96; Wong, *Norske utvandrere*, 49–51, 225.

[25]*Skandinaven*, June 28, 1866, July 11, 1867, June 1, July 13, 1875, May 18,

1876, July 9, 1878, July 8, 1879, April 25, May 23, 1882, May 19, 1886, May 21, 28, 1890; *Scandia*, May 14, 1927, April 7, 1938.

[26]*Skandinaven* (daily), February 28, 1909; *Scandia*, May 20, June 17, 1911; *Aarsberetning for Det norske Nationalforbund*, 1911, 4.

[27]*Chicago Daily Tribune*, May 18, 1914.

[28]Lovoll, *A Folk Epic: The* Bygdelag *in America* (Boston, 1975), 99–103; *Skandinaven*, January 29, February 3, 10, June 8, 1904; *Aarsberetning for Det norske Nationalforbund*, 1914, 5–8; Strand, *Norwegians in Illinois*, 532–533.

[29]See Jerry Brondfield, *Rockne: The Coach, the Man, the Legend* (New York, 1976).

[30]*Skandinaven*, August 22, 1900, May 18, 1908; *Aarsberetning for Det norske Nationalforbund*, 1908, 2; Strand, *Norwegians in Illinois*, 206–207; Osland, *Long Pull from Stavanger*, 53–54.

[31]*Norden*, December, 1930; *Norge Ski Club 25th Anniversary Review*, 1930.

[32]See Leif Hovelsen, *The Flying Norseman* (Ishpeming, Michigan, 1983). This history was given to the author as a gift from Hovelsen, a son of Carl Howelsen. Norge Ski Club members elected to the National Ski Hall of Fame in Ishpeming are: Eugene Petersen, Harry Lien, Le Moine Batson, Ragnar Omtvedt, Fred Bruun, Guttorm Paulsen, Lawrence Mourin, and Arthur Knudsen. Ole Besseberg and Robert Immens, both of whom have served as presidents of Norge Ski Club at Fox River Grove, gave permission to copy extensive scrapbooks and provided other material on the club.

[33]*Norden*, December, 1930, November, 1932; *Norge Ski Club 25th Anniversary Review*.

[34]Several brochures and advertising material produced by the Northland Manufacturing Company are in the archives of the Minnesota Historical Society in St. Paul, located by Deborah Miller, research supervisor at the Society. Norlie, *History of the Norwegian People in America* (Minneapolis, 1925), 475; Wong, *Norske utvandrere*, 193, 209.

[35]*Nordvesten*, October 13, 1904.

[36]Lovoll, *A Folk Epic*, 1–23; *Skandinaven*, January 29, February 3, 1904. Eikundasund was organized in 1910, Karmsund in 1919, Oslolaget and Nordmørlaget in 1921, and Stavangeren in 1924. See *Scandia*, April 7, 1938; Haugesunds Foreningen "Karmsund" minutes in NAHA archives; *Souvenir Program Haugesunds Society "Karmsund" of Chicago, 1919–1939*; *Souvenir Program Oslolagets dramatiske Klub Ten Year Jubilee, 1924–1934*; *Oslolaget of Chicago, Annual Fall Festival, 1931*; Stavangeren papers in the NAHA archives, given NAHA by Stavangeren through the courtesy of Hazel Egeland; *Adressebog 1925 af Foreningen Eikundasund*.

[37]Wist, *Norsk-amerikansk festskrift*, 275–276; *Skandinaven*, July 5, August 2, 1893; *Souvenir Program Forty Years Celebrated by Singing Society Bjørgvin*, March 26, 1922.

[38]Carl Hansen, "Northern Music in America," in *American Scandinavian Review*, January–February, 1916, 38–43; *Minneapolis Tidende*, January 7, 1932; *Skandinaven*, July 13, 1934; Strand, *Norwegians in Illinois*, 315–316; interview with Knute Hansen, September 21, 1985. See also Gjerset file in NAHA archives on Norwegian-American musicians.

[39]*Scandia*, April 7, 1938. Interview February 1, 1987, with Sylvia Brightstone, Irene Bjorvik, and Mildred Moe of the Grieg Ladies Singing Society. Mrs. Moe also provided additional material.

[40]Minutes of Den norske Læseforening and a typescript history in NAHA archives.

[41]Minutes of the Federation of Norwegian Women's Societies in NAHA archives. The Federation had its own building at 2512 North Kimball Avenue and published its own newsletter, the *Bulletin*. See Helga M. Ruud, *A History of the Norwegian Woman's Club* (Chicago, 1942). Interview with Vera Beutlich February 1, 1987, and documents and published accounts provided by her about her parents Anton and Emilie Beutlich.

[42]Osland, *Long Pull from Stavanger*, 40–41. The Norwegian Society (Det norske Selskab) was a literary and patriotic club of Norwegian students and literary figures

in Copenhagen, organized in 1772 and dissolved in 1813. In 1818 the society was reestablished in Oslo as a social club.

[43]Osland, *Long Pull from Stavanger*, 42. See *Chicago Norske Klub 1890–1950* (Chicago, 1950).

[44]*Skandinaven*, November 28, 1894; Bertram Jensenius, "Norsk teaterliv blusser påny i Chicago," in *Nordmanns-Forbundet*, July, 1942, 176–179; Eleonora and Ethel Olson, *Yust for Fun* (Minneapolis, 1925).

[45]*Scandia*, April 7, 1938; *Skandinaven*, February 14, 1900; Emil Biørn scrapbook in NAHA archives.

[46]*Scandia*, April 14, May 5, 1938.

[47]See *Aarsberetning for Det norske Nationalforbund*, 1912.

[48]*Skandinaven*, May 19, 1886, May 22, 1889.

[49]*Skandinaven*, December 14, 1875, May 22, 1889, May 29, 1896, May 30, 1917.

[50]*Skandinaven*, April 28, 1894; *Skandinaven* (daily), May 6, November 1, 1900; Strand, *Norwegians in Illinois*, 436–437; Paul Kleppner, *The Cross of Culture: A Social Analysis of Midwestern Politics, 1850–1900* (New York, 1970), 51–53; Allswang, *House for All People*, 207.

[51]*Skandinaven*, May 2, 1916, June 5, 1931. The John Anderson Papers in NAHA files contain letters from politicians soliciting *Skandinaven*'s endorsement.

[52]*Skandinaven*, July 2, 1892, April 15, 1896, November 10, 1897; *Skandinaven* (daily), May 6, 1900; *Scandia*, April 14, 1938; Wist, *Norsk-amerikanernes festskrift*, 54–55; Strand, *Norwegians in Illinois*, 396–397; Kleppner, *Chicago Divided: The Making of a Black Mayor* (DeKalb, Illinois, 1985), 15–31.

[53]*Skandinaven*, April 15, 1895, April 15, 1896, October 12, 1904, April 7, 1905; Strand, *Norwegians in Illinois*, 391–392; Allen F. Davis, *Spearheads for Reform: The Social Settlements and the Progressive Movement 1890–1914* (New York, 1967), 163–166; Edward R. Kantowicz, *Polish-American Politics in Chicago 1888–1940* (Chicago, 1975), 57–60. See also William T. Stead, *If Christ Came to Chicago* (1894, reprint ed., New York, 1964).

[54]*Scandia*, April 19, 1913, May 1, 1926, April 7, 1938; *Skandinaven* (daily), January 7, 1921; Minutes and Membership Records of the Bjørgvin Singing Society in NAHA archives.

[55]*Skandinaven*, January 24, 1908; Wist, *Norsk-amerikanernes festskrift*, 179. See Kaare Fostervoll, *Arbeiderskandinavismen i grunnleggingstida* (Oslo, 1935).

[56]N. Juel Christensen, a radical Danish-American socialist leader, wrote a brief history of the socialist movement and the Karl Marx Club titled *Arbejderklubben Karl Marx Chicago, Illinois. En kortfattet beskrivelse om foreningens virksomhed gennem 36 aar 1904–1940* (Chicago, 1940); Tore Pryser, "Gesell og rebell?" in Langholm and Sejersted, *Vandringer*, 211–214. See also *Skandinaven*, April 23, 1922; Hillquit, *History of Socialism*, 260–278, 301–314; Henry Bengston, *Skandinaver på vänsterflygeln i USA* (Stockholm, 1955), 58–59, 64–65. Margit Fredrickson, the daughter of Henry Bengston, provided the author with a copy of her father's book and additional information on the movement in which he was involved.

[57]*Revyen*, April 23, 1903; *Nordisk Tidende*, November 11, 1948; *Decorah-Posten*, June 16, 1949; *Svenska Amerikanaren Tribunen*, January 15, 1942; Gjerset Papers in NAHA archives; Bengston, *Skandinaver på vänsterflygeln*, 89–93; Allswang, *Bosses, Machines, and Urban Voters* (Baltimore, 1977), 95–96. See also Bernard J. Brommel, *Eugene V. Debs: Spokesman for Labor and Socialism* (Chicago, 1978).

[58]Christensen, *Arbejderklubben Karl Marx*.

[59]Bengston, *Skandinaver på vänsterflygeln*, 92, 161–166.

[1]*Skandinaven*, June 8, October 10, 1917, May 3, 1918; *Skandinaven* (daily), October 20, 1918; *Scandia*, January 24, 1920; *Aarsberetning for Det norske Nationalforbund*, 1919, 5–6.

[2]*Skandinaven*, April 21, 1917, June 19, July 3, 10, 1918. See also *Aarsberetning for Det norske Nationalforbund*, 1917.

[3] *Skandinaven*, April 18, 1917; Haugen, *The Norwegian Language in America: A Study in Bilingual Behavior* (Bloomington, Indiana, 1969), 252.

Chapter 8

[4]Lovoll, ed., *Cultural Pluralism* versus *Assimilation: The Views of Waldemar Ager* (Northfield, 1977), 102; *Beretning om Den norsk lutherske Kirkes første ekstraordinære fællesmøde avholdt i Fargo, North Dakota fra 6te til 12te juni 1918* (Minneapolis, 1918), 516–540; *Skandinaven*, December 16, 21, 1917; Ruud, *Norwegian Woman's Club*, 9.

[5]Carl H. Chrislock, "Name-Change and the Church, 1918–1920" in *Norwegian-American Studies*, 27 (1977), 194–223; Haugen, *Norwegian Language*, 255–257.

[6]Haugen, *Norwegian Language*, 257; *Viking*, April 24, 1947; *75th Anniversary History of St. Timothy*. Tella Guttelvik, who came to Chicago from Norway in the mid-1920s, where she resided in the Fullerton Avenue district, commented in an interview on September 24, 1985, on low attendance at the Norwegian services, but living in that area she still had a sensation of being in a Norwegian environment. The statistics on Norwegian divine services are based on the parochial reports from the congregations in the annual reports of the Norwegian Lutheran Church in America for 1918, 1920, 1925, and 1929. In these statistics the large St. Paul's Church, which at first joined the new church body, is not included as its forceful and conservative minister G.A. Gullixson separated the congregation from the new union over doctrinal differences, in the process losing such prominent members as Dr. George A. Torrison and Lasse Grundeland. See Parish Protocol St. Paul's Lutheran Church.

[7]Ernest W. Burgess and Charles Newcomb, eds., *Census Data of the City of Chicago,1930* (Chicago, 1933), xi–xiii.

[8]Taylor, *Pioneering*, 219; " 'Protection of Immigrant Girls on Arrival at Interior Points,' from the First Annual Report of the Immigrants' Protective League of Chicago, pp. 13–18," in Feldstein and Costello, *The Ordeal of Assimilation*, 86–90; papers of The Immigrants' Protective League in the Special Collections of the University of Illinois, Circle Campus, Chicago.

[9]Backer, *Ekteskap*, 159; Burgess and Newcomb, *Census Data of the City of Chicago*, 626–634, 660–661.

[10]Hoyt, *Land Values*, 237, 249; George Soule, *Prosperity Decade From War to Depression: 1917–1929*, vol. 8 of *The Economic History of the United States* (New York, 1947), 113. Robert J. Boucek, "Examination of the Effects of Branch Banking" (MBA thesis, DePaul University, 1966). Helen Fletre and Alan Strom of the Continental Bank identified sources and provided information on banking facilities and services in Chicago.

[11]Osland, *Long Pull from Stavanger*, 223; Wigeland Papers in NAHA archives; Leola Nelson Bergmann, *Americans from Norway* (New York, 1950), 278–279; John A. Higgins *et al.*, *The First Fifty Years 1913–1963* (Chicago, 1963), 15–18, 31–38.

[12]Bjork, *Saga in Steel and Concrete*, 128–129, 441–442; *Year Book Chicago Norwegian Technical Society 1924*.

[13]Bjork, *Saga in Steel and Concrete*, 363, 478; Wong, *Norske utvandrere*, 207; *The Pioneer Social Club of Chicago*, 19–20, 43–44.

[14]*Scandia*, April 7, 1928; Katherine S. Janega, *An Historical Guide and Service Directory to Logan Square and Avondale* (Chicago, 1979).

[15]Burgess and Newcomb, *Census Data of the City of Chicago*, 660–661, 686–687; *125th Anniversary Immanuel Lutheran Church 1853–1978*; Johnson, "Swedes of Chicago," 15; Kastrup, *Swedish Heritage*, 380. The Chicago History Committee hired Christian D. Nøkkentved to look into the origin of the naming of "Andersonville," and his report is the main source for these conclusions. See also *Svenska Amerikanaren Tribunen*, October 7, 1964.

[16]J.R. Christianson, "Scandinavia and the Prairie School: Chicago Landscape Artist Jens Jensen," in *The Bridge*, 5/2:5–18 (1982); Janega, *Historical Guide*, 19–20.

[17]Helen Fletre, using yearbooks and other publications of the Chicago Norske Klub, traced the residential mobility of the club's members.

[18]Janega, *Historical Guide*, 15; *Community Fact Book*, 55–58.

[19]Interview with Dr. Oscar Olsen, May 25, 1986; interviews on several occasions with J. Harry and Josefa Andersen. Jens T. Anker of Minneapolis has provided copies, originals and his own translations, of his mother's letters from Chicago in the 1920s.

[20]Wong, *Norske Utvandrere*, 197, 215. J. Harry and Josefa Andersen have

provided information on Norwegian restaurants. Josefa Andersen is a daughter of Edward Hansen.

[21]Allswang, *Bosses, Machines, and Urban Voters* (Baltimore, 1986), 92; Donald R. McCoy, *Coming of Age: The United States During the 1920's and 1930's* (New York, 1973), 17–23.

[22]Allswang, *House for All People*, 119; Kenneth Allsop, *The Bootleggers: The Story of Chicago's Prohibition Era* (New Rochelle, New York, 1961, new ed., 1968), 45, 122–123; Andrew Sinclair, *Prohibition: The Era of Excess* (Boston, 1962), 126–128; interview with Bert Benson, September 29, 1985.

[23]*Skandinaven* (daily), May 14, 1920. Colosimo was an avid opera fan and benefactor.

[24]Allswang, *House for All People*, 119–120; Sinclair, *Prohibition*, 163, 335–336; *Reform*, January 6, 1920, November 11, 1926, November 17, 1927; *Lutheraneren*, January 28, 1920; *Scandia*, May 28. 1927, December 7, 21, 1929; *Skandinaven*, January 17, September 14, 21, December 19, 1923, May 5, 1925; interview with Elmer Abrahamson, February 1, 1987.

[25]Allswang, *House for All People*, 188–189; Nielsen, "Halvfems aar," 72–74; *Chicago Norske Klub*, 16.

[26]Allswang, *Bosses*, 98, 145; *Scandia*, March 4, 1922.

[27]Allswang, *House for All People*, 144, 175–176; Allswang, *Bosses*, 96–98; Osland, *Long Pull from Stavanger*, 52; Lloyd Wendt and Herman Kogan, *Big Bill of Chicago* (New York, 1953), 100–119, 132; Alex Gottfried, *Boss Cermak of Chicago: A Study of Political Leadership* (Seattle, Washington, 1962), 199–237; *Nordisk Tidende*, April 4, 1919; *Chicago Daily Tribune*, April 1, 1924, March 29, 1927; *Scandia*, February 26, April 2, 1927, April 2, 1931; *Skandinaven*, April 6, July 18, 1923, April 9, October 28, 1927, February 27, April 10, 1931. *Chicago Daily News Alamanac 1928*, 762–770, and *Chicago Daily News Almanac 1932*, 278–280, 704–713, have complete voting information by precincts. Precinct maps issued by Board of Election Commissioners in Chicago.

[28]Osland, *Long Pull from Stavanger*, 65–69; K.H.J. Orm, "Leif Erikson Saken," in *Norden*, December, 1928, 17–18; *Aarsberetning for Det norske Nationalforbund*, 1923, 4–5; letters, clippings, and other documents in the Berthe C. Petersen Papers in NAHA archives; *Skandinaven*, April 9, 1927, August 18, 1931; *Scandia*, April 2, 1927, April 7, 1938. *Scandia*, December 21, 1929, reports on the completion of the Leif Eriksen Drive to Jackson Park. Some sources suggest that Leif Eriksen Drive extended north to Randolph Street. *Chicago Tribune*, August 30, 1978, identified Achsah Bond Drive as the northern limit; this information was located by Martin W. Reinhart. The unorthodox spelling of the Norse discoverer's name was due, to quote from Osland, *Long Pull from Stavanger*, 69, to the fact that "Norwegian-American language zealots from Chicago and elsewhere bombarded the South Park board with hundreds of letters advising how the name Leif Ericson should be spelled." In order to avoid adopting any of the controversial spellings the board adopted its own "and that is the insipid and incorrect way in which the drive is officially spelled today," Osland concluded in 1945. On June 17, 1946, the drive was renamed Lake Shore Drive in order to give the entire stretch along the lake the same name. "By unanimous vote the park board struck off the maps and street signs the complexity of names that had weighted down the expressway," the *Chicago Tribune* stated in June 18, 1946.

[29]Orm, "Leif Erikson Saken," 17–18; *Skandinaven*, June 17, July 1, 1925; Lovoll, *A Folk Epic*, 166–167, 169. O.J. Kvale was likely President Coolidge's authority on Norse discovery.

[30]*Skandinaven*, July 1, 1925.

[31]*Scandia*, January 29, April 16, 1927, April 16, 1931; translation by Josefa Andersen of article in *Vinland*, December 11, 1958.

[32]The catalogs produced for the Chicago Norske Klub exhibitions are in the NAHA archives. I am greatly indebted to Helen Fletre, Rolf Erickson, and Vera Beutlich for information and documents, including lectures and papers they have prepared, relative to the Norwegian-American artists in Chicago.

[33]Erickson, "Norwegian-American Artists' Exhibitions Described in Checklists and Catalogs," in *Norwegian-American Studies*, 31 (1986), 284–290, 299–301;

Sverre Arestad, trans. and intro., "Sigbjørn Obstfelder and America," in *Norwegian-American Studies*, 29 (1983), 284; *The Palette & Chisel*, September 1926, January, February, 1931; Strand, *Norwegians in Illinois*, 491.

[34]Excerpt from family history in a letter from George E. Hanson, May, 1951, in NAHA archives; J.W. Young, *Lars Haukaness Exhibition* (Chicago, 1913).

[35]*Sanger Hilsen*, October, 1954; Wong, *Norske utvandrere*, 57–58.

[36]Olga Graff, "Norsk Kunst i Amerika," in *Nordisk Tidende*, July 14, 1927; *Norsk kunstnerleksikon* 2 (Oslo, 1986), 169–170.

[37]Josefa and J. Harry Andersen have donated programs and other material on the different singing societies. See *Normændenes Sangforening of Chicago Sixtieth Anniversary Concert at Logan Square Masonic Temple Thursday, October 30, 1930*; *Vinland*, February 4, 1982; interview with Knute Hansen, September 21, 1985.

[38]*Norwegian Singers' Association of America Sangerfest in Chicago 1926*; *Viking*, April 27, 1950; interview with Knute Hansen, September 21, 1985. The Norwegian Singers' Association of America was organized at Sioux Falls, South Dakota, in 1891 as the Scandinavian Singers' Association. In 1908 the name was changed to Northwestern Norwegian-Danish Singers' Association, and in 1910 to its present one.

[39]*Skandinaven*, January 6, 1931.

[40]*Skandinaven*, January 24, 1923, April 22, 1925, March 30, 1929, January 6, 1931, March 10, 1933; Lawrence M. Nelson, ed., *From Fjord to Prairie: Norwegian Americans in the Midwest 1825–1975* (Chicago, 1975), C34.

[41]*Scandia*, March 1, 1930; *Skandinaven*, July 3, August 7, 21, November 13, 1931, March 10, 1933.

[42]Nielsen, *Halvfems aar*, 42; Mayer and Wade, *Chicago*, 178; *Dedication Program of the United Evangelical Lutheran Congregation of Chicago, Sunday, November 11th, A.D. 1928*; interview with Tella Guttelvik, September 24, 1985.

Index

Index

Credits for Illustrations

361

190 *Top:* Courtesy Margaret Buxton.
 Bottom: Thallaug and Erickson, *Our Norwegian Immigrants*, 137.

192 Thallaug and Erickson, *Our Norwegian Immigrants*, 146.

194 *Top:* Courtesy A.G.H. Anderson.
 Bottom: Strand, *Norwegians in Illinois*, 224.

196 Cavling, *Fra Amerika*, 222.

199 Two photographs at top by J. Harry Andersen.
 Bottom: Gjerset, *Norwegian Sailors*, after page 60.

204 *Top:* Courtesy Lawrence M. Nelson.
 Bottom: Courtesy Elmer E. Abrahamson.

207 *Top:* Photograph by J. Harry Andersen.
 Bottom: Courtesy Mrs. James E. Vaughn.

214 *Top:* Courtesy Sister Magdalene Rosene.
 Bottom left: Cavling, *Fra Amerika*, 290.
 Bottom right: Thallaug and Erickson, *Our Norwegian Immigrants*, 143.

216 Both photographs from *History of the Norwegian Lutheran Children's Home Society, 1896–1936, Edison Park — Chicago — Illinois*, by Millie Hendricksen.

220 Quales Estate. Courtesy Josefa and J. Harry Andersen.

223 Courtesy Lawrence M. Nelson.

227 Chicago Historical Society.

228 *Top:* Chicago Historical Society.
 Bottom: Vesterheim, the Norwegian-American Museum.

232 Chicago Historical Society.

233 Map by Alan Ominsky.

234 In *Centennial Celebration of Norway's Independence, May 16th and 17th, 1914, Chicago.*

238 Photographs by J. Harry Andersen.

242 Photograph by Douglas Gilbert. Courtesy Lawrence M. Nelson.

244 *Top:* Strand, *Norwegians in Illinois*, 318.
 Bottom: *Skandinaven*, June 9, 1905.

246 *Top:* Thallaug and Erickson, *Our Norwegian Immigrants*, 138.
 Bottom: Courtesy Ingrid Stenvik.

247 *Norwegian American Athletic Association Fiftieth Anniversary*, 13.

250 *Top:* Norwegian-American Historical Association.
 Bottom left: Vesterheim, the Norwegian-American Museum.
 Bottom right: Courtesy Josefa and J. Harry Andersen.

251 *Top left:* Courtesy Josefa and J. Harry Andersen.
 Top right and bottom: *Norge Ski Club 25th Anniversary Review*, 12 and 18.

254 *Top:* Courtesy Josefa and J. Harry Andersen.
 Bottom: Courtesy Bergljot Raaen.

256 *Top:* Photograph by J. Harry Andersen.
 Bottom: Courtesy Josefa and J. Harry Andersen.

259 Thallaug and Erickson, *Our Norwegian Immigrants*, 152.

261 *Top and bottom left:* Courtesy Rolf Erickson.
 Bottom right: Courtesy Ingrid Stenvik.

262 *Top: Forum. Det Litterære Samfunds Årbok* (Chicago, 1926), after page 104.
 Bottom left: Cavling, *Fra Amerika*, 144.
 Bottom right: Emil Biørn's Scrapbook.

264 The Norsemen's Federation, Oslo, Norway.

271 *Top:* Norwegian-American Historical Association.
 Bottom: Photograph by Odd S. Lovoll.

274 *Top:* Chicago Historical Society.
 Left: Scandia, May 5, 1917.

278 Chicago Historical Society.

280 *Top:* Chicago Historical Society.
Two bottom: Skandinaven, June 9, August 30, 1929.

282 *Top:* Courtesy Rolf Erickson.
Bottom: Bjork, *Saga in Steel and Concrete,* after page 132.

283 Thallaug and Erickson, *Our Norwegian Immigrants,* 136.

285 Photograph by J. Harry Andersen.

287 *Top:* Courtesy Genevieve Hagen.
Bottom: Courtesy Marielyn Arntzen Frazier.

288 *Top left:* Courtesy Josefa and J. Harry Andersen.
Top right: Skandinaven, December 22, 1917.
Bottom: Thallaug and Erickson, *Our Norwegian Immigrantes,* 141.

292 Courtesy Marilyn Halvorsen.

296 Courtesy Alice Norman.

297 In *Leif Erikson Festival, September 12th, 1926.*

300 *Left:* Courtesy Lawrence M. Nelson.
Right: Courtesy Rolf Erickson.

303 Vesterheim, the Norwegian-American Museum.

304 Courtesy Lawrence M. Nelson.

305 Courtesy Vera Beutlich.

306 Courtesy Helen Fletre.

307 Courtesy Knute Hansen.

308 Courtesy Knute Hansen.

310
–311 *Top: Noregian-American Athletic Association Fiftieth Anniversary,* 22–23.

311 *Bottom:* Courtesy Josefa and J. Harry Andersen.

List of Donors

Major Gifts to the Norwegian-American Historical Association

Arthur Andersen Company, Chicago
Josefa and J. Harry Andersen, Chicago
Theodore C. Blegen Fellowship Fund
E.S. Gandrud, Owatonna, Minnesota
Harriet Hustvedt, Highwood, Illinois
Lutheran Brotherhood, Minneapolis
Minnesota Historical Society, St. Paul

Gifts to the Chicago History Committee
One thousand dollars or more:

Dr. and Mrs. Alf Altern, Glenview, Illinois
Archie R. Boe, Chicago
Rolf H. Erickson, Evanston, Illinois
John and Dorothy Erland, Antioch, Illinois
Harriet Hustvedt, Highwood, Illinois
Arve Kilen, Wilmette, Illinois
Mr. and Mrs. William J. Korsvik, Wilmette, Illinois
Mr. and Mrs. Charles D. O'Kieffe, Wilmette, Illinois
Sivert Klefstad, Boca Raton, Florida
Harry J. Williams, Kenilworth, Illinois
Anonymous Friend

Five hundred dollars to one thousand:

Mr. and Mrs. Elmer Abrahamson, Chicago
American Scandinavian Association of Illinois
Peer and Esther Gulbrandsen, Niles, Illinois
Mr. and Mrs. Lawrence O. Hauge, Edina, Minnesota
Martin Reinhart, Chicago
Mrs. Evelyn K. Richie, Chicago

Two hundred dollars to five hundred:

Bert Benson, Chicago
Mr. and Mrs. L. Charles Brewick, La Grange Park, Illinois
Eric A. Hallén, Glencoe, Illinois
Gertrude Torgersen Harris, Park Ridge, Illinois
William J. Jacobson, Cape Coral, Florida
John and Josefa Kallestad, Niles, Illinois. In Memoriam
Robert L. Lillestrand, Edina, Minnesota
Lowell E. Olberg and Family, Wheaton, Illinois
Ambassador and Mrs. Sidney Rand, Minneapolis
Sandra Sundfør-Fulscher, Riverside, Illinois
Eunice L. Thompson, Pontiac, Illinois

One hundred dollars to two hundred:

Ann Sather's Restaurant, Chicago
Joseph G. Aaberg, Chicago
Margret Altern, Chicago
Hazel S. Anderson, Chicago
Bjornar and Florence Bergethon, Champaign, Illinois
Dr. Kenneth O. Bjork, Northfield, Minnesota
Else M. Bjornstad, Chicago
Marijane Carr, Wilmette, Illinois
J.R. Christianson, Decorah, Iowa
Lucy Bassoe Davis, Evanston, Illinois
Ole T. and Margaret A. Diesen, Skokie, Illinois
Mrs. Philip Duff, Jr., Red Wing, Minnesota
Florence E. Dybdahl, Chicago
Mr. and Mrs. Roger E. Elmer, Chicago
Earl Richard Ensrud, Champaign, Illinois
Dorothy Erickson, Evanston, Illinois
Marielyn Arntzen Frazier, Bellingham, Washington
Nettie Ramberg Gillette, Wheaton, Illinois
Mr. and Mrs. George Grimsrud, Evanston, Illinois
Margaret B. Grondahl, Woodstock, Illinois
Mrs. Alma E. Hofstetter, Starbuck, Minnesota
Mr. and Mrs. Wyatt Jacobs, Chicago
R.I. Jacobson, Sun City, Arizona
David Martin Andrew Jensen, Des Plaines, Illinois
Lucinda Jondahl, Des Plaines, Illinois
Gareth N. Johnson, Kenner, Louisiana. In Memory of
    Harvey N. and Shirley J. Johnson
Leif Edmund Kallestad, Niles, Illinois
Esther M. Kjorstad, Starbuck, Minnesota
Marion E. Knapp, Schaumburg, Illinois
Bertha Kobbeltvedt, Fyllingsdalen, Norway
John Larson, Chicago
Rose I. Lindrup, Chicago
Arline G. Magnor, Oak Park,, Illinois
Mildred E. Magnor, Oak Park, Illinois
Elsie M. Melby, Duluth, Minnesota

Leon Muller, Chicago
Gerhard B. Naeseth, Madison, Wisconsin
David and Betty Nelson, Decorah, Iowa
John and Arlene Nelson, Waukon, Iowa
Mr. and Mrs Lawrence M. Nelson, Glenview, Illinois
Gladys Geerlings Niemann, La Grange, Illinois
The Nora Lodge, No. 415, Chicago
Dr. Eugene J. Nordby, Madison, Wisconsin
Norwegian Information Service, New York
Alfred D. Olson, Dallas, Texas
The Rev. Dennis B. O'Neill, Chicago
Muriel W. Pedersen, Oak Park, Illinois
Richard W. Ronvik, Evanston, Illinois
Reidar Rosenvinge, Chicago
Inez Schaefer, Rochester, Minnesota
Ingrid Semmingsen, Oslo, Norway
Gerald R. Sime, Duluth, Minnesota
Ole I. Stangeland, McCanna, North Dakota
Stavangeren, Chicago
A. Garfield Stensland, Chicago
Ben Stevenson, Chicago
Kathleen M. Stokker, Decorah, Iowa
Chrystal F. Thompson, Pontiac, Illinois
Judith Torvik, Porsgrunn, Norway
Darrell F. Treptow, Chicago
Florence L. Van Valkenburgh, Northfield, Illinois
George T. Van Valkenburgh, Chicago
Mr. and Mrs. P. Rolf Westnes, Brookfield, Illinois

Below one hundred dollars:

Agnes I. Andersen, Glenview, Illinois
Carlyle E. Anderson, Evanston, Illinois
Sylvia Iverson Barber, South Beloit, Illinois
Kenneth and Eleanor Brown, Arlington Heights, Illinois
Lester Caltvedt, Elmhurst, Illinois
Eleanor Cooper, Montebello, California
Det Litterære Samfund (DeLiSa), Chicago
Eunice Engebretsen, Palatine, Illinois
Peter A. Gramsborg, Chicago
Joe Halter, Chicago
Michael Hoiland, Brookeville, Maryland
Beata C. Kamp, Chico, California
Gunnar Knutson, Chicago
Col. and Mrs. Richard Kuiper, Fairfax, Virginia
Harvey J. Landers, Jr., Lubbock, Texas
T.P. and Janice Minehan, Las Vegas, Nevada
Mr. and Mrs. Sigurd Olsen, Chicago
Kari Rice, Excelsior, Minnesota
Elizabeth Hirsch Schonbrun, Chicago
Mr. and Mrs. Myles Stenshoel, Minnetonka, Minnesota
Carl W.W. Sorenson, Dallas, Texas
Vera Wilk, Oak Lawn, Illinois